Unreliable Witnesses

Unreliable Witnesses

Religion, Gender, and History in the
Greco-Roman Mediterranean

ROSS SHEPARD KRAEMER

OXFORD
UNIVERSITY PRESS

2011

BL
815
.W6
K73
2011

OXFORD
UNIVERSITY PRESS

Oxford University Press, Inc., publishes works that further
Oxford University's objective of excellence
in research, scholarship, and education.

Oxford   New York
Auckland   Cape Town   Dar es Salaam   Hong Kong   Karachi
Kuala Lumpur   Madrid   Melbourne   Mexico City   Nairobi
New Delhi   Shanghai   Taipei   Toronto

With offices in
Argentina   Austria   Brazil   Chile   Czech Republic   France   Greece
Guatemala   Hungary   Italy   Japan   Poland   Portugal   Singapore
South Korea   Switzerland   Thailand   Turkey   Ukraine   Vietnam

Copyright © 2011 by Oxford University Press, Inc.

Published by Oxford University Press, Inc.
198 Madison Avenue, New York, New York 10016

www.oup.com

Oxford is a registered trademark of Oxford University Press.

All rights reserved. No part of this publication may be reproduced,
stored in a retrieval system, or transmitted, in any form or by any means,
electronic, mechanical, photocopying, recording, or otherwise,
without the prior permission of Oxford University Press.

Library of Congress Cataloging-in-Publication Data
Kraemer, Ross Shepard, 1948–
Unreliable witnesses: religion, gender, and history in the Greco-Roman Mediterranean / Ross
Shepard Kraemer.
    p. cm.
Includes bibliographical references and index.
ISBN 978-0-19-974318-6
1. Women and religion—Rome. 2. Women in Judaism—Rome. 3. Women in Christianity—Rome.
4. Rome—Religion. I. Title.
BL815.W6K73   2010
200.82'0937—dc22   2010009174

For Honey Kraemer, with love
And for Jerry Kraemer, in loving memory

Acknowledgments

Given that in some ways I have been writing this book my entire academic life, the list of persons to whom I owe thanks is unending. It begins with my teachers at Smith College in the late 1960s, especially the late Jochanan Wijnhoven, and then at Princeton, especially John G. Gager. It extends to the students I have taught over the last thirty-five years, both undergraduate and graduate, especially those in courses where I have tried out, with varying degrees of persuasiveness, many of the ideas in this book.

I am particularly grateful to the students in my seminar on religion and gender in the ancient Mediterranean at Brown in the spring of 2004 and 2009. Both classes were a joy to teach, and their fruits are apparent, at least to me, throughout the book. The students in 2004, however, deserve special thanks for sustaining me through the trials and exhaustion of treatment for breast cancer. Every week, they reminded me of why I love teaching at Brown.

As an anonymous reader for Oxford remarked on seeing how often I cited them, I have an especially wonderful community of colleagues at Brown. The work of several of my colleagues, including Stanley Stowers and Michael Satlow, figures prominently in these pages. The expertise of Matthew Bagger, Saul Olyan, and John Bodel was invaluable, whether in print, in conversation, or both. Susan Ashbrook Harvey inspires me daily and is a fount of fabulous bibliographic references. I also thank all the members of the Brown seminar on culture and religion in the ancient Mediterranean, and of the Judaic Studies Faculty Colloquium, especially Marcy Brink-Danan and Ronald Florence, for responses to drafts of several chapters.

Jennifer Eyl and Goran Tkalec put in hours of thankless checking of references, chasing down footnotes, and the other drudgeries of manuscript preparation; Jennifer also did much of the index preparation. My discussion of numerous points is enhanced by their insights, and those of Jon Aronchick, Jesse Goodman, Curtis Hutt, Kevin McGinness, Jordan Rosenblum, Karen Stern, Diana Shifrina, Dan Ullucci, Robyn Walsh, and Heidi Wendt. Special thanks are due to Kate Goldberg for her work on the archaeological sites on Minorca (and her companionship on our research trip there in spring 2007).

Colleagues outside Brown offered generous critique of various parts of the manuscript and provided various assistance: Mary Rose D'Angelo, Carol Delaney, Robert Doran, Troels Engberg-Pedersen, Paula Fredriksen, Robert A. Kraft, Joshua Levinson, Hindy Najman. Thanks also to the two anonymous readers at the *Journal of Early Christian Studies* for helpful critique of the chapter on Severus of Minorca. No project succeeds without the assistance of fine librarians, and I thank those at Brown, as well as Judith Leifer, at the library of the Katz Center for Advanced Judaic Studies at the University of Pennsylvania, who continues to rescue me from a distance. The gracious hospitality of colleagues at Alfred University, New College, St. Joseph's, the University of North Carolina Chapel Hill, Vassar College, and Washington University afforded me the opportunity to try out various forms of the arguments in this book.

I cannot imagine my life without the love and support of my husband of forty years, Michael, whose willingness to relocate to New England a decade ago changed both our lives for the better. Nor can I imagine it without the joy of our incomparable daughter, Jordan. At age eight, she already perceived that the book of Genesis had multiple authors, brought together by an editor. At age thirty-two, she is becoming a scholar in her own right in her chosen field of anthropology. Our many long conversations about the intersections of religious studies, gender studies, and anthropology are a parent's delight. Our family has been enriched immeasurably by her devoted life-partner, Channing Moore, on whose expertise in biophysics and neuroscience I hope to draw as I pursue my interests in cognitive science and religious studies.

I finished the last substantial revisions of this manuscript in the summer of 2009, forty years after the death of my mother, Harriet Plager Shepard, in July 1969 and twenty years after the death of my father, Herman (Ship) Shepard, in August 1989. I am indebted to them forever for the immeasurable love they gave me, for their unfailing faith in my abilities and their unwavering support of my studies while they were alive. Whatever gifts of intellect and language I may have, I inherited from them.

Since my mother's death, four women in my family have nurtured me with their love, support, and friendship. Three are cousins—Isadora Weiss, Rachel (Deb) Weissler, and Naomi Friedman, who was my mother's contemporary and her best friend—and I thank them all here. The fourth is my mother-in-law, Honey Kraemer, who has been an exemplary surrogate mother for the last four decades. This book is dedicated to her, and to my late father-in-law, Jerry Kraemer, a very token recognition of everything they have meant to me.

Contents

Abbreviations, xiii

1. Introduction, 3

2. Four Short Stories: A Bacchic Courtesan, the Reporter from Hell, the Daughters of Rabbis, a Roman Christian Matron, 29

3. Spouses of Wisdom: Philo's Therapeutrides, Reconsidered, 57

4. Thecla of Iconium, Reconsidered, 117

5. Artemisia of Minorca: Gender and the Conversion of the Jews in the Fifth Century, 153

6. Veturia of Rome and Rufina of Smyrna as Counterbalance: Women Office Holders in Ancient Synagogues and Gentile Adopters of Judean Practices, 179

7. Rethinking Gender, History, and Women's Religions in the Greco-Roman Mediterranean, 243

Works Cited, 275
Index of Ancient Sources, 305
General Index, 311

Abbreviations

ACW   Ancient Christian Writers. 1946–.

AE   *L'Année Épigraphique*

ANF   *Ante-Nicene Fathers*

ANRW   *Aufstieg und Niedergang der Römischen Welt. Geschichte und Kultur Roms im Spiegel der neueren Forschung.* Edited by H. Temporini and W. Haase. Berlin, 1972–.

ANT   *The Apocryphal New Testament.* Edited by J. K. Elliott. Oxford, 1993.

b. Niddah   *Tractate Niddah of the Babylonian Talmud*

BAR   *Biblical Archaeology Review*

BDB   F. Brown, S. R. Driver, and C. A. Briggs, *A Hebrew and English Lexicon of the Old Testament.* Oxford, 1907.

BHG   *Bibliotheca Hagiographica Graeca.* Brussels, 1977.

CBQ   *Catholic Biblical Quarterly*

CCSL   Corpus Christianorum, series Latina, Turnhout, 1953–

CHJ   *Cambridge History of Judaism.* Edited by W. D. Davies and Louis Finkelstein. Cambridge, 1984–.

CIJ   *Corpus Inscriptionum Judaicarum.* Edited by J. B. Frey. 2 vols. Rome, 1936–52.

CIL   *Corpus inscriptionum latinarum*

CIRB   *Corpus inscriptionum regni Bosporani*

CPJ   *Corpus Papyrorum Judaicarum.* Edited by V. Tcherikover. 3 vols. Cambridge, 1957–64.

CSEL	Corpus scriptorum ecclesiasticorum latinorum
DSD	*Dead Sea Discoveries*
EPRO	Etudes préliminaires aux religions orientales dans l'empire romain
FC	Fathers of the Church. Washington, D.C., 1947–.
GCS	Die griechischen christliche Schriftsteller der ersten [drei] Jahrhunderte
GRBS	*Greek, Roman and Byzantine Studies*
HSCP	*Harvard Studies in Classical Philology*
HTR	*Harvard Theological Review*
IAph	*Inscriptions of Aphrodisias*
IGR	*Inscriptiones graecae ad res romanas pertinentes*
IJO	*Inscriptiones Judaicae Orientis*
JAAR	*Journal of the American Academy of Religion*
JAC	Jahrbuch für Antike und Christentum
Jastrow	M. Jastrow. *A Dictionary of the Targumim, the Talmud Babli and Yerushalmi, and the Midrashic Literature.* 2nd ed. New York, 1903.
JBL	*Journal of Biblical Literature*
JECS	*Journal of Early Christian Studies*
JFSR	*Journal of Feminist Studies in Religion*
JIGRE	*Jewish Inscriptions from Greco-Roman Egypt*
JIWE	*Jewish Inscriptions from Western Europe*
JSJ	*Journal for the Study of Judaism in the Persian, Hellenistic and Roman Periods*
JSP	*Journal for the Study of Pseudepigrapha*
JPS	Jewish Publication Society
JRS	*Journal of Roman Studies*
JSOTSup	*Journal for the Study of the Old Testament* Supplement
JTS	*Journal of Theological Studies*
KJV	King James Version translation of the Bible
Lampe	G. W. H. Lampe. *A Patristic Greek Lexicon.* Oxford, 1961–68.
LCL	Loeb Classical Library
Lewis and Short	Charlton T. Lewis and Charles Short. *A Latin Dictionary.* Oxford, 1879.
LSJ	Henry George Liddell and Robert Scott, revised and augmented by Henry Stuart Jones. *Greek-English Lexicon.* Oxford, 1968.
LXX	Septuagint

NJPS   New Jewish Publication Society

NRSV   New Revised Standard Version

NTA   *New Testament Apocrypha*. Edited by Edgar Hennecke, Wilhelm Schneemelcher, and R. McL. Wilson. Revised English edition. Louisville, 1991–92.

P. Ant.   *The Antinoöpolis Papyri*

P. Oxy.   *The Oxyrhynchus Papyri*

PGM   *Papyri graecae magicae: die griechischen Zauberpapyri*. Ed. K. Preisendanz. Leipzig, 1928–31.

PIR   *Prosopographia Imperii Romani*. Berlin, 1933–.

PL   Patrologia latina. Edited by J.-P. Migne. 217 vols. Paris, 1844–64.

RBL   *Review of Biblical Literature*. Online at http://www.bookreviews.org.

REJ   *Revue des études juives*

RSV   Revised Standard Version

SBLSP   *Society of Biblical Literature Seminar Papers*

SC   Sources chrétiennes. Paris, 1943–.

SEG   Supplementum epigraphicum graecum

Sophocles   Sophocles, E. A. *Greek Lexicon of the Roman and Byzantine Periods*. Boston, 1870.

SWR   Studies in Women and Religion

S.V.   sub verbo

TAM   *Tituli Asiae Minoris*, Österreichische Akademie der Wissenschaften, 1901–.

t. Megillah   Tractate *Megillah* of the Tosefta

TSAJ   Texte und Studien zum antiken Judentum

WHR   *Women's History Review*

WIS   *Women in Scripture. A Dictionary of Named and Unnamed Women in the Hebrew Bible, the Apocryphal/Deuterocanonical Books, and the New Testament*. Edited by C. Meyers, T. Craven, and R. Kraemer. Boston: Houghton-Mifflin, 2000.

WRGRW   *Women's Religions in the Greco-Roman World*. Edited by R. S. Kraemer. Oxford, 2004.

WUNT   Wissenschaftliche Untersuchungen zum Neuen Testamentum

y. Sotah   Tractate *Sotah* of the Jerusalem Talmud

ZPE   *Zeitschrift für Papyrologie und Epigraphik*

Unreliable Witnesses

I

Introduction

For a number of years, the Society of Biblical Literature sponsored a session at its annual meetings at which a senior scholar was invited to reflect back on her work and views. Were it not such an egregiously generic title, this book might easily be called by the title of that session: "How My Mind Has Changed, or Remained the Same." It bears, in ways that I find somewhat startling, a striking resemblance to the outlines of my doctoral dissertation, so much so that another title might well be, "The dissertation I would have written thirty-three years ago, had I only known then what I know now."

In the early 1970s, as a neophyte graduate student in a new doctoral program then called History of Religions: Greco-Roman, at Princeton University,[1] I took an imaginative course on ancient Mediterranean religions in which we attempted to pursue as many of the sources and issues as possible in E. R. Dodds's major work, *The Greeks and the Irrational.*[2] Dodds's study included an appendix on Maenadism, the ecstatic worship of the Greek god Dionysos, attributed primarily to women in art, in Euripides' play *the Bacchae,* and in

---

1. For some sense of the significance of this title for a program that encompassed the full range of the religions of Greco–Roman antiquity, including but scarcely limited to early Christianity and ancient Judaism, I recommend Smith 2004b. Although this essay, "When the Chips Are Down," chronicles Jonathan Z. Smith's intellectual biography, it contains highly relevant remembrances of the major currents in my field in the late 1960s and early 1970s, the years I was in college and then graduate school.

2. Dodds 1951.

various other sources. Struck by what seemed to me the gross inadequacy of Dodds's explanation of Maenadism in terms of the greater irrationality of women, I focused my seminar paper on a critique of his arguments, and a preliminary exploration of alternative explanations. That seminar and that paper set the course of my scholarly agenda for the last thirty-five years in ways that I could, of course, never have foreseen at the time. That paper would form the core of my doctoral dissertation, a series of case studies on the functions of religious activities for women in the Greco-Roman world.[3] There, I argued that certain religious practices functioned as critiques of socially assigned roles for women and men, and they allowed women temporary, and sometimes permanent, actual social alternatives, from ecstatic devotion to Dionysos, to the adoption of Christian asceticism, to the contemplative life that Philo of Alexandria attributes to a group of monastics called Therapeutae. I drew heavily on the recent work of anthropologists such as I. M. Lewis's (1971) analysis of contemporary possession cults, and Kenelm Burridge's (1969) observations about gender arrangements in contemporary millenarian movements.[4]

In the early 1970s, feminist study of religion was barely a gleam in its foremothers' eyes. Much research was related to the then-active debates about the ordination of women to ministerial and priestly offices in contemporary Christian communities, themselves fueled by the resurgence of the women's movement in the last third of the twentieth century.[5] Partly because these debates often focused on questions of historical precedent (Did Jesus appoint women apostles? Did women ever serve as priests in early Christian churches? What antecedents might there have been in the practices of others?), they were certainly of interest to me. Yet it was also clear that my own central interests were not widely shared. I was interested in the recovery and accurate description of what women themselves did and thought within contexts that could be labeled "religious,"[6] as well as in theoretical models that, like those of Lewis and Burridge, might enable me to analyze and explain whatever differences I might find when I concentrated my research on women. Even ten years after I began my dissertation research, the reasonably comprehensive bibliography of a review essay I published on women in the religions of the Greco-Roman

3. Kraemer 1976. The majority of the dissertation was eventually published in somewhat revised articles: Kraemer 1979; 1980; 1989.

4 Lewis 1971 [2003]; Burridge 1969.

5. For a more detailed discussion of this period, with bibliography, see Kraemer 2008, esp. 474–79.

6. The complexity of the terms *religion, religious,* and so forth are helpfully explored in Smith 1998; see also Wilson 1998. On the emergence of a category of religion in antiquity, see Boyarin 2004; Mason 2007; Elliott 2007: see also chapter 7 for more detailed discussion. For my own current sense of this, see what follows.

Mediterranean had only about 250 entries,[7] and few of them focused on these particular issues.[8]

Similarly, in the early 1970s, the major problems associated with historical reconstruction seemed to be the relative absence of sources either by or about women, and the difficulty of assessing the reliability of those that are available. If we only had enough sources by women themselves, and/or enough sources by trustworthy male authors, we would be able to reconstruct a reasonable portrait of women's lives and self-understandings in the ancient world. Unfortunately, of course, for women's beliefs, there is virtually no first-hand, direct data (in the sense of trustworthy first-person accounts comparable to the wealth of those available for elite, educated men). Few writings survive from women themselves.[9] For women's behaviors, there is both material evidence and the accounts of elite, literate authors, mostly, if not entirely, male. The problems with explanation, of course, were another story: lacking the ability to interview our subjects or to observe directly the social workings of antiquity, we were left to arguments from analogy, a method, if not also a theory, that drew frequent criticism.

Fifteen years later, I revisited the data of my dissertation and extended my analysis, including considerable additional data, and focusing in particular on the correlations between ancient religious practices, gender constructions, and ancient social locations.[10] I drew extensively on the critique and arguments of Mary Douglas concerning religion as compensation for social forms of deprivation, as well as on Douglas's own work on the correlations between social constraints and cosmology (constructions of the universe).[11]

---

7. By contrast, the bibliography for this study contains close to two hundred entries concerned extensively with women's religions and gender in antiquity, most of them written after that essay, and it is by no means comprehensive, nor is it that really feasible any longer. It is no longer possible to read comprehensively in any of these areas, despite the fodder this inevitably provides for critics. The scholarly literature in this and most fields has become largely unmanageable. Even in the interval since I finished the basic manuscript (in 2008), numerous highly pertinent works have appeared, only a few of which I have been able to note, at best briefly.

8. When I was struggling to compose the introduction to my dissertation, after I had written the remaining chapters, I came across a file folder containing a version I had written the prior summer, and then obviously forgotten. I was both amused and relieved to find that it was far better than the newer draft I was finding so difficult to write. One can only reinvent the wheel so many times; some of my discussion here repeats, in only moderately reworked form, my remarks in the introduction to my 2004 anthology of sources pertaining to women's religions in the Greco-Roman world (abbreviated throughout as WRGRW).

9. Few women are securely known to have produced literary compositions in the Greco-Roman period, on which see Snyder 1989; see also Lefkowitz 1991. For consideration of the possibility that some anonymous or pseudonymous works may have been composed by women, see, e.g., Kraemer 1991b. On Christian women authors, see Wilson-Kastner 1981; see also Kraemer and Lander 2000 and Perkins 2007 on the authorship of the Martyrdom of Saints Perpetua and Felicitas.

10. Kraemer 1992.

11. Douglas 1970; 1978.

Her Share of the Blessings opened with the claim that it was a commonplace in antiquity that religion was women's business, and that this was not a compliment. This was true enough. Yet it missed or at least did not emphasize sufficiently a major point, to which this project attends more carefully. Although in *Her Share of the Blessings* I may still have been too optimistic about our ability to describe ancient social realities, particularly the practices and experiences of women, the real problem was precisely the gendered nature of "religion," as perceived by the elite male authors whose judgments these are (not to mention the elite male scholars of the nineteenth and twentieth centuries who largely concurred).[12] The terms regularly employed in Greek and Latin to designate women's cultic devotions, such as *deisidaimonia* and *superstitio*, were characterized by negative, gendered traits: uncontrolled, undisciplined, lacking self-control, irrational, illogical, traits that were both constructed or construed as feminine and seen to be natural to actual women. This could be (and was) contrasted with practices that exemplified masculine traits of detachment, self-discipline, rationality, and so forth, and/or that exemplified proper feminine comportment, and/or encoded or replicated masculine ideas/ideals about women. When, however, particular practices that can be called religion are gendered as male, "religion" is no longer so obviously predominantly the realm of women.

In the intervening years, it has become much clearer to me that interwoven problems of data and theory attend any attempt at the accurate reconstruction and subsequent redescription and explanation of women's religious behaviors and beliefs in Greco-Roman antiquity encounters. (The term *redescription* here refers to the use of "etic" categories and concerns shaped by the investigator's interests and perspectives to "re"-describe native practices[13]). Responding to work in literary theory, new historical criticism, cultural criticism, critical theory, and the like, many ancient historians and scholars of ancient religion have become deeply skeptical about the use of ancient texts, narrative or otherwise, for historical reconstruction and theorizing. Far from corresponding easily and usefully to women's experiences and lives, ancient sources are presently seen to deploy ancient ideas about gender, mapped onto female characters, to explore a range of issues of concern to their largely elite, male authors and initial audiences. As I shall elaborate shortly, recent scholarship seems to be of the opinion that, although it is difficult to write women's history, it is much easier to write a history of ancient constructions of gender, and of the uses of gender in

12. This point was well made in the review by Beard 1993.

13. In "When the Chips Are Down" (2004b:29), Jonathan Z. Smith claims to have first used the term in "Sacred Persistance: Toward a Redescription of Canon" (Smith 1988). See also especially McCutcheon 1998 and Mack 2001.

a wide range of ancient discourses. There is, in fact, extensive evidence for ancient ideas about gender, but this, too, must be extracted largely from the writings of elite male authors, although it is visible in various practices, which are known through authors' descriptions and archaeological evidence, architectural relations, and so forth. Such ideas are inextricably linked with systems of privilege and prestige: they tend to serve the interests of men in general, and certain elite, powerful men in particular, both in their subordination of women to male interests in heirs and property, and in their use of a gender hierarchy to subordinate other men (and women).

Although numerous scholars have written about the difficulties of extracting women's history from ancient texts,[14] the work of Elizabeth Clark, a scholar of late antique Christianity (including those writings long known as "patristic") has been particularly influential. In a series of articles on the representation of women in various ancient Christian male authors, Clark has argued vociferously that we cannot write women's history from these sources or social history, at least of a particular sort; at best, she proposes, we can write a certain kind of intellectual history, including a history of ideas about gender, and the uses of gender in ancient power contests.[15]

For Clark, the problems of using ancient accounts of women, particularly those in the high literary productions of (male) Christian writers from the second through the fifth centuries C.E., are very much grounded in theoretical concerns. Scholars in the field, she charges, have utilized ancient texts to write histories of ancient Christianity, including histories of ancient Christian women, without sufficient attention to the theoretical presumptions behind such enterprises. It has been standard practice in the study of ancient Christianity to operate from the theoretical perspective of a phenomenologically grounded, hermeneutical approach, in which texts are presumed to have an original meaning, located in the intentions of the author, and explicable only against a particular historical context. Although Clark does not spell this out, this perspective is hermeneutic in the sense that it seeks to interpret the text, by comprehending or understanding what the author would have meant (and

14. See, e.g., Cameron 1980; Halperin 1990; Winkler 1990; Beard 1995; Cooper 1996; Martin and Miller 2005. The idea that already in the Hebrew Bible, stories about women are really about relations between men is argued by Niditch 1991[1998]:39. Of rabbinic texts, Daniel Boyarin writes: "Many critics have realized that these texts are essentially literary, that is fictional, accounts about men and (occasionally) women who probably lived but functioned primarily as signifiers of values within the culture, as exempla," in Boyarin 1993:11. Similarly, Michael Satlow argues that "Palestinian rabbinic stereotypes [about women as magicians, as domestic, as meddlesome, gossips, devious, etc.] have little to do with real women, but much to do with men, and how rabbinic men defined themselves as men," in Satlow 2002:227. See also Levine 1992.

15. E.g., Clark 1994; 1998a; 1998b; 1998c; 1999; 2000. These arguments are developed at length in Clark 2004. For additional bibliography, see Kraemer 2008.

thought, and felt), and by appealing to the notion that subsequent readers can access that authorial intention, and sympathize, if not empathize.[16] It is phenomenological in the sense that it presumes sufficient commonality of human experience to make such sympathy, if not empathy, possible. Because there are "essential" elements (or qualities, or experiences) of being human, such interpretation is both desirable and feasible (given a minimally sufficient knowledge of language, history and so forth). The goal of interpretation, then, is fully understanding what the author intended, often with the further goal of appreciating, if not also validating, the author's views. This is, of course, often, but not always the case. Most interpreters of ancient Christianity have been Christians, often predisposed to read Christians sympathetically, although some have been critics of Christianity, predisposed to read "un-orthodox" texts sympathetically.

Such assumptions, clearly visible in scholarly practices but rarely acknowledged or defended, may be contrasted with the critiques of contemporary literary theorists. Particularly instructive for Clark are the arguments of Jacques Derrida, who argued against any inherent connection between a text and its context, as evidenced in the fact that texts are "readable" even in the absence of any context. Rephrasing Derrida, Clark writes, "the peculiarity of the written sign lies in its break with its (original) context: it is 'readable' even if the circumstances of its production and authorial intent remain unknown."[17] For Derrida, this is true of *all* written works (provided, one presumes, that a reader knows the language sufficiently to read in any sense at all). Because texts are readable apart from their initial context, context cannot be determinative of meaning or, at least, context cannot bear the weight of explanation. This does not render authorial intention useless, but it does (or should) mean that texts are inevitably multivalent, and that authorial intention provides, at best, one set of possible meanings. Derrida argued further that appealing to authorial intention as the locus of meaning was itself a political claim, functioning to authorize or privilege certain interpretations and readings over others.[18] Although Clark herself does not entirely want to dispense with the role of authorial intention in the reading of texts,[19] her point seems at least to be that scholars of ancient texts have read in particular ways without sufficient attention to or

16. For an overview of hermeneutics, see Green 2008.

17. Clark 2004:142.

18. Clark 2004:144, quoting Derrida 1989:841, 821.

19. "Thus contextualism both broadly and narrowly construed . . . appears inadequate as a model of historical explanation and interpretation. For scholars of 'high' philosophical and literary texts such as those of early Christianity, whose precise original contexts are often a matter of sheer guesswork, appeal to context as explanatory has definite limitations—although, I concede, perhaps not so many as Nietzsche's famously indecidable sentence ['I have lost my umbrella'—found on a scrap of paper among his writings] might suggest." Clark 2004:145.

defense of their theoretical implications. One may extrapolate, then, that assuming that meaning resides only in authorial intention, and that authorial intention is itself ever accessible, carries with it a whole host of political implications, in that privileging a particular interpretation inevitably gives authority to some persons and positions and not others. To privilege authorial intention is not only to engage a whole series of assumptions about consciousness (including conscious or deliberate intentionality), but also to then ignore, or at least miss, the ways in which texts exercise power, authority, domination, resistance, and any number of social relations that may or may not have been present in the author's self-awareness.

Alternative reading strategies, although not denying that authors have intentions and purposes, refuse to privilege authorial intentions and purposes. Instead, they attend to other things: to seeing the ways in which texts function regardless of authorial intention. One of these alternative practices, poststructuralism, explains narratives, texts, myths, and so forth in terms of structures that are inherent in human thinking but not consciously present (although perceptible to trained observers). The binary oppositions (e.g., good and evil, light and dark, right and left, soul and body, rationality and emotion, activity and passivity, masculine and feminine) that occur in many of the texts I treat in this study are aspects of these structures. This in turn is a theory of human activity that claims we do things without being fully conscious of them; that we utilize symbols, for instance, without a conscious awareness of what they are or how they work. Some theorists, particularly but not only the influential French sociologist, Pierre Bourdieu, have further argued for the centrality of "misrecognition," to which I return in the last chapter. Humans engage in various practices that we explain in one set of terms even while they are clearly, at least to observers (and sometimes perhaps even to us), doing something else.[20] For Bourdieu, misrecognition is specifically the "misrecognizing" of one's interests in competitions for cultural and symbolic capital in diverse fields.[21]

Clark charges that, relatively insulated from the debates about literary theory, scholars of ancient Christianity[22] have tended to read many texts as relatively transparent and corresponding not only to the thoughts and beliefs of

---

20. It is not entirely clear to me what happens once one becomes aware of such strategies; for example, what is the impact on practice once a theory of practice is articulated?

21. See, e.g., Bourdieu 1993 [1977]:75.

22. Clark actually sees this as truer of scholars of what used to be called patristics and has now come to be called ancient Christianity: she thinks it is less true of scholars of the New Testament. Although it may be true that many scholars of the New Testament have utilized literary theory, and perhaps even cultural theory, much of the study of women in the New Testament continues to see accounts of women, especially in the gospels, as historically useful.

actual persons (which, to some extent, they are by definition as the work of some human agents), but also corresponding unproblematically to the experiences, events, and practices of actual persons. Of particular significance have been appeals to verisimilitude, the discounting of fabulae and miracles that strain the credulity of contemporary scholars in general notwithstanding.[23] The details of ordinary life within a text have regularly been invoked as useful for historical and social reconstruction. Clark draws on the work of critics, such as Roland Barthes, to caution against such arguments and approaches. Verisimilitude itself can be a rhetorical device, functioning not to tell us about real social detail, but to persuade the reader of the truth of the text's constructions.[24] "The very details that social historians argue give veracity to a text are here repositioned as a creative artist's attempt to create an illusory reality in the reader's imagination."[25] Verisimilitude lures us in with a façade of reality: "we are led to accord considerable truth to the account because so many 'effects of the real' have been summoned up."[26] From all this, Clark concludes that texts taken to be usable representations of women turn out to be men talking about women for entirely different purposes.

Beyond misconstruing verisimilitude as providing reliable access to aspects of ancient life, scholars of ancient Christianity have been inattentive to the functions of narrative as a whole. Here Clark draws on the work of various theorists to propose that the actual functions of narrative are the furtherance of particular social values and not the provision of "accurate" and "reliable" representations of the past, which is itself inaccessible by its nature.[27] Historical narrative, despite its appearance, is little more reliable than novels and is, itself, a kind of fiction.[28] Clark concedes that historical "recovery" at least of ancient (Christian) women has had its uses, which were themselves political. They "constitute[d] a celebratory move that lauded our 'foremothers'."[29] But her current view is far more pessimistic: "the voices of real women are so appropriated by male authors in Christian texts that we are

23. This last is my observation, not Clark's.

24. Clark 1998a:419–21.

25. Clark 1998a:420.

26. Clark 1998a:422. She continues: "How far should an historian press such a hermeneutics of suspicion? What kind of histories will they write if what they took to be social detail is now recast as literary construction?"

27. On the functions of narrative, Clark quotes Hayden White: "to produce notions of continuity, wholeness, closure, and individuality that every 'civilized' society wishes to see itself as incarnating," Clark 1998a:421, from White 1987 [1980]:87. "[H]istorians work over the 'traces' of past events—to the events themselves we have no access—and endow them with 'symbolic' significance." Clark 1998a:421, quoting White 1980:102, and White 1984; no pp. given.

28. Clark 1998a:421.

29. Clark 1998a:430.

unlikely to be able to hear them." At best, she suggests, "interesting work may continue to examine how 'woman,' how gender, is constructed in early Christian texts, but will also move beyond purely linguistic concerns to explore the social forces at work in these constructions."[30] How and why those same literary sources that Clark finds so inhospitable for historical reconstruction can nevertheless facilitate reconstruction of social forces goes unexplained here.

Cognizant of these discussions, my more recent work attends far more carefully to the degree to which the rhetorical uses of gender obscure our vision of antiquity. At the same time, it is important to acknowledge that I am equally cognizant of the extent to which some, if not much of the "theory" that Clark invokes, is now on the wane, or even rejected.[31] Thus, I should clarify that when I characterize my interests as theoretical, I mean not the particular constellation of what is often meant by "theory," namely, postmodernism, "literary-critical" theory, and Marxist-based "cultural" theory, among others. Rather, I mean theory as explanation, or at least, as the endeavor to explain: to account for why this and not that.[32] In this project, I revisit much of the evidence for women's behaviors and beliefs, in order to focus more on particular theoretical, explanatory issues, that is, on the relationships between those behaviors and beliefs and ancient constructions of gender.

Another way in which this study differs from my prior work is in my further attention to categories and definitions. These issues have, in fact, engaged my work since my undergraduate days, but I realize that I have not always been as explicit as I should have been about definitions, in particular of the key categories of women, gender, and, of course, religion. All these have been contested, some more so than others. I make no claims here for the ontological status of my definitions, which I do not claim to correspond to something like ideal platonic phenomena. Rather, they serve as working delineations, themselves subject to revision.[33]

30. Clark 1998a:430.

31. See, e.g., Hoff 1994; Ramazangolu 1996; Hoff 1996; Latour 2004; Menand 2005; Boyd 2006; Slingerland 2008:1–4.

32. Put more formally and elegantly by Stowers 2008:7: "Explanation is a form of redescription. Most often it involves taking a subject matter described in native, folk, and local terms and redescribing it in terms designed by the researcher to answer the researcher's questions, to broaden the scope of the data, and to understand it systematically, if possible."

33. In doing so, I think I mean to align myself with the view that there is, for instance, no platonic ideal "religion," nor of "gender"; that there is only a humanly determined category imposed on particular phenomena. Our perception of meaningful similarity and our formation/formulation of definitions is what imposes categories.

Women

In this study, I utilize the term *women* as broadly and inclusively as possible to encompass those persons in antiquity whom we would recognize as such by twenty-first century methods of discerning anatomical and genetic difference.[34] Further, I use the plural category *women* rather than the singular *woman* to avoid aligning myself with arguments that there are any fundamental, inescapable, essential characteristics inherent in being a woman. I intend the term *women* to signal adult status, while recognizing that such status is itself culturally determined.

In the Greco-Roman Mediterranean, the terms we generally translate as *woman* or *women* usually encode numerous and complex elements of social identity, including distinctions of physical and social maturity, of rank and class, of licit marriage, and so forth.[35] In Greek, *gunē* denotes both an adult female, and one who is married.[36] So, too, *anēr* denotes both an adult male and one who is married. The distinction must often be inferred from the context; sometimes this is ambiguous, rendering translation difficult. This usage is not entirely unlike our own, however, where the terms *woman* and *man* are sometimes synonyms for wife and husband, although much less frequently (or else our sensitivity to nuance makes it easier for us to discern connotation).[37] In Greek, *paidiskē* designates a free female child, as well as a female servant or slave. As was also true of the designation of adult women slaves in the American South as *girl*, so, too, in antiquity, the use of the same term for these different social identities points to the infantilization of enslaved adults.

The range of terms in Latin is somewhat greater. The Latin *femina/feminae* can signify femaleness generically, but unlike the somewhat equivalent Greek *thēlus* (*thēleia*), which denotes femaleness, but not persons, it is often used to denote, not only females, but specifically women. Frequently, however, the common term for women in Latin is *mulier/mulieres*. The relevant Latin vocabulary for marital partners is unquestionably larger, pointing perhaps to a more

34. For some discussion of the category, see Riley 1988 and Oyewùmí 2001. See also the brief discussion in Brooten 1996:15.

35. Hanson 1990; 1999.

36. All of this was verified (or in some cases determined) by using the English to Latin and Greek functions on Perseus, searching definitions in Lewis and Short for Latin; and LSJ for Greek. A search of Greek produces no approximate synonyms for γυνή. The primary other differentiations are γραῦς (an old woman, with negative connotations); κόρη or κοράσιον (a young girl, or "maiden"); and τριβάς (a woman who has sex with other women: literally one who rubs)!

37. This dual usage persists in French, for instance, where the word for wife is regularly "femme," although the ordinary term for a husband is "mari," not "homme."

complex classification system than that available in Greek. Latin has a specific term for a wife, *uxor*, for which there is no simple masculine equivalent. As is true also in Greek, the principal Latin term for a man, *vir*, regularly also connotes a married man. Although a feminine form of *vir*, *vira*, is attested,[38] it occurs most commonly in the complimentary designation *univira*, the woman married only once (perhaps more literally a "one-man woman") and the *bivira*.[39]

In Latin, class distinctions are also discernible, not entirely unlike the connotations of the English *lady*. This is clearly true with the Latin term *matrona* (often translated with the cognate *matron*), which connotes free status and licit marriage. Conversely, *puella*, regularly used of young females, frequently carries with it connotations either of low social status or nonmarital sexual relations, or both, when applied to persons no longer considered children.[40]

Beyond these various distinctions of status, additional meanings appear to be encoded. Holt Parker, for instance, has proposed that a better definition of a *femina/puella* is precisely a person who is sexually penetrated in the vagina.[41] Persons liable to such penetration who refuse or renounce it would seem, then, to be no longer female, but male. Parker's argument has ramifications for understanding the Roman category of *virgo* and perhaps also the Greek category of *parthenos*. Both are ordinarily translated in English as *virgin*. As in English, the unmarked virgin is female (requiring the locution "male virgin"); so too, in Greek, *parthenos* ordinarily refers to females. Virgins may then be persons capable of being vaginally penetrated who have not (yet) been so. As I shall develop, particularly in chapter 4, on Thecla, the possibility that virgins constitute a separate category distinct from women undergirds certain early Christian discourse about women holding office and exercising masculinity authority. The Greek *gunaikes*, too, may, then, at least sometimes, be understood not so much as a reference to married women, as a reference to adult females who are subject to vaginal penetration.

Although I have no interest in assenting or subscribing to these ancient distinctions, they may be relevant for thinking about the relationships between religion and gender in the ancient world, not the least for the ways in which, as we shall see, some religious behaviors and beliefs participate in the formation and maintenance of these very distinctions.[42]

---

38. The only instance given in Lewis and Short is from Isid., *Orig.* 11.2.33: *quae nunc femina, antiquitus vira vocabatur*: what [or perhaps: she who] is now called *femina* was in ancient times called *vira*.

39. The term *maritus* also frequently signifies a married man; it has a feminine counterpart, *marita*.

40. Although interestingly, Lewis and Short claims that *puella* only rarely denotes a female slave. The discussion here is my own; for a far more detailed consideration, see Santoro L'Hoir 1992, who demonstrates the elite class connotations of *vir* and *femina* versus the generic *homo* and *mulier*.

41. Parker 1997:49. His language is considerably coarser, but the point is clear enough.

42. See, e.g., Cole 2004; Goff 2004; Takács 2007. I return to this issue in the last chapter.

Gender

Gender as both a concept and a topic of inquiry within the study of the ancient Mediterranean is relatively recent.[43] In the mid-1970s, anthropologists, historians, literary scholars, and those in what was then called women's studies had begun to focus on gender as a category of analysis. A profoundly influential collection of essays published in 1974 acknowledged the reality of biological difference, but posited that the interpretation of that difference was cultural: "what is male and what is female will depend upon interpretations of biology that are associated with any culture's mode of life."[44] The first use of the language of "the sex/gender system" appears to occur in an essay in another anthropology anthology published the following year, whose editor wrote that "[r]ecent studies in the biological bases of sex difference and on human gender systems have revealed flexible, culturally influenced structures."[45] Feminist anthropologists quickly produced numerous studies of gender, such as MacCormick and Strathern's *Nature, Culture, Gender,* or Ortner and Whitehead's *Sexual Meanings: The Cultural Construction of Gender and Sexuality,* whose preface defined "sexual meanings" as a "symbol, or system of symbols, invested with culturally variable 'meanings.'"[46] This definition had tremendous potential: "seeing sex and gender as symbols liberates this whole area of inquiry from constraining naturalist assumptions and opens it to a range of analytical questions that would otherwise not be asked."[47]

By the late 1980s, these insights and arguments began to infiltrate the scholarship both on the ancient Mediterranean generally, and on the study of religions more specifically.[48] Yet as Harraway pointed out some years ago, as "a concept developed to contest the naturalization of sexual difference in multiple arenas of struggle," gender is thus itself highly liable to contestation.[49] Defining and theorizing gender was and remains contentious.[50]

---

43. In the first explicitly feminist treatment of women's lives in ancient Greece and Rome, (Pomeroy 1975) the term *gender* occurs rarely, only in reference to grammatical usage. My review essay on women in the religions of the Greco-Roman Mediterranean (Kraemer 1983) contained no studies by scholars of antiquity that utilized gender as a central category of analysis.

44. Rosaldo and Lamphere 1974:5.

45. Rubin 1975 in Reiter 1975. For the identification of Rubin's formulation as the earliest, see Harraway 2001[1991]; see also Harding 1983 (in Harraway 2001[1991]:73).

46. MacCormack and Strathern 1980; Ortner and Whitehead 1981.

47. Ortner and Whitehead 1981:ix.

48. E.g., Winkler 1990; Rawson 1986; Bynum, Harrell, and Richman 1986.

49. Harraway 2001[1991] 53.

50. See, e.g., Wittig 1983; Bynum 1986; Scott 1986; Butler 1990; 1993; 2004; King 1995; Boyarin 1998; Castelli 2001; Bourdieu 2001 [1998]; Kuefler 2001.

In my own work, I have tended to use gender to designate culturally constructed meanings assigned to or associated with biological sex that vary considerably from one cultural context to another, whether in difference places, different communities, different historical periods, and so forth. Although I have understood gender as the product of human activity, something humans create, sustain, reinforce, and reinterpret, in the cultures I study, these meanings are almost always taken to be natural rather than cultural. Further, I understand gender as necessarily relational: ideas about femininity and masculinity never stand in isolation, but rather are always integrally linked to one another. Feminine is a category that has no meaning except in relation to masculine, and vice versa.[51]

There are unquestionably difficulties with this kind of definition. A prominent French gender theorist, Monica Wittig, argued over twenty years ago that "there are not two genders. There is only one: the feminine, the 'masculine' being not a gender. For the masculine is not the masculine but the general."[52] Wittig insisted that the production of ideas about sex "conceal[s] the fact that social differences always belong to an economic, political ideological order."[53] Extending Wittig's analysis, Daniel Boyarin has proposed that "[i]t is the socioeconomic needs of particular groups of people that generate the necessity for reproductive sexual intercourse, and that necessity is best served by the ideology of sexual difference, of sexual dimorphism as the primary salient feature for the classification of human beings, and the charge of desire for intercourse that it is designed to produce."[54]

Another highly influential gender theorist, Judith Butler, observed some years ago that inherent in definitions like this is the notion that sex is natural and biological, and that gender is cultural. Such a definition both relies on and replicates a dichotomy between nature and culture that has played a significant role in the subordination of women to men. Thus, Butler argued that "gender is . . . the discursive/cultural means by which 'sexed nature' or 'a natural sex' is produced and established as 'prediscursive,' prior to culture, a politically neutral surface *on which* culture acts."[55] More recently, in a fascinating study of the role played by redefinitions of masculinity in the success of Christianity, Matthew Kuefler asserts that "attempts to distinguish neatly between sex and

---

51. This definition is similar in some respects to that of David Halperin: "socially and ideologically significant distinctions [mapped] onto biological differences between the sexes," 1990:264. This definition doesn't, unfortunately, define biological difference and presumes the existence of [two] sexes, but it might work well enough as a description of how elite male Greeks authors thought.

52. Wittig 1983:64, cited in Kuefler 2001.

53. Wittig 1992:2, cited in Boyarin 1998:118.

54. Boyarin 1998:118.

55. Butler 1990, cited in Boyarin 1998:117.

gender are outdated,"[56] even while, ultimately, he construes his own project as "about the social construction of gender," which he defines briefly as "the social meaning given to this differentiation."[57] And as I will pursue further in the last chapter, Pierre Bourdieu has recently tried to argue that it is not biological difference that generates the category of gender, but, on the contrary, prior paradigms of gender difference that are projected onto perceptions of the biological.

Three decades of feminist scholarship, particularly in classics, has greatly illuminated the prevailing constructions of gender in the ancient world, and associated constructions of sexuality, as well as the centrality of gender in the organization and structure of ancient social life.[58] Central to these constructions is the notion that men are properly active (and penetrating): women are properly passive (and penetrated); gender is always hierarchical, and is an overarching means of expressing hierarchy in other domains (e.g., slavery, human/divine relations, etc.). That scholarship has also demonstrated that gender difference permeated all aspects of ancient social life: meals and foods, dress, sexual practices, bodily comportment, war, education, politics, commerce, and those practices we categorize under the label of religion.

Although the languages in which ancient elite males wrote lack a vocabulary that corresponds easily to the English terms *gender* and *sex*, a widely held theory of human reproduction associated with Aristotle, Hippocrates, Galen, and various other medical writers reveals some of implicit central elite theories about both gender and sexual difference. As many contemporary scholars read these texts (and, perhaps, in accord with Wittig's view), there was really only one sex, of which males were the more perfect form.[59] As Joshua Levinson puts it, in this model, "sexual difference is a matter of degree and not kind, and thus a woman is an undercooked or parboiled man," because a crucial difference between men and women was the amount of heat.[60] Both men and women produced reproductive seed of either sex. The dominant seed determined the biological sex of the resulting child, but the degree of masculinity or femininity of the child was a function both of the quality of that seed,

---

56. Kuefler 2001:5. It is somewhat unnerving to have a 1995 Ph.D. see the work of scholars twenty years earlier as belonging to "older generations."

57. Kuefler 2001:14.

58. The literature here is now extensive: readers may peruse the Bibliography at the conclusion of this book for many relevant entries, which themselves contain a wealth of additional bibliography.

59. The view that a one-sex theory undergirds this reproductive theory is associated particular with LaQueur 1990. Although Joshua Levinson, for instance, supports this view (Levinson 2000), others, like Kuefler read the same reproductive theories as pointing to an underlying paradigm of "opposite sexes" (Kuefler 2001:22, citing Rousselle 1988).

60. Levinson 2000. Levinson is by no means the only person to consider these issues, but his discussion is particularly clear and elegant.

and of the child's "education and habits" (to quote Hippocrates).[61] Since both women and men could produce male and female seed, seed itself could be of four types: male/masculine; male/feminine; female/masculine and female/feminine. The combining of these four types, though, produced not four but rather six possibilities. Masculine seed from a man combined with masculine seed from a woman produced an ideal man. Similarly, feminine seed from a man combined with feminine seed from a woman produced an ideal woman. But masculine seed from a man combined with feminine seed from a woman could produce either an ordinary man, if the masculine seed dominated the feminine, or a highly feminized male, if the feminine seed dominated. Masculine seed from a woman combined with feminine seed from a man similarly produced two possibilities, both androgynous, but tending more toward one than the other.

The combination of seed was not, however, the only factor accounting for the identity of the resulting child. Rather, the actual gestation process was thought to play a significant role. According to the third-century rhetorician, Lactantius, males were thought to be properly gestated in the right side of the womb and females in the left. Male seed implanted in the left side of the uterus or female seed implanted in the right side produced admixtures. This theory provided an explanation for observed realities: men and women with perceived characteristics of the other, such as stature, voice, and so forth, as well as persons with ambiguous genitalia and other ambiguities.[62]

Kuefler points out that this theory of gestation was seen to account for all other elements of gender differentiation: virtue/vice; dominance/submission, hard/soft, aggression/passivity, and so forth. In his phrasing, "sexual difference became social difference."[63] Yet this same theory had an inherent difficulty: "if the only thing separating male and female was the direction in which the male seed drifted after intercourse, then the all-important dividing line between male and female, and the social privileges that followed from that dividing line, were quite tenuous indeed."[64]

This theory of reproduction served as an explanation for ancient perceptions of the spectrum of possible gender identities. It correlates particularly well with the extensively documented anxiety felt particularly by elite Roman

---

61. Hippocrates, *On Regimen* I.xxviii, cited in Levinson 2000.

62. Persons with ambiguous genitalia were generally classed as male, an assignment that reflects the concept of the masculine as general and universal. The absence of male genitalia makes the person female; otherwise, even given ambiguities, the person is still male, see Kuefler 2001:24.

63. Kuefler 2001:21.

64. Kuefler 2001:22.

males over the fragility of their masculinity, and their constant need to assess the masculinity of other men, and demonstrate their own.[65] If women worried about the degree of their true femininity, we have virtually no indication of this. Instead, we have some occasional evidence for women's interest in emulating masculinity, or perhaps more accurately, evidence for male authors who envision women with such interests.

As Levinson reads it, the combination of male and female seed in all persons meant that everyone was, to some degree, androgynous. The gendered identity of individuals did not, then, map easily onto their apparent anatomical sex. Some degree of what I have tended to think of as "slippage" was always possible. Further, as Levinson also considers, the relationship between male and female seed was an integral part of ancient ideologies of power. "Gendered dichotomies," he writes, "inevitably invoked the postures of ruler and ruled, master and slave, dominant and subordinate peoples." These particular reproductive theories thus "reproduced *in utero* the sexual politics of domination and submission, where to be female was to be imperfect."[66] Metaphors of warfare and mastery were commonly invoked to describe the struggle for a child's identity.

Along similar lines, Parker has argued that ideas about male and female, active and passive can be mapped on a four-quadrant grid (like that of Levinson's reproductive possibilities). Although activity was coded positively, and passivity coded negatively, gender qualified these valuations. Of the resulting four possibilities, the active male and the passive female were both coded positively, whereas the passive male and the active female were both coded negatively. For Parker, these valuations undergird or, at least, correlate with well-documented ancient views about social relations, including sexuality. He proposes that at least for the Roman elite, sex could be defined as an active male penetrating an orifice of a passive (and subordinate) other with his penis, whether that other was male or female.

Parker's grid raises some particularly germane issues. To some extent, all four types are heuristic devices, but more so the passive man and the active woman. Parker argues that the notion of the *cinaedus*, the man who (inappropriately) finds pleasure in being penetrated and humiliated, is a necessary correlate to the active man who (appropriately) takes pleasure in penetrating subordinates. Similarly, he argues that the *tribas*, the woman who is sexually active and penetrating (as best she can be, lacking a biological penis) is also a necessary correlate to the passive woman. Whether, however, such persons

---

65. See, e.g., Gleason 1995; 1999; C. Williams 1999; Gunderson 2000; McDonnell 2006.
66. Levinson 2000.

actually exist, or are merely required by the grid, he is uncertain. Because the system requires the construction of negative monstrosities, the passive man, and the active woman, it is possible that no such persons corresponding exactly to these categories really existed in antiquity. Rather, they are accusations leveled against suspect persons, opponents, and so forth. Parker concedes that there probably were persons (men, in this case) who enjoyed being the passive recipients of other men's penetration, but who would not own the label *cinaedus*. The analogous question is whether there were women who corresponded to their imagined grid correlates.

Although for Parker, the active female is always coded negatively, in some philosophical circles, and in ascetic Christian contexts, actual women could be active and positively coded, but only under certain circumstances. They needed either to be celibate and/or constructed as male or masculine, that is, not subject to the subordination and passivity that typified ancient constructions of femininity. At the same time, of course, the construction of women as male was ordinarily accomplished by their renunciation of femininity and sexuality through a variety of mechanisms, including celibacy, and the attainment of a postmenopausal state (itself perhaps presumed to be the equivalent of celibacy). Numerous instances may be adduced here, from Philo's characterization of the Therapeutic women philosophers (considered in chapter 3), to the ascetic celibacy of Christian women like Thecla (considered in chapter 4), to the transvestite saints who populate the late antique Christian imagination (and who seem always to be women in male clothing, rather than men in female clothing).[67] This raises questions, however, about whether such women continued to fall within the category of women, or whether the combination of activity and femaleness was sufficiently "monstrous," as Parker calls it, to require redefining such persons.

Further, implicit Roman definitions of sex as a man penetrating a passive subordinate were not universally shared. Although ancient rabbis, also, seem to have defined sex in terms of male penetration, for them, the truly masculine man (i.e., the rabbi) does not penetrate men, let alone allow himself to be penetrated.[68] For Philo, too, no sex between men is acceptable, regardless of the other hierarchical social relationships.[69] We might explain this divergence as a function of their reading of biblical prohibitions against sex between men (but not, interestingly, between women), regardless of whether contemporary

67. E.g., Anson 1974; Davis 2002.
68. Satlow 1994.
69. Szesnat 1998.

authors are right that what the author(s) of Lev 18.22 and 20.13 intended to prohibit is being the passive partner.[70]

Further, although Parker doesn't parse this, constructions of masculinity, if not also femininity, varied according to social class and other status indicators, particularly the distinction between free persons and slaves.[71] Regardless of their anatomical bodies, in their relations with free persons, slaves were always feminized, if, perhaps, some more so than others. At the same time, of course, it's interesting to reflect on how much non-elites shared these categories. Did, for instance, enslaved persons understand their own relationships with each other in these terms? Did their mutual status as slaves mean that neither a male slave nor a female slave could claim a hierarchically dominant role, or did they reproduce the system imposed on them onto their own arrangements? Was a male slave who was subjected to the sexual desires of his master nevertheless the dominant penetrator of his female partner? Lacking reliable sources from the perspective of enslaved persons, these questions remain mostly cautionary.

Religion

For a professor of religious studies with three degrees from departments of religion, I have rarely written directly on problems of definition, although, as a teacher, I engage them regularly. Few speakers of English seem to find the term *religion* the least bit ambiguous or in need of careful precision. Like Justice Potter Stewart's famous characterization of obscenity,[72] they are sure that they know it when they see it, even if they can't define it. Yet the number of competing definitions of religion put forth in the last century alone is daunting. Among the better known are Edmond Tylor's "the belief in Spiritual Beings," or William James's "the feelings, acts and experiences of individual men in their solitude, so far as they apprehend themselves to stand in relation to whatever they may consider the divine," or Émile Durkheim's "a unified system of beliefs and practices relative to sacred things, that is to say, things set aside and forbidden—beliefs and practices which unite into one single moral community called a Church, all those who adhere to them."[73] To these relatively early

---

70. See Olyan 1994; Boyarin 1995; Milgrom, 2000; Walsh 2001 (a critique of Olyan). In another instance, *The Sentences of Pseudo Phocylides* 213–14 (van der Horst 1978) worries about guarding one's sons from the lust of men, but doesn't explicitly prohibit being the active partner.

71. See, e.g., Saller 1998; Glancy 2002.

72. *Jacobellis v. Ohio*, 378 U.S. 184 (1964).

73. Tylor 1871:1.383; James 1902:34; Durkheim 1965 [1913]:62.

formulations may be added a plethora of subsequent attempts at refinement and precision, including the oft-cited, somewhat torturous definition by Clifford Geertz that I find particularly unhelpful: "a religion is: (1) a system of symbols which acts to (2) establish powerful, pervasive, and long-lasting motivations in men by (3) formulating conceptions of a general order of existence and (4) clothing these conceptions with such an aura of factuality that (5) the moods and motivations seem uniquely realistic."[74]

In explicit criticism of Geertz' universalizing definition, Talal Asad has argued that the very concept of religion as a discreet arena of human thought and behavior, separable from other arenas of human thought and behavior, such as politics, art, economics, or philosophy, emerges at a particular moment in western European history, where a distinction between religion and politics, in particular, functions to circumscribe and thus limit the authority and power of the Christian Church. In this view, religion is itself an ideological category that cannot, or rather should not, function as a universal category of human practice.[75] While agreeing that the formulation of the category religion has its own discreet history, Daniel Boyarin has argued that the marking off of certain practices into a realm separated from other arenas of practice is rather a late antique (Christian) phenomenon.[76] Boyarin argues that the rabbinic ruling that even the rejection of major rabbinic beliefs and practices does not exclude one from membership in "Israel" effectively "refuses" this category.[77] Steve Mason has more recently argued that Christians invent a category of religion in the

---

74. Geertz 1973:90. James Frazer, in his famous *Golden Bough* (1922:58–59), defined religion as "a propitiation or conciliation of powers superior to man which are believed to direct and control the course of nature and of human life." More recent definitions include that of: Christian (1964:61): "Someone is religious if in his universe there is something to which (in principle) all other things are subordinated. Being religious means having an interest of this kind. A belief is a religious belief if it is about something taken in this way"; or that of Smart (1983:1): "the systems of belief which, through symbols and actions, mobilize the feelings and wills of human beings"; or that of Spiro (1966:96): "an institution consisting of culturally patterned interaction with culturally postulated superhuman beings"; or Klass (1995:38): "Religion in a given society will be that instituted process of interaction among the members of that society—and between them and the universe at large as they conceive it to be constituted—which provides them with meaning, coherence, direction, unity, easement, and whatever degree of control over events they perceive as possible"; or Stark and Bainbridge (1987:39): "systems of general compensators based on supernatural assumptions." On the history of these definitions see Smith 1998 and Wilson 1998: for a brief, general critique of these kinds of monothetic definitions, see Stowers 2008:8.

75. Asad 1993. Asad's argument itself, construing the category of religion as the product of particular, western, historical and political circumstances, may be intended (and I mean here to invoke conscious authorial purpose) to remove Islam and perhaps other non-Western practices from at least certain kinds of scrutiny, weakening the force of his position.

76. Boyarin 2004.

77. Although fascinating, as is all Boyarin's work, I'm unsure that he has demonstrated that this rabbinic view constitutes a real refusal of the category, although it might represent an argument that *Jewishness* (a term that doesn't exist in Aramaic/Hebrew) isn't identical to *religion* (and perhaps, then, raise questions about the category of Judaism, on which see now Mason 2007 and Elliott 2007). For a brief critique of arguments concerning the history of the category, see Stowers 2008:17 n.15.

mid-late second century C.E. They do so, Mason argues, in order to create both "Christianity" (a religion separable from distinctive ethnic devotions) and the counter-religion of "Judaism." In the process, Mason contends, they also create the religious category "Jew" as distinct from the prior ethnic category, Judean, an argument whose significance I will explore further in chapter 7.[78]

Definitions of religion have at least sometimes been interwoven with gender issues. They have been drawn, often, from observations about the practices and beliefs of men as normative. One can see this, I think, in the definition of William James, whose use of the phrase "individual men" probably was largely gender specific, even if unreflexively so. Furthermore, historically, debates about distinctions between religion and other similar kinds of practices have been closely linked to issues of gender. For instance, certain rituals exercising control over extrahuman beings, such as spirits or demons, may be designated "magic" or "witchcraft" when performed by women, particularly outside institutional control that is usually male. Identical or similar rituals may be considered religion when performed by men inside those same institutions.[79]

The plethora of competing and contested definitions of religion, themselves usually if not always ideological, might well encourage the refusal of the term, although perhaps not the category, even now. Recent highly innovative work in cognitive science, however, shows much promise in cutting through the debates about definitions of religion, explanations of religion, and even about the history of the category.[80] This work sees religion as "the concatenation of human activities centered on supernatural agents."[81] Religion, in turn, arises from human cognitions that are themselves the product of our evolutionary history, namely a predisposition to detect other agents, and a predisposition to think that these agents themselves have intentions and thoughts (usually called "a theory of mind"). Obviously, not all agents that we envision qualify as gods. Rather, gods are nonhuman agents, with intentions, who interact with humans, and who have certain counter-intuitive properties, for instance, omnipotence, omniscience, immortality, and so forth. They differ from humans (and from other nonhuman agents) in that, while humans have limited and flawed information and access to knowledge, gods have full access to the strategic knowledge that humans want.[82]

78. Mason 2007, on which see further, chapter 7; see also Elliott 2007.

79. On the problem with the category of magic, see Smith 2004a.

80. E.g., Hinde 2001; Pyysiäinen 2001; Boyer 2001; Tremlin 2006; Luomanen, Pyysiäinen, and Uro 2007; Slingerland 2008. I particularly recommend Tremlin 2006 for a clear, accessible yet rich discussion of these theories, which here I can only sketch minimally. For some critique, see B. H. Smith 2009.

81. Tremlin 2006:144.

82. Tremlin 2006:111–13.

These "god thoughts," however, are not in themselves religion. Rather, religion, including systematized reflections, rituals, and communities, emerges out of human social relations. Cognitive theorists argue that being social is itself evolutionary. The human mind is predisposed to social actions because social actions are adaptive. Living in groups and cooperating provides numerous survival benefits, such as protection from predators, maximally efficient hunting and foraging, response to illness and injury and other forms of mutual aid, shared childrearing, and so forth.[83]

A definition of religion grounded in this emerging research, and developed by my colleague at Brown, Stanley Stowers, is particular instructive as a viable delimiting of particular human activities to be scrutinized and analyzed. Stowers proposes that

> *Religions* are the often linked and combined practices (i.e., doings and sayings) of particular human populations (e.g., imagined as cultures, societies, ethnicities, groups, global movements) that involve the imagined participation of gods or other normally nonobservable beings in those practices and social formations and that shade into many kinds of anthropomorphizing interpretations of the world. *Religion* is the unfolding activity (including thinking and believing) involving those practices that postulate participation with and make reference to gods, normally nonobservable beings and anthropomorphizing interpretations of the world.[84]

Grounded particularly in practice theory,[85] Stower's definitions focus on the things human beings do (including things people say) as groups. They understand religions and religion to be practical; that is, they are oriented to "get[ting] things done, mak[ing] things right, and . . . keep[ing] them that way,"[86] as well as fundamentally social. This differs from some conceptions of religion as primarily about individual persons—as, for instance, William James's definition of religion as "the feelings, acts and experiences of individual men [sic] in their solitude."

In his acknowledgment that religions involve the "imagined participation" of various "normally non-observable beings," Stowers obviously agrees that

---

83. Tremlin 2006:107.

84. Stowers 2008:8–9. It is important to note Stowers's elaboration on the term "normally nonobservable," which "should not be taken in a positivistic way. It is not a claim about the reality and epistemological status of these beings, but about a characteristic of native conception. Gods, ancestors, and such are typically conceived as not in public view most of the time for various reasons, even if emanations, incarnations, visible instantiations, and representations of the full reality are common," Stowers 2008:9. This language improves significantly over the less precise "non-obvious beings" used by Guthrie 1993 and others.

85. Stowers 2008:18 n. 22.

86. Tremlin 112.

religions incorporate what we might consider "mental" activities—thinking about and assenting to certain ideas. Many people in North American/western European culture seem to think of religion primarily in terms of belief (by which we often mean not merely assent to particular propositions, but assent to such propositions in the absence of confirming evidence, or even in the presence of seemingly disconfirming evidence), that is, belief as opposed to knowledge. This emphasis on belief (over against, for instance, ritual) as central to religion itself has a history: the "faith versus works" opposition, which is both present in early Christian writings, debated fiercely there, and which plays a crucial role in the Protestant critique of Roman Catholicism in the sixteenth century and subsequently. (It is also regularly mapped onto Christian-Jewish dichotomies, aligning Christian, Protestant, and faith with Jewish, Catholic and works). Unlike Tylor's famous definition, Stowers's definition does not emphasize, let alone privilege, the category of belief. Still, it is important to note that in emerging cognitive theory of religion, cognitive processes, that is beliefs, and specifically beliefs in the existence of gods and their relations to humans, are the necessary prequisites for the social phenomenon of religion.

For Stowers, as for cognitive theorists of religion, these things people do (which includes things people say and things people think) are distinct from other kinds of human practices (doings, sayings, thinkings) because they involve "the imagined participation of gods and other normally non-observable beings in those practices . . . and . . . shade into many kinds of anthropomorphizing interpretations of the world."[87] Stowers's definition is about what humans, as populations do; it is not about the effects of those doings.[88] Stowers's definition has much to recommend it, particularly in its account of religion as a "class of practices," "a human activity, a social/cultural phenomenon," that in many instances is "imbedded in a rather seamless social and cultural whole," and cannot be easily separated from other spheres of human practice.[89]

Although cognitive theory of religion is an emerging field, it has tremendous implications for many issues. Cognitive theory provides a different basis for comparative religion[90] in its assumption that religion is endemic to humans. Yet where the master of comparative religions, Mircea Eliade, also assumed

87. In this regard, his definition differs from those of Geertz or Klass that make no explicit reference to gods or other "normally non-observable" beings and agrees, with modest modifications, with Spiro's insistence on the centrality of "culturally postulated superhuman beings." Stowers explicitly borrows the term "culturally postulated" from Spiro: Stowers 2008:18 n.18.

88. It differs from those of Geertz, Klass, and others as well in its avoidance of claims about any inherent or necessary function of religion.

89. Stowers 2008:10.

90. Tremlin 2006:146.

that humans were fundamentally, essentially religious, cognitive theory of religion offers a completely "natural," evolutionary explanation for religion that accounts both for its pervasiveness and its diverse cultural forms. Unlike Eliade, who thought that secular persons were deluding themselves and denying their innate religiosity, cognitive theory of religion also offers legitimation for contemporary secularists, because this same model of the propensity for religious thought also allows us to see that it originates, not in the existence of divine beings, but in our propensity to imagine them. It is, in this sense, completely nontheological. At the same time, it does not inherently rule out the possibility that such beings exist; it only argues that we would imagine them regardless of whether they existed. And in this sense, it provides a better explanation both for the pervasiveness of religion and for its diversity—while also arguing that, in fact, religious ideas, at least, are relatively limited and constrained by their cognitive origins.[91] Further, in its insistence that both religious thoughts, especially thoughts about gods, and religion are human universals, cognitive theory suggests that debates about the origins of the category of religion are only of limited value. In this model, there is always religion, although its particular forms may be historical, and even our debates about the category have historical explanations.

With regard to religion, then, I would like to think that my regular appeal to naturalist theories and theorists of religion from my dissertation on has been sufficient to signal my own naturalist and often explicitly reductionist theoretical stances. Here, although I am only beginning to consider the ramifications of cognitive science, which seems to me highly promising, my views have not really changed in any fundamental way. I see religion as the product of human thought, agency, and activity, and I continue to find naturalist, and sometimes reductionist theories, to have particularly compelling explanatory power. Inherent in my own work has been the view, explicit in Mary Douglas's work, that religions participate in the construction of alternative and competing cosmologies, which religions themselves often serve to explain and legitimate. Recently, this view has been challenged by the scholars who argue that humans all share fundamentally similar cosmologies, without which communication would be impossible, a debate to which cognitive theory may well be able to contribute.[92] But while I concede the necessity of some shared assumptions about how the universe works, in my view, it is still the case that people co-exist at practical levels while holding to vastly different views of the cosmos,

---

91. Tremlin 2006:161.

92. See, e.g., Frankenberry 2002, a collection of essays responding to the arguments especially of Davidson.

its operations, and our place within it, and that these divergent views help to illuminate the range of religious practices and concomitant cosmologies in Greco-Roman antiquity.

Another terminological, if not definitional, note is in order. As I noted briefly earlier, and will return to in chapter 6, Mason and others have recently made the case that the better translation of the Greek and Latin terms *Ioudaios* and *Judeus* (and their various permutations of gender and person, as well as their adjectival forms) is Judean, not Jew, thereby signaling their ancient connotation of ethnicity (including devotion to particular deities), rather than religion. In this study, I have generally used Judean for the period before the second century C.E., and Jew (Jews, Jewish) for the late fourth century C.E. on. For the second century through the fourth, I have generally still preferred Judean, but with perhaps less consistency. In addition, I have generally retained the translation of Jew, Jews, Jewish when presenting the work of other scholars who utilize that terminology.

I am well aware that this usage is contentious, and that it produces some awkwardness. Because the evidence for *Ioudaioi* and *Judaei* extends from the Hellenistic period through the late Roman period, well into the Byzantine and early medieval periods, choosing the right term is often difficult when discussing material that cannot be dated precisely within this range. Even scholars who accept the translation of Judean for the earlier period are not entirely sure when it becomes more appropriate to speak of Jews, whether from the perspective of insiders or outsiders. Mason thinks that Christians begin developing the category of "Jew" as a religion by the mid-second century, yet one might reasonably argue that they are unsuccessful in imposing this scheme until at least the late fourth century, and even then, a shift from ethnicity to religion is complicated. Doubtless, some scholars will see these difficulties as sufficient justification for retaining the translation of Jew, Jews, and Jewish for all of Greco-Roman antiquity. But in my view, the rethinking that the translation Judean compels is worth the occasional inconsistency.

To make this book friendlier to readers who do not know the ancient languages, particularly those written in non-Roman fonts, I have transliterated Greek and Hebrew throughout the main body of the book: in the footnotes, I have made more use of specialized fonts. In both the main discussion and the notes, I have generally preferred English titles for ancient works, both for accessibility and also because, in many cases, the titles used by scholars are themselves Latin designations for works originally composed in Greek. In a few cases where English titles are awkward (such as Epiphanius' *Panarion*), I have retained the more standard scholarly conventions. I have also not provided references for standard editions and translations of well-known ancient sources (except where quoted directly) or sources that I only cite incidentally, since all this may be found easily in this digital age.

Although this study, then, differs in many ways from my earlier work, the resemblances are still discernible to any remotely attentive reader. Only after completing the manuscript did I realize that virtually all my cases are about conversion in some sense, or at least about voluntary religious practice, as opposed to the domestic and civic practices learned from early childhood on.[93] Some of this may be due to the interests of the authors of ancient accounts themselves. Women are most visible and of most interest (to men) when they exercise autonomy, an exercise that frequently threatens the social order. The changes they make are themselves often socially dangerous and require explication. Further, as I argue in several chapters, conversion itself is often coded as feminine, and, thus, female figures serve as particularly useful exempla.

Still, it is important to note that some of this may reflect my own choices. In this volume, for reasons of space, but also of idiosyncratic interest, I exclude further consideration of my recent work on Herodias and Salome,[94] on Berenice and Babatha;[95] and do not return to my older work on women's goddess devotions (some more freely chosen than others). Nor, with the relatively brief exception of Livy's account of the Bacchanalia considered in chapter 2, do I examine further women's devotion to Dionysos, which was the initial trigger for my realization, in my early graduate studies, of how poorly generations of prior scholars had attended to women's practices.[96] Further, in contrast to *Her Share of the Blessings*, most of the material in this book is about Judean and Christian women, or at least, about Judean and Christian practices, since some characters in my texts, such as Thecla, begin life as practitioners of their own other native devotions.

The chapter after this introduction attempts to illustrate the methodological and theoretical concerns of this project with four short case studies. The first revisits Livy's well-known account of women's roles in the importation of Bacchic rites to Rome in the second century B.C.E. The second examines an episode I have not previously discussed: the visions ascribed in the apocryphal *Acts of Thomas* to a resurrected Christian woman who tried, with limited success, to avoid heterosexual intercourse. The third considers rabbinic debates about the appropriateness of teaching women (to study) Torah. The last case

93. For further discussion of some of the theoretical issues around conversion, see chapters 6 and 7.
94. Kraemer 2006.
95. Kraemer 1999c; 2003.
96. Considerable subsequent work has been done on these topics, e.g., Lyons 1997; Staples 1998; Cole 2004; Goff 2004; Takács 2007.

analyzes a fascinating tale in the writings of the second-century Christian apologist, Justin Martyr, of a Roman matron whose husband bitterly opposed her attempts to take up the ascetic Christian life. Returning to the texts of my dissertation thirty-some years ago, chapter 3 revisits Philo's account of the Therapeutae, and then chapter 4 revisits the *The Acts of (Paul and) Thecla*, a text that has since become quasi-canonical in the academic study of early Christianity. In addition to the new case studies in chapter 2, chapter 5 also treats new material: a particularly compelling if vexing account of the coerced conversion to Christianity of the Jews on the island of Minorca in the early fifth century, which focuses especially on the resistance of Jewish women.[97]

Chapter 6 of this study moves away from an exclusive focus on literary materials, and their particular challenges, to two issues for which the sources are particularly (although not exclusively) epigraphical: non-Judean women's adoption of Judean religious practices, and Judean women's service as synagogue officers in diaspora Judean communities. Although *Her Share of the Blessings* explored this second issue in some depth, here I take up some of the critics of the view that women held such offices, as well as offering an explanation of some of the issues of the gender dynamics that may have been at work in antiquity. Finally, chapter 7 explores in some depth the implications of the various cases treated for the larger questions of the relationships between gender and women's religions in the Greco-Roman Mediterranean.

---

97. Ironically, although this represents some of the newest work in this project, this chapter appeared in the *Journal of Early Christian Studies* (Kraemer 2009) prior to the publication of this book, with the consent of the *Journal* and OUP.

2

Four Short Stories

A Bacchic Courtesan, the Reporter from Hell, the Daughters of Rabbis, a Roman Christian Matron

A Bacchic Courtesan

In the early second century B.C.E., the Roman Senate issued a decree banning the observance of certain rites devoted to the deity Romans called Bacchus and Greeks called Dionysos or Bakxos: a copy of this *Senatus Consultum* survives in inscriptional form.[1] It orders the immediate dissolution of existing Bacchic associations and outlaws private ownership of places where Bacchanalia are celebrated. Roman men are forbidden to be Bacchants (*Bacas*). No men may be priests in Bacchic service, and neither men nor women may be *magistri* (officers in charge of the affairs of a cultic organization). Bacchic rites may only be performed with permission of the urban prefect (*praetor urbanus*), and no more than five persons may participate. Of these, no more than two may be men; no more than three may be women. The urban prefect may, however, grant exceptions to these rules.

The circumstances that apparently led to the issuance of this decree are narrated in the *Annals* of the Roman historian, Titus Livy, a century or so later.[2] Woven into Livy's account are not only highly inflammatory and derogatory descriptions of rites said to have

---

1. *CIL* I² 581. The Senatus Consultum is presently in the Kunsthistorisches Museum in Vienna, inv. no. ANSAIII168, reproduced in Takács 2007:90.

2. Livy, *Annals of Rome* 39.8–18, WRGRW 102.

originated in Greece, but also several competing and somewhat contradictory explanations of how these came to be practiced, first in Italy outside of Rome, and then in the very city of Rome itself. In his first telling, "a nameless Greek (man)" brought the rites to Italy, where both women and men participated.[3] In the account put into the mouth of Hispala, a freedwoman and courtesan, whose lover had become a Bacchic, she tells the consul Postumius that the rites were first restricted entirely to women, until a Campanian woman named Pacula Annia initiated her own sons, and subsequently other men.[4] In the final version, Livy has Postumius himself tell an assemblage of Roman citizens (understood to be men) that the majority of Bacchic practitioners were women, and men "very like the women." Their rites were instituted by women, performed at night, by men and women together, and included drunkenness and indiscriminate sexual activities. Bacchic devotees were responsible, in fact, for all fraud and crimes committed in recent years, and their ultimate goal was control of the Roman state. Participation in these rites made young men effeminate and rendered them unfit to be soldiers defending the chastity of the wives and children of the male citizenry to whom the speech is addressed.

A few decades ago, this account, like numerous other accounts of women's activities, seemed tantalizing evidence for describing and analyzing the religious practices and experiences of women in ancient Mediterranean. Such inquiry was, in the early 1970s, terra incognita. Certain difficulties with these sources, of course, were obvious even then, historical skepticism being hardly a creation of the last thirty years. In addition to Livy's three somewhat contradictory accounts of how the Bacchic rites were first imported from Greece into Italy, his version of the Senatus Consultum differs at various points from that of the extant inscription.

Still, as I and others scholars began to scrutinize a plethora of ancient sources referring to women that had up to that point been vastly underanalyzed, it seemed reasonable to think that they provided some useful windows into ancient women's lives. Pioneering studies in women's history were beginning to demonstrate the extent to which women actors had been erased from many historical narratives and sources. Despite the obvious polemical uses to which Livy puts the narrative, perhaps women *were* the originators, leaders, and primary participants in the second-century B.C.E. Roman Bacchanalia. And if so, it should be possible to formulate some arguments about why these particular rites appealed to women, how women's leadership roles were authorized, and other comparable questions. Because my own training and interests

3. Livy, *Annals of Rome* 38.8.
4. Livy, *Annals of Rome* 38.14.

were already very much grounded in the larger field of religious studies, I, in particular, was interested in what difference such evidence would make to explanatory theories of religion, both religion in antiquity and religion more broadly.

Although it remains within the realm of possibility that women played some significant role in the importation of Bacchic rites from Greece to Italy in the second century B.C.E., several major shifts of perspective and analysis in the last thirty years have vastly refocused the scholarly gaze. Responding, as noted in the Introduction, to work in literary theory, new historical criticism, cultural criticism, critical theory, and the like, discussed in somewhat more detail later, many ancient historians and scholars of ancient religion have become deeply skeptical about the use of ancient texts, narrative or otherwise, for historical reconstruction and theorizing. Three decades of feminist scholarship on sources pertaining to women in the ancient Mediterranean, in concert with women's studies and gender studies more broadly, has greatly illuminated ancient understandings of gender, and the centrality of gender in the organization and structuring of ancient social life. Together, these developments strongly suggest that far from corresponding easily and usefully to women's experiences and lives, ancient sources deploy ancient ideas about gender, mapped onto female (and male) characters, to explore a range of issues of concern to their largely elite male authors and ancient audiences.

Livy's account of the importation of the Bacchanalia into Rome provides an excellent illustration of the implications of these challenges to older scholarly analysis, including, to some significant degree, some of my own work. It is rife with gendered elements. Virtually everything about the rites themselves may be plotted on one side of the binary (structural) oppositions coded as feminine. They are foreign, practiced by women and effeminate men. Bacchic devotees are perhaps leaderless, or led perhaps by women, itself a shameful reversal of gendered hierarchy. The rites are shameful, held at night in illicit gatherings where an improperly mixed group of men and women engage in lust, fraud, murder, madness, error, and impiety. Their performance emasculates unsuspecting young men, rendering them unfit for masculine military service, perhaps by involving them in homoerotic encounters. Proper Roman matrons engage in wholly improper practices. Bacchic men prophesy in a frenzied state, a characterization that invokes gender in several ways. Frenzy itself involves a lack of proper masculine self-control. Although men may certainly be prophets, prophesy flirts perilously with gender transgression: the very notion of prophesy relies on a gendered model of divine penetration of the human, constructing the deity as the male penetrator, and the human prophet as the passive recipient.

The address of the consul Postumius to an audience of concerned male citizens of Rome constitutes the structural opposite of the Bacchanalia. Postumius, a lawfully appointed official of the Empire, calls together the male citizenry in a lawful assembly held by day, in the open. He reads to them the decree of the lawfully constituted Roman Senate, and he contrasts the Bacchanalia with proper, licit, native Roman religion that relies upon edicts of the pontiffs, decrees of the Senate, and properly taken auspices as its guarantors of truth.

The punishments reported in Livy conform to Roman notions of gender. Convicted men were either imprisoned or publicly executed, whereas women were turned over to relatives or legal guardians for private punishment, reproducing a fairly fundamental construction of masculinity as public and femininity as domestic or private. Despite their participation in the same illicit rites, male offenders deserved public censure, implying the public weight of their offense. Women were disciplined privately, a distinction that might even be construed as a rebuke in itself: women's private punishment returns them to the private sphere and reinscribes on them the code of gender their Bacchic rites have challenged.

In both Livy's version and the extant inscription, the *Senatus Consultum* imposes restrictions that are both hierarchical and gendered. Henceforth, Roman men may not participate in the rites at all; men may not be priests, and no one—man or woman—may serve in the capacity of *magister* for a Bacchic association. By implication, foreign men and women, both foreign and Roman, may participate, and women may serve as priests, but no one can serve as *magister*, thus apparently depriving Bacchics of any real organizational structure. Bacchic rites can only be private, limited to no more than five persons, and even then only with the permission of the appropriate Roman authorities, the urban prefect, and the Senate.

Alien rites may thus be performed only under the most limited and controlled circumstances that, in their very marginality and constraints, contribute to the construction of religion itself as profoundly gendered. True, proper religion affirms the authority of the state and a gendered moral order, in which women are subordinate and feminine; men are superior and masculine. False religion comes from outside, challenges the authority of the state, fosters military weakness, and inverts gender relations. Gender inversion is accompanied by madness, disorder, and heinous crimes of all sorts. Roman gods themselves abhor it, and military vulnerability results: otherwise strong young men will no longer be able to defend women and children, and Rome itself will be at risk.

By itself, of course, none of this demonstrates that women were not to some degree involved in the importation and spread of Bacchic rites from Greece to Italy. Epigraphic evidence suggests, if not demonstrates, the regular participation of women in various Bacchic associations in Greece and Italy over hundreds of years.[5] But what seems unavoidable at this point is that the women actors in Livy's narrative function to condemn Bacchic rites and their adherents by tarring both with the taint of femininity and of dangerously transgressive gender inversion. Blaming the Bacchanalia on women is a rhetorical device to defame the rites that then provides us with little if any useful access to women's actual practices.

Livy's account is thus a textbook case of the problems of reconstructing and redescribing ancient women's religious devotions. Because associating foreign, disordered rites with women serves Livy's rhetorical agenda so well, it is difficult to assess whether Bacchic practitioners were in some self-conscious way critiquing ancient social hierarchy, including gender, or whether Livy's account is polemic directed against rites perceived to be threats against the social and political order whose assault on gender is offered only as demonstration of their assault on the entire social (and cosmic?) order. Yet not inconceivably, it is actual underlying social practice that affords Livy this rhetorical opportunity.

Further, Livy's account raises questions of contemporary reading strategies. One way to read the text is as a reflection of Livy's particular intentions, which are seen to be located in the specifics of his own time and interests. Numerous scholars have pointed out that Livy wrote this account at a time when the importation of foreign cults, particularly that of Cybele, into Rome was very much an issue,[6] and those scholars have suggested that his conscious intent was to defame present-day foreign rites by association with the catastrophe of the Bacchic rites several centuries earlier. Read in this way, the episode of the Bacchic rites clearly functions as a kind of polemical, cautionary tale.[7] Further, it seems highly likely that Livy's extended use of gender to defame the Bacchanalia and its participants is deliberate and self-conscious: he knew he was portraying them as both female and feminized; he knew he was portraying them as a threat to Roman masculinity; and he knew that gender hierarchy and the social order were integrally related.

Yet at the same time, the richness and complexity of Livy's description raises questions about just how conscious all this is, and just how much his account reflects underlying gendered structures and associations that were

---

5. Cole 1980; des Bouvrie 1997; Henrichs 1978; Goff 2004.

6. Livy, *Annals of Rome* 29.14, *WRGRW* 126B.

7. Hänninen 1998; Takács 2000; 2007:90–97. For Hänninen, gender is central to this account: she sees the Senate responding to a moral crisis, exemplified by women's public performance of transgressive cultic acts. Takács focuses less on the centrality of women and more on the Senate's desire to exert political authority. See also Levene 1993.

almost certainly not conscious. Conceivably, Livy has absorbed these associations to such a degree that they are ready to hand in his attack on the threat to Roman social order, and he is not entirely aware of the degree to which he incorporates gender into his polemic. This, in turn, raises questions about the basis of the numerous structural oppositions that Livy deploys so well: day and night, male and female, native and foreign, licit and illicit, public and private, true and false, and so on. Do we employ them largely without realizing that we do so, and if so, why?[8]

The Reporter from Hell

The degree to which constructions of gender are implicated in the representation of women in ancient narratives is further demonstrated through a second example. An anonymous Christian work now known as the *Acts of the Apostle Thomas* (or just the *Acts of Thomas*) incorporates a relatively brief tale of a woman murdered by her former lover after she refuses to join him in his abandonment of illicit sexual practices in favor of Thomas's brand of ascetic Christian chastity.[9] With Thomas's aid, she is resurrected by her repentant murderer, and narrates for them the torments of hell she had seen before their intervention rescued her. This vision of afterlife torments reveals persistent and widely shared ancient understandings of gender, authorized by religion, with what appear to be some particular Christian twists.

Guided by "an ugly-looking man, entirely black . . . whose clothing was exceedingly filthy" she is shown first souls who "exchanged" the intercourse of man and woman (or husband and wife).[10] Next to them lie the children of these souls, "heaped upon each other, struggling and lying upon each other, . . . placed here for a testimony against them." Next, she is shown a chasm with "mud and worms sprouting forth, and souls wallowing there." These are the souls of adulterous women; no mention is made of a chasm for male adulterers.

In the next chasm, the repulsive guide shows the woman souls hung by various bodily parts, which are causally related to their sins. Those hung by the tongue are "slanderers who have spoken false and disgraceful words and are not ashamed." Those hung by their hair "are the shameless, who are not ashamed at all, and go about with uncovered heads in the world." Souls hung by their hands both used them for evil, stealing from others, and failed to use them for

---

8. On the presence of structural elements, see further chapter 3, on the Therapeutae.

9. *Acts of Thomas* 51–61, *WRGRW* 33.

10. *Acts of Thomas* 55, transl. mine.

good: "[they] never gave anything to the poor, nor helped the afflicted." So, too, for those hung by their feet, who "lightly and eagerly walked in wicked ways and disorderly paths," and failed to visit the sick and tend to the dying and dead.[11]

Despite its association with the apostle Thomas, much of this story invokes the numerous New Testament writings in the name of Paul intertextually, and may, at least in part, be understood as interpretation of various Pauline passages. The sins articulated in the *Acts of Thomas* are part of lists of vices enumerated particularly in Paul's Corinthian correspondence, such as 1 Cor 6.9–10,[12] in which Paul advises the Corinthians to shun those who will not inherit the kingdom of God: those who engage in illicit sex (*pornoi*); idolaters (*eidōlolatrai*); adulterers (*moixoi*); persons called by the somewhat problematic terms *malakoi* and *arsenokoitai*, to whose translation I'll return in a minute; thieves (*kleptai*); the greedy (*pleonektai*); drunkards (*methusoi*); revilers; (*loidoroi*) robbers (*harpages*). Ancient lists of virtues (itself derived from the Latin *vir*) and vices, including those here and in the pseudo-Pauline Pastoral epistles, 1 and 2 Timothy and Titus, are heavily gendered; vices correspond to lack of proper masculine traits, somewhat modified for women, whereas virtue lists cohere with positive gender expectations.

In Paul's writings, these categories appear directed primarily (although not exclusively) at men. Theft, robbery, drunkenness, and greed are rarely vices associated with women in the ancient world (although interestingly the Pastoral epistle Titus includes excessive drinking as something women should avoid).[13] The first three terms—those engaged in illicit or inappropriate sexual practices (*pornoi*), idolaters, and adulterers—might conceivably envision women as well as men, although my unverifiable suspicion is that, in fact, Paul here has in mind primarily male offenders. The next two terms are particularly interesting, for they both designate male sexual practices that Paul considered deviant and have everything to do with gender conformity. The term *malakoi*, which the NRSV translates, somewhat oddly, as "male prostitutes," literally means "soft ones," and carries the widespread negative connotation of femininity. It draws not only upon the association of women with physical softness, but the association of men with hardness, both generally and specifically with regard to phallic erection. Some scholars have suggested that a translation more in line with both the author's intentions and the initial audience reception would construe *malakoi* as men who are penetrated by other men sexually, which the NRSV

11. *Acts of Thomas* 56.

12. Others include 1 Cor 5.11; 1 Cor 11.21; Rom 1.29–31; Gal 5.20; Col 3.5–8; Eph 5.5; 1 Tim 1.9–10, 6.4; 2 Tim 3.2–4; Titus 3.3. See also Mark 7.21–22 (twelve items); Matt 15.19 (six items, perhaps conforming more closely to those in the ten commandments). For Paul's use of these lists, see Brooten 1996:260–62.

13. Tit 2.3.

editors suggest in a note. Similarly, *arsenokoitai*, which the NRSV awkwardly and circumlocutiously translates as "sodomites," literally designates men who are the sexual penetrators of other men.[14] Thus, in a Pauline catalogue of vices, sexual acts that invert the presumed natural order of gender hierarchy and cast men in the role of women with other men are seen as particularly egregious. Even idolatry may have gender implications, for in the Judean scriptures so familiar to Paul, Israel's idolatry is regularly constructed as a wife's infidelity to her (divine) husband: men who worship other gods are as a woman who has sex with a man not her lawful husband.

The torments shown to the resurrected woman in the *Acts of Thomas* are sins disproportionately focused on gendered norms. Consider the first group of suffering souls she sees (55), those who have "departed from, or exchanged (*metallaxasai*) the intercourse of man and woman [or perhaps: husband and wife]." This may very well be an intertextual invocation of a famous passage in Paul's letter to the Romans where, because human beings have failed to honor God properly and have instead worshipped images, God gave them up to "dishonorable passions." In Rom 1.26, Paul writes, "the females among them exchanged (*metēlallaxan*) natural intimacy (*chrēsis*: literally, usage) for that which is contrary to nature, while similarly the males, relinquishing natural usage of females, were consumed with passion for one another, and engaged in shameless acts, males with males."[15]

As numerous scholars of sexuality in antiquity have demonstrated, these notions of natural and unnatural sexual practices are inextricably bound up with hierarchical notions of gender.[16] Normative sex was understood to be the insertion of a penis into the orifice of another human being. Such a practice allowed both for the expression and inversion of social hierarchy. A man who inserted his penis into the orifice of a social inferior (a woman, a younger man, a slave of either sex) was appropriately replicating the social order: he was the active party, while the woman, younger man, slave, and so forth was the appropriately passive recipient. An older man who allowed himself to be penetrated by a younger man inverted the correspondence of sex and social hierarchy: he was passive when he should have been active, and the younger partner was active when he should have been passive. In such cultural logic, women cannot actually have "sex" with each other, not only because they lack a penis to insert

---

14. Petersen 1986; Wright 1984; 1987. Contemporary slang for these among gay men are "a top," and "a bottom," which itself derives from a stereotypical notion of heterosexual intercourse, with the man on top and the woman on the bottom, that itself effectively encodes gender hierarchy.

15. Transl. mine. For a detailed treatment of this passage, see Brooten 1996:189–302.

16. See especially Foucault 1978–1988; Halperin 1990; Parker 1997. The rabbis, at least, only share some of this; for them, sex between men is never acceptable: see the Introduction.

into someone else, but because being "naturally" passive, they cannot perform an act that requires the expression of activity and passivity at the same time. The point is not whether women could, in practice, engage in what we modern persons would clearly call sexual activity with one another: ancient writers on these subjects were well aware of the possibilities, including the use of artificial phallic devices. Rather, such an act was particularly incongruous and problematic, having, as it did, no social meaning, or perhaps challenging, as it did, the whole set of social meanings of sex.

Sexual intercourse between women and men afforded similar means of enacting or violating gendered hierarchy. The woman on the bottom and the man on the top reproduces the allegedly "natural" or divinely ordained domination of women by men, whereas the woman on top and the man on the bottom, for instance, inverts that domination. Similarly, such intercourse is understood to afford women a more active role; and men a more passive role, which, again, inverts the associations of activity with masculinity and passivity with femininity.

If this passage in the *Acts of Thomas* intentionally invokes Rom 1.26–27, it is both sharing the general notion that sexual acts express appropriate and inappropriate social relations, particularly gender relations, and diverging, as did most, if not all, early Christian writers, from the view that intercourse between males was acceptable, provided it continued to express dominance and subordination appropriately.[17] Rather, for this text, only certain intercourse between a man and a woman (or perhaps husband and wife—the Greek terms are identical) was permissible, and all other intercourse landed one in this particular chasm of torment.

Interestingly, it is impossible to tell from this passage whether the souls here tormented are both men and women who have engaged in inappropriate sex, or whether only women are intended. Because the Greek term for soul, *psyche*, is feminine, and the text repeatedly describes the persons in torment as souls, grammar alone is no help. Also noteworthy is the presence of the otherwise innocent children, whose own suffering is intended to intensify the torment of their parents. The ramifications of this are clear: conforming to gendered norms and gender hierarchy will be rewarded after death, whereas deviations from those norms and failure to acquiesce to gender hierarchy not only lands one in eternal torment, but convicts one's otherwise innocent children as well. Such visions provide strong incentives and disincentives for particular social behaviors.

---

17. On early Christian opposition to male homosexuality, see Boswell 1980; but see also the critique in Brooten 1996; for additional bibliography, see Brooten 1996:9 n. 15, as well as her bibliography.

Next on this particular ancient tour of hell are the souls of adulterous women. (Whether this specification means that otherwise, we should take the tormented souls to be those of both women and men is possible, but hardly certain). Adultery in antiquity is also rooted in concepts of appropriate gendered relations: fathers and then husbands have sole rights to the reproductive capacities of their daughters and wives. Adultery was essentially a crime against a husband's rights, and raised the dreadful possibility that a man might pass his name and inheritance to men who were in fact someone else's sons (e.g., Ben Sira 23.22–27). Unlike contemporary American law, in which either spouse commits adultery by engaging in heterosexual intercourse outside the marriage, in Greek, Roman, and Jewish law and practice, adultery was defined as heterosexual intercourse between a married woman and a man not her husband.[18] It was not inherently illicit for a married man to have sex with a woman who was not his wife, although the particulars of forbidden and permissible (or at least not explicitly impermissible) relations vary. Biblical law outlawed sex between a man and many of his kin (although it has been noted that these long lists in Lev 18.6–23 and 20.10–21 never explicitly prohibit sex between a man and his daughter). Roman law at various times forbade a whole raft of sexual liaisons, and the ideal of Roman male marital fidelity was much touted, if often honored more in the breach.

Early Christian sources are unusual in Greco-Roman antiquity for their apparent equitable prohibition of adultery on the part of either spouse.[19] Later in this same story, the apostle Thomas enjoins all followers of Christ to avoid adultery: "The adulterers [here a masculine plural—*moichoi*] are no more to commit adultery, lest they give themselves up to everlasting punishment. For with God adultery is an evil exceedingly wicked above all other evils."[20] Nevertheless, as I remarked earlier, it is interesting that the murdered woman is shown only a hell for women adulterers.

The next set of souls the woman sees, those strung up by their offending body parts, might seem, on first glance, to be far more gender neutral: people

18. Adultery was a specific form of the more general *stuprum*, sexual immorality. The Augustan *Lex Julia* established adultery as a separate but not equal offense: that is, intercourse between a man and a married woman who was not his wife. Sex between a man and a marriageable woman was technically *stuprum*, although as Gardiner notes, it was not always adjudicated in public, and the definitions of licit and illicit sex in Roman law are quite complex: see Gardner 1986:121–31, and the much more extensive treatment in Treggiari 1991:262–98; see also Grubbs 1995:203–60; Arjava 1996:193–229. For sources, see Treggiari 2002:187–218. On Greek law, see also Sealey 1990:28–29.

19. So for instance, Paul's command of the Lord in 1 Cor 7. Mark 10.10–27 *may* equally constrain both spouses, but may also be read to refer to men who have sex with other men's wives. That is, in Mark, a man who commits adultery may not offend his own wife; but rather only offends the husband of the woman with whom he commits adultery.

20. *Acts of Thomas* 58.

who slandered with their tongues, or who used their hands to rob, or their feet to walk in ways of wickedness. Yet a closer analysis suggests that gender remains very much at the forefront of these sins and punishments.

Although the description of the tormented souls in the first chasm plays off Paul's letter to the Romans, the following passage evokes an intertextuality with prescriptions for appropriate gendered behavior in the Pastoral epistles. The Pastorals, in fact, as well as two other letters attributed to Paul—Colossians and Ephesians—are rich illustrations of the uses of religious authority in the implementation or enforcement of ancient constructions of gender,[21] but I will for now only discuss those passages that illuminate the vision in the *Acts of Thomas*.

Those hung by the tongue are "slanderers who have spoken false and disgraceful words and are not ashamed" (*Acts of Thomas* 56). In the Pastorals, false speech is very much associated with women, both its utterance and its acceptance. Women are more likely to speak falsehoods, because they are inherently deceitful, and also because they lack the necessary intellectual capacity to discern truth from falsehood, and thus are more likely to repeat falsehoods. They are also more likely to accept falsehoods, again because they lack sufficient critical acumen (e.g., 2 Tim 3.6, which asserts that "ditsy" women [*gunaikaria*] are always being instructed yet can never acquire knowledge of truth). Thus, although polemical Christian writings often accuse particular men of uttering and perpetrating falsehoods, these accusations have a gendered component to them: to the degree that truth is associated with masculinity and falsehood with femininity, accusing men of speaking falsehood always invokes, in antiquity, the specter of femininity and the violation of gender norms. True men (that is properly masculine men) only speak truth; false men (that is, femininized men) speak falsehood.

The invocation of shame is also disproportionately associated with women. Those souls hung by their hair are "the shameless, who are not ashamed at all, and go about with naked heads in the world."[22] Almost certainly this passage refers only to women: I know of no ancient Christian texts that advocate head coverings for men. It is, thus, forceful in its identification of deviation from gender hierarchy as sinful. Women who do not cover their heads in public will suffer a corresponding torment in the afterlife.

The ancient Mediterranean view that women, at least free women, should cover their heads was rooted in associations between the hair on women's heads and the hair on their genitals (just as constructions of women's public

---

21. Glancy 2003; D'Angelo 2003a.
22. *Acts of Thomas* 56. Gk: γυμνοκέφαλοι, which Elliott translates as "uncovered."

speech as inappropriate drew on associations between women's mouths and their vaginal opening).[23] Just as a respectable woman whose sexuality belonged properly to her father and then her husband would not dream of exposing her genitals in public, so she should not also display the hair on her head in public.[24]

Artistic representations of women's elaborate hairstyles in the Roman period strongly suggest that elite women did not universally cover their heads in public, and that failure to do so was not necessarily construed as a violation of gendered norms.[25] Nevertheless, when women did cover their heads, it appears to have been routinely construed as a symbol of their subordination to male authority, and an expression of gender differentiation. It may also have been used to differentiate among social classes, particularly between free women and enslaved women, as well as between "respectable" women, and those women whose sexuality was available to men not their licit husbands, such as courtesans and prostitutes.

This torment may also allude to another famous and much-scrutinized passage in the Pauline corpus, 1 Cor 11.3–11. There, Paul's attempt to persuade Corinthian women prophets to cover their heads when they pray and prophesy is, in fact, a two-pronged argument: women should cover their heads during such practices but men, Paul says, should not. Gender differentiation needs to be maintained in the Corinthian assembly. It has occasionally been suggested by scholars for whom authorial intention is determinative that Paul's opposition to male head coverings is here an attempt to distinguish between the practice of his Corinthians and that of Roman men who covered their heads while sacrificing (particularly the Emperor and the pontifex maximus).[26] This misses what may well be the same gendered, hierarchical, and implicit cultural logic: even the Emperor, when sacrificing to the gods on behalf of the empire, adopts a position of subordination vis-à-vis the gods that carries with it an inevitable element of feminization.

The remaining punishments in *The Acts of Thomas* focus on those hapless souls who also sinned in their failure to use these parts for good: giving to the

23. On which see also chapter 3.

24. See, for example, D'Angelo 1995:131–64, see also Carson 1990 on the covering and uncovering of the bride's head in Greek weddings as a symbolic representation of her husband's uncovering of her genitals, signaling his legal right to have sex with her. Modern brides would probably be horrified to realize that similar cultural ideas undergird the veiling of brides, and the granting of permission to kiss the bride in many western weddings. Cynthia Baker makes the important point that women's headcoverings were part of the larger process of rendering women invisible in public, something that required not so much physical absence, but rather "that the *subject* be disregarded or *unperceived* as such" (Baker 2002:62). Baker also suggests that head-coverings specifically render women invisible by obscuring their faces.

25. See, e.g., Thompson 1988.

26. E.g., Oster 1988. See also the intriguing suggestion that bull's testicles are at issue here: T. Martin 2004.

poor, helping the afflicted, tending the sick and the dying. Although these seem like moral obligations easily incumbent on women and men alike, in the Pastoral epistles these are particularly the obligations assigned to women. In 1 Tim 5.9, for example, those widows eligible for communal support must have brought up children, shown hospitality, washed the feet of the saints, helped the afflicted, and done good in every way.

The torments in the *Acts of Thomas* are thus clearly associated with violations of gender norms. Not only are the vices from which people should abstain themselves gendered to varying degrees, but conformity to gender roles is itself imbued with moral significance. Implicit here is the view explicit in the Pauline corpus that gender roles are divinely ordained; explicit here is the view that failure to conform to them results in postmortem suffering, made known through a tour of hell witnessed by a woman.

Read in this manner, this vignette is very much about the authorization of gender difference and gendered norms; and not, or only incidentally, about women converts to Christianity. Its presence in the *Acts of Thomas* is somewhat intriguing, though, and may point to underlying social realities of some sort. In its pervasive attack on sexuality and marriage, the *Acts of Thomas* can be construed as critiquing or negating gender constructions. Particularly interesting is another, somewhat better-known story of a newlywed couple whom Jesus, in the guise of Thomas, persuades to refrain from consummating the marriage and to remain celibate. This celibacy, then, appears to reconfigure the traditional husband-wife relationship as one of parity rather than one of dominance and subordination. The morning after the unconsummated wedding night, the bride's mother is astonished to find her sitting with her face uncovered, unashamed, as though she had been married for many years.[27] It may be tempting to propose that the function of the narrative of gendered postmortem torments warns against taking the rest of the *Acts of Thomas* to legitimate much in the way of gender critique, suspension, or reversal, an argument that itself may point to actual conflicting interpretations with consequences for women members of these communities.

The Daughters of Rabbis

Roughly around the same time stories of the apostle Thomas were formulated and collected, that is, the early third century, the collection of Jewish legal traditions and explorations known as the Mishnah incorporated a relatively brief

27. *Acts of Thomas* 13.

discussion of whether or not women could, or should, engage in that most highly valued rabbinic practice, Torah study. The question arises as an offshoot of an exchange concerning the ritual prescribed in the biblical book, Num 5.11–31, for a wife suspected of adultery. Brought before the high priest, the woman was obligated to drink a potentially poisonous drink composed largely of water and dirt from the Temple floor. If she was innocent, the drink would have no effect, but if she were guilty, the physical effects would be obvious. The three rabbinic authorities said to be participating in this discussion consider the possibility that previous meritorious deeds can nullify the effects of the drink, so that an adulterous woman who had otherwise behaved in a meritorious fashion might not, in fact, suffer any harm. Ben Azzai proposes that a father should teach his daughter Torah in case she has to undergo the rite. If she is guilty, but does not suffer the predicted consequences, she will know it is because merit has averted the decree.[28]

R. Eliezer's response is sharp: "If anyone teaches his daughter *torah*, it is as though he taught her sexual impropriety." The implicit logic here is that teaching a daughter this particular *torah*, at least, will encourage her to engage in illicit sex, knowing that she can avert its consequences through other meritorious deeds. R. Joshua concurs with the view that women are predisposed to sexuality in the first place; presumably, then, anything that would encourage this "natural" tendency to sexual excess should be discouraged. Other later rabbinic traditions also associate R. Eliezer with opposition to women studying Torah: he is said to have said, "They shall burn the teachings of *Torah* rather than convey them to women."[29] Another rabbinic tradition invokes a gender-specific reading of Deut 11.19 ("you shall teach them to your sons") to demonstrate that it is not obligatory to teach daughters Torah: this means, it says, "your sons and not your daughters."[30]

Another relatively early rabbinic Jewish compilation, the Tosefta, (or the supplement or appendix) broaches a related question—whether women may read from the actual scrolls of the Torah in public—asserting that while women may be included in the quorum of seven persons necessary for the public reading of Torah on the Sabbath, "one does not bring a woman to read [the Torah] in public."[31]

The question of women studying Torah actually arises quite rarely; these passages from the Mishnah and Tosefta are virtually the only direct treatments

---

28. I have taken this description from my earlier work: Kraemer 1992:97–98.

29. *y. Sotah* 3.4, 19a, cited in Ilan 1995:191.

30. *Sifre Deuteronomy* 46, cited in Ilan 1995:191, from the edition of Finkelstein, p.104.

31. *t. Megillah* 3.11, cited in Wegner 1988:158. On the relationship between Mishnah and Tosefta, see Mandel 2006, with additional references.

found in early extant rabbinic collections. Most of rabbinic preoccupation with women had little to do with their participation in these practices, and might be taken to mean that, at least in limited rabbinic circles, the question rarely arose. Most contemporary discussions of these texts (often, although not always, undertaken in service to debates about contemporary practice) have focused on to what extent women may, in fact, have engaged in Torah study and public reading, as well as on the internal rabbinic logic and the possible motives of the rabbinic interlocutors. Rarely has anyone analyzed the underlying cultural logic of gender difference that I think pervades and to some extent explains rabbinic responses.

In an insightful and fascinating article, Michael Satlow argued that, for the early rabbis, Torah study is constructed as the ultimate masculine activity.[32] To undertake Torah study requires many of the same masculine virtues valued in the larger Roman environment: education; mastery over one's household; self-mastery, including moderation in practices of diet and sexuality; and so forth. Where the rabbis diverged from the common culture was, Satlow argues, in their repudiation of traditional masculine pursuits of war, government service, and athletics, and their view that "being a man means using that uniquely male trait, self-restraint, in the pursuit of the divine through Torah study."[33]

It was not merely, however, that the study of Torah was privileged as masculine (thus rendering it problematic, at the least, for women). It was, and is, also, that Torah itself becomes feminized and sexualized, so that its study and more specifically the reading of Torah scrolls themselves, becomes gendered and sexualized.

A brief redescription of the reading of Torah in most modern Jewish synagogues makes it almost shockingly clear how gendered a practice this presently is, if not always was. Torah scrolls are normally kept out of sight of the congregation in a closed box, often an ornate and beautiful cabinet (the holy ark: the *aron ha-kodesh*) that is itself in full view of the congregation. Each Torah scroll is tied with a cord and covered with a cloth wrapping that is often made of luxurious fabric, and beautifully embroidered. The poles to which the scroll itself is affixed are often adorned with elaborately worked and expensive silver casings, and a similarly elaborate and expensive breastplate is hung from these poles.

The reading of the Torah begins with the opening of the ark, and the removal of the scroll. It is then paraded around the synagogue for all to see, and for men to touch (traditionally, a man touches his prayer shawl to the Torah and then kisses the shawl; he does not touch the Torah directly). Carried back to the altar,

32. Satlow 1996.
33. Satlow 1996:20.

the *bimah*, from which it will be read, the Torah is first undressed (this is the actual language employed) by removing the silver and other precious ornaments, and the cloth cover. The undressed Torah is then laid out on the bimah, and untied, after which it is unrolled to the day's portion. The reader of the Torah does not touch the text with his fingers, but finds his place and follows the portion to be read with a long pointer, often made of silver or other precious metals, and is itself often hung around the poles of the Torah. This pointer is called a yad, a Hebrew term for hand that has a long history of being a euphemism for the penis: some actually have a casting of a hand and a pointed finger at the end.

At the conclusion of the reading, these acts are reversed. The yad is withdrawn, the Torah is rolled up and retied shut, the scroll is dressed again in its beautiful clothes and jeweled ornaments and held up again for public display. Then the Torah is returned to the box, and the box is closed from view. In traditional Jewish practice, men performed all these acts, while women watched, if at all, from an upper balcony or behind a barrier. This redescription makes clear that the Torah scroll is thus analogous to the body of a woman: lavishly adorned, ordinarily secluded from sight, and displayed on occasion to her licit male viewers. Reading the Torah is analogous to the performance of sexual intercourse.

Although ancient rabbinic arguments for why women are exempt from many commandments incumbent on men are often couched in seemingly practical terms (women should not be required to attend synagogue, for instance, because their childcare responsibilities impinge on their ability to do so, and an obligation should not be imposed on them that they inherently cannot fulfill), Satlow's work suggests that such explanations are an act of misrecognition.[34] In rabbinic constructions of femininity and masculinity, women generally lacked much of the capacity necessary for Torah study, including sufficient self-discipline, critical discernment, and so forth.

Satlow proposes that for the rabbis, women reading Torah was always dangerous, for they lacked, by definition, the self-restraint necessary to do it properly[35] (as did the Gentiles).[36] His insightful analysis makes clear why ancient rabbis would have resisted the idea of women either studying Torah generally or, although he does not extend his own argument quite this far, reading Torah scrolls specifically: their doing so posed a fundamental contradiction in gendered terms. How can women engage in the fundamentally masculine activity of Torah reading and Torah study? Torah reading in particular carried with it

---

34. Or what my late mother used to call "a good reason, but not the right reason."

35. Satlow 1996:36.

36. Satlow 1996:33.

associations of sexual intercourse that made women's reading deeply transgressive and culturally illogical. Perhaps at best women could do so in some
private context, as the passage in the Tosefta implies for women reading Torah
(just as perhaps, in private, women can engage in sexual behavior with one
another that, unseen, doesn't pose a challenge to the gendered social meanings
of sex). And even if women can be counted in the Sabbath quorum, they cannot
lead the prayers, for to do so might construct a woman as the hierarchical
superior of the praying males.

Satlow points out that rabbinic ideas about masculine self-restraint had
other implications, particularly for rabbinic ideas about sexuality. The rabbis
are often lauded for their seemingly positive views both of heterosexuality and
of women's sexual pleasure (particularly when contrasted with the long history
of Christian critique of sexuality and ambivalence about the body). One notable
example is the rabbis' insistence that a man was obligated both to have sex with
his wife on a regular basis, and also to make sure that she found the experience
pleasurable.[37] Satlow's work suggests that the rabbis' views here are closely
linked to their assumptions about masculinity as self-restraint that extended to
restraint in sexuality. Sexual activity itself, when performed with self-restraint,
may be constructed as masculine; otherwise, in the very lack of restraint that it
involves, it is constructed as feminine. This illuminates the rabbinic view that
a man who restrains his own orgasm while facilitating that of his wife will have
male children, while the man who lacks sufficient restraint will instead father
female children.[38]

Both of these discussions, debates about teaching daughters Torah, and
rabbinic views of the links between the order of orgasm and the gender of the
children conceived, exemplify the dilemmas of modern readers. Some contemporary commentators clearly think that it would be good to find that at least
some Jewish men taught their daughters some degree of Torah and that the
seemingly positive views of the rabbis concerning sexuality are laudable.[39] Certainly the utility for such historical evidence in debates about what is permissible, if not also desirable in contemporary Jewish communities, is obvious.

Yet merely because some women may have studied, or even read Torah,
does not mean that the underlying gender systems that generally forbade women

37. For the second point, *B. Niddah* 31a–b. Interestingly, the same logic appears to underlie a passage in the
Genesis Apocryphon (1QGenAp ar) found at Qumran and thus several centuries earlier than the redaction of the
Babylonian Talmud. There Lamech appears concerned that the son born to his wife Bitenosh, namely Noah, is
not his own, but was rather fathered by one of the sons of God, or a giant. To prove her claim that Lamech is the
father of Noah, Bitenosh implores him to remember the great sexual pleasure that she experienced, apparently
appealing to the logic that a woman's orgasm leads to the conception of sons.

38. Again, *B. Niddah* 31 a–b.

39. See, e.g., Hauptman 1998.

from doing so, or impeded the ability of all but a few, did not remain very much in place. If, for instance, as may be argued for the present case, the purpose of teaching a daughter Torah is to inculcate in her, or has the effect of inculcating in her, gender expectations, themselves understood to be the product of divine authorization, we moderns should be extremely careful about the valuation we impute to such practices. Similarly, rabbinic promotion of female sexual gratification may have been licensed (if not also motivated) not by their concern for women, but, on the contrary, by their concern for gender conformity. A man who restrains his own orgasm while causing his wife to have one has re-enacted a gender paradigm in which men have self-restraint and women do not.

These remain, of course, complex issues. Some rabbis may have praised the man who restrains his own orgasm because they saw this as consistent with their overarching (and unarticulated) understandings of gender difference. Yet ironically, this view may have served women's interests in several ways. First, it facilitated their sexual pleasure, rewarding women for conforming to particular gender expectations and constraints (women should be passive and unrestrained, giving themselves over to bodily desires). Second, it promises them a culturally valuable reward for doing so, namely the conception of sons. Conversely, it warns women that the consequences of nonconformity are substantial—the conception of daughters instead of sons (and implies that women themselves are the products of parental imperfection). What all this has to do with social reality, though, is difficult to gauge, and one wonders whether anyone subjected these theories to reality testing.

Similarly, rabbinic debates about women studying Torah may or may not tell us virtually anything about whether women did so, let alone how women themselves might have thought about this. Yet once women gain the capacity to study the authoritative texts of their traditions, who knows what alternative, transgressive, and transformative interpretations they may find or formulate? Study of Torah might be dangerous, not only for its violation of gendered order, but for its capacity to undermine that very order through alternative readings. By itself, though, Torah study by women need not do anything more than confirm and authorize an existing gendered hierarchy, just as a system that promulgated women's sexual pleasure might not, in fact, do so out of any valuations of women or any egalitarian impulses.

A Roman Christian Matron

One last instance exemplifies the concerns of this project. In the mid-second century C.E., a convert to Christianity who came to be known as Justin Martyr (d.c. 165 C.E.) sought to demonstrate the irrational treatment Christians received in the Roman legal system with the story of a Roman matron whose acceptance of Christianity ultimately led to the dissolution of her marriage and the demise of her (male) Christian teacher.[40] As Justin narrates it, an unnamed woman and her equally anonymous husband once both lived morally reprehensible (*akolastos*) lives.[41] Through unspecified circumstances, the woman came to know "the teachings of Christ" and renounced her former way of life. She tried to persuade her husband to join her in living "soberly and with right reason," warning him of the eternal torments that awaited those who failed to do so. Failing in this attempt, she wished then to divorce him, but friends initially prevailed on her to remain married. Eventually, though, when her husband left Rome for Alexandria and reports reached her that he was continuing to engage in egregious (but unspecified) sexual practices, she separated from him,[42] sending him the Roman document known as a *repudium*.[43]

In response, her husband alleged that his wife was a Christian. She, however, requested and received a legal stay from the emperor. This apparently effectively terminated her husband's action against her, for she disappears from the story at this point and we learn nothing more of her fate. Instead, her husband then instigated the interrogation and prosecution of the matron's teacher, a Christian named Ptolemaeus. Brought before (Q. Lollius) Urbicus,[44] the urban prefect, Ptolemaeus confesses to being a Christian and is led away to punishment, presumably martyrdom, although no account of his death is given.[45] A second Christian named Lucius, present at the proceedings, decries the judgment as "irrational" (*alogos*). For his trouble, Lucius, too, is suspected

40. Justin Martyr, *Second Apology*, 2. Text from Wartelle 1987; English translation in Barnard 1997; additional text in Krüger and Ruhback 1965:14–15; and in Musurillo 1972:38–41. Text and translation also in K. Lake's text and translation of Eusebius, *Ecclesiastical History* 4.17 (LCL). Eusebius takes Justin to be demonstrating that there were other martyrs before himself (4.17.1). Justin simply designates the unnamed woman "γυνή," but her obvious social rank (her divorce case is adjudicated by the emperor) and marriage clearly warrant the designation of *matrona*.

41. ἀκόλαστος is difficult to translate smoothly into English. The opposite of σωφροσύνη, in philosophical discourse it seems to have connoted complete or absolute moral failure (see Wasserman 2008, esp. 1–14). The translation by both Barnard and the *ANF* of ἀκόλαστος as intemperate and σωφροσύνη as temperate accurately reflects their oppositional meanings, but doesn't have much resonance in contemporary English. Lake's translation is "dissipated"; Musurillo's is "evil life." LSJ (s.v.) defines it as "licentious, intemperate."

42. *Apology* 2.6. ἐχωρίσθη. The same verb is used a few verses earlier, where the matron wishes τῆς συζυγίας χωρισθῆναι, to separate from their union.

43. Literally, "what is called among you a *repudium*, τὸ λεγόμενον παρ᾽ ὑμῖν ῥεπούδιον.

44. Called Urbicius in Eusebius' version, he was urban prefect from 150–163 C.E.; see *PIR* 2.240, cited in Musurillo 1972.

45. The Greek here appears somewhat ambiguous: καὶ τοῦ Ουρβικοῦ κελεύσαντος αὐτὸν ἀπαχθῆναι (2.15). To what fate, exactly, is Ptolemaeus led away? Wardell translates this as "Urbicus donna l'ordre de l'emmener au supplice," and Barnard (1997) translates: "When Urbicus ordered him to be led away to punishment." Lake, from the same Greek, translates: "When Urbicius ordered him to be executed. . . ."

of being a Christian, readily confesses, and is similarly sent off. Finally, a third unnamed person also comes forward to the same fate.

Justin's account exemplifies the dilemmas posed by ancient narratives about women. At first glance, it is straightforward enough, and entirely plausible: a Roman matron adopted the teachings she learned from a Christian named Ptolemaeus, renounced her former dissolute life, encountered resistance from her husband, filed for divorce, and was accused by her husband of being a Christian. Although she managed to avoid prosecution, her teacher was implicated and sentenced. The story contains not even a tinge of the miraculous to raise our eyebrows,[46] and it all seems comprehensible within the framework of elite second-century Roman society. Why should we not consider it a reliable account that offers us a window into the social realia of elite urban Christians and their opponents in the second century C.E.?

Only twenty years ago, the eminent historian of ancient Christianity, Robert Grant, read the story in precisely this manner, as did Peter Lampe a few years later.[47] Neither Grant nor Lampe appears to have given any thought to the possibility that the story was not true, although Grant does consider briefly whether the wife or the husband was the source of Justin's information.[48] His detailed analysis attempts to situate the story within the context of various second-century issues and practices, including Roman mores, popular Stoic morality, and a legal system whose details Justin largely omits (presuming, perhaps, a sufficiently familiar audience).

Justin, for instance, tells us only that once the wife sent the *repudium* to her husband, he accused her of being a Christian. Grant attempts to supply the missing connection between these two actions. To be legally tenable, the wife's divorce petition would have included an accusation of sexual impropriety that would have required the husband to return the wife's dowry.[49] His counteraction, accusing of her being a Christian, was a diversionary legal tactic intended, in Grant's analysis, to avoid having to pay. Her successful petition to the emperor would have effectively ended her husband's counter suit and led her apparently frustrated husband to seek revenge against his wife's teacher. Grant also

---

46. Miraculous elements often signal to modern readers, although perhaps not ancient ones, that authorial imagination is at work. Yet the lack of seemingly fictive embellishment, including but not limited to miraculous elements, is hardly proof of historicity, although the absence of such elements frequently seems to ensnare contemporary scholars, who take it as an indication of historicity when they shouldn't.

47. Grant 1985; Lampe 2003:237–40. I read this only after formulating my initial argument.

48. Grant 1985:463.

49. Grant 1985:466–67. Kirsopp Lake made similar, but less detailed observations in his notes to the LCL edition of Eusebius, *Ecclesiastical History* (vol. 1, 366–67 n. 1). Musurillo interprets this somewhat differently:

considers the probability that the matron's teacher was the same Ptolemaeus who wrote the *Letter to Flora*,[50] an identification argued more forcefully by Lampe.[51]

Grant further attempts to situate the matron's efforts to convert her husband and, failing that, to separate herself from him and his illicit practices, within the context both of Stoic teachings about self-control, including those of Musonius Rufus, and of various early Christian writings. For instance, 1 Cor 7.13–15 advocates that believers should stay with unbelievers in the hopes of saving them, while the Shepherd of Hermas considered at what point an offending spouse's sexual transgressions corrupted an innocent spouse.[52] Grant points out that from a Roman perspective, the husband's pursuit of his unseemly erotic passions outside of marriage would often have been viewed sympathetically.[53]

Yet a close reading of the narrative suggests that various rhetorical strategies are at work that may call into question the veracity of the episode. It fits well within Justin's overall intent, not merely to portray Roman legal prosecution of Christians as irrational, but to portray Christianity as the truest form of ancient philosophy, and Christians as living the philosophical life, in response to well-documented second-century attacks on Christianity as irrational and antithetical to reason, such as those of Celsus. Throughout, both Christianity and Christians are presented in the language of philosophical teachings and virtues.

---

assuming that the *repudium* "had to be accompanied by the actual cessation of common life," he infers that the husband had replied that the divorce was without cause, rendering his wife liable to financial penalties (1972:39 n.1). Grant proposes that the wife had petitioned the emperor for control of her own estate, including the returned dowry she claimed due her (Grant 1985:467) and cites what he considers a legally comparable case in Valerius Maximus 8.2.3 and Plutarch, *Life of Marius* 38.3–4. If actual legal actions underlie the story, Musurillo's analysis might make somewhat more sense. According to Treggiari, *repudiare/repudium* was the normal terminology for the male actor in a divorce (1991:436), but there is evidence (apart from the story in Justin) for wives or their fathers sending a *repudium* to a husband (1991:437). Wives most often had just cause to divorce if their husbands engaged in sexual misconduct, which would seem to apply here (462–63). If serious moral offences were proved against the husband, he would have been liable for repayment of the dowry within six months (Treggiari 1991:464).

50. Grant 1985:468–69.

51. Lampe 2003:239–40. His argument rests partly on an apparent consonance between Ptolemaeus' interpretation of why the Mosaic law allows divorce and the situation in Justin. "A divorce appeared to Moses to be more advantageous than to be forced through a torturous marriage into injustice and badness, 'from which might result complete corruption.' (33.4.9)." (Lampe 2003:240). Lampe's principal interest in the passage seems to be its utility for determining the woman's social standing. From the "artful and theoretical exposition" of Ptolemy's *Letter*, he infers that she must have been "an interested and educated woman" (Lampe 2003:240), thus eliding the implied recipient with an actual and intended recipient. See also C. Munier 1994:27–28, esp. n. 91.

52. *Commandments* 4.1.5–9, following Ehrman's choice of title for what is traditionally translated as *Mandates* (Ehrman 2003).

53. E.g., Plutarch's view that a wife whose husband does so should consider this his respect for her: *Coniugalia praecepta* 16–17, 140b–c, cited in Grant, 465.

The term Justin uses to characterize both the matron and her husband, *akolastos*, is, after all, the polar opposite of the cardinal philosophical virtue of *sōphrosune*. Once she knows "the teachings of Christ," however, the woman acquires *sōphrosune*, and seeks to convince her husband to live in this manner as well. She repeatedly acts thoughtfully, deliberately, and with obvious self-control. Having curbed her own desires for illicit sexual practices or, at the very least, her willingness to engage in them, she also curbs her initial desire to divorce her husband. Only after she is confronted with evidence of his intractable infidelities, does she take legal action, believing that not to do so implicates her in evil. Her husband, on the other hand, continues to demonstrate his lack of self-control, in everything from his rampant promiscuity in Alexandria, to his irate prosecution of his wife, and then of her teacher.

Juxtaposed to the husband is Ptolemaeus himself, who exemplifies the virtues of self-control, love of truth, and honest speech.[54] When asked directly whether he is a Christian, his fidelity to "the teaching of Christ" compels him "to confess the teachings of divine virtue" (*ton didaskalion tēs theias aretes homologesen*). His prosecution is Justin's prime example of irrationality on the part of the Roman administration. Lucius's objections to the judgment against Ptolemaeus are couched precisely in these terms: they are irrational, unreasonable (*alogos*). "This judgment," he says to Urbicus, "befits neither the Emperor Pius, nor Caesar's philosopher son, nor the holy Senate."[55] Lucius's own fate, and that of the unnamed third Christian are similarly implicitly equally irrational: Lucius has done nothing apart from rightfully object to the injustice he sees.

Yet other resonances may be perceived. Particularly intriguing are the precise and striking concordances between the story, and 1 Cor 7.12–16, where Paul expresses his views about the proper response of believers married to unbelievers. Paul advocates that the believing spouse should stay with the unbeliever if the unbeliever consents (1 Cor 7.12–13). So, too, counseled to do so by friends, the woman initially remains in the marriage even though her desire is for separation. Paul proposes that believing spouses may yet save their unbelieving spouses (1 Cor 7.16); so, too, the woman remains in the hope that her husband might change. And finally, Paul concludes that if the unbelieving spouse separates (*chōrizō*) from the believer, the believing spouse is no longer bound by the marriage (1 Cor 7.15); so, too, the woman only separates (*chōrizō*) and presents her husband with a bill of divorce after he leaves her in Rome,

---

54. *Apology* 2.11; see also 2.13–14.

55. Translation mine. Lake and Barnard take this as a reference to the Emperor Antoninus Pius, but Wartell translates merely "the pious Emperor."

and goes to Alexandria, where, she learns, he continues to engage in offensive practices.[56]

This neat, if not convenient, conformity with 1 Corinthians certainly provokes suspicion. In Grant's brief discussion of 1 Corinthians 7, he suggests only that Paul's letter might have influenced the matron's decisions, citing 1 Clement as evidence that Christians in Rome took Paul's letters as authoritative by this time.[57] Yet alternatively, one might argue that, sensitive to early Christian anxieties and debates about mixed marriages and divorce, Justin, or perhaps his source for this story, has shaped it to conform to Paul's dictates.[58] In this form, it thus demonstrates that Christians, in general, and this woman, in particular, are both rational in their beliefs and faithful to the positions of their esteemed teachers. Such a representation challenges hostile characterizations of Christianity as irrational and Christians as mostly persons lacking rational capacity and self-control, including women, slaves of both genders, children of both genders, and illiterate or poorly educated men.[59]

One might even take a more extreme view that, as I have argued for certain other tales, an authoritative text, in this case, 1 Cor 7.12–16, itself generates at least the first part of the story, through the divorce. Although the subsequent material seems difficult to generate from Paul's letter, one portion does have

56. The use of χωρίζω in both texts reinforces the suspicion that early Christian writings, including 1 Corinthians, undergirds Justin's account, especially since a wide range of other terms is regularly used for divorce. Searching *divorce* on the Perseus English to Greek tool produces a long list, of which χωρίζω is relatively unusual. In Mark's account of Jesus' teaching on divorce, the verb is almost always ἀπολύω, but χωρίζω occurs once. In Mark 10.2–9, the Pharisees ask Jesus whether it is permissible for a man to divorce (ἀπολῦσαι) his wife, and quote Deut 24.1, 3, that a man writes his wife a "bill of divorce" (βιβλίον ἀποστασίου) and divorces (ἀπολῦσαι) her. Jesus replies, however, that because a man (here ἄνθρωπος) leaves his father and mother, and he and his wife become one flesh, God desires that the man not separate (χωρίζω). Subsequently, Jesus tells his disciples privately that a man who divorces (ἀπολύσῃ) his wife and marries another commits adultery against her, while a woman who, having divorced (ἀπολύσασα) her husband, marries another, commits adultery (Mark 10.10–12). Matthew's version of this (Matt 19.3–9; see also 5.31–32) follows Mark in its verbal patterns; Luke's highly attenuated version (Luke 16.18) of the saying of Jesus on remarriage after divorce as adultery employs only ἀπολύω. See also note 58, below.

57. Grant 1985:465. Obviously recognizing the consonance between 1 Cor 7.13–16 and the advice given to the woman by "her people," Lampe also wonders whether those persons counseling her were "influenced" by the Pauline text, but does not develop the point.

58. Justin's unproblematized depiction of a Christian woman divorcing her unbelieving husband suggest that in his circles, at least, Paul's views of separation/divorce were shared. The woman's actions are also consistent with a reading of Mark 10.10–12 as envisioning both men and women instigating divorce. The key issue in all three synoptic sayings of Jesus is that of remarriage: in Mark it is unambiguously adultery against the divorced spouse. In Matthew, as is well known, in cases of πορνεία, a man who divorced his wife and married another apparently is exempt from the charge of adultery. It has been suggested that in Matthew, πορνεία may actually connote marriages with unacceptable outsiders, which would, of course, be relevant here. In any case, though, it has often been observed that Matthew omits Mark's provision for women who divorce: see, e.g., Brooten 2000a; 2000b; 2000c; 2000d.

59. The most famous expression of this view is probably Celsus, in Origen, *Against Celsus* 3.44, on which see M. MacDonald 1994.

interesting Pauline resonances, namely Lucius' objection that Ptolemaeus was neither an adulterer, nor one who engaged in illicit sex, nor a murderer, a thief, or a robber. In fact, he had been convicted of no crime at all. The list is similar, although not identical to 1 Cor 5.11 and 6.9, which identify deeds that exclude one from inheriting the *basileia* of God.[60]

Justin's intriguing tale has received surprisingly little scholarly attention. It receives a very different, if brief, read a decade later from Kate Cooper, in a study exploring late antique Christian idealization of virginity and Roman adoption of that ethos.[61] Cooper's work was informed by newer trends in ancient studies, including rhetorical criticism, and the work of Michel Foucault and others on the history of sexuality, including particularly her Princeton teacher, Peter Brown.[62] As I will consider again in chapter 4, for Cooper, stories like that of Justin's matron were not primarily, if at all, stories about women's interest in early Christian ascetic practices. Rather, they were stories about the conflicts between competing male figures of authority: the morally superior Christian apostle on the one hand, and the elite male representatives of civic power on the other.

In Cooper's analysis, the primary function of the Christian wife in Justin's narrative is "to emphasize . . . Christian vulnerability and moral excellence by comparison to the complacency and vested interest of the powers that be," while the "dissolute husband is adduced precisely to illustrate the bad faith of the man who opposes the Christian message," whose real interests are not, as he claims, a concern for civic order, but his own dominant position.[63] Both the artifice of the story and its real purpose are evident, for Cooper, in the story's sudden shift from the wife to her husband's prosecution of her teacher after 2.8.[64] By contrast, for Grant this shift reflects comprehensible, plausible, and probable legal maneuvers, although he seems to concur that Justin tells the story to demonstrate the philosophical respectability of Christians and to defame its opponents as irrational and lacking appropriate self-control.

Cooper takes no explicit position on whether the story has any historical basis, probably because, for her purposes, it's the use of the parties—the

---

60. Paul's list in 1 Cor 6.9 includes idolatry and drunkenness, contains more detailed sexual transgressions, and omits murder; his shorter list in 1 Cor 5.11 also includes idolatry and again omits murder. The absence of idolatry, at least, in Lucius' objections makes perfect sense, since it would hardly have offended the Roman administration. Grant notes (1985:470), that Lucian's list is based on a slightly expanded Christian version of the ten commandments, although all equally recall widespread ancient vice lists.

61. Cooper 1996.

62. This connection is noted especially by Matthews 2002. For details, see the following.

63. Cooper 1996:62.

64. Cooper 1996:62.

vulnerable, morally excellent wife versus the bullying, morally flawed husband—that matters. Furthermore, gender matters here: the tale of the wife who attains moral excellence and is thus the source of conflict between two men functions in a way that tales of morally excellent polytheist men converting to Christianity and disdaining their polytheist wives presumably would not. Although she is not explicit on this point, the Christian convert is here apparently a woman, because it is Christianity itself that is being gendered as female, the better to demonstrate that Christianity imbues the least likely persons with the most masculine virtues, namely, discernment and knowledge of truth. In Cooper's reading, then, we would be ill-advised to take Justin's story as useful evidence for the experiences of women attracted to, and adopting, ascetic Christian practices in the mid-second century, in Rome or elsewhere, let alone as evidence for this particular if unnamed matron.

Most recently, Carolyn Osiek and Margaret MacDonald offer a brief discussion of the account, which they take as more or less historically reliable.[65] In keeping with MacDonald's earlier work on the rhetorical strategies at work in the representation of early Christian women, they do comment that "[i]t is precisely the superiority of the Roman matron's morals in comparison to that of her profligate husband that serves to enrich Justin's portrait of the tragic circumstances of the first Christians."[66] Like Lampe, they read the details of the story as indications of the matron's social circumstances: she was financially well-off, as demonstrated by the leisure time she previously had to engage in sexual misconduct with servants and "hirelings"; the reference to "her people" (*hoi autēs*); her ability to petition the emperor; the husband's residence in Alexandria; and so forth. They remark on what they characterize as the "surprisingly public dimension [of] the Roman matron's circumstances. . . . Despite its potentially lethal consequences, she is presented as making no effort to conceal her Christian allegiance from her husband; instead, she actively tries to evangelize him." (For others, this might index the fictive character of the account.) They also comment that the woman exhibits "the kind of independence in domestic matters, including the initiating of divorce, that was associated especially with elite women."[67]

How does one adjudicate these competing explanations and what difference does it make? After all, the mere utility of Justin's story as a vehicle for ancient (male?) Christian responses to issues of power and identity in a

---

65. Osiek and MacDonald 2005:42–45. Their discussion cites Grant 1985 (as well as Grant 1988:72), but not neither Lampe nor Cooper, although Cooper's book appears in their bibliography: Lampe does not.

66. Osiek and MacDonald 2005:43.

67. Osiek and MacDonald 2005:44.

pre-Constantinian, and often hostile, Roman empire, does not inherently demonstrate that it is a fabrication, even though it might suggest that reverse cases might have been less useful to Justin. Even if the story serves Justin's rhetorical interests, it seems somewhat arbitrary to insist that it has no historical grounding. If the basic plot is true, it demonstrates that, at the very least, some second-century adopters of Christian practices did experience these kinds of social and legal conflicts. And even if the particular story of the woman, her husband, and her teacher Ptolemaeus, is fictive, or no longer extricable from its rhetorical purposes in the *Apology*, the very fact that Justin tells it in this form suggests that he expects his readers to find it plausible, appealing to a social dynamic they will recognize and affirm. In either case, it points to actual conflicts between male Christian teachers and the husbands of their female students, as well as conflicts between Christian women and their non-Christian spouses.

In my own present view, it seems quite possible, if ultimately undemonstrable, that there was such a case, although perhaps embellished in numerous ways, and probably shaped by concern for Pauline, and perhaps other similar or related Christian positions about believers married to unbelievers. Justin's desire to counter critiques of Christianity as irrational and to represent Christians as the true exemplars of "right reason" unquestionably structures his representation of all the parties concerned. That, here, a woman can exemplify such virtues may serve to highlight just how superior Christianity was, for it enabled, not only elite men trained in philosophy, presumably like Ptolemaeus himself, to achieve ultimate virtue, but also more ordinary (if still elite) Roman matrons, who lacked the innate intellectual and self-disciplinary capacities of men. Beginning with such deficiencies may have made women all the more effective exemplars of transformation.[68]

These four instances, then, exemplify the issues raised by diverse accounts of women's religious practices in the Greco-Roman Mediterranean, in which it becomes increasingly difficult to extract reliable historical evidence from the entanglements of gendered concerns that underlie all these narratives. Livy's account of women's foreign, disordered rites with women serves his rhetorical agenda all too well, even while the existence of the Senatus Consultum tantalizes us with the possibility of some access to women's practices and their construal. The tale from the *Acts of Thomas* says far less about the experiences of women who adopted Christianity, and far more about the authorization of gender difference and gendered norms, authorized by a vision attributed to a resurrected woman. Rabbinic debates about teaching daughters Torah say little

---

68. I argue this with respect to Aseneth (Kraemer 1998:193–96); see also Lieu 1998.

about whether at least a few women in rabbinic circles were able to study and much more about the anxieties women and gender caused the rabbinic formulators of these debates. Even the seemingly straightforward narrative of a woman whose adoption of Christian philosophy triggers the unjust death of her teacher seems less a reliable account of a Roman matron's interest in the self-controlled Christian life, and more the use of women as evidence of the superiority of Christianity (which could make even women chaste and virtuous) in the face of the extraordinary irrationality and injustice of imperial Rome. In the chapters that follow, I consider other examples in more depth.

3

Spouses of Wisdom

Philo's Therapeutrides, Reconsidered

Introduction

An extensive test case of the issues this study considers may be found in a treatise attributed to Philo of Alexandria, customarily entitled *On the Contemplative Life*.[1] This account appears at first glance, and has long been taken by many scholars to be the description of a community of contemplative monastic Judean men and women living on the shores of the Mareotic lake outside Alexandria in the first century C.E. My entire discussion presumes that Philo was the actual author of the treatise, but as we shall see, this presumption is not completely secure.[2]

The best known of ancient Judean philosophers, Philo came from a prominent family with extensive ties to the ruling Roman elite in the first century B.C.E./C.E. The exact dates of his life are not known, but he describes himself as an "old" man when he went to Rome in the late 30s of the first century C.E. to plead the cause of Judeans in Alexandria before the Emperor Caligula.[3] According to Josephus, Philo's brother,

---

1. In Latin, *De Vita Contemplativa*. Editions include Cohn, Wendland, and Reiter, 1915; Conybeare 1895; Daumas and Miquel 1963; and Colson (LCL) 1941 [1967]. English translations are available in Conybeare 1895, Colson 1941; Winston 1981; and Corrington 1990. A partial translation by Joan Taylor is available in Taylor 2003:349–58, with selections in *WRGRW* 13. For discussion of the likely Greek title of the initial work, including discrepancies between manuscript titles and the title in Eusebius, *Ecclesiastical History* 2.17–18, see Taylor 2003:31–41.

2. See later, pp. 63–64 on disputes about authorship.

3. *Embassy to Gaius* 1.1. In *On the Soul* 58, Philo refers to a horse race thought to have taken place c. 47 C.E.

Alexander, was a high-ranking official (*alabarch*) in Egypt, while his nephew, Tiberius Julius Alexander, was procurator of Judea, prefect of Egypt, and a staff general for the future emperor Titus during the siege of Jerusalem.[4] Philo's lengthy allegorical interpretation of Judean scriptures (which he read in his native Greek) was extremely attractive to later generations of Alexandrian Christian biblical exegetes and his writings were ultimately preserved not by Jews, but by Christians.[5]

Among his prolific writings are a small number of apologetic treatises that appear to contain significant historical content, including *On the Contemplative Life*. Explicitly presented as a companion to a description of the Essenes as exemplars of the virtuous active life, *On the Contemplative Life* details the make-up, practices, and ideas of a group of philosophical monastics who, Philo says, are called *Therapeutae* (masc. pl) and *Therapeutrides* (fem. pl). *Therapeuō* generally means to attend or serve, particularly a divine being; as well as to heal or cure: its nominal form, *therapeia*, is the basis of the English *therapy*. Philo says this name derives either from their curative, therapeutic care of the soul, or from their worship of the divine being, which they have learned from both nature and the holy laws.[6]

According to Philo, conventicles of Therapeutae could be found all over the ancient world,[7] but the best of their communities was to be found in a compound on the shores of the Mareotic Lake, not far from Alexandria itself (*Cont. Life* 22). There, a community of both women and men spent six days a week secluded in small individual dwellings, "reading the sacred writings and interpreting allegorically the ancestral philosophy" (*Cont. Life* 28).[8] In addition to Judean scripture, the Therapeutae also read the writings of "men of old, those who began the school"[9] (*Cont. Life* 29), and composed their own psalms and hymns to God (*Cont. Life* 29). They prayed at dawn and sunset, ate only at night, fasted routinely for days at a time (*Cont. Life* 34–35) and wore the most plain and basic clothing (*Cont. Life* 37).

On the seventh day, Philo says, they came together to listen to a philosophical discourse by the senior member of the group (*Cont. Life* 31), and to eat a modest day-time communal meal of bread seasoned with salt or perhaps hyssop, accompanied by spring water (*Cont. Life* 37). He devotes considerable

---

4. See, e.g., *Antiquities* 18.259; 19.276; 20.100. On Tiberius Julius Alexander, see Kraft 1991.

5. For fascinating discussion of the transmission of Philo by early Christians, see Runia 1993.

6. *Cont. Life* 2; for the debates about this, see Taylor 2003:55–66.

7. *Cont. Life* 21.

8. Translation Taylor 2003. Although I often follow Taylor's translation, I do not always do so, especially in the discussion in the latter part of this chapter.

9. παλαιῶν ἀνδρῶν οἱ τῆς αἱρεσέως ἀρχεγέται: "The founders of their way of thinking" (Colson [LCL]).

length to their celebration of a festival of seven sevens (or the Festival of Fifty).[10] It began on the eve of the fiftieth day, fifty being the most sacred (*hagiōtatos*) number (*Cont. Life* 65). Dressed in special white robes, the Therapeutae lined up in order, eyes and hands raised to heaven, and prayed to God that their feast might be acceptable (*Cont. Life* 66). At the conclusion of this prayer, the elders, or seniors (*hoi presbuteroi*) reclined for the banquet according to their seniority in the community (*Cont. Life* 67). Although their high status, by virtue both of birth and philosophical training, should have entitled them to soft, comfortable couches, all sit on hard benches of ordinary wood, covered with what seems to be shredded papyrus (*Cont. Life* 69). No slaves attend the diners, who are served instead by *eleutheroi* (literally free persons), junior members of the association chosen for their virtue and character. The food here is more or less identical to the seventh-day meal. No water is served, but only wine; no meat but only leavened bread, seasoned with salt, or perhaps hyssop.

Like their seventh-day observance, the Feast of Fifty was preceded by a lengthy learned lecture by the president of the community, this one explicitly devoted to scriptural interpretation (*Cont. Life* 75). What particularly differentiates the Feast of Fifty from the weekly assembly was an all-night vocal performance. This began with predinner individual performances, first by the president, then by other members, apparently in order of their seniority in the community. They sang either compositions of their own, or those from a communal repertoire (*Cont. Life* 80). As each sang, the others listened in complete silence, except when it was necessary to chant the closing lines or refrains.

After dinner, all the members joined together in two gender-segregated choirs, each with its own leader. They sang for hours, until they ultimately blended together into a single choir, replicating the rejoicing of the ancient Israelites on the shore of the Red Sea (*Cont. Life* 83–88). In an ecstatic but decorous state, they greet the dawn. After morning prayers, they returned again to their individual cells for their regular routine (*Cont. Life* 89).

What is particularly striking about Philo's account is the repeated emphasis he places on the equal participation of women in these practices. At the outset, he relates that the vocation of these philosophers is immediately apparent in the names by which they are called: Therapeutae and Therapeutrides. But having established that the community is comprised of men and women, he makes no explicit mention of the women again until he comes to describe the weekly assembly of the community, and all his discussion of the Therapeutrides

---

10. There is debate about whether this festival should be construed to recur at 50 day intervals throughout the year, or whether it purports to describe a yearly event. The plain meaning of the text would seem to favor the first reading, but its superficial similarities with the Jewish festival of Pentecost, fifty days after Pesach have led some interpreters to construe it as a yearly event. See Leonhardt 2001:48–50.

specifically comes within the context of either the weekly gathering or the Feast of Fifty.

Philo describes the communal room in which they gather (to koinon semneion—perhaps an intentional contrast to the individual semneion in each dwelling),[11] as a diplous peribolos, a "double enclosure," one part men's space, the other part women's quarters.[12] There, he says explicitly, the women, too, "customarily participate in listening, having the same zeal and the same purpose."[13] A wall extending only part-way to the ceiling, he says, separates the men and women, preserving the women's modesty while allowing them to hear clearly everything that was being said.

Philo's fullest description of the Therapeutrides comes in his account of the Feast of Fifty. Just as he emphasized the equal attention of the women during the seventh-day discourse, so, too, here, he is explicit about the inclusion of women,[14] who are

> mostly elderly virgins (pleistai gēraiai parthenoi). They strongly maintain the purity, not out of necessity, as some of the priestesses of the Greeks [do], but out of their own free will, because of a zeal and yearning for Wisdom: being eager to espouse her, they take no heed of the pleasures of the body, and desire not a mortal offspring, but an immortal one, which only a soul which is loved by God is able to give birth to, by itself, because the Father has sown in it lights of intelligence which enable her [the soul] to see (theorein) the doctrines of Wisdom." (Cont. Life 68)[15]

---

11. According to LSJ, s.v., the term is unique to Philo, derived from the fairly common σεμνός. Some scholars speculate (e.g., Inowlocki 2004) that it derives from Therapeutic designation of their space. See, however, n. 92 for the associations of σεμνεῖον with the number seven. Similar claims are made about his use of the term μοναστήριον for their individual cells (Colson 519–20, who also cites Conybeare 1895; see esp. Taylor 2003:279–82).

12. My translation of ὁ μὲν εἰς ἀνδρῶνα, ὁ δὲ εἰς γυναικωνῖτιν: Colson's translation loses the subtlety of this language, as does Winston's "one part set off for the men, the other for the women" (1981:47); and Taylor's "one part is set apart for men, and the other [is set apart] for women" (2003:352). On the use of these terms, especially γυναικωνῖτις, see later.

13. Cont. Life 32, transl. Taylor, slightly altered.

14. Cont. Life 66: συνεστιῶνται δὲ καὶ γυναῖκες. Taylor's translation, "Women eat together [here] also," appears to derive συνεστιῶνται from συνεσθίω (to eat together) but it is from συνεστιάω, to banquet or feast (at the hearth ἑστία) together, as reflected in the translations of Colson ("The feast is shared by women also,") and Winston 1981:53 ("The women, too, take part in the feast").

15. Cont. Life 68. Translation of this section is taken from Taylor, except for the phrase "being eager to espouse her, they . . ." which reflects my translation of ἡ συμβιοῦν σπουδάσασαι (and Troel's Engberg Pederson helpful observations about syntax, in personal communication). Taylor's translation, "which they are eager to live with," obscures the marital and sexual connotations of συμβιοῦν. Colson's rendering "Eager to have her for their life mate," is closer to the meaning of συμβιοῦν, but with a fairly chaste tone (which was perhaps intentional on his part): somewhat more subtly in tune with the erotic connotation is Winston, "Eager to enjoy intimacy with her," (1981:53).

In several details of the Feast of Fifty, Philo further emphasizes the presence and participation of both women and men. The diners at the feast, he says, recline in a gender-segregated arrangement: men on the right, and women on the left (*Cont. Life* 69). Interestingly, he makes no mention here of the partial wall used in the *semneion* on the seventh-day gathering. The junior members of the society serve their elders at the banquet as sons serve their real mothers and fathers (*Cont. Life* 72). Describing the response of the audience to the singers before the banquet, he notes that they listen in complete silence, except when it is necessary to chant the refrains or closing lines: all the men (*pantes*) and all the women (*pasai*) join in these communal responses (*Cont. Life* 80). As I shall explore at some length later on, Philo is explicit that the Therapeutae form into two choirs, one of men; one of women (*Cont. Life* 83) and that both men and women are filled with divine inspiration (*Cont. Life* 87).

How much more of Philo's description of the community as a whole may extend to the women is uncertain. For instance, he says of the Therapeutae in general that

> through their longing for the deathless and blessed life, they consider
> their mortal life to have already ended, and they abandon their
> belongings to sons or daughters or even other relations, voluntarily
> giving them an advance inheritance, while those who do not have
> close family [give] to companions and friends. . . . (*Cont. Life* 13)

Those who joined this community are here represented as free, relatively wealthy, and somewhat mature in age (old enough to have children; young enough, perhaps, to still have living parents). Those who have children to receive their estates are presumably also represented as married: those who do not could be understood either as married and childless, or (presently) unmarried. Nothing in the passage restricts this description to men, nor explicitly extends it to women. In a subsequent passage, though, Philo says that

> [t]hen, when they have rid themselves of their belongings, no longer
> enticed by anything, they flee away without turning around, leaving
> behind brothers/sisters, children, wives, parents, numerous
> relations, friendly companions, and the native areas in which they
> were born and raised . . ."[16]

The explicit reference to wives (*gunaikes*) left behind represents the Therapeutae as exclusively male. Philo could have used here the more generic term

16. *Cont. Life* 18; translation Taylor. *siblings* might be better for "brothers/sisters." ἀδελφούς raises questions of gender inclusivity again: Does Philo here intend siblings of both sexes, or merely the masculine plural *brothers*? See Kraemer and Eyl, forthcoming.

for spouse (*sumbios*) which he does use in a verbal form in the passage quoted earlier when he says that the "mostly elderly virgins," desire to "espouse" [*sumbioun*] Wisdom. His failure to use it here may suggest that he really does mean to construe the Therapeutae as male, or, at the very least, suggests that this particular description is not to be extended to the Therapeutrides.

Other seemingly generic descriptions of the Therapeutae may also be read more narrowly as applying only to the men. Describing the group as it stands for the opening prayers of the Feast, Philo says only that "they stand in a regular line in an orderly way" (*Cont. Life* 66), and that after these prayers the seniors (*hoi presbuteroi*) recline according to the order of their admission" (*Cont. Life* 66). Philo subsequently refers several times to these *presbuteroi* (literally elders).[17] That we are to take these elders to be all male seems apparent from the use of the term *enēbēsantas*, with its allusion to the male ephebate, to describe their maturing. It may also be implied in the force of the contrasting *de* in the phrase just discussed, which follows immediately: "Women, too, also partake of the feast (*sunestiōntai de kai gunaikes*).[18] If, however, the women are not included in this description (and I think it possible that Philo does not have them in mind here), it does raise questions about where we are to situate the women while the men are praying.

Only in the last hundred years or so has *On the Contemplative Life* been read more or less uniformly as a genuine writing of Philo of Alexandria, describing an actual contemporaneous community of Judean contemplatives.[19] In the fourth-century C.E., in his *Ecclesiastical History*, Eusebius of Caesarea reproduced portions of the Philonic account, adducing the Therapeutae as the earliest Christian community in Egypt, and reporting that Philo himself had met with early Christian notables, including the apostle Peter.[20] Particularly noteworthy is the fact that Eusebius defended his insistence that Philo describes Christians (who, he concedes, are not so named) by adducing the presence of the women virgins, who, he says, can only be Christians.[21]

Filtered through this lens, the Therapeutae were long presumed to be early Christian monastics.[22] Such a reading was facilitated by the transmission of

---

17. Note that this is not the term he uses for the women, whom he calls γηραιαὶ, not πρεσβύτεραι.
18. *Cont. Life* 67.
19. For a brief survey of the history of the text, see Taylor 2003:31–34.
20. *Ecclesiastical History* 2.17.24.
21. *Ecclesiastical History* 2.17.20.
22. Inowlocki points out that Eusebius does not himself describe the Therapeutae as monastics, but subsequent Christian writers made that identification 2004:307. For a full treatment of Philo in Eusebius and other early Christian writers, see Runia 1993. I thank my ever-helpful former colleague at the University of Pennsylvania, Robert A. Kraft, for calling both these studies to my attention.

Philo only through Christian channels and bolstered, perhaps, by the fact that *On the Contemplative Life* never explicitly states that the Mareotic community was Judean. This understanding was sufficiently widespread that Conrad Beissel, the founder of the Ephrata cloister in Lancaster County, Pennsylvania, in the early eighteenth century, could explicitly pattern some of the practices and physical arrangements of his own utopian community around *On the Contemplative Life*.[23]

In the late nineteenth century eminent German scholars initially found persuasive the thesis advanced by Ernst Lucius that the account of the Therapeutae was a third-century C.E. Christian forgery intended to provide legitimation for emergent Christian monasticism.[24] F. C. Conybeare's 1895 refutation of Lucius, arguing that *On the Contemplative Life* was an authentic work of Philo's describing an actual Jewish group, was quickly accepted by most scholars, with the notable exception of Emil Schürer, and it became twentieth-century dogma.[25] That these are, in fact, somewhat separate issues (whether Philo wrote *On the Contemplative Life*, whether it describes an actual group, and whether that group was Judean) has been largely obscured in twentieth-century discussion, despite Philo's own coyness on this last point. Further, as R. A. Kraft points out, very little attention has been paid to the potential problems with the transmission of *On the Contemplative Life* in particular. Although it is true that portions of the description in Eusebius conform closely to our present text(s) of Philo, this suggests only, in Kraft's words that "[i]t is highly probable that Eusebius knew and used a text that agrees with the later MSS . . . [and that] it is not demonstrable that there had been no Christian editing of the text

---

23. I discovered this on a visit to the Cloister in about 1991, where I must have read it in one of their exhibits. The Cloister web site does not mention this, nor do other extensive sites on Beissel.

24. Lucius, 1879.

25. For details, see Runia 1993; see also the lengthy arguments of Conybeare himself, "Excursus on the Philonean Authorship of the De Uita Contemplatiua," 1895:258–358. Conybeare's detailed comparison of the language of the text with other writings of Philo is more germane than his endeavors to argue on the grounds of plausibility, as when he claims, 1895:xliii, that the Therapeutae must be Jews because they do nothing not in accord with Philo, and Philo was himself a devout Jew. Conybeare obviously felt some pressure to locate Philo's description of the women within normative Judaism, and does so in creative ways: their presence at the Feast, for instance, is not at all troubling, since the Feast is Pentecost (Shavuoth) and Deut 16.11 requires the presence of women at that Feast (1895:279). Philo's general reliability on these matters is proved by such odd examples as 1 Cor 11.5, which Conybeare takes to demonstrate that "Jewish women wore veils in public," and which Philo himself says, in the *Embassy to Gaius* (1895:308). His indiscriminate use of Talmudic references to describe first century Alexandrian Judean practices is at once typical of the era in which he wrote, fascinating and distressing. He argues, for instance, that the Therapeutae must have sung the great Hallel (Ps. 113–18) because that is what the Talmud says was sung on Pentecost (*Erechin* 10.1: 1895:308). They ate leavened bread at their feast because that's what Lev 23.17 specifies for Shavuoth. Interestingly, only a year earlier, in his edition of the *Acts of Saint Eugenia*, Conybeare at once disdained arguments that the Therapeutae were Christians, yet also failed to say explicitly that they were Jews, and he proposed that, ultimately, they became Christians: "We may with great plausibility suppose that the community which Philo describes had lasted on and become Christianised, for the transition from the one to the other was easy" (1894:154).

before it reached Eusebius."[26] Whether, in other words, we actually have what Philo wrote, or whether we have a work redacted by subsequent Christian tradents, is impossible to determine.[27]

In my own initial reading of *On the Contemplative Life*, I was enthralled with its highly unusual and seemingly positive description of women members of the community, a feature that had been largely neglected by Philo scholars. Philo's description seemed to provide important evidence that at least some Judean women, in Alexandria, if not elsewhere in the Mediterranean, were well-educated in both Judean scriptures in Greek and probably other Greek philosophical writings as well, and they had sufficient autonomy and probably also financial resources to leave their families and devote themselves to the contemplative life.

In my 1976 doctoral dissertation on the functions of religious activities for women in the Greco-Roman world, the Therapeutrides merited a lengthy appendix. There, taking Philo's characterization of these women as "mostly elderly virgins," to be reasonably accurate, I argued that unmarried and/or childless women of sufficiently elite status might have been particularly drawn to the monastic philosophical life as both compensatory and enabling. It would have been compensation for not participating in the mainstream definitions of women as wives and mothers. It would have enabled women whose lives did not conform to these expectations to engage in activities and roles not available to other women, and normally reserved for men. My argument was informed particularly by the then relatively recent work of anthropologist Kenelm Burridge, whose refined model of certain religious practices as compensation for deprivation located deprivation not necessarily in economic terms, but more subtly and significantly in terms of measures of worth and access to prestige that seemed particularly conducive to analyzing the Therapeutrides as described by Philo.[28]

In 1989, I published an article in a special volume of the relatively new journal of feminist studies, *Signs*, where I expanded my analysis in several ways, perhaps most significantly arguing that despite his views of women as expressed or implicit elsewhere in his writings,[29] Philo could valorize the women Therapeutae because he understood them to be, in crucial respects, no

---

26. Kraft 2001:383.

27. One could go far down this path arguing what kinds of alterations and fabrications Christian authors might make, including the argument that one would expect more egregious Christian editing, but such arguments quickly become tangled up in the same kinds of theoretical issues this whole study engages; they depend upon assumptions about the ancient redactors that are impossible to adjudicate. In addition it's clear that the text as it stands was more than sufficient for Eusebius to read it as Christian.

28. Burridge 1969; see also the earlier work of deprivation theorists such as Lanternari 1963.

29. See, e.g., Sly 1980; Wegner 1991. Earlier studies of Philo included Baer 1970, a useful and important study published the year I began my graduate work.

longer female, but rather virgin and/or male.[30] An abbreviated and modestly reworked version of this article appeared a few years later within a chapter of *Her Share of the Blessings*, bolstered by working out the description of the Therapeutae from the perspective of Douglas's grid/group theory.[31] In all of these, I took Philo's narrative to be "rooted in social reality," even while I remarked on the useful consonance between Philo's allegorizing of gender and the actualities of the Therapeutae.[32]

Shortly thereafter, Philo's Therapeutae became the subject of increased scholarly scrutiny.[33] Taking *On the Contemplative Life* to be an authentic treatise of Philo's, these subsequent studies have tackled two significant and related issues. The first is whether the Therapeutae actually existed, or whether they are more or less a figment of Philo's fervent imagination.[34] Therapeutae are mentioned nowhere else in Philo's writings,[35] and are uncorroborated by any other ancient evidence, literary or archaeological. No other writers testify independently to the existence of Therapeutae, and no remains of their alleged settlement have ever been excavated.[36] By contrast, the Essenes, whom Philo also treats in several works (*That Every Good Man Is Free* and the *Hypothetica*) are also described by several additional ancient authors.[37] Many scholars also believe that the Dead Sea Scrolls and finds at Qumran provide archaeological evidence for their presence (although the topic continues to provoke shouting matches at scholarly conferences).[38] By itself, of course, this situation proves

30. Kraemer 1989a. In Kraemer 1992, I argue for more parity between Philo's understanding of becoming male and becoming virgin, and I think this is consistent with Harrison 1996 (who doesn't appear to have read my article).

31. Kraemer 1992:113–17.

32. Kraemer 1992:114.

33. E.g., Riaud's extensive overview: Riaud 1987. My own work (which is cited in virtually all subsequent studies of the Therapeutae) appears to have spurred some of this subsequent interest. The Therapeutae were the subject of several sessions of the Philo Seminar of the Society of Biblical Literature. Among these was an important paper by David Hay (1992). Hay is here concerned to refute the thesis that the Therapeutae constitute Philo's ideal society by demonstrating the numerous points at which Philo appears elsewhere to disagree with practices and ideas of the Therapeutae. His analysis is predicated on the historical existence of the Therapeutae, but, as we shall see, it is possible to account for the discrepancies Hay identifies in different ways. See also Hay 2003; 2004.

34. As I noted earlier, in the nineteenth century, Lucius attributed the fabrication of the Therapeutae, which he saw as intentional deceit, to Christian ideological interests. That they might be Philo's own construction seems to be a newer argument.

35. Although some scholars see allusions to the Therapeutae in occasional references elsewhere in Philo.

36. Taylor 2003:75–89 thinks, however, that she has identified the site of the Mareotic conventicle, but this is based on its consonance with Philo's description, not on any archaeological excavation. That there is a site that matches Philo's account only demonstrates that the site Philo describes was consistent with an actual location known to him.

37. E.g., Josephus, *Antiquities* 13.171ff; 13.298; 13.311–13; *War* 2.119–61; Pliny the Elder, *Natural History*, 5.17.

38. The literature on this question is extensive: see, e.g., Betz 1999. See Cansdale 1997; Golb 1995 for critiques of the identification; Schiffman 1994; Magness 2003 for support.

nothing: our knowledge of antiquity is far too limited and serendipitous for this particular absence of evidence to be evidence of absence. Nevertheless, the lack of corroboration is essential for the argument that Philo has entirely imagined the Therapeutae.

The second current issue is whether, even if Therapeutae did exist, Philo conforms his description to his own apologetic agendas to such a degree that it hampers, if not incapacitates, our ability to use Philo's account to reconstruct (and then analyze) the practices (and perhaps associated beliefs and ideas) of the community in general, and its women in particular.

In the case of the Therapeutae, and more particularly, the Therapeutrides, my mind has changed considerably on two major issues. First, I now think it likely that Philo has either entirely invented the Therapeutae, or has so radically shaped his representation of some actual ancient persons as to make them virtually inaccessible to us. Second, I think that this representation is generated out of a combination of Philo's exegetical interests, especially in Exodus 15, the Song-by-the-Sea, Genesis 1–3 (and perhaps, also, less central texts such as Joel 2.28) on the one hand, and a series of logical problems generated by his imagination (or perhaps representation) of them, particularly of women philosophers. In two other regards, my thinking has not so much changed as moderated. First, I continue to think that Philo deliberately represents the Therapeutrides as masculinized, but I argue in this study that this is part of a larger pattern of de-emphasizing many aspects of ancient gender norms both for the women and for the men. Second, despite my present view that we cannot proffer Philo's account as reliable evidence for Judean women's philosophical practices, I also think that, *were* his description to correspond to some actual women and their ancient social locations, my earlier arguments about the consonance between social experience and Therapeutic ideals and practices might still have some utility. Here, too, though, I offer some caveats.

The Historicity of the Therapeutae

The most explicit recent challenge to the historicity of the Therapeutae, and the artificial nature of Philo's treatise came in an article by Troels Engberg-Pedersen entitled, "Philo's *De Vita Contemplativa* as a Philosopher's Dream."[39] A specialist

---

39. Engberg-Pedersen 1999. For a much less theoretically sophisticated response that does not really engage the substance of Engberg-Pedersen's argument, see Beavis 2004. Beavis compares Philo's representation to the demonstrably utopian fantasy of Iambulus' Islands of the Sun (the Heliopolitans) in Diodorus Siculus 2.55–60, and concludes that Philo's account is "a utopian construction of a real . . . community," 2004:41, a position similar in some ways to that of Taylor, discussed at length later.

in ancient philosophy at the University of Copenhagen, Engberg-Pedersen argues that the Therapeutae conform far too closely to Philo's own philosophical ideals. He reads *On the Contemplative Life* as the work of a philosopher imagining "what *theoria* [the life of contemplation] practiced in a concrete form would actually look like,"[40] albeit a philosopher who wishes ultimately to demonstrate that perfection is to be found only "in Philo's own *therapeutai*, the Judean ones."[41] To do this, he posits, Philo has employed the well-known genre of a moral philosophical treatise of a type established by Aristotle on the various "lives" available to the ethical person to construct what is actually a *"plastheis mythos,"* a fictional story written for a serious purpose.[42] Such practices, he argues, are evinced in the writings of Philo's much-admired Plato, and perhaps also in Josephus.[43]

He then proposes to test his hypothesis by seeing whether it produces a "maximally coherent" reading, on the assumption that if the work is factual, it is actually *less likely* to cohere maximally with the rhetorical purposes of its author.[44] In his effort to demonstrate this coherence, he relies heavily on the work of anthropologist and theorist Pierre Bourdieu to offer a poststructuralist analysis of some of the key oppositions in Philo's account that he thinks demonstrate the artificial nature of Philo's description. Engberg-Pedersen remains agnostic on the question of whether Therapeutae actually existed, but he is adamant that scholars are justified in speaking only of "Philo's Therapeutae" and not of the Therapeutae themselves, to whom *On the Contemplative Life* provides no useful access.[45]

Contrary to Engberg-Pedersen, Joan Taylor, a scholar of ancient Judeans, argues in a lengthy 2003 monograph that much of what Philo says about the Therapeutae is derived from their actual practices, which were reasonably well known to Philo, although his rhetorical interests frequently compel him to obscure, misrepresent, and otherwise refashion the Therapeutae in a suitable image. Taylor shares with Engberg-Pedersen the general view that the purpose of *On the Contemplative Life* was to demonstrate that Judeans live in accordance with prevailing philosophical norms of the good, as exemplified by the Mareotic community.[46] But where Engberg-Pedersen sees Philo's work as an exercise

---

40. Engberg-Pedersen 1999:56.
41. Engberg-Pedersen 1999:50.
42. Engberg-Pedersen 1999:43.
43. Engberg-Pedersen 1999:43–47.
44. Engberg-Pedersen 1999:48.
45. Engberg-Pedersen 1999:64.

46. Taylor 2003:342, 346 and passim; see also the view of David Hay: "The main thesis of the treatise might therefore be summed up like this: 'The virtue that leads to the highest happiness is contemplation [theoria], and it is practised to an extraordinary degree by a Jewish community in Egypt,'" 1992:677.

in utopian vision, imagining the ideal life for a more general apologetic thrust, in Taylor's view, Philo probably wrote *On the Contemplative Life* as part of a larger apologetic ensemble to accompany a delegation of elite Alexandrian Judean men who went to Rome to plead the cause of their community before the Emperor Claudius c. 41 C.E.[47]

Philo himself tells us that he led a delegation to the Emperor Caligula a few years earlier. Although he says nothing about his role in a second embassy to Claudius, Eusebius says that Philo wrote *On the Contemplative Life* after he had been in Rome during the reign of Claudius, and Taylor's argument rests to some degree on reports in Eusebius. Taylor also points out that another contemporaneous work apparently by a member of the Egyptian delegation to Claudius, Chaeremon, extols the exemplary life of Egyptian priests in language and details strikingly similar to that Philo uses for the Therapeutae.[48] Chaeremon's work survives only in epitomes in Porphyry and Jerome. For Taylor, these similarities suggest that the two authors (and ambassadors) were engaged in a rhetorical contest to depict their respective communities as the exemplars of virtue. "The specific correspondences between Chaeremon's text . . . and *Contempl.* are striking down to small details concerning their diet."[49] One might expect these correspondences to make Taylor more wary of reading the details in Philo as historically reliable, rather than artificially generated. Somewhat to the contrary, implicit in Taylor's analysis is the argument that the reality of Egyptian priests bolsters the historicity of the Therapeutae. "Both . . . use a real religious group in order to argue that their lifestyle was philosophical and good."[50] Chaeremon's ideal priests are only men, who do marry and have children (like, apparently, the male Therapeutae), but abstain regularly from sex. Philo's insistence on the presence of women may have some relationship to the absence of women either in Chaeremon (if Philo was directly engaging his work) or the cluster of practices found in the Egyptian writer, regardless of how Philo knew them.

The debate between Engberg-Pedersen and Taylor is very much one of theory. Engberg-Pedersen's (post)structuralist approach locates meaning largely in universal and unconscious structures and oppositions. Taylor's contextual approach locates meaning in particular historical and social situations. For Engberg-Pedersen, this detaches the text from historicity; for Taylor, it grounds the text in historicity.

---

47. She notes that the noted Philo scholar of the mid-twentieth century, E. R. Goodenough, thought that Philo had written the *Embassy to Gaius* for an embassy to Claudius, and argues that *Cont. Life*, too, is comprehensible in the same context, Taylor 2003:39–40, with fuller discussion, 35–42.

48. Taylor 2003:44–45.

49. Taylor 2003:45.

50. Taylor 2003:44.

Although Engberg-Pedersen would appear to be offering a reading more aligned with contemporary literary critical theory and poststructuralism (hence his use of Bourdieu), both he and Taylor ground their reading in what they take to be Philo's intentions, intentions that for Engberg-Pedersen are accessible to the contemporary reader in the very form of the text itself.[51] Both ground their assessments of Philo's intentions in the textual and grammatical features.[52] But whereas for Engberg-Pedersen, these signal Philo's artifice, particularly the latter, for Taylor, they signal the existence of lost treatises that bolster her historical contextualization. Taylor's theory of Philo's intentions enables her, so she argues, to differentiate between his rhetorical strategies and the underlying realities of the Therapeutae themselves. Their divergent stances and interpretations produce significantly different readings of *On the Contemplative Life* and its representation of the Therapeutae, which, of course, can be adduced in support of arguments (such as those of Clark, laid out in the introduction) that the meaning of a text is produced in the intersection between the reader and the text, rather than determined by the intentions of the author.

Numerous examples illustrate their divergent readings. Consider Philo's physical location of the Therapeutae. For Taylor, Philo's precise siting of the conventicle outside the city of Alexandria on the shores of the Mareotic lake reflects its actual location, which Taylor believes she has identified.[53] At numerous points, she contests Engberg-Pedersen's argument that *On the Contemplative Life* is a utopian fiction precisely because it locates the Therapeutae in a specific, easily accessible and verifiable locale, whereas ancient utopias were located in places far beyond the civilized world.[54] Engberg-Pedersen acknowledges this general characteristic of ancient utopian fiction. In Philo's case, however, this seemingly specific location is a particularly clever artifice that nevertheless itself signals the fictive character of the work. Philo's rhetorical purposes, to demonstrate "that [the] ideal state was one to which only one

51. "[Philo] *wanted* . . . to show these terms being put to use in practice—exactly in the way Plato aimed in the *Timaeus* to present his ideal state in "acting practice," "Philo *wanted* to give a description. . . ." (emph. mine), both from Engberg-Pedersen 1999:57; "Philo . . . wishes to connect his own *therapeutai* . . ." Engberg-Pedersen 1999:50.

52. Taylor relies heavily on the manuscript designations of *On the Contemplative Life* as "the 4th part, on the virtues," whereas Engberg-Pedersen discounts the weight of the title and subtitle on the grounds that it is impossible to adjudicate among the various extant manuscripts, and that in any case, it is unclear that these titles originated with Philo himself (Engberg-Pedersen 1999:40). By contrast, Engberg-Pedersen makes much of the opening and concluding portions of the extant text. The latter appears to envision a subsequent but missing section; whereas Taylor takes this as probable, Engberg-Pedersen takes this to be a conceit that is itself part of the "true" genre of the work, 1999:42–43.

53. Taylor 2003:75–93, with a map indicating their probable location on 85.

54. Taylor 2003:8–11, where she approvingly cites my own earlier claim that the Therapeutae were locatable and, therefore, verifiable; 2003:77; 345.

actual people in the world, the Jewish one, could be said to be aspiring,"[55] required him to locate the Therapeutae within the boundaries of the civilized world, for otherwise they would have no relationship with actual Judeans. Philo's program required him "to present his ideal state as a historical fact . . . *without* admitting its fictitious character . . . and to locate it *within* the confines of the known world."[56] Engberg-Pedersen does not address the issue of verifiability, nor does Taylor, for her part, discuss the fact that in her own reading, the Roman audience for whom the treatise is written would not have been immediately or easily able to verify the existence and location of the Therapeutae.

A second example concerns the routine practices of the Therapeutae. For Taylor, Philo's description of the Therapeutic disciplining of the body with regard to clothing, sexual abstinence, sleep and other related practices is reasonably accurate. She thinks it probable that they ate a minimal ascetic diet, abstained from meat and wine, and might well have fasted regularly, if not the routine three and six day fasts that Philo describes. In a detailed, deft analysis of the garments Philo says they wear, she argues that the women's simple garments may not have been adequate to conceal their bodies from their brother monastics, prompting the need for the partial barrier in the communal *semneion* on the seventh day.[57]

That they spend six days out of seven in solitary study of ancient writings and commentaries, and composition of hymns, is also for Taylor what the Therapeutae do. Similarly reliable, in general outline, is Philo's description of their weekly gathering on the seventh day, in a communal room divided by a partition, that allowed the women to hear the discourse of the president of the conventicle, but prevented the men from seeing the women and vice versa.[58]

---

55. Engberg-Pedersen 2003:46. It is mildly unhelpful that Taylor somewhat mischaracterizes his argument on this point.

56. Engberg-Pedersen 2003:46.

57. "If the women wore *himatia* and always properly covered themselves up by their clothing there would have been less reason for the wall that separated the men and the women in the *semneion*," Taylor 2003:295; "the women may have been more neglectful in their clothing than Philo may have wished. Had the women covered up their bodies in a modest fashion, it would not have been so necessary for Philo to emphasize these spatial separations which serve to protect their modesty," Taylor 2003:302. The whole discussion runs from 287–302. Taylor does not here consider the fact that mention of the barrier disappears in the description of the Feast of Fifty, although she does note that Philo has the women and men sit separately for the meal there. Following Taylor, this might be because the special white garments the Therapeutae wore for the Feast were more concealing, but this line of argument depends on the assumption that actual practices are described here.

58. From my perspective, the disappearance of the barrier at the Feast of Fifty, without any explanation on Philo's part, is susceptible to other readings, including the possibility that it serves his apologetic interests well in the case of the seventh-day observance, but is an impediment to his representation of the unified choir at the Feast of Fifty (how, exactly, would the singers become one choir with that barrier in their midst?). Taylor's explanation for this, though, appears to be that the seventh-day activities and the feast take place in different rooms (precisely because Philo's description of the latter makes no mention of the barrier), Taylor 2003:283.

So, too, Philo's far more detailed description of the banquet and all-night choral and dance performance at the evening Feast of Fifty.

In Engberg-Pedersen's reading, by contrast, essentially all of Philo's description is generated from his imagining of how the theoretical life would work if practiced. It represents the expression and resolution of some fundamental binary oppositions: city and countryside; night and day; solitude and fellowship; female and male; inequality and equality; injustice and justice; slavery and freedom; Gentile and Judean (although not in these last terms explicitly). For him, it is this "underlying system of abstract terms"[59] that actually generates Philo's description of the Therapeutae. Their movement from the city to the lakeside and their routine of six days of solitary day-time study and night-time eating, a seventh day of communal day-time study and day-time eating, and a fiftieth day of communal day-time study, day-time eating and night-time singing and dancing are best read structurally, as "a move from non-solitude *via* solitude to a kind of fellowship . . . which is as far as could be from life in the city."[60] Underlying the alleged practices of the Therapeutae is a concern to express and resolve dangers associated with food, gender, and night. Hence, the Therapeutae remain in their individual houses six days out of seven, eating only at night. When they come out of their houses and gather together on the seventh day, they eat together during the day, but gender division remains: a partial wall separates the sexes physically and visually. Only on the fiftieth day are all oppositions overcome and resolved: food is taken during the day; night is conquered along with all its dangerous associations. Gender division is again initially present but ultimately overcome. The Therapeutae recline separately for the banquet (69), men on the right and women on the left (an alignment that will surprise no one even remotely acquainted with structuralism). In the performance that follows the banquet, men and women initially sing in separate choirs, led by a person of the same sex, but ultimately, as we have seen, a blended, unified choir greets the dawn at the conclusion of the festival.[61]

Numerous scholars have commented on the degree to which On the Contemplative Life repeatedly contrasts the practices of the Therapeutae with those of the Greeks and Italians.[62] Philo's account of the banquet on the Feast of

---

59. Engberg-Pedersen 1999:57.

60. Engberg-Pedersen 1999:59.

61. Philo does not explicitly say whether this unified choir has one or two leaders, although his description of it as a μίμησις of the Red Sea choir, with the men led by Moses and the women by Miriam seems to imply this. See later extensive discussion of this material. Engberg-Pedersen does not comment on this question, and its possible implications for his representation of the dissolution of gender difference.

62. That Philo repeatedly ascribes the more negative practices to Greeks *may* relate to his intended (and actual?) audience(s), and also to his characterization of contemporary banquets as Italian (rather than not Roman).

Fifty is preceded by a lengthy, critical description of apparently contemporaneous banqueting practices, as well as by a comparison of the problematic after-dinner discourses in Plato's and Xenophon's respective *Symposia* with the ideal discourse of the Therapeutae. For Taylor, this comparison clearly serves Philo's rhetorical purposes, but it is grounded in the actual practices of the Therapeutae, from which Philo picks and chooses to critique Greek practices and cast the Therapeutae as the best exemplars of the *bios theoretikos*. By contrast, for Engberg-Pedersen, this is "a utopian style comment on the devious practices of [Philo's] day."[63] The contemporaneous practices of others, which he wishes to critique, actually generate Philo's vision of what the Therapeutae (would) do. The Greeks (and Italians) eat lavishly and drink wine excessively, wear elaborate clothing and recline on soft couches. The English translations of this passage frequently obscure the gendered associations of these couches, for the term *soft* here, *malakōteros*, connotes the softness associated with women and with effeminate men. They are served by male slaves decked out to delight the eye of the male guest and even elicit homoerotic desires.

The Therapeutae eat only bread, seasoned minimally if at all, drink only water, recline on hard couches, wear only coarse, basic clothing that provides a modicum of modesty and protection from the weather of the season, and are served by junior members of the community who regard the Therapeutae and Therapeutrides as their fathers and mothers, not as either masters or potential pederastic lovers.

These differing readings have substantial implications, not the least for scholars interested in women's history and the study of women's religions in antiquity. Taylor's Philo offers us reasonably reliable, if heavily rhetoricized, evidence for (Judean) women philosophers in the first century. Engberg-Pedersen's Philo offers us only idealized fantasies that permit no conclusions about women's practices, and that, on the contrary, represent only male imaginings of women with little if any correspondence to real women. Hence we need to look in considerably more detail at what each has to say about Philo's description of the Therapeutrides.

Much of Taylor's analysis of the Therapeutrides hinges on an extremely close reading of *On the Contemplative Life* 68, where, in the context of describing the Feast of Fifty, Philo characterizes the women as *pleistai gēraiai parthenoi* (which she translates as "mostly elderly virgins"), as well as on his subsequent remarks that the women have deliberately chosen celibacy, seek Wisdom for their *sumbios*, and prefer immortal rather than mortal offspring.

63. Engberg-Pedersen 1999:54.

Particularly important for Taylor is Philo's use of the qualifying *pleistai*, "mostly." If the Therapeutrides are "mostly" elderly virgins, then at least a few must not be: they must be either young, married, or both.[64] Yet Philo chooses, in Taylor's view, to emphasize the "elderly virgins" and say virtually nothing about the women implicit but obscured in the word *mostly*. Taylor proposes that this characterization derives from Philo's need to avoid a crucial problem that married women philosopher contemplatives pose. As she demonstrates in a lengthy preliminary chapter, ancient representations and discussions of women philosophers make clear that women who practiced philosophy could easily be seen to violate widely held notions of a gendered "Good."[65] In particular, married women who practiced philosophy were only seen to be exemplifying the Good if their practice of philosophy was consistent with their performance of their duties as daughters, wives, and mothers. If studying philosophy makes women better wives, mothers, and examples to other women who know them, it is acceptable and consistent with the general function of philosophy to teach humans to live properly. If, however, philosophy led women to abandon those roles, it was wholly inappropriate.[66] (Precisely this debate is visible in the writings attributed to Philo's approximate contemporary, the Roman Stoic philosopher Musonius Rufus, who takes the position that contrary to the views of others [rhetorical, actual, or both], the pursuit of philosophy does not cause women to abandon appropriate femininity or be inappropriately masculine, but on the contrary trains them to be the best wives and mothers possible).[67]

Taylor proposes that married Therapeutrides threatened Philo's project to demonstrate that the Therapeutae as a whole are the best exemplars of the virtuous contemplative life, for a woman who was truly "good" would not leave her family responsibilities. Apparently, however, "good" men could leave their families, once they had discharged their obligations appropriately, including (albeit implicitly) the obligation to procreate.[68] Philo masks the presence of the problematic married (and perhaps also younger) women by his characterization of the Therapeutrides as largely older, childless, and celibate. Such women

64. Taylor 2003:263 and passim.

65. Taylor 2003:173–226.

66. Taylor 2003:264.

67. Musonius Rufus, "That Women, Too, Should Study Philosophy," and "On the Education of Daughters," in Lutz 1947. Daniel Ullucci, Brown Ph.D. 2009, demonstrated in a seminar paper that the attribution of these to Musonius is somewhat less secure than one might wish (Ullucci 2004).

68. *Cont. Life* 13 and 18, where "they" make appropriate financial provisions for their families before entering the monastic life; see earlier for my argument that Philo seems here to mean specifically, and perhaps only, the men, which is supported by his claim that "they" leave siblings, children, parents and wives (γυναῖκας), but not, apparently, husbands.

would have had, conveniently, no children to desert, and perhaps also no husbands either, if the connotation of *parthenoi* extends beyond abstinence from (hetero)sexual intercourse to abstinence from marriage as well. Elderly virgins are rhetorically acceptable.

In Taylor's view, Philo minimizes the potential challenge posed by women contemplative monastics, and bolsters the acceptability of the Therapeutrides by constructing them with maternal imagery. This is apparent, she argues, in his casting of the senior women as mothers (and the senior men as fathers) to the junior members of the society. Similarly, she sees the emphasis on their spiritual procreation as highlighting their maternal qualities. The Therapeutrides have not rejected conception and motherhood; they have merely preferred one sort of children, the immortal kind, to the lesser mortal kind. Philo's emphasis on the modesty of the Therapeutrides[69] further conforms them to his rhetorical desire to represent them as "good" women.

Although Taylor is generally highly attentive to the potential rhetorical purposes of Philo's description of the women, she reads as largely reliable Philo's report that the women themselves chose celibacy, rather than having it imposed on then. For her, it points to the practices and mores of a larger circle of Alexandrian allegoricist philosophers, where daughters were raised to think they could make such decisions, over and against the extensive general ancient evidence to the contrary.[70] Precisely because nothing in Philo suggests that this is problematic, she infers that actual underlying social attitudes and practices are at work.

Yet this, too, could easily be explained as part of a rhetorical program. As Taylor suggests, Philo needs the Therapeutrides to be childless so that, in joining the community, they have no children to abandon. However, in construing them as childless another problem emerges that Taylor misses. In antiquity generally, and in some ancient Judean circles specifically, the failure to conceive had moral implications, particularly for women.[71] It was often seen as the consequence of adultery (despite the fact that adultery is actually apparent precisely because it leads to pregnancy). The childlessness of the Therapeutrides could, of course, be seen simply as a function of their being *parthenoi*, but then again, their being *parthenoi* itself might be troubling. If the Therapeutrides are simply elderly virgins, they could easily have been vulnerable to the critique that their failure to marry, conceive, bear and rear children successfully challenges, again, the claim that they are exemplars of the "good," understood,

---

69. *Cont. Life* 33 and 69.

70. Taylor 2003:260; also 261–62.

71. This seems implicit in Philo's own discussion of the wife accused of adultery (Num 5.28) in *Special Laws* 3.62: see my discussion in Kraemer 1992:116.

always, to mean the good woman. Hence, Philo's insistence that they choose this state deliberately may contain the implicit denial that their virginal, childless state is due to any deficiency on their part. But if his rhetoric is any clue to his concerns, there is still another issue—one of compulsion versus free will—for he contrasts the Therapeutrides' choice of virginity with Greek priestesses whose chastity is imposed on them by others.

Taylor concludes that despite the mask of Philo's rhetoric, some useful historical and social data is perceptible. The Therapeutae and Therapeutrides come particularly from a larger Alexandrian Jewish philosophical milieu that utilized extreme allegorical readings of Jewish scripture, and may not have felt obligated to practice the law in a literal sense.[72] This, she thinks, is certainly suggested by the practices of the Therapeutae themselves, which, while perhaps not inconsistent with other readings of Jewish law, are not identical to it, either. (This would have differed from Philo's own more tempered and oft-cited stance, in which the allegorical meaning was the ultimate meaning, but the literal instructions of the law were still to be practiced).[73] In these Alexandrian Jewish circles, girls received education in scripture and allegorical exegesis, and were raised to have a considerable degree of autonomy. She bases this, in part, on speculation about what would have happened to the wives and children left behind by men who joined the movement.[74] The financial resources bequeathed or provided to them would have afforded them some autonomy, as well as the ability to provide the support structures necessary for even the modest lifestyle of the Therapeutae. Taylor does not note that Philo actually speaks only of inheritances to children (although he does specify both sons and daughters), and not to wives specifically,[75] but in her reading some of the women could have been the recipients of inheritances from their own fathers, giving them some personal and financial autonomy. In Taylor's reconstruction, the majority of the Therapeutrides may or may not have been elderly virgins, although she appears to think that Philo's description is not completely rhetorical either, so that at least some of the women are elderly virgins. And at least some were, on the contrary, among the juniors of the group.[76]

---

72. I use the terminology *Jewish* here, despite my reservations about it laid out both in the introduction, and in more detail in chapter 7, because it more accurately reflects Taylor's language and conceptualization.

73. Taylor 2003:262–63.

74. *Cont. Life* 13 and 18.

75. *Cont. Life* 13: unless one wants to argue that ἄλλοις συγγενέσιν (other relatives) includes wives, but I doubt it.

76. In this reconstruction, possibly, also, some had been at some point married, and perhaps also borne actual children?

The claim that some of the women were juniors seems hard to support from the text itself, methodological and theoretical issues aside. Philo's actual description of the "juniors" seems definitively male. Therapeutae are served at the *"hieron symposion"* not by slaves, but by free persons (*eleutheroi*). These, he says, are not just any free persons appointed for these purposes, but *"hoi neoi,"* who serve the others as though "sons to their real fathers and mothers." In short order, Philo repeats this characterization. During the presidential discourse *hoi neoi* stand by (*Cont. Life* 77); after the discourse *hoi neoi* bring in the food (*Cont. Life* 81).[77]

Conceivably, *hoi neoi* and *hoi eleutheroi* can be read as gender-inclusive masculine plurals, but the designation of the attendants as "sons" to their parents really argues for their being construed as male. Philo could easily have presented mixed-sex attendants as *tekna*, or even as "sons and daughters," in keeping with his practice, noted earlier, of mentioning both women and men at various points in the text. Further, the servers at ancient banquests do seem to have been routinely, if not exclusively male. Apart from this passage, Taylor's only real argument for the existence of junior women as well as for senior women who are not *parthenoi* is her interpretation of *pleistai*.

In Taylor's reading, then, the presence of women among the Therapeutae is bolstered by a methodological principle akin to the so-called criterion of dissimilarity: the largely celibate, autonomous women who join the movement pose a serious dilemma for Philo's rhetorical program. He wants to laud the Therapeutae as the ultimate example of Jewish adherence to pervasive elite norms of the "good," but the presence of these women threatens that representation and forces him to misrepresent them somewhat in order to accomplish his rhetorical goal. But this means, although Taylor doesn't explicitly say this, that he cannot possibly have invented the women altogether, for had they not existed he would either have imagined them in perfect conformity to his goals or omitted them from his account altogether. After all, as Taylor does note, Philo had no trouble describing the Essenes, his exemplars of the active life, as a community of only men, who intentionally refrain from marriage even for the purposes of procreation.[78] Hence, at the very least, Taylor's Philo truly believes both that there are women Therapeutics and no women Essenes, whatever the historical reality may have been. Taylor, however, is willing to go further and say at least that there are Therapeutrides; whether Philo is right that there are no female Essenes is, as Taylor is well aware, a far more complicated

---

77. These attendants are actually called διάκονοι: *Cont. Life* 75.
78. *Hypothetica* 11.14–17.

question, given the statement of the Judean historian Josephus, writing a half-century or more later, that some (male) Essenes marry for procreative purposes only.[79]

Taylor's attempt to refute Engberg-Pedersen's thesis focuses on two issues. The first is that Philo's account is far too detailed, specific, and verifiable (to ancient readers) to be the product of utopian fantasizing, as in the case of their location outside Alexandria, discussed earlier.[80] The second is that Engberg-Pedersen posits far too radical a dichotomy between historicity and rhetoric. Instead, throughout the book, Taylor endeavors to demonstrate how Philo's rhetoric shaped, extensively, his portrait of the nevertheless quite factual Therapeutae.[81]

To date, Engberg-Pedersen has not replied to Taylor in print, although we have all participated in scholarly meetings together, where it has been clear that Taylor's objections to his arguments do not generally persuade him. In both public exchanges and in private correspondence, Engberg-Pedersen has argued, for instance, that Taylor's reliance on Philo's use of *pleistai* (mostly), to qualify the "elderly, virgin" Therapeutrides, seriously overreads Philo. For Engberg-Pedersen, *mostly* does not mean that some Therapeutrides are not elderly virgins. Rather, it is understatement: it means something more like "mind you: they are elderly virgins."[82] Another instance of this occurs in *On the Contemplative Life* 1, where Philo first says that the Essenes excel in all arenas of the active life, and then immediately moderates this claim to say that they excel in most (*pleistois*) of its arenas. Engberg-Pedersen takes this as rhetorical modesty on Philo's part, not as a claim that the Essenes are only excellent in some areas, but not others. Given how central this language is to Taylor's reconstruction of the Therapeutrides, this is not trivial.

Yet, unfortunately for a study concerned with issues of women's religions in antiquity, Engberg-Pedersen actually says very little about Philo's precise description of women. He focuses almost entirely on the structural aspects of

---

79. For a brief overview on the question of female Essenes (and women at Qumran), see Kraemer 1999b:67–69. For a more detailed discussion of both texts and archaeological evidence, including recent analysis of skeletal remains from the Qumran cemetaries, see Schiffman 1994:127–43; Schuller 1994; 1999; Davies and Taylor 1996; Cansdale 1997:49–57; Ilan 1999; Taylor 1999; Zias 2000; Magness 2002:163–87; Sheridan 2002; Crawford 2003; Grossman 2004; Wassen 2005.

80. The argument from specificity is one other scholars raise as well.

81. It is a little tempting, if facile, to view this dispute as a battle of male dualism versus female attempt at negotiation and synthesis.

82. I am deeply grateful to Engberg-Pedersen for his generous reading of this chapter in manuscript, and for this and other significant points in personal correspondence by e-mail, in the winter of 2009. Although I think the phrase πλεῖσται γηραιαὶ παρθένοι remains somewhat ambiguous, I find his argument here highly appealing, and consistent with Philo's general caution about overstatement. Perhaps one might translate this as "they are pretty much elderly virgins."

the presence of women at the weekly assembly and at the Feast of Fifty, reading both together as elements of a central structural opposition, gender, that requires resolution, which is attained in the final merged choir. Although he is not explicit about this in the article, his poststructuralist analysis of gender in the text seems to suggest that women are present precisely (if not only) to serve as the vehicle by which gender oppositions are expressed and resolved.[83]

Engberg-Pedersen also fails to articulate *why* gender oppositions are central for Philo.[84] Rather, he invokes Bourdieu's poststructuralist analysis of the North African Kabyle house as "organized in a series of binary oppositions whose fundamental division was that of gender."[85] The presence of such oppositions in Philo appears to be precisely because such symbols are so natural and so structurally useful.[86] These natural oppositions "invariably" come to "symbolize and refer to the whole abstract, cultural order of a society's values and interpretive morality, which is itself also organized in the form of binary oppositions."[87] Hence a (post)structuralist analysis will illuminate their logic and function.

There is, however, a tension here between Engberg-Pedersen's insistence on Philo's intentions as central to his rhetorical program and the assumption of (post)structuralism that the use of structuralist oppositions is basically unconscious. Engberg-Pedersen doesn't explain how these elements come to be present in Philo: whether because Philo, in imagining the Therapeutrides unconsciously introduces them, or consciously does so, or whether groups like this inherently make use of such oppositions. Bourdieu, and probably Engberg-Pedersen with him, would not see these as conscious: the whole point of structuralism is that the use of these oppositions is unconscious and largely naturalized. In Bourdieu's work on Kabylia, structural oppositions are projected from the body onto the arrangement of the house, as well as derived from the relationship of the embodied person to the physicality of the house—as in oppositions of up and down, outside and inside, and so forth. Engberg-Pedersen may presume that as the product of an analogously organized culture, Philo, too, works within the framework (the *habitus?*) of such largely unconscious oppositions.

In any case, one test of Engberg-Pedersen's proposal is whether *On the Contemplative Life* is maximally coherent with regard to the presence and

---

83. Which, again, he confirms in personal correspondence.

84. In correspondence, he responds that "I just think they were 'central to Philo,' as it were, in general."

85. Engberg-Pedersen 1999:56.

86. Engberg-Pedersen 1999:57. One might even have expected him to invoke Mary Douglas's use of "natural symbols," but he doesn't: Douglas 1970.

87. Engberg-Pedersen 1999:57.

description of the Therapeutrides. Is a poststructuralist analysis sufficient to account for the presence of women in Philo's vision? Is some other rhetorical need met by envisioning the presence of women? And even if the answer to both of these is yes, why does Philo describe the Therapeutrides in precisely the way that he does, namely, as "(mostly) elderly virgins" who deliberately choose *sumbios* with Wisdom and immortal children over the ordinary sort.

Engberg-Pedersen might argue that Philo imagines women among the Therapeutae as a device to express and then resolve gender opposition. One could argue that Philo not only needs Therapeutrides, he needs them at the banquet for the Feast of Fifty in order for it to serve as the site where gender is both dichotomized and then unified. Once, however, Philo has posited their existence for structural reasons, he might well need to address precisely some of the problems Taylor postulates. The Therapeutrides would need to be presented as women philosophers who do not violate fundamental notions of the good, the theoretical life, and so forth.

As I noted earlier, Engberg-Pedersen argues that much of Philo's description is driven by a comparison (an *antitaxis*) with both the representations of banquets in Greco-Roman literary traditions and contemporaneous banqueting practices that Philo styles as particularly Italian. Philo's Therapeutae avoid the offensive practices of others (lavish food, ornate clothing, wine, enticing male slaves as servants, and so forth), and practice only the good (plain bread, modest clothing, water, chaste free men as servers, and so forth). Jonathan Brumberg-Kraus observes that Philo's account eliminates one of the most central features of literary symposia, namely the verbal contestation, argument and competition. Instead, in the Therapeutic banquet, the president discourses and the Therapeutae listen in appreciative silence, nodding approvingly, and ultimately signaling their pleasure with applause. In fact, he argues, the Therapeutic banquet is not so much a *symposion* as it is a *deipnon*, or rather, the after-dinner practices of the Therapeutae are different from those of the classic *symposion* not merely in their abstemiousness, but in their very practice of the inebriated yet sober singers.[88]

What then, if anything, is the relationship between the presence or absence of women at ancient literary symposia, in actual first-century banqueting practices, and the representation of the Therapeutrides at the Feast of Fifty (and to a lesser extent, at the seventh day observance)? As many scholars have noted in

---

88. In a presentation of work in progress on the contrast between the Therapeutic banquet and other Greco-Roman banquets, particularly literary symposia, presented to the Seminar on Culture and Religion in the Ancient Mediterranean (CRAM) at Brown University, February, 2005. Brumberg-Kraus thinks that *Cont. Life* 75 implies some active questioning on the part of the listeners, but I disagree: I think this refers only to the topic on which the president discourses: an issue in scripture, or a question posed at some point other than the banquet.

recent years, the only women represented as present in Greek symposia were either support staff of a sort (flute players and other entertainers) or educated companions (*hetairae*) there to stimulate the men both intellectually and sexually. There seems to be a general consensus that regardless of the artifice of these literary depictions, "respectable" women in Greek cultural contexts did not generally attend such male gatherings. On the other hand, there is also a general consensus that, by the Roman period, it had become more acceptable, although not necessarily routine, for elite married women to attend dinner parties in the company of their husbands.[89]

In an important article, David Halperin argued over twenty years ago that the character of Diotima in Plato's *Symposium* was a necessary rhetorical construction that demonstrates the uses men might make of female voices, but says nothing about the existence, presence, and voice of such women in actuality.[90] In the mode of Engberg-Pedersen, how might we read the presence of the Therapeutrides at the two communal meals?

Is their very presence, for instance, explicable not necessarily in terms of structural oppositions, but in terms of the presence of women at literary symposia? Is it explicable in terms of what Philo knew actual contemporaneous practices to be? Would his intended audience expect such a meal to be attended by both women and men, all the more so if it is an exemplary one?

But if the answers to both these questions are yes—Philo depicts women at the communal meals of the Therapeutae because women are present both in literary depictions and in actual first-century banquets, his description of them may also be governed by contrast with the representations of these other women. The women present at literary symposia are generally young and beautiful, whether as slaves in support roles, or as clever, engaging, courtesans. Their clothing, coiffure, and demeanor, all signal their sexual availability (and thus their lack of respectability). So, too, probably, does their singing and speech in the presence of men, drawing on widespread ancient associations of women's mouths with their genitalia. They are hardly to be construed as the respectable wives or mothers of the men in attendance.

The general representation of the Therapeutrides would certainly suit Philo's rhetorical purposes. Six days out of seven, the women, like the men, live in complete isolation, never leaving their huts, and thus being invisible to any man. Certainly, Philo does emphasize that the Therapeutrides are present at both communal events, the celebration of the seventh day, and the Feast of Fifty, and that they share the same devotion to philosophy and Wisdom as their

89. Theissen 1991:81–97, esp. 91; Corley 1993; D. Smith 2003.
90. Halperin 1990.

male counterparts. But unlike women at literary symposia, they are modest, not sexual. At the seventh day gathering, they sit separated from the men by that partial wall whose purpose Philo says is to preserve their modesty while allowing them to hear everything that is said. Unlike the women at literary symposia, they are never explicitly presented as speaking. That the women sing communally, as members of the chorus, is without dispute, but Philo does not ever say explicitly that the women sing individually during the initial phases of the musical performance of the Feast of Fifty. At the celebration of the seventh day (where the enactment of gender unity does not appear to take place), Philo's Therapeutrides are distinguished by their modesty, their invisibility to men and their apparent silence.[91] Even at the Feast of Fifty, where the necessity of enacting unity would seem to require them to be visible to the men, and ultimately to sing with them, the men and women dine separately on opposite sides of the room, and there is still no indication that individual Therapeutrides ever speak.

Philo's characterization of the Therapeutrides as "elderly virgins" may also be seen as the diametric opposite of the women usually associated with male banqueting, who are generally young, sexually experienced, and available. Interestingly, Philo never actually says anything about whether the Therapeutrides are beautiful in form. His description of them as "old" might appear to characterize them as physically unattractive, but we should be careful about such a reading. The notion that physical beauty and the beauty of the soul are integrally related was a pervasive one in antiquity, and his implicit argument that the Therapeutrides are the ultimate exemplars of the good might well mean either that they were beautiful in form, or at least that Philo would avoid any explicit representation of them as other than beautiful! Furthermore, despite the fact that he explicitly calls the Therapeutrides "elderly" and "virgin," Philo is also at pains to present them as maternal, as Taylor elucidates. This, too, forms a contrast with the women usually associated with banquets. Thus it seems that rhetorical interests and prevailing types *could* generate at least some of the details of Philo's description, which, for Taylor, require an historical explanation.

It is particularly striking that Philo's explicit discussion of Therapeutrides comes at two points: the seventh day observance and the Feast of Fifty. The correspondence between the women and the numbers seven and fifty is at the least quite intriguing. For Philo, seven is a particularly holy and virgin number,

---

91. See above for my argument that only when Philo is explicit about the participation of women should we infer their activity in this text.

neither begetting nor begotten, like the motherless, virgin Nike (Athena).[92] As humans, the Therapeutrides are obviously not unbegotten, but it is quite interesting that Philo says nothing about their parentage and lineage, and emphasizes their deliberate abstinence from physical childbearing. The consonance between the number fifty and the Therapeutrides at its feast is even more striking. Philo says explicitly that the number fifty is the most perfect: it is *hagnē kai aeiparthenon*, chaste and eternally virgin.[93] So, too, are the Therapeutrides, whose description as *gēraiai* might extend the correspondence to their age (fifty?).

Engaging and substantial as Taylor's study is, it does not, then, provide a sufficient invalidation of Engberg-Pedersen's hypothesis. Much of Philo's description of the Therapeutrides *can* be seen as maximally coherent, although whether such coherence must be explained as the product of utopian fantasy rooted in (post)structuralist elements seems less clear to me, as I will elaborate later. Yet Engberg-Pedersen's argument lacks an explanation at the very least of why Philo would employ the specific structural oppositions Engberg-Pedersen identifies and does not address in detail the question of why Philo would characterize the Therapeutrides as "mostly elderly virgins" when entirely "elderly virgins" would seem to better satisfy his own criterion of a maximally coherent reading.[94]

It is my present view that the Therapeutrides (if not also the male Therapeutae) are far more of an artifice than Taylor's analysis recognizes and that I myself once thought. Unlike Engberg-Pedersen, however, I do not think that their description is sufficiently generated by the factors he identifies. Rather,

---

92. *On the Creation of the World* 100: Philo devotes sections 89–128 to the properties of this special number. Interestingly, Philo associates the number seven with the term σεμνός: the very words for seven in both Greek and Latin are derived, he claims, from the Greek σεμνός and σεβασμός (*On the Creation of the World* 127). The use of this name for the individual cells of the Therapeutae as well as for their common space thus coheres well with numerous elements of Philo's description.

93. *Cont. Life* 65.

94. But see earlier, especially note 82 for his response, since I initially wrote this, that this is rhetorical modesty on Philo's part. Engberg-Pedersen also fails to address the argument of Hay 1992, elaborated by Taylor, that there appear to be significant discrepancies between Philo's own views, as expressed elsewhere in his writings, and those he assigns to the Therapeutae, an argument that would seem to undercut Engberg-Pedersen's theory of maximal coherence. Whereas for Hay, the payoff of this is a refutation of the more moderate claim that the Therapeutae are Philo's ideal, for Taylor these discrepancies substantiate her rejection of Engberg-Pedersen and her claim that the Therapeutae are historical and perceptible even through the dense layering of Philo's rhetoric. Engberg-Pedersen might respond, however, that any such discrepancies simply highlight the differences between Philo's disciplined imagination, and the actualities of his life. The Therapeutae can live the perfect *bios theoretikos* where he himself cannot. Further, as I will argue later, reading what Philo says in this one treatise against the amalgamation of his entire corpus is methodologically flawed. It reifies what he says elsewhere as his "real" and constant view, rather than allowing for inconsistency in his views, change over time, and so forth.

I think that neither Taylor nor Engberg-Pedersen has paid sufficient attention to the role that biblical texts play in Philo's formulation. In the discussion that follows, I will argue that Philo's engagement with key biblical texts, including especially Exodus 15, Genesis 1–3, and perhaps even Joel 2.28, taken together with the elements discussed earlier (such as the Therapeutrides as the antithesis of banqueting women, and as representatives of the Good) is probably sufficient to generate his entire description of the Therapeutrides, calling into question their correspondence with actual historical persons.

Exodus 15, Philo, and the Therapeutrides

> Then Moses and the sons of Israel sang this song to the LORD, and they spoke, saying:
> I will (or: let me) sing to the LORD, for he has triumphed gloriously: horse and rider he has thrown into the sea. (Exod 15.1b-2)

> Then the prophet Miriam, Aaron's sister, took a [musical instrument] in her hand, and all the women went out after her with [a musical instrument] and with dancing. And Miriam [sang] to them:
> Sing to the LORD, for he has triumphed gloriously: horse and rider he has thrown into the sea. (Exod 15.20–21)

Exodus 15, the rejoicing of the newly rescued Hebrews at the shore of the Red Sea, plays a major role in Philo's thinking, and his allegorical reading of the events celebrated in this chapter is quite clear. For Philo, Egypt is the quintessential symbol of the passions, and the drowning of the riders in the sea and the departure of the Israelites from Egypt symbolize victory over the passions.[95] In his description of the Mareotic Feast of Fifty, Philo is explicit that the unified choir of the Therapeutae and Therapeutrides is an imitation (*mimēma*) of the one set up of old by the Red Sea, in acknowledgment of the wondrous occurrences there.[96]

---

95. E.g., *Allegorical Interpretation* 2.102, where Philo says that that the casting of the horse and rider into the sea is God's casting into the abyss of "the four passions and the wretched mind mounted on them," and that "this is indeed practically the chief point of the whole song." See also *On Dreams* 2.269–70; *On the Posterity of Cain*. 155–57; *On the Migration of Abraham* 151, 154, *On the Preliminary Studies* 104; Taylor 2003:325.

96. *Cont. Life* 85.

Exodus 15 is treated extensively elsewhere in Philo's corpus.[97] Two passages in the *Life of Moses* describe the choirs by the sea, while a lengthy passage in *On Agriculture* presents an explicitly allegorical interpretation of that scene. Although all four passages (these three and *On the Contemplative Life*) have elements in common, they also have some interesting and perhaps significant differences. Only in his description of the Therapeutic festival, however, does Philo claim that the two choirs, one of men, the other of women, merge into a single choir.

Taylor, who devotes considerable discussion to some aspects of this question, has argued that this difference derives from actual differences between Philo's interpretation of Exodus 15, and the interpretation and practices of the Therapeutae themselves.[98] It is, thus, particularly important to arguments about whether Philo has accurately described the practices of an existing community or constructed them. In this section, I will explore the degree to which Philo's description of the musical performance at the Therapeutic festival coheres with Exodus 15, and propose that it is possible to generate Philo's entire description of these actions from that text alone.

Exodus 15 in Hebrew

To do this, we must begin with the Hebrew text as we now have it. There has been extensive scholarly investigation arguing that the present text reflects an intentional process subordinating both Miriam and her Song to that of Moses,[99] but for my purposes, what matters is only how the text is likely to have read in the first century C.E.

In the present critical edition of the Masoretic text of Exodus 15, Moses and the sons of Israel (*b'nai Yisrael*) sing a song of praise to God that extends from 15.1b-18.[100] The hymn opens with the word *ashirah* "I will sing: *or*, let me sing," and continues the use of the first person singular through 15.2. This is followed by verses that address God directly and whose speaker could be either singular or plural. At the conclusion of the song, in 15.20, Miriam the prophetess (*ha-neviah*), called the sister of Aaron (but not Moses), takes up her musical instrument,[101] and all the women go out (*v'tatzen*) after her, shaking their

---

97. These include *On Agriculture* 79–82 (an English translation I prefer over the older *On Husbandry*), *Life of Moses* 1.180; 2.256; *Allegorical Interpretation* 2.102; *On Drunkenness* 111; *On Dreams* 2.269–70; *On the Confusion of Tongues* 36.

98. Taylor 2003:324–34. Note that Taylor's use of *On Agriculture* 79–82 is primarily focused on the question of who sings how many hymns, and thus misses a close reading of the consonances between the two texts that potentially undercuts her argument.

99. See Taylor 2003:327–28, with helpful references.

100. v.19 is in prose form: whether it forms part of the hymn is irrelevant for my concerns.

101. NJPS: timbrel; NRSV: tambourine.

instruments and dancing. In 15.21, Miriam *ta'an lahem* the same words that occur back in Exod 15.1b. Although the NRSV translates this simply as "Miriam sang to them," the phrase *ta'an lahem* is more ambiguous and problematic than initially appears.

Taylor and others read Exodus 15 to say that, not only Miriam, but also the women sing.[102] Taylor does not specify whether she thinks the women sing only the two lines of Exod 15.20, or the entire song, although she does argue, in a note, that Miriam's singing of only the first two lines implies the rest.[103]

Contrary to what these scholars assert, Exod 15.20–21 in Hebrew simply does not explicitly say at all that the women sing with Miriam, whereas it is quite clear in Exod 15.1a that both Moses and the sons of Israel sing. And nowhere does the Hebrew text say that the women and the men sing together. Thus, Philo's account of the Red Sea performance would appear to be somewhat at odds with the biblical text, at least in Hebrew, and thus not directly derivative.[104]

A closer analysis of the present Hebrew text allows us to see the potential ambiguities that might allow for divergent readings of the passage in antiquity. These include the following questions:

1. Is the term *b'nai Yisrael* gender exclusive or gender inclusive?

2. Do Miriam's actions come after those of Moses (and the *b'nai Yisrael*) or at the same time?

3. Why is a different verb is used for the action of Moses and the *b'nai Yisrael* on the one hand (*shr*), and Miriam on the other, *anah*, and what, exactly, is meant by *anah*?

4. What is the referent of *lahem*? That is, to whom does Miriam do whatever she does?

5. Why does the version of the song that Moses sings begin "*ashirah l'adonai,*" whereas that of Miriam begins "*shiru*"?

---

102. E.g., Taylor, "In the Masoretic Hebrew text, Moses composes the song by means of heavenly inspiration, and the women, led by Miriam, echo the song, though also by means of heavenly inspiration" (2003:326). I also fail to see anything in the Hebrew that imputes divine inspiration either to Moses' song or to that of Miriam, and thank my colleague in Hebrew Bible, Saul Olyan for confirming my reading. That Philo does so, though, is another matter. In another recent study of Philo, Jutta Leonhardt also takes Exod 15.20–21 to mean that the women sing, when she writes that Philo's description of the double choir singing the same hymns in *On Agriculture* 82 "does not follow the biblical text, which shows the men as singing the verses 1(b)–19 and *the women as singing the verse 21b.*" Leonhardt 2001:164, emphasis mine.

103. Taylor 2003:325 n. 41, where her argument is derived from later Jewish liturgical practices.

104. Leonhardt 2001:164. Colson, too, comments on what he sees as a different discrepancy in this same text (*On Agriculture* 82), namely, that Philo seems to imply that only some of the women sing, when "in Ex xv.20, *all* the women sing the song. Perhaps Philo's memory of the passage misled him." (LCL 5.491). On the contrary, perhaps it is Colson's memory that is in need of correction.

Whether the term *b'nai Yisrael* is gender exclusive or gender inclusive is a complex question, obscured for modern readers by relatively recent inclusive language translation practices. The NRSV and the NJPS both render it simply as "Israelites," which modern readers generally take to be gender nonspecific.[105] Sometimes, of course, this is reasonable: the traveling of the *b'nai Yisrael*, for instance, clearly includes the entire community of men, women, and children. But in many instances, the term really is gender specific, pertaining only to adult males. In other words, the term had the potential, long before contemporary interests in inclusive language, for multiple interpretations. Taylor reads later Jewish liturgical incorporation of the Song of the Sea to subsume women under the category *b'nai Yisrael*,[106] but this does not in any way resolve the question of how Philo and his immediate contemporaries read it.[107]

Whether Miriam's actions come after those of Moses (and the *b'nai Yisrael*) or at the same time is perhaps even more ambiguous. The very placement of Miriam and the women in verses 20–21, after the verses recounting the singing of Moses and the *b'nai Yisrael*, certainly supports a temporal sequence. In such a reading, the words of Miriam merely echo those of Moses and the men. But it is by no means dispositive, and the sequencing of verses (and shared content) *could* also be construed to mean that the singers are singing together, in some fashion.

The choice of a different verb for what Moses (and the men) do—*ashir*, as opposed to what Miriam does (*ta'an*)—easily lends itself, given the exceedingly close scrutiny to which the biblical texts were subjected in antiquity, to the interpretation that there is some distinction between the two actions: the men sing, but Miriam does something not quite the same. This is visible in some contemporary English translations, such as the NJPS, which has Moses "sing," while "Miriam chanted for them."

The Hebrew verb *anah* has a range of connotations. Its frequent meaning, to answer, or respond, is reflected in the old KJV, which reads, "Miriam answered them." It does also sometimes have musical connotations, reflected in the NRSV translation, "Miriam sang."[108]

---

105. The older RSV translated this as "then Moses and the people of Israel. . . ."; the 1917 JPS translation read: "Then sang Moses and the children of Israel this song unto the LORD, and spoke, saying: . . ." or the KJV: "Then sang Moses and the children of Israel this song unto the LORD, and spake, saying. . . ." Note that these are more literal, accurate translations of the verse as a whole than the NRSV, which eliminates the somewhat awkward duplicative verbs: "Then Moses and the Israelites sang this song to the LORD."

106. Taylor 2003:326.

107. Taylor also notes that Josephus writes only of the "Hebrews" singing hymns at the sea, eliminating any specific mention of the women: *Antiquities* 2.346; Taylor 2003:325.

108. BDB, s.v. actually gives this as its only definition; Jastrow, s.v. however, gives both the definition of "answer, respond," and also the musical definition, "to sing." ענה seems to mean "sing" in biblical texts, see below: ענה also has a third definition, to be afflicted, which certainly seems irrelevant here.

Also of some significance for construing the passage is the use of the preposition *le*. Whatever it is Miriam does, she does *to* (or perhaps *for* [?]) someone else. Conceivably, this also supports a reading that *Miriam* does this, and "they" do not. That is supported by the use of the singular verb, as well as the absence of any explicit statement that the women did anything other than go out after Miriam, playing their instruments and dancing.

Who, however, is implied by the pronoun *them*? The context might suggest the women who have followed Miriam "out." Although one might then expect the feminine plural (*la*)*hen*, such a usage is apparently quite rare.[109] Instead, we have a masculine plural, which then allows the objects of Miriam's actions to range from the women alone,[110] to Moses and the *b'nai Yisrael*, to Moses, the men, and the women all together.

Exodus 15 in Greek

However ancient readers of the Hebrew text might have construed it, some possible ancient interpretations are suggested by the extant ancient Greek translation. Where the Hebrew of Exod 15.1b used a singular verb, "I sing [or: let me sing], for Moses, and the imperative "Sing!" for Miriam in 15.21, the Greek uses for both the first person plural *aisōmen*, "let *us* sing." In the case of Moses, this translation might have been prompted by a desire to conform the verb of the song to the action of 15.1, where Moses and the now *huioi Israēl* sing (*ēsen*—plural). Whatever prompts the translation, it is carried over into Miriam's verse as well, with interpretive implications I will consider shortly.

Of particular significance is the choice of *exarchein* to translate *anah*. *Exarchein*, too, has a range of meanings. Its primary usage seems to denote beginning or initiating, and some instances of this include musical references.[111] Further, *exarchōn* can denote the leader of a chorus, and *exarchōntes* are lead(ing) singers in a chorus. Although it sometimes takes a dative (and does, in fact, do so in some musical instances), *exarchein* more commonly takes a genitive, as it does in Exod 15.21: *exarchein de Mariam autōn*. This introduces even more ambiguity than the Hebrew *lahem*, since *autōn* is both the

<hr/>

109. I rely here on the professional assessment of my colleague in Hebrew Bible at Brown, Saul Olyan.

110. In practice, להם might have been taken by ancient readers to refer just to the women, even though in a narrow sense, it shouldn't. I thank my colleague Saul Olyan for this information.

111. LSJ s.v. ἐξάρχ- [588]; with examples from Theocles 8.62 (fourth/third centuries, B.C.E., so somewhat contemporaneous with the LXX translation) and the *Homeric Hymn* 27.18 (with no date given). These usages, however, take the dative, whereas ours takes the more common genitive. It can also mean to teach, or to dictate, both of which would be interesting in this context.

masculine and feminine plural genitive of *autos/autē* and there is no way to determine what is meant other than contextually.[112]

The effects of this translation are quite considerable (whether the translation generates the interpretation, or whether the choice of *exarchein* already reflects an interpretative tradition that Miriam is conducting in some sense).[113] First, one can easily construe this to say that Miriam conducted a chorus. Second, the greater inherent grammatical ambiguity of *autōn* permits the reading that it is a feminine plural and so the chorus Miriam leads consists only of women. Third, one connotation of *exarchen*, to *begin* the singing, implies that Miriam's actions are only the beginning, permitting the reading that Miriam sang the first two lines, and the chorus she led then sang additional lines.

This reading is strengthened by another textual feature of the Greek, already noted, namely, the substitution of the first person plural *aisōmen*, "let us sing," where the Hebrew had only *shiru*. This substitution implies that Miriam sings with whomever is construed by *autōn*. It thus permits diverse readings: Miriam invites, or commands, the women to sing with her, the men to sing with her, or both.

It seems then, that for whatever reasons, the extant Greek translation of Exodus 15 produces a somewhat different reading that is, I will argue, more consonant with Philo's interpretations of the Song of the Sea and its singers.

Philo's Accounts of the Song and Its Singers

Philo's discussion of the Song by the Red Sea and its singers range from a relatively brief and unallegorized description in *Life of Moses* 1.180, to a fairly lengthy, allegorized presentation in *On Agriculture* 79–81. It would be helpful to know the order, if not the actual dates, in which these discussions were written, but the sequencing and dating of Philo's works is notoriously difficult and there is no scholarly consensus on these questions (nor would a consensus

---

112. Interestingly, there are quite a few medieval manuscripts that read αὐταῖς for αὐτῶν—making the object of Miriam's actions unequivocally only women. These readings seem to come particularly in one or two families, and point, perhaps, to circles in which someone wanted to clarify the ambiguity of αὐτῶν, or bring it into line with an interpretation of this passage. The reading αὐτῶν, however, is quite old, and αὐταῖς an obvious and late alteration. Quite a few of these seem to be "hexaplaric."

113. ἐξάρχειν translates ענה Exod 32.18; 1 Sam 18.7; 21.11 (12); 29.5, apparently based on the lead-sing aspect. Notwithstanding these musical connotations, Horbury gives the far more literal "governed," arguing that the LXX enhanced Miriam's role as "choir-mistress," Horbury 1999:379. He also notes that Clement of Alexandria (*Miscellanies* 4.19) considered Miriam the "fellow general" of her brother Moses, and that Martin Hengel concluded from Philo that "the model of Moses and Miriam may have been followed not only among the Therapeutae, but also in communal practice," Hengel 1971:163 n. 25, in Horbury 1999:380; and n. 60.

necessarily be definitive). Only the few works that deal with actual known historical events can be dated with any security, including the *Embassy to Gaius* and *Against Flaccus*. Taylor argues at some length that Philo wrote *On the Contemplative Life* in the late 30s C.E., toward the end of his career, although other scholars would place it earlier. The *Life of Moses* is sometimes thought to be a product of Philo's middle work, while the fullest allegorical interpretations, such as *On Agriculture*, or *On Dreams*, are taken to be his later productions. But these arguments appear to depend, in part, on the thesis that Philo's work moves from earlier less allegorical studies to more complete allegorization, and it has been difficult to develop a schema for dating his writings that relies on some independent characteristics.[114] In this discussion, then, I will work through Philo's briefest treatment in *Moses* 1.180; his much longer and significantly different treatment in *Moses* 2.256; the allegorical presentation in *On Agriculture* 79–82, and conclude with a consideration of the salient similarities and differences in his representation in *On the Contemplative Life* 85–88.[115]

LIFE OF MOSES 1.180. In this relatively brief treatment, Philo says that having seen the great, marvelous work (of the destruction of the Egyptians), the Hebrews set up (*stēsantes*) two choirs, one of men, one of women, to sing (*aisō*) thanksgiving hymns (*eucharistikous humnous*). The men are conducted (*exarchontos*) by Moses. The women are conducted by his sister, whose name is not given, and who is not called a prophet. These two (*houtoi*) served as leaders (*hegēmones*). This account is perfectly consonant with the Greek text of Exodus 15, although it certainly uses language not found there and makes explicit the two choirs that are at best still implicit in the biblical text.

LIFE OF MOSES 2.256–57. In the second part of the *Life of Moses*, 2.256–57, Philo gives a much fuller and quite divergent account. Here, it is not the Hebrews who set the choirs up, but Moses himself who divides the people into two choirs, one of men and one of women, as in the prior passage. He does so to honor the Benefactor with thanksgiving hymns (here *eucharistois humnois*). Further, Moses himself leads (*exarchei*) the men, and appoints (*kathistai*) his sister, again unnamed, to lead (*exarchon*) the women.

---

114. I owe this general schematization to R.A. Kraft, in personal conversation. Kraft thinks that Philo's usage of certain terminology, like Chaldean for Hebrew, characterizes earlier work, tied to particular cultural situations, but concedes that he has been unable to work out the thesis in detail (for lack of time, not because it fails, such as it is).

115. Whether this allows an argument for sequencing I will leave to others.

In comparison to the brief earlier passage in Moses 1.180, Philo here elaborates that Moses forms these choirs that they might sing hymns to the Father and Creator harmoniously, through the blending of *ethon kai melous*. The meaning of *ethos* is not, in fact, obvious: Colson translates it as "temperaments" and notes that perhaps "feelings" would be better.[116] When the blending of the bass of the men and the treble of the women is done symmetrically, it produces the most harmonious melody. The voices of women and men are required to produce the most harmonious sound.

Having said, though, that Moses forms the choirs to sing hymns (plural), Philo then says that Moses persuaded all these myriads to sing, in accord, the very same hymn (note the singular: *ton auton humnon*). Rejoicing at their joy, the prophet himself led off the song (*katērche tēs ōdēs*). And those hearing him, sang (*sunēdon*) the story of these events with him, in two choirs.

In this passage, then, Moses plays a far more authoritative and authoritarian role, and his unnamed sister is explicitly subordinated to him. The order and content of the singing is more precise. Having divided the people into two choirs, and appointed his sister to lead the women while he leads the men, Moses then leads off both choirs: having heard him, two choirs then sing the same, single hymn or song, with him.[117] Philo's switch from the plural hymns to the singular hymn (also called song/ode) sung by both choirs creates somewhat of a tension in the text. Is he suggesting that first the two choirs sang various hymns, but then, under Moses' inspired leadership, sang the particular singular hymn, in unison? Or is he suggesting that Moses formed the choirs for the purpose of singing hymns but then, in an inspired state, persuaded them to sing the identical hymn that he himself leads? The latter is somewhat closer to what the text actually says, but it's not actually obvious how Philo would answer this question, were we able to ask him.

ON AGRICULTURE 79–81. Philo's treatment of Exodus 15 in this treatise is by far the longest, with explicit allegorical interpretation and numerous significant details. It is a difficult passage to translate because the terms Philo uses are highly multivalent and opaque. Subtle distinctions produce significantly different readings that are themselves potentially quite important for the interpretation of *On the Contemplative Life*. It is set within a larger discussion of the allegorical associations of horses and riders, and triggered by what Philo describes as Moses' saying in his (Moses') *Protreptikon*: "If you go out to war

---

116. Colson writes "The thought is that while men and women have their different characteristics, here for the moment they are entirely united. The phrase is often used by Philo as a synonym for ὁμόνοια and the like." (LCL 6.578–9, note a.).

117. Or perhaps, repeat after him.

against your enemies and see horse and rider and a multitude of people, do not be afraid, because the Lord God is with you."[118] Commenting on this, Philo says:

> There is a divine army, the virtues, fighters on behalf of souls that love God, for whom it is fitting, when they see the adversary vanquished, to sing (*adein*) a totally beautiful and completely fitting hymn (*humnon*) to the victory-bringing and beautifully glorious God. Two choirs, one from the men's quarters (*andrōnitidos*) and one from the women's quarters (*gunaikōnitidos*),[119] standing, begin to sing harmonious sound and counterpoint (*antēchon kai antiphōnon . . . harmonian*).[120] The choir of the men has as its leader, (*hēgemon*) Moses, who is Mind Perfected (*nous teleios*) while that of the women has Miriam, who is Sense-perception wholly purified (*aisthēsis kekatharmenē*). For it is right (*dikaios*), using both mind and

118. My translation, from Philo's text. Colson identifies this as Deut 20.1, but the quotation here is not identical to the LXX (and Colson's translation actually elides the two a little: he translates κύριος ὁ θεός μετὰ σου as "the Lord thy God is with thee"). The LXX contains the second pronoun κύριος ὁ θεός σου μετὰ σοῦ.

119. The Greek here is somewhat puzzling: ὁ μὲν τῆς ἀνδρωνίτιδος, ὁ δὲ τῆς γυναικωνίτιδος ἑστίας. Colson translates this as "one from the quarters of the men, one from those of the women," perhaps thus taking ἑστίας as "quarters." This seems, however, redundant: since γυναικωνῖτις already means women's quarters, or apartments, by itself. So, too, ἀνδρωνῖτις (= ἀνδρῶν) means men's quarters, or, in some instances, a men's banqueting hall. As Harrison notes (1996:523), it occurs in Plato's *Timaeus* 69–70, in the context of a discussion about the tripartite soul: the irrational soul is divided into the θυμός and ἐπιθυμία just as "in a house the men's quarters are divided from the women's." Whether it ever had this usage of men's banqueting hall in Judean contexts is debated. It occurs in Josephus, *Antiquities* 16.164, within his quotation of an edict of Augustus, penalizing theft ἔκ τε σαββατείου ἔκ τε ἀνδρῶνος. For discussion, see Horbury 1999:384–86, who thinks, partly on the basis of Philo's description of the Therapeutic banquet, that it should not be gender exclusive! In any case, Yonge translated ὁ μὲν τῆς ἀνδρωνιτιδος, ὁ δὲ τῆς γυναικωνίτιδος ἑστίας as " two choruses, the one proceeding from the conclave of the men, and the other from the company of the women." Interestingly, LSJ (s.v. ἀνδρών) gives precisely this text as an instance of the adjectival use of ἀνδρωνῖτις: "As Adj., ἀ. ἑστία." Yonge, however, perhaps takes ἑστίας to apply only to the women, which is grammatically feasible. In any case, I continue to be intrigued by the banqueting associations of this language, and wonder whether one couldn't translate this either as "one from the banquet hall of the men, one from the banquet hall of the women" (with LSJ, applying ἑστία to both), or perhaps even arguing that ἀνδρωνῖτις already bears the connotation of men's dining hall, while it needs to be supplied more explicitly for the women, since I think there's some merit to Yonge's construal. For ἑστία as banquet or feast, see also the definition and instances cited in Lampe, s.v. ἑστία = ἑστίασις (551).

120. *On Agriculture* 79–80. This technical language is not easy to translate accurately. According to Jeffery 2004:170, antiphonal harmonies refers to singing in parallel octaves, not to singing in alternation, as it comes to mean in Christian musical tradition. The significance of this becomes clearer below. Jeffery's discussion of Philo on music is particularly instructive. He argues that Philo was quite knowledgeable about ancient musical practice and theory (2004:156). Interestingly, although he doesn't elaborate, Jeffery alludes to the possibility that the Therapeutae are fictional, even while he proceeds to analyze Philo's account of their choral banquet practices as factual (2004:155). His discussion also points out some intriguing gender dimensions. Long syllables and long notes conveyed grandeur, solemnity, and even masculinity (2004:161, citing an ancient music theory treatise by Aristides Quintilianus [late third to early fourth century C.E.?]), for whom spondaic meter recalled people who are "stable and manly in character." For other treatments of Philo and music, see Feldman 1986–1987; Levarie 1991; also Wilson 1998. I thank Susan Harvey for the references to Jeffery and Wilson.

sense-perception,[121] to produce (*poieisthai*)[122] hymns and blessings (*eudaimonismous*) to the Divine without delay.[123]

Continuing the musical metaphor, Philo goes on to say that it is appropriate to use each of our instruments, *nous* and *aisthesis* "in thanksgiving and honor to the only Savior (*sōter*)."[124]

Philo then transitions from this somewhat more general image (which still mentions Moses and Miriam) to the precise biblical example of Exod 15.[125]

> All the men, for their part (*men*), then, sing the "song-by-the-sea" (*tēn . . . paralion ōdēn*), not with blind understanding, but, led by Moses, seeing most clearly;[126] while the women who are truly the best,[127] having been enrolled in the *politeuma* of virtue, also sing, with Miriam leading them off.[128] The (very) same hymn (*humnos*) is sung by both choirs, having a most marvelous refrain (*epōdon*), which is beautiful to repeat.[129]

After providing the words of Ex. 15.1b and 21 (LXX), Philo moves on to the association of vices and passions with horses and says nothing further about the song and its singers.

---

121. This is another difficult phrase: νοητῶς και αἰσθητῶς. This adverbial use is rare (see LSJ s.v. 42, which does not here adduce Philo). "Thoughtfully and perceptively" carries with it the grammatical structure, but probably loses the sense.

122. ποιεῖσθαι can mean more specifically to create or compose (LSJ s.v. 1428), and this is significant both for this passage and *Cont. Life*: see below, pp. 93–94.

123. Translation mine.

124. *On Agriculture* 80.

125. This may not be the most accurate characterization of the movement in the passage: it comes partly from Colson's note that Philo often uses γοῦν to introduce the biblical story which an allegory explains (LCL 3:491).

126. Another tricky translation: ὀξὺ καθορῶντες. καθορῶντες has a more precise meaning than just to see: it means to see distinctly, to perceive (and the adverb here is thus also somewhat redundant or perhaps emphatic). Colson notes, rightly I think, that this plays off Philo's understanding of the men as Israel—those who see God.

127. αἱ πρὸς ἀλήθειαν ἄρισται. Colson translates this as "the women who in the true sense are the best," and seems to take it as a subset of women, a reading he nevertheless thinks is curious. But his logic here is somewhat flawed, as noted earlier: he thinks it's odd because he thinks that Exod 15 says that "all the women sing the song" and suggests that Philo's memory has here failed him. (LCL 3:491). As I noted also earlier, the person whose memory (or whose reading) is flawed is actually Colson. This, however, doesn't resolve the issue of whether he's right that "the best" refers to a subset of women, or whether these women are in fact "the best" (of a larger set—say, all women in the world). Conceivably, Colson's translation is here affected by how he reads the end of 79. Perhaps he thought that the choirs could be understood to be drawn from the ranks of women and men, and thus not comprise all of them, so that here he understands Philo to clarify, by saying that all the men, but only some of the women, sing. Yonge's translation reads: "and women sing, who are in good truth the most excellent of their sex . . ."

128. The use of ἀφηγέομαι rather than ἐξάρχω here is noteworthy. Colson's translation of the earlier description in 79 is a little misleading: "[the choir] of the women shall be led by Miriam,"—for the English "shall be led" is implicit in the Greek, and actually refers back not to a verbal form (as it does in *Moses* 1.180), but to the nominal *hegemon*. A closer translation would be "the men have Moses as their *hegemon*; the women have Miriam."

129. *On Agriculture* 81–82, translation mine.

This passage has some salient features. It introduces a divine army of the virtues, which is either identical to that of the two choirs, or is perhaps a heavenly (platonic?) version of some sort. It lacks any indication of how the choirs come to form, and may suggest, although this is not entirely clear, that the choir of the women is a smaller subset of women,[130] while all the men sing. It is most fitting for the divine army to sing hymns (plural) to God, although whether the army actually sings is ambiguous: the only demonstrable singers in the passage are the two choirs, whose relationship to the army is similarly ambiguous.

The allegorical meaning of the two choirs and their leaders is, however, quite explicit. Just as throughout Philo, Mind is male and Sense-Perception is female, so here Moses represents perfected Mind and Miriam represents purified sense perception. Together, they represent the perfect harmony, which is replicated in the harmonious singing of the clear-sighted seers (the men) and the most virtuous women.

What exactly, is sung in this passage? *On Agriculture* 80 asserts that "it is right to produce [or: compose][131] hymns and blessings" without delay, and this might imply that this is what the two choirs do. The only thing that is clearly sung in this passage is the singular "Song-by-the-Sea," (79), which, in 80, Philo says is sung by both choirs, and whose marvelous refrain is identical to Exod 15.1b and 21. The passage appears to say, then, that the choirs sing a hymn whose refrain is those lines, and thus consists of more (presumably but not definitively the remainder of Exodus 15). The last phrase of *On Agriculture* 81, "with Miriam leading them (fem. pl) off" can be construed to mean that Miriam sings first, and the women then follow. As with the passages from *Life of Moses*, this can be seen as consonant with the Greek translation of Exodus 15, while introducing an allegorical interpretation, and clarifying its potential ambiguities.

It's also interesting to note that produce or compose (*poieisthai*) is the verb Philo uses in *On the Contemplative Life* 29 to describe the Therapeutic composition of hymns and psalms, as well as his adjective in *On the Contemplative Life* 83 for the hymns the two choirs sing.[132] Philo appears to be suggesting that the proper response to the events of Exodus 15, either historically or allegorically, is the composition of hymns, as he says the Therapeutae do. This in turn supports a consonance between Philo's ideals, and what he says about the Therapeutae, that poses a challenge to the thesis that Philo's account of the Therapeutae is

---

130. See earlier, n. 127.

131. See above, n. 122. The spontaneous response of the army to the sight of the vanquished enemy might, however, imply a similarly spontaneous and even divinely inspired process of production, rather than the studied process of musical composition modern readers might envision.

132. They sing πεποιημένους ὕμνους.

grounded in fact. In this passage from *On Agriculture*, however, there may be a tension between this reading, which may have the singers compose the hymns, and the implication that the singers sing the hymn of Moses' inspiration.

One of the most striking and somewhat puzzling differences between this text and the others we have considered so far is Philo's characterization of the choirs as not simply made up of men and of women (as in *Life of Moses*), but rather from "the men's quarters" and the "*hestia* of the women's quarters" (or perhaps "from the *hestia* of the men's quarters and of the women's quarters").[133] This has tantalizing associations with banquet language, both because *andrōnitis* often means men's dining rooms,[134] but also because *hestia*, which often signifies a hearth and, by extension, the home, can also denote a banquet. In its verbal form, it has a range of meanings from "receive at one's hearth," to feast, banquet, and so forth. These implications are lost in Colson's translation, but they are enormously intriguing, since they then bring this passage into even closer conformity with *On the Contemplative Life*, sequencing banqueting, standing, and the singing of a singular hymn, perhaps preceded by the singing of multiple hymns, and probably also invoking the composition of hymns and blessings.[135] Thus they suggest that Exodus 15 may itself generate not just the description but the whole concept of a Therapeutic feast.

This passage is also of interest for the presence of certain details and the absence of others. In contrast to the *Life of Moses*, Miriam is named here, but neither she nor Moses is called a prophet, and Miriam is not identified as Moses' sister. God is called by epithets not found in the *Life of Moses*, including "Victory-bringer," and "Gloriously Victorious," as well as "the only Savior." In contrast to Exodus, Moses is said to lead (*exarchō*) the male singers. In contrast to Exodus and the *Life of Moses*, a different verb, to lead off, or start off (*aphēgeomai*) is used for what Miriam does with the women.

EXODUS 15 IN *ON THE CONTEMPLATIVE LIFE*. Philo's depiction of the Therapeutic chorus that becomes a copy of the one at the Red Sea begins in *On the Contemplative Life* 83. After dinner, they stand up (*anistantai*) together in the middle of the room (having previously dined on opposite sides) and form themselves first in two choirs, one of men (*ho men andrōn*), one of women (*ho de gunaikōn*). Each has its own leader and conductor (*hegemōn de kai exarchōn*), chosen both for their respect in the community and their musical talents. Interestingly, Philo does not say here that their respective leaders are male and female, nor does he explicitly identify them with Moses and Miriam.

---

133. See earlier, n. 119.
134. See earlier, n. 119.
135. See earlier, n. 119.

These two choirs then sing multiple hymns, "in many meters and melodies, both sounding together (*sunechountes*) and also with antiphonal harmonies (*antiphōnias harmoniais*) gesturing with their hands (*epixeironomountes*) and dancing (*epourxoumenoi*)."[136] Then, when they are in a sufficiently ecstatic state, they mix/intermingle (*anamignunta*) and become "one choir out of the two, a copy of the one set up [or standing: *sustantos*] of old beside the Red Sea, in acknowledgment of the wondrous occurences there."[137] This now single choir of the men and the women, sings hymns of thanksgiving (*tous eucharistērious humnous*) to God their savior (*ton sōtēra theon*). The bass of the men and the treble of the women produces a truest harmonious music (*Cont. Life* 88).

This description shares much with Philo's other accounts of the Red Sea singing. Its designation of Moses as a prophet (absent in Exodus 15 but certainly present elsewhere in the Bible) also occurs in the *Life of Moses* 2.256. Its use of the verb *exarchein* for Moses' leadership of the singers, again absent in Exodus 15, occurs in all four passages. The characterization of the hymns as "eucharistic," while absent from Exodus 15, is shared with both accounts in the *Life of Moses*, although it is absent in *On Agriculture*. The two choirs sing multiple hymns in all of Philo's passages. Verbs of standing describe the activity of the singers in *On the Contemplative Life*, Moses 1.180 and *On Agriculture*. Philo attributes the composition of hymns both to the Therapeutae and to somewhat ambiguous persons (perhaps the divine army of the virtues, perhaps the singers by the sea) in *On Agriculture*. The Therapeutae sing hymns to God who saves (*ton sōtēra theon*). Philo similarly calls God savior (*ho monos sōter*) in *On Agriculture* 81.

In *On the Contemplative Life* 83, Philo says that one of the two choirs is composed of men (*ho men andrōn*) and one of women (*ho de gunaikōn*), as he does also in *Life of Moses* 1.180 and 2.256. However, as discussed at some length earlier, in *On Agriculture*, he says rather that the two choirs come one from the men's quarters (*andrōnitidos*) and one from the women's quarters (*gunaikōnitidos*). Interestingly, when describing the double *peribolos* in which the Therapeutae gather for their seventh-day observance, he says that it is divided into two parts:

---

136. Here I defer to Jeffery's translation (2004:170), including his observation (noted earlier) that antiphonal harmonies refer to two pitches sung an octave apart. He writes: "In short, Philo was describing what naturally happens when men and women attempt to sing in unison: the differences in their natural ranges produces two concurrent renditions an octave apart" (2004:171).

137. *Cont. Life* 85. Philo then goes on to describe the parting of the sea that, in Exodus, enables the Israelites to pass through on dry land, while the pursuing Egyptians drown in the returning waters. Interestingly, he names neither the Israelites nor the Egyptians, whom he calls only "the enemy." This, however, is consistent with the Song of the Sea itself, which never mentions the Israelites explicitly, and refers to the "enemy" and to the chariots and army of Pharaoh, but not explicitly to Egyptians, either, although the bracketing lines, Exod 15.1a and 15.19 do explicitly refer to Israelites, and the immediately preceding lines of Exod 14.31 explicitly name both Egyptians and Israelites.

ho men eis androna, ho de eis gunaikōnitin (32). The subtlety of this description is obscured in the translations of both Colson and Taylor, but in Greek, the language common to both texts is apparent.

On the Contemplative Life lacks a few elements found at least once in the other accounts. But these absences are never unique. In *Life of Moses* 2.256, the choirs sing both hymns (plural) and the same singular hymn/song. In *On Agriculture*, Philo again emphasizes the singing of the same singular hymn/song by the double choir. Whether here the choirs sing hymns in the plural is somewhat ambiguous: Philo says only that it is appropriate for the divine army of the virtues to compose hymns. (Who, if anyone, in *On Agriculture* performs those hymns is not explicit). In *On the Contemplative Life*, the two choirs sing many hymns, and the unified choir also simply sings hymns (plural). This, however, is identical to Philo's relatively brief description in *Life of Moses* 1.180 where the choirs simply sing hymns and there is no mention of a singular hymn or song.

Consider also the designation of Moses and Miriam as *hegemones*. *Life of Moses* 1.180 employs it, *Life of Moses* 2.256 does not. Philo also uses it in *On Agriculture* but only for Moses. It does not occur in *On the Contemplative Life* 87, where Moses and Miriam are explicitly named, but describes the actual leaders of the two choirs formed following dinner at the Therapeutic banquet. It does not appear in Exodus 15.

Only in one respect is the description in *On the Contemplative Life* truly unique, from both explicit elements in Exodus 15 and Philo's other treatments of Exodus 15. It explicitly has the two choirs become a single choir. In all other respects, its details are paralleled in one or more of Philo's treatments of Exodus 15.[138]

Philo's Exegesis of Exodus 15 and his Representation of the Therapeutae

Central, if not crucial, to Taylor's argument is the distinction she sees between Philo's representation of the singing in *Moses* 2.256 and *On Agriculture* on the one hand, and the practices of the Therapeutae as described in *On the Contemplative Life*, particularly 87, on the other. Taylor aggregates Philo's discussion in all the passages other than *On the Contemplative Life*, to arrive at his own view. In her reading, Philo's Moses composes the Song of the Sea, and the women led by Miriam merely repeat it, actions Philo interprets allegorically as "mind that is active in initiating and composing the song, and sense-perception

---

138. It is also the only place in these passages that Philo calls Miriam a prophetess, but this is explicit in Exod 15.20.

(Miriam) provides an echoing response."[139] According to Taylor, Philo insists that the Israelites sing one song; Moses leads the men and appoints his sister to lead the women—Miriam takes no initiative but simply does what Moses has assigned to her (and the women).

Relying particularly on Philo's use of the plural *hymns* both in *Moses* 1.180 and in *On the Contemplative Life* 87, Taylor speculates that Philo is attempting to counter an alternative tradition in which there were two songs, not one, and Miriam functions as an independent prophetic leader of inspired song. For her, it is this alternative tradition that undergirds the practice of the Therapeutae:

> There is a subtle but significant difference in what Philo states regarding the Mareotic group and what he states elsewhere, and it seems likely to me that he is in fact reflecting the notions of the group despite his own different viewpoint. There is one inspired choir, which sings hymns composed by Moses and Miriam. Miriam's own identity as a prophetess and composed of song would justify the *therapeutrides* using her as a model . . . *For the Mareotic group, though not actually for Philo* (italics mine), Moses—as inspired prophet— leads the men. . . . Miriam—as inspired prophet—does likewise with the inspired women.[140]

She also points out that Philo's description of the singing of the Therapeutae is at odds with his own understanding of the Israelite experience, where the men lead and the women echo. Instead, in *On the Contemplative Life*, all the Therapeutae are one inspired harmonious unity.[141]

There are several serious problems here. One is methodological. Taylor's argument relies on an amalgamated reading that actually creates, or attempts to create, a single static interpretation ascribed to Philo. Such a move obscures some of the significant differences between those various readings that I have laid out earlier, and will return to later, and fails to allow for fluidity in Philo's thinking, change over time, and even contradiction.

Further, Taylor's attempt to extract a single summary of Philo's own view of the Red Sea singing runs somewhat roughshod over the complexities of these passages. Her insistence that for Philo, the Israelite men led and the women followed does not seem to me to be borne out in the actual passages. Both the *Life of Moses* 2.256 and *On Agriculture* are far more ambiguous in their representation of the singing by the Sea than Taylor's summary of Philo's view would suggest.

139. Taylor 2003:332.
140. Taylor 2003:333.
141. Taylor 2003:333–34.

Life of Moses 2.256–57 is amenable to several readings. In 256, Moses him-self divides the people (*to ethnos*) into two choirs, leading the men himself while appointing his sister to lead the women *hin'adōsin humnous eis ton patera*: "in order that they might sing hymns to the Father," or perhaps "for the pur-pose of singing hymns to the Father." Philo then goes on to explain how the blending of male and female voices produces the sweetest and most completely harmonious melody. This language, which closely resembles that of *On the Contemplative Life* 88, suggests not the sequenced singing of the men, followed by the echoing women, but a choir of voices ensemble.[142] Further, the use of *hina* creates an ambiguity: the purpose of the creation of the two choirs, one of men, one of women, is this ensemble of *ethos* and *melos*, *treble*, and *bass*. But is that purpose realized? If it is, then this passage describes two choirs, one led by Moses, one by Miriam, singing hymns (plural). After they sing in this form, apparently, Moses persuades these many persons to sing one and the same hymn, *ton auton humnon* (which appears to be Exodus 15 or some version thereof, since it recounts the marvelous events related in Exodus 14 and 15). Overjoyed at their joy, Moses himself leads off the song (*katerxē tēs ōdēs*). And his hearers, assembled[143] into two choirs, sing together (*sunēdon*). Alternatively, while the purpose of dividing these two choirs was to have them sing multiple hymns, Moses is so overcome by their joy that he changes plans, as it were, and leads them instead in the singing of the singular hymn. But even then, the passage says only that Moses leads off and the choirs sing all together (*sunēdon*), not that the men sing first and the women follow. It is not clear to me how we might choose among these readings (although I probably prefer the first as more natural,—an admittedly dangerous category).

On Agriculture is even more ambiguous (or ambivalent). For whereas in *Life of Moses* 2.256–57, all the singers are clearly the men and women miracu-lously saved by God, rejoicing on the shore of the sea, in *Agriculture* 79, the first choirs described are those of a divine army of the virtues, drawn not from men and women, but from the male and female "quarters."[144] As noted earlier, how these choirs form is unstated, but they come into being because it befits the

---

142. Jeffery 2004 would seem to support this.

143. Colson translates εἰς δύο χορούς ἁλισθέντες as "massed in two choirs," reading ἁλισθέντες from ἁλίζω, to assemble, mass, etc. But it is intriguingly close to ἁλιτενής—"stretched out along the sea," which would actually make more sense: the two choirs, arrayed along the sea, although there does not seem to be man-uscript evidence to support such an emendation.

144. Perhaps this is because such a divine army is not made up of actual men and women, but rather denizens who are nevertheless gendered in some way. This is an interesting line to pursue, if an odd one, because it *might* suggest that Philo here envisions a heavenly court of male and female beings. However, this is undercut by Philo's reversion to a more simple description in the next line: the chorus of men is led by Moses; the chorus of women is led by Miriam.

divine army, on seeing the enemy vanquished, to sing commemorative hymns to God. The repeated use of infinitives in this portion of the passage seems to me to be (perhaps deliberately) ambiguous. It describes what we might take for a Philonic (platonic) ideal pattern: it is fitting for the divine army to sing hymns; it is right (*dikaios*) to compose (*poieisthai*) hymns and expressions of happiness,[145] but whether this describes the actions of the saved Israelites by the Red Sea is not so clear. And in any case, the passage sheds no light on the order of singing by the male and female denizens of the army.

What is somewhat clearer is the subsequent portion, which describes, with allegorical interpretation, the actual singing by the sea. Here, too, Philo shifts from a discussion of the hypothetical singing (and composition) of multiple hymns (and blessings) to God, to the specific performance of the singular song by the sea (*tēn paralion ōdēn*). Moses leads the men, Miriam leads off the women, and both choirs sing the same hymn, whose refrain is so marvelous. Here again, nothing in the passage compels conclusions about who sings in what order, other than the suggestion that Miriam "leads off" (*aphēgoumenēs*) the women. For Taylor, however, it is the explicit allegorical interpretation that is crucial: "In this allegorical passage [*On Agriculture* 80], it is clear that it is mind that is active in initiating and composing the song, and sense perception (Miriam) provides an echoing response."[146] Although Philo's view of mind as active and sense perception as passive and derivative could possibly support such a reading, I see nothing in the passage that compels this.

Taylor chooses to privilege the *Life of Moses* 2.256–57 and *On Agriculture* as Philo's "real" view of the Exodus singing, with what she takes to be their insistence on the singing of the singular hymn, and to see *Life of Moses* 1.180 as pointing to the alternative tradition Philo seeks to oppose. *Life of Moses* 1.180 corresponds far more closely with what Philo says in *On the Contemplative Life*: two choirs sing thanksgiving hymns to God, with Moses leading the men and his sister leading the women. It says nothing about a singular hymn or song; nothing about whether the men sing first, and the women echo, and so forth. At the very least it supports the possibility that Philo did not have a fixed and static interpretation of Exodus 15.

Taylor is right that *Life of Moses* 2 and *Agriculture* do emphasize the singing of the same singular hymn, over and against both *On the Contemplative Life* and *Life of Moses* 1, where only plural hymns are mentioned. But she is not right that the sequence of singing in either of those privileges the men over the women.

---

145. εὐδαιμονισμούς: Colson translates this as "blessings," and that may be right in some general sense, but it's also one of those terms that's actually incredibly vague and doesn't indicate what, exactly, Philo or his readers would have had in their heads.

146. Taylor 2003:332.

On the contrary, even in those passages in which Philo insists on the singing of the same hymn, the women and men appear to be singing in concert, not in hierarchical sequence. Particularly in *On Agriculture*, this unified singing has allegorical implications (and in fact, might have led Philo to go one step further, ultimately, and envision a single unified choir that is an even better expression of the union he envisions).

Taylor's thesis that the Therapeutae utilized alternative Miriam traditions that distinguished their interpretation of Exodus 15 from that of Philo hinges particularly on Philo's statement that the Therapeutae sing hymns to God as Savior (*ton sōtera theon*). This epithet also appears, in Hebrew, in a small fragment from Qumran that may be an alternative and longer version of Miriam's Song in Exodus, and Taylor speculates that this points to traditions employed by the Therapeutae.[147] Yet this same epithet occurs in *On Agriculture* 81, where God is called *ho monos sōter*. The Qumran fragment does not offer us an explanation for the language Philo attributes to the Therapeutae that cannot be found both elsewhere in Philo and as a derivative of Exodus 15 (as I shall argue later).

Finally, it is not clear to me at all why we cannot, or should not, take *On the Contemplative Life* itself to be as viable a representative of Philo's "real" interpretation of the passage as any of his other treatments of Exodus 15. That is, when Philo says in *On the Contemplative Life* that the original choir by the sea was a single choir, and that the single choir formed by the Therapeutae is a *mimēsis* (an instantiation?) of that original choir, why is this not an equal contender for a view Philo himself held, at least at the point at which he wrote *On the Contemplative Life*? I understand Taylor's attempt to control for what Philo says in *On the Contemplative Life* by reading it against what he says elsewhere, on the supposition that, if it's different, it's attributable to the Therapeutae, not to Philo. Because she really does think that the Therapeutae existed and had such practices, Taylor segregates out *On the Contemplative Life* 83–88 from Philo's other treatments of Exodus 15, and sees its distinctive features as a reflection of real divergences between the Therapeutae and Philo. However, this is another instance of the kinds of literary dilemmas theorists have identified. Merely because the single choir is absent in *Life of Moses* and *On Agriculture* does not require us to see it as the Therapeutic view, rather than Philo's, particularly in the absence of any explicit statement to this effect, and in the presence of Philo's own claim about both the original choir and the Therapeutic one. It is, of course, possible that here Philo represents the views of the Therapeutae rather than his own, but there is no way to triangulate their views, and both

147. Taylor 2003:32932, with text and translation of the Qumran fragments on 330–31.

readings are, in fact, plausible. In other words, there seems to be no way to distinguish between views and practices that actual Therapeutae might have held and Philo's representation(s) of them.

Consonances and Engagements with Exodus

Although I did not begin with this position, it now seems to me that all of Philo's treatments of the Exodus singing, including his description of the Therapeutic singers and their choirs, is integrally related to his interpretation of Exodus 15 in Greek. Although, as I have laid out in detail earlier, these four passages are hardly identical, and do sometimes diverge from one another, read synoptically, they produce a reasonably coherent picture of exegetical engagement with Exodus 15.

Presuming, of course, that the text we have corresponds reasonably closely to the version(s) Philo knew, some of the particular details of Philo's various accounts of Exodus 15 are derived directly from the text itself, particularly from 15.1 and 20–21. Exod 15.1 says that Moses and the sons of Israel sang "this song" (tēn tautēn ōdēn). Throughout Philo's accounts, Moses and a choir of men sing. In Life of Moses 2 and On Agriculture, the singers sing a specific song (ode, singular). Exod 15.20 explicitly calls Miriam a prophetess, as does On the Contemplative Life. Exod 15.21 has Miriam "lead" someone, and the same verb occurs in On the Contemplative Life and Life of Moses 2, while in Life of Moses 1, one occurrence governs the activity of both Moses and his sister. Only in On Agriculture does Philo use a different verb for Miriam's actions. In Exod 15.2, the singer says that God has become "my helper" for salvation, which coheres with Philo's claim that the Therapeutae sing hymns to God as Savior, and the epithet "the only Savior" in Agriculture 81.

Far more intriguing than these relatively straightforward correlations are the places where Philo's treatment seems to reflect ancient interpretive dilemmas posed by the Greek version of Exodus 15. Philo's consistent depiction of, at least initially, a male choir and a female choir, affords one example. Exod 15.1 is explicit that the sons of Israel sing: reading this phrase as gender specific easily produces a choir of men. As I have argued earlier, although the Hebrew text does not say that the women sing, the Greek translation of Exod 15.20–21 strongly implies that they do, and Philo clearly reads it that way. All of his accounts envision two choirs, one of men and one of women, for at least some of the singing.

Although Philo is also consistent that the men are led by Moses and the women by Miriam, variations from text to text seem to respond to interpretive dilemmas. The variations in the description of Miriam, for instance, mirror variations in the biblical texts. In Exod 15.20–21, Miriam is named, called prophetess, and said to be the sister of Aaron. In Exodus 2, the story of Moses' birth, the figure of his sister is unnamed (as is, in fact, every other character except the baby Moses). Although Miriam appears in Numbers 12 (and dies in Num 20.1) the explicit identification of Miriam as the sister of both Aaron and Moses comes only in the geneaologies of Num 26.59 (and 1 Chron 6.3).[148]

In *On the Contemplative Life*, Miriam is named and called prophetess, following Exod 15.20, but she is not said to be the sister of Aaron. In the *Life of Moses* 1 and 2, Philo omits Miriam's name, calling her only "the sister of Moses." This may also be read as an implicit correction, or at least clarification of her identification in Exod 15.20 as "the sister of Aaron." In *On Agriculture*, she is named, but without any further qualification, either in terms of her brothers, or her role as prophet.

The variations in Philo's descriptions construct the relative status and authority of Moses and Miriam somewhat differently. In *On the Contemplative Life*, Miriam and Moses are portrayed relatively equally: she is a prophetess, as she is in Exod 15.20, and he is a prophet. This may reflect Philo's discomfort that Exod 15.20 calls only Miriam, but not Moses, a prophet. In Philo, at least, if Miriam is a prophet, Moses must be also. This suggests, however, that at least in Philo, the relatively balanced representation of Moses and Miriam is derived more from Philo's desire to correct a potential apparent imbalance which favors Miriam than from any egalitarian impulse. In any case, the converse appears not to obtain: Moses can be a prophet, whereas Miriam is not explicitly so (*Life of Moses* 2). In *Life of Moses* 2 and *Agriculture*, the net effect of Philo's exegetical choices is to subordinate the figure of Miriam to Moses, by omitting her name and identifying her only as "the sister of Moses" (*Life of Moses* 2) or by omitting her designation as prophetess (*Life of Moses* 2 and *On Agriculture*).

Several of the strategies that Philo deploys to subordinate Miriam to Moses, however, point again to exegetical dilemmas. Exod 15.21 uses the verb *exarchein* to describe Miriam's actions, but not those of Moses. Philo, too, uses it for Miriam directly in *On the Contemplative Life* and *Life of Moses* 2, and indirectly in *Life of Moses* 1. At the same time, Philo supplies *exarchein* explicitly for the actions of Moses in all four instances, deriving it, in my view, from its initial characterization of Miriam in Exod 15.20. Anything Miriam does, Moses does, too (if not better), or, put differently, Moses can be superior to Miriam, but Miriam cannot be superior to Moses.

In *Life of Moses* 2, Philo makes a claim absent anywhere else, that Moses appoints his sister to lead the women. This retains the biblical statement that

148. For useful discussion and bibliography, see Trible 2000.

Miriam "led" but subordinates her leadership to his; Miriam can only lead because Moses has authorized her to do so.[149] Yet this may be part of a larger pattern of readings in response to the question, How did these choirs come into being? Exodus 15 says nothing about how the sons of Israel come to sing with Moses, while Miriam and the women do whatever it is they do. Philo's various writings offer different answers. In *On the Contemplative Life*, the choirs of the Therapeutae form themselves; in *Life of Moses* 1, the "Hebrews" set up the two choirs. In the highly arcane scenario of *On Agriculture*, it is the divine army of the virtues that simply has two choirs, whose origins are unarticulated. Only in *Life of Moses* 2 does Philo maintain that it is Moses himself who is responsible for dividing the people. This claim, of course, is not actually irreconcilable with what he says elsewhere, but it is certainly far more explicit.

The use of *exarchein* in the Greek Exodus to describe Miriam's activity poses numerous potential dilemmas. The repeated English translation of the term as simply "led" obscures the musical connotations as well as the ambiguities. Philo's use of *aphēgeomai* in *On Agriculture*, whereas elsewhere he always uses *exarchein*, might be construed as part of his program to subordinate Miriam, if he (and his readers) would take *aphēgeomai* to have less hierarchical meaning. But there are other possibilities here. The precise meaning of *exarchein* depends, not only on its various ancient resonances, but on the referent of *autōn*, that is, who Miriam "led," as well as on the exegetical questions concerning what, exactly, is sung, either by women, or by men. Who is included in the gender ambiguous *autōn*? The women with Miriam, who, in Exod 15, play instruments and dance? The men? The women *and* the men? Further, when Miriam sings, "Let us sing," in Exod 15.21, who is the implied "us"? The ambiguity of *autōn* can easily extend back to *aisōmen* (let us sing), allowing it to mean again anything from the women alone, to the men alone, to both the women *and* the men.

These readings affect how one reads the sequence of singing. If one construed *exarchein* to mean that Miriam "began" the singing, one might conclude that Miriam sang the lines of Exod 15.21, followed by whoever is included in *autōn*. If, on the other hand, one construed *exarchein* to mean that Miriam led "them" in the sense of conducted them, one would envision a different sequence, in which Miriam and "they" sing altogether.

Philo's treatments, including *On the Contemplative Life*, suggest that he takes Miriam's invitation to be directed to the women, and for women to be the referent of *autōn*. Yet he is less clear about whether Miriam sings first, followed

---

149. This may also relate to Philo's allegorical interpretations of Moses as mind and Miriam as sense perception and their proper hierarchical relationship, enmeshed in gender hierarchies. Sense perception should not initiate and be active on its own, but should be under the direction of mind, just as women should not be active on their own, but subordinate to appropriate male authority.

by the women, or whether Miriam merely "leads" (and perhaps also sings with them). *Life of Moses* 1 and *On the Contemplative Life* give no indication of what Philo might envision here. Philo's change of verb for Miriam, in *On Agriculture*, however, could be construed to signal exegetical precision on Philo's part, assuming, as noted earlier, that *aphēgeomai* more precisely indicates that Miriam sings first and the women then follow.

Similar problems pertain to the sequencing of the men's singing. As I noted earlier, the first person singular of Exod 15.2 supports a sequence of Moses singing by himself, followed by the sons of Israel. That Moses might sing with them is implied in his invitation "*aisōmen*," but the matter is open to interpretation.[150] Interestingly, Philo does appear to address this issue at least once, in *Life of Moses* 2, where he explicitly says that Moses, overjoyed at the joy of those on the seashore, leads them off (*katerchē*, not *exarchen*) himself, while those hearing him, sing with him.

Yet other questions of sequence remain. What is the relationship between the singing of the men and the singing of the women? Does the order of the text reflect a sequencing of singing? Did Moses and the men sing first, together, followed by Miriam and the women? Did Moses sing first, then the men, followed by Miriam, then the women? Moses, then the men with Moses, followed by Miriam, then the women with Miriam? It is easy to read *Life of Moses* 2 to say that Moses leads off, and then the men and the women together join in, whereas Philo's description of Miriam leading off the women in *Agriculture* seems to conjure up a slightly different sequence. It is, of course, impossible to decide what Philo's real position on these questions might have been, as though he had one singular, immutable view. His treatises, however, diverge in their details precisely along these lines of textual ambiguities.

Enmeshed in questions of sequencing is another dilemma. What, exactly, comprises "this song" that Exod 15.1 claims Moses and the sons of Israel sang? All of what follows (i.e., Exod 15.2–18)?[151] If the song that Moses and the men sing comprises all of verses 2–18, why does verse 2 seem to presume a singular speaker? Does "this song" perhaps only include 1b? Ancient readers might adduce Exod 15.21 in support of this narrower reading: the "song" is what the women also sing. But if "song" refers only to Exod 15.1b, what then is Exod 15.2–18? If it is not "this song," is it still a song? A different song? Something else that can be sung (i.e., hymns)? One can also easily imagine that the identity of verses 1b and 21 would have prompted speculation concerning whether

---

150. And Taylor's discussion of the singing of the hymn in later Jewish liturgy supports my general point that the text is susceptible to these kinds of readings.

151. I will for now omit the problem of whether to include verse 19, which is found in the *Odes*, although the remainder of Exodus 15 is not.

Moses, the men, Miriam, *and* the women all sang the same thing. And if so, how, precisely?[152]

As I have detailed earlier, there is considerable tension in Philo's accounts between the singing of hymns, and the singing of one particular song, which is also called a hymn. Philo makes no reference to "this song" in either *Moses* 1 or *On the Contemplative Life*, whose singers only sing unspecified "hymns." He is explicit in *Life of Moses* 2 and *On Agriculture* that the two choirs sing the same song (singular). In *On Agriculture*, he goes even further, specifying that this hymn, which they all sing has a most marvelous refrain (*epōdē*), whose words are precisely those of Exod 15.1b = 15.21. Thus, one might read this passage to say that the Song-by-the-Sea consists of Exod 15.1b-18, of which 15.1b = 15.21 is the refrain.[153]

These exegetical quandries seem to me to provide a sufficient account for much of the specific variations in Philo's representations of Exodus 15. The implication of this is highly significant, for it undercuts Taylor's argument that the differences between what Philo says in *On the Contemplative Life*, on the one hand, and these other passages, on the other, should be attributed to real differences between Philo's interpretations and the enacted interpretations of the Therapeutae. This is true not only for relatively minor details, such as the designation of God as Savior, but for what Taylor takes to be a major discrepancy between the singing of plural hymns in *On the Contemplative Life* and *Life of Moses* 1, and the singing of the identical singular hymn in *Life of Moses* 2 and *Agriculture*.[154]

The crucial question, however, is whether this is sufficient to account for what is unquestionably a unique feature of Philo's account of the Therapeutic performance, namely, their merging into a single choir. Based on the analysis and argument I have offered here, I see no reason not to think that it is. It is certainly true that Philo never says elsewhere that the two choirs by the Red Sea ever merged into one. But as I have argued earlier, I see no reason to require him to do so. It is sufficient in my view that here he explicitly says not merely that the Therapeutae do so, but that the ancient singers by the sea did so: at the sight of the enemy drowned, "filled with divine fervor (*enthousiōntes*), both men and women became one choir, and sang hymns of thanksgiving to the salvific

---

152. Here again, Jeffery is extremely helpful in his arguments that throughout his writings, Philo describes the singing at the Red Sea always with a similar vocabulary that describes a harmonic mixture of male and female voices. "The most detailed such passage (*Life of Moses* 2.256–57), accurately interpreted, confirms that Philo imagined men and women blending simultaneously, not alternating . . ." as turns out to be what medieval Christian singers did, and maybe even what they thought Philo meant: 2004:173.

153. It is interesting to think about the significance of Philo's description earlier in *On the Contemplative Life* of the singers, women and men, who join in the refrains of the hymns sung by the individual singers.

154. Taylor sometimes seems to read these plural hymns as dual (one the song of Moses, one the song of Miriam) although I see nothing in Philo that requires this.

God, the men being led by Moses the prophet, while the women (were led) by Miriam the prophetess."[155] That is, as I have suggested earlier, here Philo presents both his reading of Exodus 15, and his representation of the Therapeutae as instantiating that original ultimate single choir. To borrow briefly from David Hay's distinction between things Philo said and did not say about the Therapeutae, we must recognize that Philo does *not* say that the earlier two choirs are a replication of the Red Sea choir. Rather, he says only that *this single* choir is mimetic. Precisely *because* Philo describes only the one choir as a *mimesis* of the original, we must conclude that that he now understands Exodus itself to imply such a fusion, or at least allow for one.

Multiple aspects of the text may have supported this particular reading for Philo. He may envision that because the women and the men sing the same words, they were one choir, whose unity can be expressed even further through the physical positioning of the singers. His failure here to refer in *On the Contemplative Life* to the singing of the one song may reflect a reading that the choirs sang both that song and others, all covered by the ambiguous plural "hymns." It is possible that reflection on the inclusive nature of the phrase "*uioi Israel*" led Philo to envision a single choir, supported, as noted earlier, by the identity of the words they sing.

There is one odd aspect to Philo's description of the single choir that Taylor does not discuss. Why is it that the single choir at the Red Sea continues to have two conductors, Moses for the men and Miriam for the women? If one is envisioning actual singers, one might propose that this is because they continue to sing different vocal parts (although anyone who has sung in a choral setting knows that this is hardly required, and can be, in fact, quite distracting). One solution is exegetical: the unified choir continues to be led by Moses and Miriam because that is what Exodus 15 explicitly requires.[156] Philo can fold the women into the choir fairly easily, but, regardless of what leads Philo to envision a singular choir, once he has done so, the description of Miriam as "leading" constrains the details. He cannot fold her into the choir without doing violence to the text as I think he reads it, and, perhaps, he cannot have Miriam leading the men (even though the ambiguity of *autōn* would allow this). Hence his conclusion is that even for his unified choir, Moses continues to lead the men and Miriam the women.[157]

---

155. *Cont. Life* 87.

156. The continued role of Moses and Miriam undercuts, I think, the claim that gender here has been entirely transcended; one might think that a truly unified choir would now only require a single (and probably male) leader. My argument here is that exegetical constraints produce this tension.

157. I continue to be unclear about whether *lead* implies an order of singing, or conducting in the modern sense, and see, e.g., Jeffery 2004:174, on the possible responses to leading.

It is also interesting to note that when Philo describes the initial Therapeutic double choir, he never explicitly says that their respective leaders are male and female, respectively. Since, however, the unified Therapeutic choir mimics the original, it seems that we should imagine it, too, to be led by two conductors, one male and one female.

It is important to emphasize that I am not here trying to argue for the definitive explanation of Philo's reading of Exodus 15 in *On the Contemplative Life* (or elsewhere for that matter). Although it seems to me quite feasible that his motivations were at least partly exegetical, other explanations are entirely feasible. Taylor makes much of Philo's failure here and in *Life of Moses* 1.180 to refer to the singular ode or hymn, but conceivably Philo writes here only of plural hymns for no particular reason; perhaps he was tired, he was in a hurry, he meant to dictate it, or write it, but forgot. I am simply trying to argue that multiple readings of these passages are possible, that they are highly amenable to being read as exegetical engagements, and that there is no way, from our twenty-first century vantage point, to adjudicate among these competing contemporary readings of Philo. Philo's representation of both the Exodus choir and the Therapeutic choir as singular need not be a function of what the Therapeutae really did, although it *could* be; it can be derived either entirely exegetically, or perhaps from a combination of the textual details and Philo's own allegorical reading of the whole narrative, which ultimately points for him to a unification that is expressed in the unification of the choirs.[158]

In their arguments, both Taylor and Engberg-Pedersen overlook the centrality of biblical exegesis in the production of Philo's description of Therapeutae, not to mention other apparently historical events. Consider Philo's description of the response of the Judeans in Alexandria on learning that Flaccus, the Roman governor of Egypt at whose hands they had suffered much torment, had himself been arrested (which Philo attributes to his dreadful treatment of the Judeans).[159] Just as the freed Hebrews rejoiced at the Red Sea over their release from Egyptian slavery, so, too, the Judeans of Alexandria celebrated their release from the abuses of the governor of Egypt, by singing hymns and conducting (*exerchon*) paeans ("songs of triumph") to God. "All night long they continued to sing hymns and songs [of praise] and at dawn

---

158. I continue to think, though, that there is a tension between this interpretation and the continued leadership of Miriam and Moses in Philo's depiction of the Exodus singers, as well as the implicit presence of the two conductors of the Therapeutic choir. The devil's advocate might argue that it's the actual Therapeutic practice that drives Philo to portray the original choir as having two leaders, but he doesn't actually describe them that way, and it seems simpler, though perhaps not dispositive, to argue in the opposite fashion.

159. *Against Flaccus* 121–22.

pouring out through the (city) gates, they made their way to the parts of the beach near at hand, since their *proseuchai* had been taken from them," and uttered a long prayer of thanksgiving which Philo quotes.

For ancient Judean readers, and perhaps some contemporary Jewish readers as well, the allusion to Exodus 15 is unmistakable. The rejoicing Hebrews go at dawn to the seashore, as did their ancestors, where they sing hymns and odes of praise to God for their release from torment in Egypt. But whether they actually did so (which is certainly possible), or whether Philo depicts them as doing so to signal the allusion to the Exodus (with its anti-Egyptian implications) cannot be determined. The consonance, however, is striking. And that the Judeans in Alexandria might have done so precisely because of the reference to the Exodus similarly cannot be determined.

Exodus 15 Elsewhere in On The Contemplative Life

Additional support for my arguments here may come from the observation that Exodus 15 undergirds more in *On the Contemplative Life* than just the description of the choirs at the banquet. I think it likely that it also undergirds the rest of the description of the singing, a process which Taylor and others have taken to approximate Therapeutic practice, but which seems to me here to be equally explicable exegetically.

The Therapeutic singing begins before dinner, with the singing of a hymn of praise to God by the president of the society, after his learned discourse (79–80). In a reading of Exodus 15 in which Moses first sings alone, this might be construed as an enactment or a replication or an instantiation of Moses' initial singing (and there are other reasons to read the president as a type of Moses). Following the president, the others (*hoi alloi*) sing individually in turn, while the rest listen in complete silence, except when they are required to chant the closing lines or refrains.[160] Then, as noted earlier, Philo says, all the men (*pantes*) and all the women (*pasai*) join in. This whole scenario itself may be read as enacting the singing by the sea, if the sequence of that singing is understood to be Moses alone, the sons of Israel (individually), and then the men and the women together chanting the common refrain of Exod 15.1b=15.21. That is, the sequence Philo describes here can be seen as a template derived from a particular reading of Exodus (although by no means the only one), that may then be imposed upon the singing of other hymns.[161]

---

160. *Cont. Life* 80.

161. And see also Jeffery 2004:165 that some Therapeutic practices, for instance individual singing by turn, and even the final "standing" are typical of ancient Greek choral practice.

This argument requires *hoi alloi*, and the masculine singular, each, *hekastos*, which follows in 81, to be read gender exclusively. As I noted earlier, throughout this treatise, Philo repeatedly takes great pains to specify when women participate, which suggests that only at these points are we justified in reading the activity or presence of women: otherwise, in fact, his use of masculine forms is gender specific. Careful as he is to specify the participation of the Therapeutrides as numerous points, Philo does not here avail himself of the opportunity to specify that they, too, stand up and sing. In this passage, then, his explicit statement that all the men and all the women sing the refrains may well mean that only men are the individual singers here.

One might wonder why a close reading of Exodus 15 would not produce the singing of a female soloist, replicating at least the singing of Miriam, if not also the (individual) women? If there is an answer to this sort of question (which there may not be), it might lie in the complex of ancient associations about women's singing, that Philo wishes to avoid. Women who sang (and danced) for men at Greco-Roman symposia are regularly represented as that "other" kind of women, whose singing (and dancing) has sexual connotations highly inappropriate for the celibate and "mostly" virgin Therapeutrides. By not representing the women as singing individually in front of men (or, for that matter, speaking in front of men), Philo may avoid all those highly negative connotations of such practices.[162]

Philo's Gendering of the Therapeutae

In my earlier work, I argued that Philo's approval of the Therapeutrides, over and against his corpus of fairly negative comments about women and femaleness, rests on his construal of them as virgin and/or masculine; as not/no longer women.[163] Taylor and Hay have both disagreed with this to some extent, arguing, among other things, that the need for a dividing barrier between the women and the men at the sabbath gathering demonstrates that Philo continues to consider them as female. Taylor's argument further relies on her view that Philo constructs the Therapeutrides not merely as women, but as "good" women, who do not violate gender norms, are maternal in spite of their apparent lack of actual children, and so forth. Her argument here focuses on Philo's need to

---

162. Philo's explication of Exodus 15 may be relevant elsewhere in his writings: *On the Drunkenness of Cain*III, where Philo explicates Exod 15.1 to mean that God "has buried out of sight the mind which rose upon the unreasoning impulses of passion. . . . and has shown himself the helper and champion of the soul which can see, to bestow on it full salvation . . ."; *On Dreams* 2.269–70, where the appropriate response to the death and casting out of the passions is to sing the hymn of Exod 15.1.

163. Especially Kraemer 1989; 1992.

respond to the possible interpretation of the actual Therapeutrides as "bad women," but the fact that they are judged by the standards of "women" seems, for her, to mean that he continues to view them as women, not men/male.

The argument from the divider that Philo says separates the Therapeutae from the Therapeutrides during their weekly gathering does not persuade me, for various reasons. First, were one to accept Taylor's reading of *On the Contemplative Life* as grounded partly in historical realia, this could conceivably be Therapeutic practice, which does not need to accord entirely with Philo's representation. Their reasons for sitting separately, with a divider, could have any number of explanations that need not be consistent with Philo's reading of them as not/no longer "women." That is, *if* he is constrained here by actual Therapeutic practice, his representation of the Therapeutrides need not be perfectly consonant with these details, and in fact, is unlikely to be so. This is, in fact, the whole methodological premise of Engberg-Pedersen's analysis, except that for him, these are all consonant. I suspect that Hay, Taylor, and Engberg-Pedersen would largely agree on the point of method: where they disagree is in what constitutes "maximal coherence."

Second, though, the lack of a divider at the Feast of Fifty seems to me to undercut this argument, and Taylor's apparent response, that they sit on opposite sides of the room, doesn't seem adequate. Why couldn't they have sat on opposite sides of the room for the seventh-day assembly if that is sufficient for whoever's purposes are at issue here? Taylor also hypothesizes that they are using a different room, but again the problem remains. If female modesty is the real reason for the dividing wall on the seventh day, why is it no longer necessary at the banquet, where, in fact, ultimately women and men will apparently stand side by side, singing in close proximity to one another. Conversely, if it's not necessary at the feast, why was it necessary previously? Engberg-Pedersen, of course, would argue it's all an artifice: on the seventh day, certain aspects of gender difference are expressed in heightened fashion, only to be overcome at the Feast of Fifty.

I also find unpersuasive Taylor's argument that, because Philo's representation of the women seems to address anxieties about whether they are "good" women, he must continue to envision them as female. As she does elsewhere, Taylor here elides Philo's views with those she thinks he feels the need to refute, either hypothetically or in actual response. Philo might well himself envision the Therapeutrides as not/no longer women, yet anticipate that others might not operate with these same constructions, and might object to his representation. And perfect consistency on these points may expect far too much of Philo, as of ourselves.

It may be more productive to consider the representation of both the men and the women in the light of what we have come to understand about ancient gender constructions, constructions that Philo clearly seems to share. In an insightful article, J. Neyrey has suggested that certain categories provide particularly salient measures of gender in antiquity, including role and status, tasks and behavior, public speech, objects, and reputation.[164] Plotted along these various measures of gender in the ancient world, the Therapeutrides appear as relatively masculine, on a sliding scale: they are rational, self-disciplined, celibate (and also childless). They do not perform the stereotypical tasks of women, namely, spinning, weaving, child-rearing, and cooking, although some of these have class dimensions as well. They do not experience one of, if not *the*, defining experiences of women (in antiquity and elsewhere): they are not penetrated by a man vaginally (let alone in any other way). Instead, like the male Therapeutae, the Therapeutrides spend their days in study, contemplation, musical composition (perhaps understood as an inspired activity), fasting, and prayer. Their clothing does not distinguish their gender.

Yet at the same time, there are stereotypical female traits to their representation. They preserve their modesty, at least at the seventh-day gathering; they do not speak in the presence of men (in fact, apart from their communal singing, they are never explicitly said to speak at all, to anyone); they remain inside, either in their individual cells or within the confines of the enclave, and do not go out into the larger world. They lack the traits that various scholars associate with idealized masculinity in the first century C.E.: they do not display physical strength, they do not engage in contestation or violence, they do not subordinate others, they do not demonstrate their prowess in powerful and persuasive speech.[165]

The male Therapeutae, on the other hand, continue to demonstrate some of the traits of idealized masculinity, while lacking others. Like the women, they display the masculine traits of discipline and self-control, as evidenced in their rigorous diet, their sexual abstinence, their general minimal attention to their bodily needs, their daily devotion to philosophy, allegory, and contemplation, and so forth. Their physical postures at the seventh-day gathering and at the Feast of Fifty appear to evidence masculine norms, or at least norms that convey their self-mastery, discipline, attentiveness, and so forth, and are in that sense gendered.[166] It's interesting that Philo does not explicitly indicate that the

---

164. Neyrey 2003.

165. E.g., Neyrey 2003, and various other essays in this volume.

166. Bourdieu observes that "honor" is "inscribed in the body in the form of a set of seemingly natural dispositions, often visible in a particular way of sitting and standing, a tilt of the head, a bearing, a gait, bound up with a way of thinking and acting . . ." Bourdieu 2001:49. On the seventh day, they "sit in order according to their age in the proper attitude, with their hands inside the robe, the right hand between the breast and the chin and the left withdrawn along the flank," *Cont. Life* 30, transl. Colson in the LCL. At the Feast of Fifty, they first "stand in a regular line in an orderly way, their eyes and hands lifted up to heaven. . . ." *Cont. Life* 66, transl. Colson (LCL).

women, too, sit in these postures. Perhaps we are to imagine that they do, but this is not one of those places where Philo is explicitly inclusive.[167]

Also like the women, the male Therapeutae display some feminine characteristics. They live their lives indoors. They have removed themselves from the idealized masculine pursuits of public contestation and honors, violence, and domination. Yet this may not be entirely so; one could read the presidential discourses as a form of masculine competition and domination, if one that is itself somewhat of a critique of the practices of the larger male elite culture, and certainly the explicit contrasts Philo makes between Therapeutic practices and those of the larger world support such a position. The wisdom of the president is revealed through its rhetorical persuasiveness, to which the Therapeutae give assent through both bodily position and ultimately applause, even as Philo contrasts the truth of this wisdom with the falsehood of empty rhetoric. Much of their daily activity does not appear to be like those of the idealized elite male. Cloistered in their cells, they apparently do not receive flattering subordinates; they neither engage in contests of physical strength nor direct the work of slaves and subordinates; they do not engage in public debate and public affairs. They do not congregate, at least ordinarily, in the company of other men, and when they do engage in communal activities, those are still radically distinguished from the superficially similar practices of elite male society. They do not do the less elite but still more masculine activities, many of them outdoors, of farming, sailing, fishing, carpentry, craftsmanship, and the range of other active tasks assigned to men in the later ancient Mediterranean.

In fact, the Therapeutae and Therapeutrides largely do precisely the same things. Their daily routines of study, contemplation, composition, and prayer are presented as identical, as is their diet, their dress, and their discipline of the body. In some respects, these activities are clearly gendered as masculine in the ancient world (study, contemplation, composition, self-discipline of the body), whereas, in some others, they are gendered as female (their seclusion from both each other and the larger world). Yet the Therapeutae and Therapeutrides may also be characterized as "gender-blenders," in their identical practices in realms ordinarily distinguished by gender difference (clothing, diet, sexual practices).

Only in a few respects are the Therapeutrides distinguished from their male counterparts: they do not appear to engage in public speech, and they are explicitly said to be (largely) elderly virgins who desire to espouse wisdom, and conceive spiritual children. It is worth noting, though, that elsewhere in Philo, the conception of spiritual children is often associated with men, rather than

---

167. And posture is connected elsewhere to both modesty and idleness.

women, and is presented as the ultimate consequence of (sexualized) union of the (feminine, but now masculinized, virgin) soul with the divine.

Thus, it may well be that both Taylor and Hay miss the point about gender and the Therapeutae. The Therapeutrides are more or less entirely removed from the system of classification as female, even while vestiges of their gender remain. They no longer function in any of the basic ways in which women function in traditional societies, including that of the first-century Mediterranean, "Greek" culture. They are not the medium of exchange for men and do not function as tokens of prestige and honor for men. They do not perform the stereotypical activities of women, and they do perform some of those associated with men. They are not differentiated from men in the numerous ways in which women and men are differentiated. They do not marry men and they do not reproduce.

These last two characteristics do, however, suggest some tension. That Philo says of the Therapeutrides that, although they do not marry, they do espouse (Wisdom), and although they do not bear children, they do produce spiritual offspring, might be construed as reflective of a need to respond, in some manner, to the deeply transgressive nature of such women. Taylor would respond, I think, that this last tension points to the historicity of the Therapeutrides, but again, I see no need to posit that explanation. Philo could just as easily be responding to perceived reactions to his depiction, or even, possibly, to criticisms raised by friends who have read his early drafts and objected. Yet again, though, our ability to imagine, let alone verify, the particular situations that might produce Philo's text, is greatly limited.

This is further complicated by the fact that elsewhere in his writings, although not here, Philo does envision men as impregnated with comparable spiritual children.[168] Verna Harrison has argued that Philo constructs union with God in gendered, sexualized language. Using imagery widespread in the ancient world and elsewhere,[169] a masculine God is the sower of seed in the perfected and perhaps divinized soul. The soul of the one who seeks to see,

---

168. Harrison argues that this paradigm is much more typical of men in Philo, 1996:521. Harrison's argument is actually quite relevant here, although she didn't pursue these issues. In her discussion of *On the Creation of the World*, she argues that "[a]s the human brokenness that *Genesis* 3 depicts is healed and as the person progresses spiritually, each of the soul's faculties has to be restored. . . . this means . . . becoming male through the intellect's active choice of virtue and self-control; becoming a virgin through the redirection of perception, desire, and receptivity toward the divine; and become one through mature harmony within the self," 1996:529. This is precisely what the Therapeutae collectively do and are: they are male, virgin, and become one (through the harmony of music). One might easily argue that these correspondences (which Harrison argues are derived at least partly from Plato) are sufficient to account for Philo's representations of the Therapeutae. Interestingly Harrison doesn't generally note the connections between her arguments about spiritual childbearing in Philo and his depiction of the Therapeutae.

169. See Delaney 1991; also DuBois 1988; Levinson 2000.

itself gendered as female, must renounce the attributes of femininity and become masculine and/or virgin in order to become able to receive God. Yet at the same time, this receptivity to divine seed is a kind of feminization. Thus the tension here may have more to do with Philo's scheme of gendered divine union than with the actual Therapeutrides themselves.

Conclusions

Philo's account of a group of male and female monastics, living the ideal contemplative life on the shores of the Mareotic lake (if not also elsewhere) has long captivated scholars, myself included. Its details are regularly adduced by historians of ancient Judaism and early Christianity as evidence for a wide range of practices, dietary, devotional, and otherwise, on the part of at least some ancient Judeans.

Yet the recent work of Engberg-Pedersen, and even to some degree Taylor has raised serious questions about how much, if any, of this description derives from the practices of an actual first-century C.E. community. Taylor has argued that, although many details of Philo's descriptions are the product of his rhetorical interests, the Therapeutae were an actual group whose practices and ideas can be discerned through the filters of Philo's rhetoric. Engberg-Pedersen has proposed that the entire account is fictive, derived from Philo's envisioning what an ideal contemplative community would look like, grounded particularly in structured oppositions of which he may not have even been conscious. It allows us to speak only of "Philo's Therapeutae," not of *the* Therapeutae.

Although I now think that Engberg-Pedersen may be right that much, if not all, of Philo's account is his own construction, I disagree that the best explanation may be found in the effects of largely universal and unconscious oppositions, coupled with Philo's own philosophical training and interests. Rather, I have tried to suggest in the second half of this discussion that a great deal of Philo's description of the Therapeutae may be derived from his own exegesis of Exodus 15, both elsewhere, and even in his account of the Therapeutae.

Although I have not attempted to work this out in detail here, other aspects of his description may come from his reading of Genesis 1–3. The Therapeutae live a life very much like that of the being(s) created in the divine image before the expulsion from Eden. They do no manual labor; they eat a vegetarian diet; they abstain from sexual activity and from human procreation, especially the majority of the women, whom Philo says prefer Wisdom to a human mate and spiritual children to the ordinary kind. Instead, they spend considerable amounts of their time on the activities envisioned in various sources for the angelic residents of the heavens: the composition and performance of hymns and odes of praise to God. In fact, it seems possible that Philo constructs the Therapeutae as a whole as the collective image of the *anthrōpos* in Genesis 1, who becomes divided into *anēr* and *gunē*, and ultimately is restored to the primordial unified image of God represented particularly in the blended choir of the Feast of Fifty.

Philo's representation of women, or at least females, in this community may thus relate as much to these texts, especially Genesis, as to the realities of an ancient monastic community. Many scholars have been puzzled by the seeming tension between Philo's relatively harsh comments about women elsewhere in his writings and his entirely positive representation of the Therapeutrides here. I argued in my earlier work that this may be a function of Philo's perception of the Therapeutrides as having become male, and this may still be true. But while earlier I took Philo to impose a paradigm of masculine transformation onto the actual women of the Therapeutae, now I think it quite likely that Philo has derived his depiction of the women from a constellation of beliefs about how gender would work itself out in the ideal human community, modeled on the pattern in Genesis 1, especially of course, Gen 1.26–27, as well as on other paradigmatic passages such as the Exodus account.

I also think it possible that Philo's representation of both the Therapeutic men and the Therapeutic women may relate to Joel 2.28–29, which envisions a future time when the divine spirit will be poured out on "all flesh," even male and female slaves; and sons and daughters both will prophesy.[170] This inclusion of both female slaves and free females in the divine spirit may further undergird Philo's expectation that the ideal Edenic community would include

---

170. "Then afterward, I will pour out my spirit on all flesh; your sons and your daughters shall prophesy, your old men shall dream dreams, and your young men shall see visions. Even on the male and female slaves, in those days, I will pour out my spirit," Joel 2.28–29; NRSV: LXX Joel 3.1–2. This passage played a central role in early Christian representations of prophets, especially women prophets. It is quoted by the author of Acts, in 2.17, with a few significant differences: "afterward" becomes "in the last days," and the slaves not only experience the spirit, but also prophesy, which they do not do in the Hebrew and LXX text of Joel. Luke's account of the early Christian community includes several women prophets, all abstaining from sexuality and procreation. An 84-year-old prophet named Anna lives in the Temple in Jerusalem (Acts 2.36—38). Married for only seven years, she has lived there ever since. Interestingly, Anna resembles the Therapeutrides in significant ways: she is unquestionably elderly; she is not said to have children; she lives an ascetic life of fasting and prayer. In Acts 21.8–9, the evangelist Philip has four virgin daughters who prophesy. In my view, Anna is a creation of the author of Luke-Acts, whose characteristics may themselves derive from a constellation of exegesis and ideas similar to those of Philo. The same may be true of Philip's daughters, although their rhetorical function is far less apparent than that of Anna, who testifies to the Christ child. Not inconceivably, this is a tradition the author knew. Both Joel and its quotation in Acts play a central role in the legitimation of later Christian prophetic movements, including those with women prophets. It opens the *Martyrdom of Saints Perpetua and Felicitas*, and may have been used by members of the New Prophecy (Montanism) in support of their practices: see Atkindon 1982; Kraemer and Lander 2000; Butler 2006.

women demonstrating the presence of the spirit, in his case through their composition (if not also their inspired singing) of hymns of praise.

Does *On the Contemplative Life* then really give us access to Judean women philosophers in first-century Alexandria? In my present view, this cannot be known. Philo's account of the Therapeutae as a whole, and the women in particular, is sufficiently consistent with philosophical ideals, Philonic interpretation of key biblical passages and perhaps even also structural oppositions that it could easily have been produced from those alone. Not inconceivably, of course, a community of philosophers might have modeled themselves on precisely those same ideas, licensed, if not also generated, by interpretation of the same biblical passages, as certainly later ascetic communities are known to have done. But the absence of any independent attestion to the Therapeutae raises the possibility that in this case, Philo's account is indeed an imaginative exercise.

At the very least, this requires us to be considerably more cautious in the use of *On the Contemplative Life* in any reconstructions of ancient Judean practices, particularly those regarding women. If I now think that Philo has largely imagined the Therapeutae, I would seem to have rendered mostly irrelevant my own earlier analysis of them that depended on some reasonable degree of sociological accuracy in Philo's depiction, particularly my analysis of how and why the contemplative life might have been appealing to educated women for whom gendered expectations of the good woman constrained their lives, or who, unable or uninterested in meeting those expectations, found the Therapeutic life literally therapeutic. Yet at the same time, were Philo's account to be some reasonable representation of actual Therapeutae, I would continue to stand by the possible utility of my earlier analysis, if perhaps somewhat qualified. And it is worth noting that Philo's description coheres with instances across many cultures of celibate women engaging in privileged activities ordinarily limited to males in those same cultures. That is, if Philo has imagined the Therapeutrides, his imagination is not entirely fantastic, and has, on the contrary, numerous actual examples. And finally, if Philo's account is not about actual women, it is still very much about the uses of gender in the construction both of ancient religious practices, and the imagining of an ideal life.

4

Thecla of Iconium, Reconsidered

I permit no woman to teach or have authority over a man: she is to keep silent.

> —The first letter of "Paul" to "Timothy" 2.12

Thecla said to Paul, "I am going to Iconium."
So Paul said to Thecla, "Go forth and teach the word of God."

> —*The Acts of (Paul and) Thecla* 41

Introduction: Women Baptizers in the Late Second Century C.E.?

A half century or so after Justin wrote his account of the Roman matron and her ill-fated teacher, a North African Christian writer named Tertullian sought to counter the claims of some late-second-century Christians that it was appropriate for women to teach the word of God, baptize, exorcize (demons), heal, and administer the eucharist. Viewed from the perspective of the early twenty-first century, Tertullian seems remarkably well aware of what, precisely, offended him about these practices. They violated his understanding of fundamental gender differences, which he took to be divinely ordained and inscribed in the order of creation. In Tertullian's view, which would have been widely shared, teaching, disputing, exorcising demons, healing and baptizing were all inherently masculine practices, involving activity, authority, speech and public performance. Precisely because these are by their nature masculine, they are prohibited, he insists, to women.[1]

Tertullian's views on this subject surface in three separate writings.[2] In *On the Veiling of Virgins*, Tertullian extends the prohibition now in 1 Cor 14.33b–36 against women "speaking" in the *ekklēsia*, to their teaching, baptizing, and making offerings. Central to Tertullian's argument here is the possibility that (Christian) virgins may not count as women and thus may engage in practices forbidden to women (here apparently defined as females who are subject to heterosexual intercourse and are under the authority of a man).[3] Ultimately, he concludes, virgins, too, are excluded from such activities and offices.

In a work entitled *On the Prescription of Heretics*, Tertullian alleges that heretical women are so bold that they dare to teach, dispute, exorcize, heal, and even perhaps baptize.[4] Years ago, in several different venues, I argued that constructing one's opponents as female and one's self and community as male was a common if not pervasive rhetorical strategy in ancient intergroup polemical writings.[5] Christian writers regularly represented their opponents as both actual women and feminized men, while denigrating women's religious practices and ideas as irregular, if not actually heretical. So contextualized, Tertullian's rant might seem no more than yet another instance of conveying the fundamental error and disorder of heretics by accusing them of transgressing gender norms.

What aroused Tertullian's ire? Is his analysis of the distinction between women (*mulieres*) and virgins (*virgines*) a response to the practices and legitimating arguments of others? Is it perhaps an exegetical exercise prompted by distinctions between women and virgins (*gunaikes* and *parthenoi*) Paul has already made in his correspondence with believers at Corinth? Is his invective about unspecified "heretics" merely a rhetorical defamation of them? Or do one or both passages reflect engagement with historical others, who not only argued that women, or perhaps at least "virgins," could engage in the disputed practices, but did so as well?

In a treatise, *On Baptism*, dated to 203 C.E., Tertullian made a more specific allegation. Those people, he wrote, who support their view that women may

1. *On the Veiling of Virgins* 9.
2. Issues of women and gender are pervasive in the writings of Tertullian, the most famous example of which may be his opening salvo, "You are the devil's gateway. . . . On account of your desert—that is, death—even the Son of God had to die," *On the Apparel of Women* 1.1. Many of his other treatises concern women's practices or matters integral to women's lives (*On the Veiling of Virgins; To His Wife; The Exhortation to Chastity; On Monogamy;* etc.)
3. On the definition of γυναῖκες as females subject to penetration in the act of vaginal heterosexual intercourse, see Parker 1997 and the Introduction, earlier in this volume.
4. *On the Prescription of Heretics* 41.
5. Kraemer 1992; 1994.

teach and baptize by appealing to a story associated with Paul about a woman named Thecla should know that it was the production of a presbyter in Asia Minor who had confessed to the forgery and subsequently left office.[6] Whereas his argument against heretics broadly might be explained as a standard polemical accusation of gender transgression on the part of one's opponents, and the discussion of the veiling of virgins as an exegetical exercise, Tertullian's defamation of a Thecla tale appears aimed at actual Christian practices and their authorization. These practices appear discernible as early as Paul's attempts to rein in the women prophets of 1 Corinthians 11, who fail to conform to gender expectations by not covering their heads when they pray and prophesy. They are also strikingly associated with a movement known as the New Prophecy, or Montanism, that began in the second century C.E. in Asia Minor, and allegedly featured women prophets in primary roles.[7] Tertullian himself was associated with the New Prophecy in North Africa.[8]

It is extremely difficult to discern precisely what Tertullian had in mind when he lambasted a story about Thecla. The text of Tertullian's treatise on baptism is itself the subject of some dispute. Until the early twentieth century, this work was known only through a sixteenth-century edition of a manuscript no longer extant.[9] According to this, Tertullian attacked "writings which wrongly go under Paul's name" that "adduce the example (or perhaps: the writing) of Thecla as license for women to teach and baptize." "Let them know (*sciant*)," he writes, that the work in question was produced by that anonymous presbyter in Asia. In 1916, a twelfth-century manuscript, Codex Trecensis 523, came to light, which explicitly refers to the discredited work as *Acti Pauli* but still does not specify who, exactly, is intended by the verb *sciant*.

In 1996, drawing on a suggestion by W. Rordorf,[10] A. Hilhorst published a short article proposing to solve some of the textual problems by utilizing Gelenius's 1550 edition of the manuscript no longer extant. This edition contains one key difference. Whereas Mesnartius's 1545 edition read "*Quod si quae Pauli perperam scripta sunt*" (But if those writings which wrongly go under Paul's name), this edition corrects *sunt* to *legunt*. The passage now reads: "But if those

---

6. *On Baptism* 17. For a translation, bibliography, and brief discussion, see *WRGRW* 105, where, regrettably, the words "in Asia" were inadvertently omitted after "presbyter"; for additional discussion, see below.

7. Sources for the study of the New Prophecy are collected in Heine 1989 and Tabbernee 1997; see also *WRGRW* 93–96 and 97, the epitaph of a female prophet, Nanas, from Asia Minor. For discussion, see Kraemer 1992:157–73; Church 1975; Klawiter 1980; Elm 1994; see with considerable caution Trevett 1996.

8. See, e.g., his account in *On the Soul* 9 of a woman prophet whose visions are subjected to private review by church authorities; in, inter alia, *WRGRW* 93.

9. Mesnartius's 1545 edition, used in Oehler's 1853 edition, with one variant. For more recent editions, see now Refoulé 1952 [2002]; Evans 1964; Luiselli 1968. For details, see Hilhorst 1996:151–52.

10. Rordorf 1990.

women who read the falsely named writings about Paul . . ." This relatively small change now supplies a feminine plural subject, *quae* (those women) for the various verbs in the passage, which previous editions lacked. Hilhorst concedes that Gelenius had no manuscript evidence for this reading, but he thinks it a plausible conjecture that solves many of the problems of the prior readings and offers it as a "better reading."[11] Hilhorst also argued against those scholars who thought that the phrase "example of Thecla" was itself an emendation that would have been missing from Tertullian's own writing.[12]

Hilhorst may well be right that Gelenius was emending the missing manuscript, and that his emendation explicitly identifying women as the misguided readers of the Thecla tale was reasonable. Yet the manuscript evidence for *On Baptism* is simply far too thin to instill confidence that we know what Tertullian might actually have written. The characterization of his opponents as "those women" might be anything from Tertullian's own writing to the accidental creation of a female subject by a scribe wishing to improve a problematic text, to the work of a scribe (of whatever date) who thought that only women would take such a view, to part of a revisionist attempt to discredit this particular reading by associating it with women. Yet as we shall see later, scholars have made much out of this particular reading.

Although the attribution of a Thecla tale to a conveniently anonymous presbyter far from Tertullian's North Africa is sufficiently useful ammunition for Tertullian's objections to both the story and the practices to be highly suspect, very little consideration has been given to the possibility that Tertullian's account is itself a fabrication, whether his own or one he knew and took, erroneously, to be reliable. Most scholars have either taken it as reliable or failed to challenge it.[13]

The Acts of (Paul and) Thecla: Contemporary Contestations

Fortunately, in this particular instance, we are not restricted to the problematic testimony of Tertullian himself. A text narrating Paul's conversion of a young elite virgin named Thecla to an ascetic form of Christianity, and his

---

11. Having solved the textual problem to his own satisfaction, Hilhorst then devotes the remainder of his article to a discussion of other issues, such as whether the passage really refers to the *Acts of Paul*; he concludes (157) that it does, but concedes that there are discrepancies between Tertullian's description and the text of Thecla as we have it (157–58), on which see later.

12. Hilhorst 1996:153–54. W. Schneemelcher, in the most recent edition of *NTA* 2:214, takes the position that the phrase "exemplum Theclae" is a scribal insertion, but his position does not seem to have much support and his discussion significantly antedates Rordorf and Hilhorst.

13. Rordorf briefly poses the question at the end, but then indicates that it is beyond the scope of his article (1990:159–60). Bremmer 1996:57 also accepts Tertullian's claim; see further n. 32.

commissioning her to "Go forth and teach the word of God," survives in Greek, Latin, Syriac, Armenian, and Slavonic manuscripts. The earliest of these appears to be a small Greek fragment from Antinoöpolis in Egypt, dating to the fourth or perhaps fifth centuries C.E.[14] Although there are signs that the story once circulated independently, it is now incorporated within a larger collection of stories about the apostle Paul known simply as *The Acts of Paul*.[15] Numerous ancient writers, particularly of the fourth century and later seem well acquainted with traditions about Thecla, including the pilgrim Egeria.[16] The secret name of Macrina of Nyssa (sister of Gregory and Basil) was Thecla.[17] Despite its mid-first-century C.E. setting, modern scholars uniformly consider the story a post-Pauline production, and virtually no one argues that it comprises historical evidence for a contemporaneous female disciple of Paul's.[18]

Thecla tells the story of a young elite woman in Asia Minor who converts to an ascetic form of Christianity preached by the apostle Paul in her native city of Iconium (modern Konya, in Turkey). Dazzled by Paul, Thecla renegs on her engagement to a prominent citizen Thamyris, is denounced by her own mother Theocleia, escapes various trials and temptations, and baptizes herself in a pool of voracious seals. Ultimately commissioned by Paul to "go forth and teach the

14. *P. Ant.* 13. Another, *P. Oxy.* 6. was found among the extensive collection of ancient papyri and manuscripts from Oxyrhynchus, Egypt, dating perhaps to the fifth or sixth centuries C.E.

15. Davis 2001:39–40, argues that it begins autonomously, is incorporated into the larger *Acts of Paul*, and then detached to circulate separately again. Until very recently, the only critical edition was that of the *Acts of Paul* in Lipsius and Bonnet 1891. A new critical edition of the *Acts of (Paul and) Thecla* appeared too late for use in this study (Barrier 2009). A new critical edition of the entire *Acts of Paul*, including the *Acts of (Paul and) Thecla*, is in preparation for the Corpus Christianorum Series Apocryphorum, edited by Willy Rordorf, but F. Bovon reports (in private correspondence) that it apparently will not be available for some time. For a description of the manuscripts, and critical discussion, see Lipsius-Bonnet 1891:1.xcix–cvi; Vouaux 1913:12–19; but note that manuscript M (Vaticanus Graecus 1190) is inaccurately reported as fourteenth century, rather than sixteenth century—see, e.g., the description in Devreese 1965. See also the detailed introduction to the *Acts of Paul* in NTA 2.213–37 and in *ANT*; Geerard 1992:117–23; see also BHG 2:267–69. Bovon 1999:23 seems to report the discovery of an additional uncial citing Rordorf 1993:148. See also Calzolari 1996–1997; 1997; Bovon 2003.

16. Egeria, *Diary of a Pilgrimage* 22–23; in WRGRW 76.

17. Gregory of Nyssa, *Life of Macrina* 2.33–34. The *Acts of Xanthippe and Polyxena* and the *Acts of Saint Eugenia* (Conybeare 1894) both of uncertain date, explicitly refer to Thecla. A lengthy reworking and expansion of the *Acts of Thecla* was composed in the fifth century C.E., *The Life and Miracles of St. Thecla* (Dagron 1978). See also Johnson 2006. For discussion of Thecla in subsequent Christian sources, see Rordorf 1984; Hague 1994; the rather bland treatment of Pesthy 1996; and most thoroughly Davis 2001.

18. The claim is occasionally made, without serious argument, that Thecla was a real person: see, e.g., Petropoulous 1995:126: "Thecla probably was a historical person, as Henri Leclercq has shown." Petropoulous does not cite LeClercq 1921, esp. 141–77, but only the reference to LeClercq in MacDonald 1983:107 n. 21. MacDonald's actual note is more judicious—it merely says, "For a discussion of the evidence for a historical Thecla, see Henri Leclercq. . . ." Schneemelcher also appears to presume that there was a person named Thecla, while discounting any of the actual events of the narrative (NTA 2:222). This position was also taken by Harnack 1908:73, who thinks the historical Thecla was converted by a missionary named Paul. Interestingly, however, there seems to have been a Queen Tryphaena, who is attested on first century CE coins as having ruled Pontus (in Asia Minor) with her son, Ptolemon II; for references, see Bremmer 1996:52 n. 56.

word of God," Thecla is said to have "enlightened many" before she dies an unremarkable death. Some versions of the text contain additional endings that narrate more of a martyr's death, and Thecla eventually acquires the epithets "protomartyr" and "*apostolos.*"[19]

Numerous scholars have seen both the Thecla story, and others with similar plots found especially in the *Acts of Peter, Thomas, Andrew,* and *John,*[20] as reflections of the actual social experiences and practices of women in ascetic Christian communities, particularly in Asia Minor and Greece, in the second and third centuries C.E. Indeed, I argued for precisely such a reading in my own early work.[21] For me, what has come to be called either the *Acts of (Paul and) Thecla* or even simply *The Acts of Thecla,* was a fictional narrative, perhaps dating to the mid-second century C.E., that invoked the authority of Paul to support women teaching (and probably also baptizing, as Tertullian suggests, even though in the forms in which we now have it, Thecla explicitly baptizes only herself, an issue to which I will return[22]). In doing so, however, it drew upon verisimilitude: like comparable stories in other *Acts,* for which it may even have been the prototype,[23] it assumed an audience would find such a woman plausible because it knew of such women.

Thecla is presented as an elite virgin engaged to be married to a man of the local ruling class. Women in these other tales were often the childless wives of local rulers or the concubines of such men.[24] My own interests lay in analyzing the descriptions of these women to formulate a theory of women's attraction to those early forms of Christianity that gave pride of place to celibacy, including the repudiation of marriage and childbearing. Drawing on late-twentieth-century social-science theories, particularly modified deprivation theories,[25] I argued that such movements would have been of particular interest to women who were either unable to marry and/or bear children,

---

19. On this ending, see Davis 2001:39–47, and later.

20. Many of these are shorter episodes, although the story of Maximilla in the *Acts of Andrew* (Codex Vaticanus 808), Mygdonia in the *Acts of Thomas* 9–13 and perhaps also Drusiana in the *Acts of John* 63–86 are somewhat longer and more complex.

21. Kraemer 1976; 1980.

22. For additional discussion, see later, p. 144.

23. The literary relationships between the various apocryphal *Acts* are much debated, but Thecla seems generally to be taken as the earliest of the stories about elite women positioned between a Christian apostle and a fiance, husband, or lover. Hilhorst actually proposes that the story of Thecla might be significantly earlier than Tertullian's report of it, although Rordorf 1989 argues that its origins are somehow related to the emergence of the New Prophecy in the second half of the second century, cited in *NTA* 2:234. Davis, too, argues for the feasibility of a Montanist context: 2001:31 n. 118.

24. E.g., Agrippina, Euphemia, Nicaria, and Doris, the concubines of Agrippa in the *Acts of Peter*: see Kraemer 1980; 1992:154–55.

25. Particularly Burridge 1969; Lewis 1971.

or who were, for reasons inaccessible to us, unwilling or uninterested in doing so.

Within a few years, the Thecla story became the focus of considerable scholarly interest.[26] Yet unquestionably, Thecla's role as teacher, and late second-century opposition to her, seemed particularly germane at a time when debates about women's contemporary Christian ministry were becoming acute in many churches in America and Europe, and the Vatican Declaration on women priests had recently been issued.[27]

A book on women in ancient texts often called apocryphal *Acts* (of various apostles of Jesus), by Stevan Davies, and an article of mine appeared in the same year.[28] While sharing my view that the story of Thecla and other women who adopted ascetic forms of Christianity reflected the composition and practices of some early Christian communities, Davies went further. Earlier scholars had seen the prominence of female heroines in Greco-Roman novels (taken to be earlier, or perhaps sometimes contemporaneous with the various apocryphal *Acts*)[29] as evidence that their intended readership was particularly female.[30] Applying this logic, that, because women were the subjects of numerous stories in the various *Acts*, women were also the intended audience, Davies hypothesized that these stories were originally formulated and circulated by women, although men may have played some role in their transformation into literary forms and their incorporation into the larger various apocryphal *Acts*. The title of his book was indicative of his views: *The Revolt of the Widows: The Social World of the Apocryphal Acts.*

Davies's argument was understandably appealing to some feminist theologians and scholars of early Christianity eager to have access to women's own voices from a period when virtually no writings by women are identifiable.

26. Some of this may have been spurred by my own work: Stevan Davies, for instance, wrote his book-length study of women in the apocryphal *Acts* after doing a summer seminar at Princeton in the late seventies with my former teacher, John G. Gager. A partial bibliography includes Davies 1980; 1986; D. MacDonald 1983; 1984; Burrus 1987; Kaestli 1989; 1990; Boughton 1991; Dunn 1993; McGinn 1994; Petropoulous 1995; Bremmer 1996; Cooper 1996; Aymer 1997; Aubin 1998; Konstan 1998; Jacobs 1999; Davis 2000; 2001; C. Burrus and Van Rompay 2003; Castelli 2004; Ng 2004; Johnson 2006; Streete 2006. For a fascinating analysis of historiographic trends in the reading of Thecla, see Matthews 2002. There is an older secondary literature on the apocryphal *Acts* that often includes Thecla, but it tended to focus on relationships between the Acts and ancient Greek novels, and rarely if ever raised the kinds of issues addressed in scholarship after 1970.

27. The Report of the Pontifical Biblical Commission concluding that women could not be ordained priests was published in 1975: a volume of responses by Catholic theologians was published two years later (Swidler and Swidler 1977).

28. Davies 1980; Kraemer 1980.

29. In fact, dating these Greek novels is extremely difficult, and sequencing these and the apocryphal *Acts* chronologically is far less secure than many scholars seem to presume, as I note in the introductions to selections from Heliodorus (*WRGRW* 22), Chariton (*WRGRW* 23), Xenophon of Ephesos (*WRGRW* 25), Achilles Tatius (*WRGRW* 29), and Longus (*WRGRW* 30).

30. E. R. Rohde, as noted in Cooper 1996:62, who points out some of the flaws in this thesis.

Nevertheless, it was seriously flawed. Davies's theory of female authorship of *Thecla* ran immediately up against Tertullian's claim that a male presbyter produced it. Davies's way around this was to offer several arguments in support of the thesis that Tertullian could not have been referring to the extant *Acts of Paul*, but rather to a now lost pseudepigraphic Pauline epistle, thus reconciling his own theory of female authorship with Tertullian's accusation of male authorship.[31] These arguments, however, are skewered in a brief article by W. Rordorf published originally in 1990.[32]

Even apart from this, the deficiencies of Davies's argument were apparent. Literary testimony and manuscript evidence suggest that both novels and *Acts* had the same elite (largely male) readership as other ancient writings.[33] Davies relied on the naïve and unsupported assumption that the apparently highly positive representation of women in the *Acts*, particularly the Thecla story, could not have been written by men, whose writings about women in antiquity were routinely, if not inescapably, negative, indeed misogynist. Even if women are positively represented in the *Acts of Thecla*, a complex question to which I shall return, ancient male writers do sometimes write quite positively about women, particularly when it meets their needs to do so for whatever reasons.[34]

A more sophisticated analysis was offered several years later by Dennis R. MacDonald, in a far-reaching book entitled *The Legend and the Apostle: The Battle for Paul in Story and Canon*. MacDonald argued that the Thecla story represented one side of a dispute over Paul's teachings about celibacy, marriage, and childbearing in 1 Corinthians, whose other side was most visible in the New Testament letters of 1 and 2 Timothy and Titus, letters that actually invoke some of the same characters and themes as *Thecla*.

In *Thecla*, for instance, men named Demas and Hermogenes oppose Paul, while Paul is refreshed by Onesiphorus and his household. Demas and Hermogenes teach that the resurrection has already come "in the children whom

---

31. Davies 1980:108; 1986.

32. Rordorf 1990:155–59. Davies argued, for instance, that according to Tertullian, the presbyter wrote his tale to augment Paul's reputation, yet the extant *Acts of Thecla* portray Paul in an extremely unflattering light. Rordorf concedes that in the Thecla portion, this is true, but not in the *Acts of Paul* as a whole (1990:158). Davies suggested that it was hard to account for the continuing and subsequent popularity of Thecla if it had been so effectively denounced by Tertullian; Rordorf counters that the *Acts of Paul* as a whole are, in fact, quickly repudiated, and that the Thecla tradition survives the taint in part by virtue of being detached from the larger work (1990:159). Rordorf particularly takes Davies to task for apparently relying on the English translation of the German introduction in Hennecke-Schneemelcher³ (1964:222), rather than any Latin edition of Tertullian (1990:155 n.19). One of Davies's arguments, however, does raise significant questions about the present text, namely, the fact that Tertullian claims people used Thecla to legitimate women performing baptisms, yet our Thecla baptizes only herself, and that under duress. On possible explanations for this, see later.

33. Wesseling 1988; Kraemer 1991; Bowie 1994; Stephens 1994; Gamble 1995; Eitzen 2000:111–27.

34. For a discussion of some of the problems in Davies's logic, see Kraemer 1991:231–33. For additional critiques of Davies' claims of female authorship, see also D. MacDonald 1984; Kaestli 1989; 1990.

we have, and . . . we are risen again because we have full knowledge of the true God" (*Thecla* 14). Paul, however, teaches that the resurrection has not yet come, and that asceticism and lack of offspring are necessary prerequisites for salvation. In 2 Timothy, men named Phygelus and Hermogenes oppose Paul (1.15), and a man named Demas has deserted Paul (4.9). One Onesiphorus and his household refresh Paul (1.16). Paul's opponents teach the godless claim that the resurrection has already come (2.17–18, where they are identified as Hymenaeus and Philetus).

The author of the Pastorals invokes Paul's authority for the claim that women are subordinate to men, and that women are explicitly forbidden to teach or otherwise have authority over men (1 Tim 2.12). These claims are themselves set within a larger complex hierarchical order of gender, social status, and age; as Christ has authority over the church, so church officials have authority over the laity, men have authority over women, parents have authority over children, elders have authority over young persons, and slave owners have authority over slaves.[35] The author of *Thecla* invokes Paul's authorization of a celibate woman to teach, and perhaps also to baptize, and gives no evidence for any significant hierarchical structures for believers in Christ.

MacDonald never argued for the historicity of Thecla, and he gave credence to Tertullian's report of a forgery by a male presbyter. He also took seriously the Pastorals' characterization of false teachings as "tales told by old women" (1 Tim 4.7) and of women as particularly susceptible to such false teachings, as evidence for social verisimilitude (2 Tim 3.6).[36] MacDonald thus provided a somewhat different basis for the proposal that women might have been responsible for the formulation of such tales, although not necessarily for their production as literary works. The author of the Pastorals portrayed women as particularly vulnerable to the teachings more positively represented in *Thecla* because women were, in all likelihood, attracted to such teachings, and were, in all likelihood, responsible for formulating such stories and sharing them with other women.[37] Their self-representation, and positive valuation of the views denigrated in the Pastorals is much more clearly visible in the *Thecla* story and others like it.

Several years after MacDonald's book appeared, Virginia Burrus, who would become a highly respected scholar of gender and late antique Christianity, published a study entitled *Chastity as Autonomy: Stories of Women in the Apocryphal Acts*, based on her master's thesis.[38] Burrus has now largely distanced

35. For an analysis of gender construction in the Pastorals, see D'Angelo 2003; Glancy 2003.
36. See also the relevant entries in *WIS*.
37. D. MacDonald 1983, esp. 34–53.
38. Burrus 1987.

herself from the positions she took in this early work,[39] while at the same time demonstrating a critical issue central to many of her own studies: authors lose control of their work, once disseminated. Like Davies and MacDonald, Burrus argued for female formulation of the stories in the *Acts*, and saw them as evidence for the experiences of ascetic Christian women, who, like Thecla, gained a highly prized autonomy through the practice of celibacy. For Burrus, this had implications as well for contemporary Christian women.[40]

As Shelly Matthews narrates in her fine article on the historiography of Thecla, the work of Davies, MacDonald, and Burrus quickly garnered a critical response from various conservative scholars disturbed, it would seem, by the various implications of their theories.[41] Lynne Boughton and Peter Dunn both wrote articles arguing that there was no ancient "women's liberation movement" discernible behind the *Acts of Thecla* and other related narratives.[42] They accused Davies, MacDonald, and Burrus of substituting contemporary feminist agendas for sober, objective scholarship. In his revised edition of the scholarly staple, *New Testament Apocrypha*, Wilhelm Schneemelcher also dismissed their work summarily. "On a sober treatment of the evidence, hypotheses [of a liberated women's movement in the Church of the second century] appear to be largely no more than the products of modern fancy, without any basis in the sources."[43]

Although Matthews devotes considerable care to analyzing the unarticulated interests of the rhetoric of Boughton, Dunn, and, to a lesser extent, Schneemelcher, their arguments have had relatively little impact, particularly

39. Her subsequent views on these issues may be found in Burrus 1994; 2005, as well as more generally in her numerous publications listed in the Bibliography.

40. Burrus 1987:113–19.

41. Matthews 2002. My own work seems to have evaded much of this critique, which I take not so much as an endorsement of my own views, but rather as evidence that they were less well known (being published in attenuated form in *Signs*, a relatively new feminist women's studies journal that scholars in my field did not routinely read), and also somewhat more modest in their claims. I did not, for instance, ever broach the question of women's authorship in my dissertation, or the *Signs* article, and took Davies (although not D. MacDonald) to task in Kraemer 1991 article for his deeply flawed assumptions about ancient male writers. My own lack of theological interests, and my disinterest in drawing contemporary conclusions from my work may also have contributed to my remaining below the radar screen, although my article was regularly cited (demonstrating at least bibliographic thoroughness).

42. Boughton 1991; Dunn 1993.

43. *NTA* 2:222; and 236 n. 19, where Schneemelcher repeats this sentiment: "Only there is unfortunately no evidence from the sources of the period which could be adduced for a 'women's liberation movement' in the Church of the 2nd century." In addition to Matthew's critique of Schneemelcher's rhetoric (his treatment is "sober"; theirs apparently the opposite—recalling, ironically, the rhetoric of Justin), Schneemelcher's invocation of a singular entity called the second-century "Church," is itself an excellent example of interested scholarship masquerading as "objective" and "sober." And although the twentieth-century label of "women's liberation movement" is undoubtedly anachronistic, the ancient sources contain substantial evidence for intentional critique of gender constructions and women's actual roles in various early Christian communities, however difficult that evidence may be to interpret responsibly. Schneemelcher wrote this before the publication of Kraemer 1992 and the many more recent studies of these issues.

on the question of whether the stories of Thecla and other women may reasonably be analyzed as verisimilitude.[44] On the contrary, Jan Bremmer has continued to explore Thecla as a window into the social and religious practices and theological concepts of second- and third-century Christian ascetics.[45]

Two decades after my initial foray on Thecla, Kate Cooper endeavored to reframe the discussion. Just as she saw the story of the matron and her martyred Christian teacher in Justin to be about Christian identity and male competition in the second century, so, too, she saw stories like that of Thecla as having little to do with actual women's interest in early Christian ascetic practices. Rather, they were stories about the conflicts between competing male figures of authority: the morally superior Christian apostle on the one hand, and the elite male representatives of civic power on the other. Playing off of popular themes in Greco-Roman novels, the apocryphal *Acts*, Cooper argued, reconfigured elite male desire for chaste heroines not as "a renewal of the city," not (as in the novels) as sexual desire channeled into appropriate civic marriage and concord, but as an expression of "the social order's claims on those [i.e., Christians] who found them intolerable."[46] Despite the seeming centrality of women in the Thecla narrative and other related tales, the real contest in these stories was between men, and the chastity of an apocryphal heroine served as a literary device to "propel the conflict."[47] Cooper also found persuasive the view that the presence of women characters indexed not interest in women themselves, but the desire to critique a male character. "[W]henever a woman is mentioned, a man's character is being judged."[48]

44. Boughton's article appears, for instance, in the bibliography of Cooper 1996 but not in Cooper's notes or discussion, and in the bibliography of Davis 2001, again with no discussion. Dunn 1993 receives no mention in either work. Nevertheless, their arguments have resurfaced recently in Ng 2004, who attempts to counter the claims that oral Thecla traditions were circulating (perhaps by women); that the Pastorals respond to Thecla, and not vice versa; that Thecla was canonical in some circles and that its intentions related to women's "liberation" or equality. Interestingly, Ng does not cite Cooper or Matthews.

45. Engaging Boughton and Dunn briefly, Bremmer 1996 agrees that Thecla was not written by a woman (he accepts the claim of Tertullian, 1996:57) but also argues that if there was no women's liberation movement behind these stories, it's because elite women like Thecla were, in fact, already wealthy, influential, and "used to a degree of independence which we do not normally associate with Greek women." He proposes that the situation of elite women in Asia Minor and North Africa were similar and that "these women could appropriate the example of Thecla and aspire to the same independence," 1996:58–59.

46. Cooper 1996:62.

47. Cooper 1996:54. She wrote: "The challenge posed here by Christianity is not really about women, or even about sexual continence, but about authority and the social order. In this way, tales of continence uses [sic] the narrative momentum of romance and the enticement of the romantic heroine, to mask a contest for authority, encoded in the contest between two pretenders to the heroine's allegiance," 1996:55.

48. Cooper 1996:19. In particular, Cooper focused on the ways in which men could be attacked by accusing them of vulnerability to undue or unseemingly womanly influence, as she had explored in an earlier article (Cooper 1992).

Cooper's work drew heavily on the idea that narrative women were a device ancient male writers employed "to think with." The phrase is actually a quotation from Claude Levi-Strauss,[49] and was invoked already in the work of Cooper's Princeton teacher, Peter Brown, an eminent historian of late antiquity, and the author of a highly influential study.[50] As Matthews points out, Brown acknowledges deriving this language from Levi-Strauss, but misses Levi-Strauss's own caution that women are not merely signs deployed by men; they are also the users and producers of signs.[51] Matthews implies that Cooper, too, misses this subtle but significant distinction.

Cooper was well aware that her arguments were antithetical to those of earlier scholars who had seen the *Acts* as verisimilitude, at the very least. They erode, she recognizes, efforts to see the apocryphal *Acts* as "expressions of a woman's world," here targeting Davies, before somewhat more gently critiquing my own reading of the stories as social and historical verisimilitude.[52] Instead, she proposes, "ancient writers dwelled on the trials of a virtuous heroine for literary, rhetorical, and even quasipornographic reasons."[53]

Interestingly, Cooper agreed with MacDonald that the counterpoint to the apocryphal heroine was the "old wives" of the Pastorals, although she demurs from his thesis about female composition. The two stereotypes embody negative and positive attributes: falsehoods are associated with garrulous old widows; truth with the raptly attentive but silent young and pure virgin.[54] Neither, for Cooper, would appear to point in any useful fashion to the actual activities of women.

---

49. Levi-Strauss 1963:61.

50. Brown 1988:153, quoted in full in Matthews 2002:47, who also points to similar arguments in a 1989 piece by the classicist, Averil Cameron (1989:191). The same basic argument occurs in Goldhill 1995: 112 ff, cited in Davis 2001:12 n. 44: "[Goldhill] argues that the representation of women in ancient novels largely reflects the concerns of 'men of a particular class and education.'"

51. Matthews 2001:51 n. 31.

52. Cooper 1996:62–63. Despite her delicacy here, no doubt attributable in part to our common Princeton training and relationships, Cooper's actual characterization of my position, is somewhat misleading. According to Cooper, I saw the "wives-first" aspect of the apocryphal Acts as verisimilitude. For me, the real issue of verisimilitude has less to do with who converts first, and more to do with the social dynamics of ascetic women in non-Christian (hostile) households and families. Although Cooper does not pursue this, some Christian feminist reconstructions of early Christian history have been particularly interested in evidence for the thesis that women were frequently or regularly the first to adopt Christianity (e.g. Schüssler Fiorenza 1983; and see now Osiek and MacDonald 2006: see also chapter 7, this volume). Whether one thinks that, were this to be true, it would have some contemporary usage and/or inherent moral value, or whether one rather sees it as a potential historical datum in need of carefully theorized explanation depends very much on one's own intellectual and cultural location. This, however, is neither my point nor my interest, and it never was.

53. Cooper 1996:62–63.

54. Cooper 2001:63.

Although not explicitly accepting Tertullian's statement as historical, Cooper invoked it as consistent with her thesis of the author's intentions, namely, the fame of the male apostle. Tertullian had claimed that the presbyter confessed that he had forged his work "out of love for Paul," mistakenly thinking that he could add something "of his own reputation to Paul's." Cooper allowed that, once written, *Thecla* may have licensed alternative views: "when the text fell into the hands of female readers, however, some of them proposed a different reading of the heroine. Be it a lack of cultural sophistication, or a deliberate, self-interested blind eye, something led at least some women to see the Christian heroine, not as an icon of obedience to the apostolic word, but as a precedent for women's clerical authority."[55] Here she again invoked Tertullian's report as evidence that "some female readers saw it as license for female authority within the Church."[56] Cooper does not here acknowledge the textual complexities of reading Tertullian's audience as either wholly or even partly female, although she alludes to them briefly in a note.[57] Nor does she consider Tertullian's possible role in either formulating or sharing this story about the presbyter, perhaps because she uses it primarily to demonstrate the plausibility of a tension between authorial intention and audience interpretation.

Despite the challenge it poses to all prior work on women in the apocryphal *Acts*, Cooper's work has not been subjected to much detailed critique. Scholars like Davis and Matthews concede, for instance, that insufficient attention had been paid to rhetorical interests in the *Acts*, but have also then argued that Cooper's antipathy to historical reconstruction was excessively pessimistic.[58]

For all its sophisticated attention to the potential rhetorical uses of stories about female Christian virgins, Cooper's argument pays little attention to debates among literary critics about the role of authorial intention in the construction of

---

55. Cooper 2001:64.

56. Cooper 2001:65.

57. Cooper 2001:155 n. 40, where she cites only Souter 1924:292, and MacDonald 1983:17ff. For the text of *On Baptism*, Cooper cites only CCSL 1.277–95 (Borleffs, translated in *NTA* 2:214): her translation reads "But if they claim writings which are wrongly inscribed with Paul's name—I mean the example of Thecla, in support of women's freedom to teach and baptize, let them know. . . ." Cooper seems most worried about to what precisely Tertullian refers and not about the question of intended female readers or hearers. Hilhorst's article arguing for reading Tertullian's intended audience as female was probably not available to Cooper, since it appeared the same year as her book, although it would actually have bolstered her argument on this point. Rordorf's earlier article goes unremarked.

58. Of the two, Matthews is perhaps the more detailed, focusing, as noted earlier, on Peter Brown's influence on Cooper, including Brown's misuse of Levi-Strauss, whereas Davies devotes only a paragraph or so to Cooper in the single chapter he devotes to the *Acts of Thecla* in his monograph on late antique devotion to Thecla as saint. Bremmer's anthology of his and other articles on Thecla was published more or less simultaneously with Cooper's book, and is more concerned to engage the issues raised by Davies, MacDonald, Burrus, Boughton, and Dunn. His work is highly positivist in many respects, and focuses often on contextualizing the details of the text in second-century Asia Minor.

textual meaning.[59] As I noted in the Introduction, many literary theorists argue that authorial intentions quickly become inaccessible to subsequent readers (if they are indeed ever accessible), and in any case have little or no effect on the way texts are subsequently read by various readers. Cooper's analysis of the apocryphal *Acts*, however, appeals directly to authorial intention to determine an, if not *the*, initial meaning of the stories and the texts in which they are presently embedded. Her argument appears to be that some particular ancient authors intended to represent the struggle between minority Christian interests and the prevailing, polytheist power structures as a battle between an apostle and an elite male for the allegiance of an elite, young woman, for the propagation of their respective values. But this argument itself relies on a connection between Cooper's reading of what the text *seems* to do, and what its author "intended." Cooper appears to argue here that authorial intention is both accessible and to be privileged over the interpretations of its readers. Hence she can characterize the women readers of Thecla as either lacking sufficient "cultural sophistication" to perceive the author's intentions (that a truly competent reader presumably would have recognized) or else deliberately construing the text in a manner antithetical to its author's purposes and interests. Where that author envisioned "the Christian heroine . . . as an icon of obedience to the apostolic word," these women adduced it "as a precedent for women's clerical authority."[60]

In Cooper's reading, then, the only historicity lies in the women readers of Thecla, who do, in fact, (mis)use it to either generate or support their arguments for women's authority, apparently with particular regard to baptism and teaching.[61] The various problems with Tertullian remain unexamined. Yet the question of Tertullian's intended, as well as actual, initial audience is here quite germane. The dichotomy between male authors and contestants on the one hand, and female readers on the other, is not nearly as pronounced in this case if Tertullian's original critique was aimed at a mixed audience of readers who supported women's right to teach and baptize, rather than one of only women who took such a stance. Thus, Cooper's assignment of the "misguided" reading of Tertullian to women (whose interests it may have served) is itself vulnerable. Further, despite Cooper's attentiveness to the rhetorical uses of the Thecla tale, she fails to inquire about the uses of Tertullian's claims as a rhetorical strategy in a particular power struggle.

For Cooper, the one audience reading we *are* able to demonstrate, namely, that of Tertullian as reader of *Thecla*, is not determinative of the intent of *Thecla's* author, and is, in fact, at odds with that intent; in that regard, after all,

59. See Clark 2004.
60. Cooper 1996:64.
61. Cooper 1996:64–65.

Cooper thinks Tertullian was essentially right. Further, for Cooper, women played no discernible role in the formation of this and related stories, although they apparently were more than happy to use them for other purposes. Having detected a utility of these stories for ancient male power struggles and contests for authority, Cooper then argues that function points to authorial intention, yet denies that their one historically attested function, the legitimation of women's agency with regard to baptism and teaching, is related to their authorial intention. Rather, their historically attested function is a misreading, where reading is determined by authorial intent (which has itself been derived from perceived function). In doing so, of course, Cooper privileges the presentation of Tertullian, who himself has a (gendered) power agenda here, and oddly, she ends up affirming the rightness of his view, subordinating what she takes to be women's interpretations to those of powerful men.

Cooper not only privileges Tertullian, but the readings of men more generally. In her own argument, women read the text wrongly; men read it rightly, where *rightly* means "as the (male) author intended." Men understand that a story about women isn't really about women; it's only women who misread the story, either out of ignorance of the relevant rhetorical genres and clues, or out of knowing disregard. This, ironically, is almost certainly not her intent,[62] but it is an effect, or perhaps a function, of her argument. This is itself an ironic demonstration of the problem of method: textual function does not necessarily point back reliably to authorial intention.

Further, Cooper appears to subordinate the only available historical evidence to her interests in (male) ideology. For Cooper, just as Justin's *Apology* says nothing about the matron whose teacher was apparently martyred nor other elite women like her, so *Thecla* says nothing about ancient Christian women except that men found it useful to tell tales about women who were adopting Christian chastity and were caught in power conflicts between apostles and elite men; in these conflicts, although the apostle is ultimately martyred, the Christian perspective is shown to be the true (and more masculine) one. Yet, oddly, Cooper's own thesis about women readers undercuts her very argument that there's no history here, because what there appears to be, in fact, is a history of women's alternative readings for their own purposes and interests. Whether, of course, that history is reliable in this particular case is hard to say, given the difficulties of the text of *On Baptism*.

Although Cooper insists that the readers whom Tertullian refutes violated the author's intentions as Cooper constructs (and privileges) them, either out of ignorance or willful misreading, Cooper's own reading of *Thecla* and other

---

62. I make this claim not so much on the basis of the book itself, but on personal acquaintance with Cooper.

apocryphal *Acts*, is, in fact, a subtle one that depends on certain highly implicit assumptions to convey to the reader that women are only incidentally the subject. Much in the *Acts of Thecla* would have supported the interpretation of Tertullian's opponents, including Thecla's active roles as a teacher (authorized by Paul); her self-baptism; her intervention on behalf of Falconilla; the support of the women, including the powerful patroness, Queen Typhaena, and so forth. Further, Cooper's approach has a puzzling inconsistency: she is quite willing to see verisimilitude in the use of the characters of Jesus's first-century disciples behind the representation of real second and third century C.E. male Christian teachers like Justin's Ptolemaeus, yet she is unwilling to consider that the female characters similarly correspond to actual persons and practices.

Because Cooper's analysis also fails to account for other significant components of the Thecla story, I turn now to some of these in detail. Consider the presence of numerous other female figures in the story. Although "virgins" in her native Iconium are among those who bring firewood for her initial trial by fire, from the moment of her appearance in front of the governor in Antioch, Thecla is repeatedly defended by a crowd of women. Immediately, they declare Thecla's punishment to be lawless, "a bitter spectacle, an evil judgment" (32). Later, in the arena, when Thecla's defending lioness dies in battle with the lion, the women mourn all the more. When yet other beasts are brought in, women wail, and throw such a profusion of flower petals that the perfume overcomes the beasts and they leave Thecla unharmed. At best, Cooper's analysis would seem to account for the presence of these women as devices by which "a man's character is being judged."[63] Certainly, the women's protestations of injustice function like the judgments of a Greek chorus against the various male authorities. Yet the extensive development of female relationships seems to point, at least, to elements in the story that would have appealed to women readers and provided license for precisely the interpretation that Tertullian's opponents took, if not to real social dynamics.[64]

Cooper's analysis further offers no means of accounting for the literary function, if not the intention, of the story of the Queen Tryphaena and Falconilla. Tryphaena's support of Thecla clearly facilitates certain key elements of the plot. Her powerful patronage assures that Thecla will remain sexually unmolested before her battle with the animals. Her fainting in the arena triggers

---

63. Cooper 1996:19.

64. Bremmer thinks the characters of the story reflect the intended audience: "the [*Acts of Thecla*] was directed not only at virgins but also at the group of women at large" (because of the role of women at the trial): 1996:51.

Alexander's petition to the governor to release Thecla, for he fears the retribution of the emperor himself, Tryphaena's relative of some unspecified sort. Yet convenient as these are, their effects could surely have been accomplished in other ways. If miracles could save Thecla from death and the shame of public nudity, they could certainly save her from assaults on her chastity.[65]

Even if Tryphaena's appearance is partially plot driven, this does not account for the complex theme of mother-daughter relations that pervades the text, a theme that has received relatively little attention.[66] Mother-daughter relations bookend Thecla's story. In the beginning, it is Thecla's natural mother, Theocleia, who is horrified by her new-found devotion to Christian celibacy, and who angrily urges the governor to "burn the lawless one . . . who is no bride in the midst of the theatre" (*Thecla* 20), as a warning to all who might follow her example. At the very end, in a scene that may have been truncated (Hilhorst actually speculates that Thecla might have even baptized her mother), Thecla returns to her mother and achieves some sort of closure, although the scene ends abruptly with Thecla's speech to her mother, and gives no indication of Theocleia's response.[67]

In this sense, at least, the story is an odd inversion of the classic ancient narrative of mother-daughter devotion, that of Demeter and Persephone. Persephone was snatched unwillingly from her mother's protection, forced to marry Hades, sought for in vain by her despairing mother, and ultimately reunited with her after Demeter used the full strength of her divine powers to force Zeus and Hades to return Persephone for a portion of the year.[68] Thecla leaves home

65. This problem does not even occur before Thecla is brought out to be burnt in Iconium, where we might imagine that her elite status was sufficient to protect her, but there is no way of knowing whether such logic was in the mind of either an author or ancient audiences. Thecla's intervention on Falconilla's behalf (which as Bremmer notes [1996:42–44] resembles in general outlines Perpetua's intervention on her dead brother's behalf) certainly serves to demonstrate Thecla's ability to work miracles, but why this particular miracle remains elusive: it does not serve, for instance, to explain Tryphaena's aid to Thecla, but constitutes at best, Thecla's *quid pro quo*, since Tryphaena aids her initially without explanation.

66. Aubin 1998 briefly discusses this, and sees Tryphaena as a surrogate mother for Thecla. Van der Weg argues that Thecla is not represented as Tryphaena's replacement daughter, because the text calls her παῖς (child), not θυγάτηρ (daughter) (1996:32–33). In any case, Tryphaena explicitly calls Thecla her "second child" and also calls Falconilla "child." Somewhat more useful is van der Weg's point that Tryphaena does not actually adopt Thecla, but I am less persuaded by her thesis that Tryphaena is here presented as Thecla's patron, not as her surrogate mother.

67. *Thecla* 43. Based on this scene, Aubin speculates that Theocleia's opposition to Thecla's refusal to marry reflects a concern that Thecla will lack the resources to care for her mother in her old age; resources that marriage, presumably, would afford her, 1998:265–66. In the end Thecla does, in fact, provide for her mother (apparently from the resources obtained from Tryphaena). Aubin thinks that Theocleia converts to Christianity (1998:271), but I think the text is ambiguous at best on this point. Some versions of the story found in other manuscripts are more explicit that Theocleia does not believe (manuscripts G, M, c, d; cited in Lipsius-Bonnet 1891:269: ἡ δὲ μήτηρ αὐτῆς Θεοκλία οὐκ ἐπίστευσε τοῖς λεγομένοις αὐτῇ ὑπὸ τῆς μάρτυρος Θέκλης).

68. See Foley 1994; see also *WRGRW* 124.

voluntarily, refuses to marry her mother's approved choice of a husband, is persecuted by her own mother, maintains her chastity and her integrity, and returns, at least briefly, to forgive her estranged mother.

The fraught relationship of Thecla and Theocleia is contrasted to the loving relationship between Tryphaena and Falconilla, as well as to the surrogate relationship of Tryphaena and Thecla. Where Theocleia sought to marry off Thecla against her will, and failing that, to condemn her to death, Tryphaena seeks to protect Thecla's virginity, and ultimately becomes the instrument through which Thecla's life is saved, when her fainting triggers Alexander's petition. Theocleia is the epitome of the bad mother, Tryphaena of the good.

Apparently present when Thecla is first sentenced to the beasts, Tryphaena takes Thecla into her protective custody, and follows Thecla as she is paraded in public on a lioness in anticipation of her battle. The dead Falconilla tells her mother in a dream that Tryphaena will have the stranger, Thecla, as her replacement, and through Thecla's intervention, Falconilla will be translated to the place of the righteous dead. Tryphaena then again takes Thecla into her protection, now as a surrogate daughter: "she loved her dearly like her own daughter, Falconilla." Asking Thecla to pray for Falconilla, Tryphaena addresses her as "my second child."[69] Thecla's impending apparent death causes Tryphaena and her household to grieve as for Falconilla. Tryphaena acknowledges that she is helpless, being a widow, lacking her daughter, who is dead, and having no (male) relative. "O God of Thecla my child," she prays, "help Thecla."[70]

When the time comes for Thecla to be led away to her death, Tryphaena refuses to stand aside, and instead holds Thecla's hand and accompanies her, saying: "My daughter, Falconilla, I brought to the tomb, but you, Thecla, I bring to battle the beasts." When Thecla is finally released, Tryphaena, now recovered, comes to greet Thecla, confessing her belief in the resurrection, and transferring her wealth to Thecla. She takes Thecla into her home a third time, to the rejoicing of her household.

What rhetorical purposes are served by the rich articulation of the love and support between Thecla and Tryphaena? The story of Thecla's natural and surrogate mothers exemplifies the early Christian critique of natal families and the corresponding construction of alternative families of believers found already in

---

69. τέκνον δεύτερον (29).

70. ὁ θεὸς Θέκλης τοῦ τεκνοῦ μου, βοήθησον θέκλῃ (30). This scene stresses that, despite Tryphaena's elite status, her ability to protect Thecla is limited to guarding her virginity: only God can truly help Thecla. This may also account for some aspects of the representation of Paul as unable to protect Thecla, either, although the contrast is significant between Paul, who denies knowing Thecla, and abandons her to Alexander's assaults, both physical and legal, and Tryphaena, who remains steadfast in her devotion to Thecla and successfully guards her virginity.

early traditions about Jesus and his relatives. It also serves as an implicit critical contrast to Paul's behavior: whereas he repeatedly abandons her to her fate, and marvels after the fact at her survival, women repeatedly support her, Tryphaena above all. It is difficult, though, to see what function might be served by this extended emphasis on female solidarity and love in a tale whose basic purpose is, as Cooper argues, to articulate competing claims of masculinity and power among men.

Cooper's reading of *Thecla* as a narrative device by which Christian men challenged the ruling male elites as arbiters of truth, authority, and masculinity is not the only way to read the uses of gender in this and related stories. The gendering of the main characters as female, and the presence of women more generally in the text serves different issues than those envisioned by Cooper. Writing roughly contemporaneously with Cooper, on the uses of gender in early Christian martyrdom narratives, both Judith Perkins and Brent Shaw have illuminated the ways in which Christians deployed gender inversion in their responses to Roman opposition and prosecution.[71] As is perhaps also true of Justin's account of the unnamed matron, the fundamental associations of femininity with weakness, powerlessness, passivity, limited intellect, and numerous other deficiencies were effectively exploited to demonstrate the ultimate power of the Christian God. Constructing themselves as female, seemingly powerless to stop their suffering at the hands of Roman male authorities, Christians in fact challenged and defied Roman claims to power.

This tactic had antecedents in the Judean scriptures that Christians, too, revered. The representation of Israel as weak, as suffering, in short, as feminine had been similarly deployed to demonstrate the true power of the God of Israel in the face of the seeming power of the nations and their deities. But as both Perkins and Shaw make clear, Christian rhetorical strategies appear deeply rooted in prevailing and contemporaneous Greco-Roman constructions of femininity and masculinity.

These insights may be fruitfully applied to *Thecla* (and other narratives in the apocryphal *Acts*). In *Thecla*, Christians and their sympathizers are frequently female: Thecla; Tryphaena; her daughter, Falconilla; Tryphaena's female servants; the mass of women in the stadium in Antioch (sometimes including their children); and not the least, the lioness who defends Thecla against various male animals in the arena. The opponents of the text's Christianity, whether polytheists or other Christians, are overwhelmingly male: Thamyris, Demas, Hermogenes, the governor at Iconium (Castellius), Alexander, the unnamed governor in Antioch, the men in the stadium in Antioch, and the various male

71. Perkins 1995; Shaw 1996.

animals sent against Thecla, including the bull prodded in his genitals. There are a few exceptions: Thecla's own mother, Theocleia, initially opposes her, although in the end, some sort of reconciliation between Thecla and Theocleia takes place. And Paul, of course, is male, as is his host Onesiphorus and his son (Onesiphorus' unnamed wife is also a Christian; they appear to have other children and perhaps household members whose gender is not perceptible).

Thus, although a few really good guys in this story are men, and one really bad guy is a woman, in general, the women are Christians, or Christian sympathizers, and the men, by contrast, are opponents of Christianity. This is entirely consistent with a use of gender inversion to express Christian critique and challenge of Greco-Roman culture and power when legal, military, economic, and social power lay overwhelmingly with non-Christians. It depends for its effectiveness, though, on the positioning of the Christian women as true exemplars of masculine virtues, and the positioning of their non-Christian male opponents as lacking such virtues.

Thecla's Transgression of Gender Norms

Many contemporary commentators on the Thecla story, myself included, have remarked on several passages where Thecla transgresses ancient gender conventions.[72] Fairly early on, after she has survived attempts to burn her in Iconium, Thecla tells Paul that she will cut off her hair and follow him wherever he goes. The use of future verbs makes it somewhat unclear that Thecla actually does ever cut off her hair, but the passage is routinely read that way.[73] Whether there is an allusion here to 1 Cor 11.6 is difficult to say, although quite intriguing. There, apparently responding to Corinthian women who pray and prophesy in the communal assembly with their heads uncovered, Paul admonishes his Corinthian audience that a woman who does not cover her head might as well cut off her hair (keirasthō), but since it is shameful for a woman to have her hair cut off (to keirasthai), or to be shaved, she should instead cover her head.[74] To an audience familiar with 1 Corinthians 11, Thecla's announcement that she will cut off her hair reads either as an intentional repudiation of Paul's instruction, or perhaps as a denial that Thecla is included in the category of "women." In any case, later, after she has survived the battle with the beasts in Antioch, Thecla

---

72. For analyses along the lines of my own here, see, e.g., Aubin 1998.

73. περικαροῦμαι καὶ ἀκολουθήσω σοι (25).

74. NRSV translates this as "if a woman will not veil herself, then she should cut off her hair; but if it is disgraceful for a woman to have her hair cut off or to be shaved, she should wear a veil." There is an enormous secondary literature on this passage.

dresses in a man's cloak and goes off in search of Paul. Whether Thecla continues to cross-dress in her subsequent travels is again not explicit.

Thecla's apparent actions here are illuminated by an awareness of ancient understandings of the gendered meanings of hair and clothing. A woman communicated her status instantly and silently by the garments and adornments she wore, the length and styling of her hair, her bodily comportment, her attendants and the public venues, if any, in which she appeared. (To a surprising degree, this remains true even in twenty-first-century American culture, although clues of class and social status are more ambiguous than they were even fifty years ago).[75] Whatever the flaws in Paul's argument in 1 Corinthians 11, he was certainly right that a woman's hair was taken to be a sign of her beauty as well as of her social standing, and that for a woman to have short or shorn hair was often a sign of social stigma.[76] As I have noted in previous chapters, artistic representations of women's elaborate hairstyles in the Roman period strongly suggest that elite women did not universally cover their heads in public, and that failure to do so was not necessarily construed as a violation of gendered norms. Nevertheless, when women did cover their heads, it appears to have been routinely construed as a symbol of their subordination to male authority, and an expression of gender differentiation. Ancient ideas and practices concerning women's hair were rooted in associations between the hair on women's heads and the hair on their genitals.[77] The underlying logic of women's headcoverings seems to have been that just as a respectable woman whose sexuality belonged properly to her father and then her husband would not dream of exposing her genitals in public, so she should not also display the hair on her head in public. Similarly, a woman's garments announced her status as a free woman or a slave; a wealthy aristocrat or a more ordinary, if still free person; a woman who was sexually available only to her licit husband, or a woman who was not.

Thecla's intention to cut off her hair and follow Paul regardless of where he goes thus has resonances in ancient culture that a modern reader might easily miss. In effect, Thecla renounces the gendered practices associated with her former identity as an aristocratic young woman on the verge of a highly respectable marriage. Cutting her hair short carries with it a range of potential meanings: for Thecla herself, within the framework of the text, it appears to

---

75. E.g., Bourdieu 2001.

76. This, though, is a complicated question: Lewis 2002:104–6 suggests that there is no easy correlation between hair length and social status in classical Greek sources, whereas Kleiner and Matheson 2000:12 note that even female slaves adopted the hair style of the Empress Livia.

77. D'Angelo 1995; see also Carson 1990.

signify her rejection of the sexuality associated with women's hair, as well as the male authority to which she was previously subject. Although her intention to follow Paul blunts this somewhat, it also demonstrates Thecla's new freedom to travel and function in public venues. Yet at the same time, these actions are liable to be read differently by unsympathetic readers and by the characters in the story who resemble such readers.

Thecla appears to subvert conventional elite femininity in numerous other ways. She repeatedly defies male figures of authority, familial and civic: her fiancé, Thamyris, first citizen of Iconium (11), who orders her to turn to him and be ashamed of her devotion to the teachings of Paul against marriage; Alexander, called Syriarches,[78] whom she publicly humiliates when he attempts to molest her; even, perhaps, Paul himself, whom she repeatedly pesters to baptize her when he refuses to do so. Numerous times, Thecla acts autonomously. She leaves her house at night, another act that could be easily misconstrued as one motivated by the intention to indulge illicit sexual desires, and goes to Paul in prison. There, the chaste nature of her desires is manifest, however amusing ancient audiences might have found the description of Paul and Thecla "bound together in affection (*en storgē*)." Ultimately, of course, Thecla takes responsibility for her own baptism, is commissioned by Paul to teach, and strikes out on her own as a Christian missionary and teacher.

Thecla willingly endures punishments intended to induce gender-related shame. Twice she is forced to appear naked in a public arena (22 and 33), reflecting the widely held ancient notion that for a respectable woman to be seen naked was deeply embarrassing: for her to be forcibly exposed to the public gaze was one of the ultimate forms of humiliation.[79] When, having survived the attack of the beasts, Thecla is ordered to dress by the astonished governor, she does not immediately do so. Instead, presumably still exposed, she

---

78. The title syriarch (head of the provincial capital of Syria) is well attested, both in legal sources, e.g., *Theodosian Code* 15.9.2; Justinian, *Novella* 18.15; and epigraphic sources, e.g., *TAM* III.118; 226; 327; 386, 429, 456, etc.

79. In the first instance, she is apparently totally naked as she is brought in to be burnt. In the second, she is stripped and thrown into the arena, but somehow takes (grabs?) a girdle—ἔλαβεν διαζώστραν—on the way in. This brief phrase seems incongruous both grammatically (coming between two passive verbs), and because the subsequent scenes seem to presume that Thecla is still naked, as she was in the earlier episode. In 34, a cloud of fire protects Thecla both from the beasts and from being seen naked; in 38, the governor offers Thecla clothing that she eventually accepts (see later). In addition, it's difficult to envision that Thecla might conveniently have seen and grabbed a garment enroute to her punishment, and that she would have been able to put it on, when the whole point of stripping her was to embarrass her. Although there's no supporting textual evidence, I wonder whether it is, in fact, a scribal emendation at some fairly early point in the textual transmission. Petropoulous argues that "this article of clothing is more than a "sop" to the Acta's prudish readers; it surely must connote Thecla's aggressive retention of her virginity and her status as a warrior pitted against the male legacy of cruelty," and here cites Atalanta's devotion to her girdle; Petropoulous 1995:134.

disdains the implication that the nakedness of her body is meaningful and requires the cover of ordinary clothing. Rather, she proclaims, true clothing comes from God in the form of salvation: "The one who clothed me when I was naked among the beasts, this same one shall clothe me with salvation in the day of judgment."[80] Only then does she take the clothes and put them on. This scene may also allude to Christian ideas about clothing as the garments of shame given to Adam and Eve after their transgression. The virgin Thecla, virtuous and obedient, has no need for such garments, and is not ashamed of her naked body, no more than Eve (and Adam) was ashamed of her nudity before she became disobedient.[81]

In a text that configures Christians as women and their opponents as men, it may be not at all surprising that it also configures exemplary Christian women as male, or at least, as demonstrating valued masculine characteristics of self-control, activity, knowledge, and so forth. It is probably also relevant that these traits are most associated with virgins—with adult females who have not been (and will not be) penetrated by a man, and are not under male authority, although Thecla's relation to Paul is complicated here.

The construction of Thecla as masculine is accomplished over time, in a narrative of subtle and progressive transformation (that may be consistent with ancient notions that masculinity was both a process and a performance?).[82] In the opening scenes, Thecla has many feminine attributes. She sits passively inside, by her window, observing and listening to Paul's teachings of celibacy (7). Her mother, Theocleia, describes her as "controlled by a new desire and a terrible passion." Although the sympathetic Christian reader understands Thecla's literal fixation differently (perhaps, indeed, as an imitation of the three days and three nights Christ spent in the tomb before his resurrection [8]), that same reader would have been alert to the underlying stereotype of women's lack of self-control over desires and passions that is implicit here. Called by Theocleia, Thecla's fiancé, Thamyris, appeals to ancient notions of female shame: "Thecla, my fiancée,[83] why do you sit like that? And what sort of passion (pathos) holds you distracted? Turn to your Thamyris and be ashamed (aisxuntheti)" (10).

---

80. *Thecla* 38, my translation. Aubin 1998:270–71, makes a similar point about Thecla's nakedness and subsequent clothing, noting also the discussion of Miles 1989:58.

81. This association is not suggested by either Aubin or Burrus.

82. On masculinity as a performance, see, e.g., Gleason 1995; 1999. Aubin also sees a progressive masculinization of Thecla (and a relative feminization of Paul), although she does not develop it in this much detail. Our analyses are developed independently (or at least, mine is independent of hers: I'm fairly sure that she is quite familiar with my work in general, although she doesn't cite it in this article).

83. νύμφη.

Thecla does not begin to assert herself until well into the narrative, when Paul is imprisoned while the governor gives more thought to Paul's defense against Thamyris' accusations. Still, her actions illuminate various features of ancient gender systems. Thecla cannot simply leave on her own accord but must bribe the doorkeeper (18).[84] Apparently, Thecla lacks access to money, for she exchanges her bracelets for the doorkeeper's complicity. A silver mirror given to Paul's jailer gains Thecla access to the prison cell. These objects are stereotypically female in antiquity. Although there's no way to determine some "original" intention behind the use of these objects, other than as plot devices, they may also be read as symbolic of Thecla's renunciation both of gendered roles in general, and of concern for bodily adornment associated with female identity and sexuality in particular.[85]

Despite the autonomy implicit in her decision to accept the teachings of Christ as taught by Paul, Thecla continues to conform to gendered expectations of elite women. Once in Paul's prison, she sits silently at his feet. Even when she is discovered in his company, she appears to remain silent, and it is her physical agitation at his removal (perhaps itself a form of lack of self-control) not anything she says, that lands her, also, before the governor. When Paul is expelled from the city and Thecla condemned to be burned, she looks around for Paul as a "lamb to its shepherd," constructing her as helpless and lost. Seeing Christ sitting in the theater, in the form of Paul, she utters her first words, apparently to herself: "As if I were not able to bear up, Paul has come to look after me" (21). Masculine intervention repeatedly rescues her, whether that of the male deity, who sends a miraculous rainstorm that quenches the fire intended to burn Thecla in the theater (22), or that of the son of Onesiphorus, who finds the now-released Thecla and takes her to Paul (23).

For Cooper, Thecla's silence contrasts with the false speech of old women stereotyped in the Pastorals and elsewhere. "The continent heroine is essentially not a speaker but a listener. . . . If falsehoods were associated with the uncontrolled speech of old women, the rapt listening of feminine youth and purity were linked

---

84. Why Thecla must bribe the doorkeeper isn't entirely clear. The text suggests that this is because the door is locked and Thecla has no authority to leave on her own. Although we might speculate that Thecla bribes the doorkeeper to purchase silence about her activities, the doorkeeper is immediately forthcoming in a subsequent scene (19), so either the bribe was to get out or the doorkeeper is easily persuaded to give Thecla up!

85. See the similar observations of Aubin, who has a brief discussion of the significance of Thecla's removal of her bracelets, which she sees as "traditional gender signifiers," and sees some irony in the contrast of Thecla's removal of her bracelets while Paul himself is shackled by the wrists: "this is our first clue to the emergence of Thecla as a figure who supercedes Paul in authority and masculine license," Aubin 1998:264. Compare this analysis to the much more positivist approach of Bremmer 1996:36–59, who remarks only that Thecla's actions "illustrate both [her] independent nature and her wealth, in that she used (golden?) bracelets and a silver mirror." For Bremmer, bribing of jailers is attested in ancient novels and martyrdom acts, and "must have been normal." Bremmer says nothing about Thecla's need to bribe her own household doorkeeper (Acts of Thecla 48).

to the truth."[86] Although Cooper does not elaborate on it, the ancient association of female silence with female chastity and female speech with illicit sexuality was widespread, and drew on analogies between a woman's mouth and her vagina (as headcoverings drew on analogies between the head and the pubic region). Yet Thecla, in fact, does speak, more and more as the text progresses, culminating in her enlightenment of "many" before her death. Now, for the first time, Thecla speaks in the presence of others (24). Still, her speech is hardly transgressive, and consists of a fairly formulaic prayer praising God for saving her from the fire and enabling her to see Paul. Further, Thecla prays not spontaneously, but in response to Paul's own prayer to God to rescue her from the fire. From this point on, Thecla becomes more and more vocal and autonomous. Announcing that she will cut her hair and follow Paul, for the first time, she asks him to baptize her. Although Paul demurs, he does take Thecla with him to Antioch.

When Thecla is there accosted by Alexander, his uncontrolled desire for her functions as an implicit critique of his lack of masculine self-control. The story does not reflect well on Paul, either (despite Tertullian's report that the alleged author intended to add to Paul's reputation).[87] When, apparently thinking that Paul has control over Thecla's sexuality,[88] Alexander offers him money and gifts for her, Paul denies not only that Thecla is his,[89] but even that he knows her. Left to fend for herself, Thecla protests vigorously, identifying herself as a slave of God (perhaps in contrast to Alexander's presumption that she is a slave of Paul's), and as "first" among the Iconians, a well-attested ancient title of prestige for both women and men.[90] Then, as noted

86. Cooper 1996:63.

87. And see earlier for Davies's argument (and Rordorf's critique) that this characterization of Paul makes it unlikely that Tertullian was referring to the *Acts of Thecla*.

88. Various scholars have proposed that Alexander's molestation of Thecla presumes that something about her makes it "reasonable" for him to think she is sexually available. Aubin 1998:267, and n. 24, cites Burrus 1987:89, that Alexander feels free to molest Thecla in public because her "departure from private space and free movement in public," communicate her sexual promiscuity. Aubin extends this to argue that Paul beats a quick retreat to avoid being seen with the wrong sort of person. More to the point may be Thecla's apparent physical appearance, particularly the shorn hair associated with prostitutes. Alexander's attempts to obtain Thecla by giving money and gifts to Paul might imply that he takes Thecla to be a whore and Paul to be her pimp. Thecla's response to Alexander, "force not the stranger; force not the slave of God" (26), may also imply that Alexander has mistaken her for a different sort of slave, perhaps one owned by Paul. These two readings are not mutually exclusive: ancient audiences might have understood Alexander to take Thecla to be an enslaved prostitute controlled by Paul. But we should also be wary of overreading this: the narrative requires Alexander to accost Thecla, regardless of what apparently motivates his character to do so.

89. ἐμή.

90. Bremmer 1996 relies on this title (which is applied both to Thecla and to Thamyris) to locate the origins of the story, but this is a common fallacy—that a seemingly well-known geographic location points to the geographical location of the author. At best, such accuracy points to authors familiar with such particulars for reasons that may, but need not, include residence at the time of writing or at some prior time. And residents of any given locale are still capable of erroneous description.

earlier, she ridicules Alexander by ripping off his cloak and the crown from his head.[91]

When Alexander brings Thecla up before the governor, she continues to assert herself. No longer silent, she readily confesses her deeds against Alexander, and asks to be allowed to remain chaste until she has to fight the beasts, a request that reflects ancient assumptions that women could routinely expect to be raped under such circumstances, another expression of male dominance and female submission.

Given over, at the queen's request, to Tryphaena's care, Thecla immediately prays for her daughter, Falconilla, as Tryphaena has asked. That her prayer is efficacious is implicit in Tryphaena's response later, when Thecla herself has been saved from the beasts, "Now I know that my daughter lives."

In the arena in Antioch, Thecla continues to exhibit masculine characteristics of public speech and autonomous action. After her protecting lioness kills various male animals sent against Thecla, and then dies herself in a battle with the lion, Thecla fears she is about to die unbaptized. She prays aloud and then baptizes herself in the only water available, a pool filled with human-eating seals.

When, ultimately, various miraculous interventions secure Thecla's freedom, she responds to the governor's inquiry about her identity with a relatively long speech proclaiming her Christian faith. Taken back into Tryphaena's household, Thecla now instructs Tryphaena, and the queen and "the majority of her female servants" also believe. Then, learning that Paul is now in Myra, Thecla dresses in male outer garb, and goes off, accompanied (as proper women should be) by a retinue of servants, male and female. After she relates to Paul and the others the events at Antioch, including her self-baptism, she announces that she is returning to Iconium. Paul then issues the statement that Tertullian's opponents must surely have loved: "Go forth," he tells Thecla, and "teach the word of God" (*Thecla* 41).

Thecla is thus gradually transformed in the story from a passive young woman inside her mother's household, content to listen to others without speaking herself, to an autonomous, self-controlled teacher of Christ, authorized by the apostle Paul himself, and capable of "enlightening" many. Yet even this transformation into masculine self-discipline, autonomous action, public speech, and so forth, has its limits. Throughout the text, when Thecla speaks or

---

91. *Thecla* 26. Aubin observes that a *chlamys* was an imperial or military mantle; and notes S. Price's suggestion that Alexander wore a priest's crown that contained an imperial image (Price 1984:124, cited in Aubin 1998:268 n. 25). For Price, this explains why Thecla is specifically charged with sacrilege, but this may miss the utility of the charge in the larger interests of the narrative. Bremmer, who may not have read Price, argues that it was Thecla's shaming of Alexander that was legally actionable. Both presume that the text needs a specific and coherent impetus for Thecla's fate.

acts in public venues, it is because circumstances compel her to do so, whether her trials in the theater and arena, or her travels to seek out Paul. Otherwise, we mostly see Thecla in the confines of private households, from that of her mother, to that of Tryphaena, to that of Hermias (41). The masculine Thecla thus nevertheless conforms to some basic ancient notions of female comportment.

Further, it's not really clear whether men are among those Thecla teaches. In Tryphaena's household, Thecla only explicitly converts the queen and "the majority of her female servants." The closest the text comes to depicting Thecla as a teacher of men as well as women appears in the one closing line that encapsulates Thecla's public career as a teacher of the word of God and gives us little sense of who Thecla might have taught, or where. "And having enlightened many (*pollous photisasa*) with the word of God, she slept a fine sleep"(43). But whether *pollous* actually includes men is ambiguous. In the accusative plural, the masculine and feminine forms are identical here, so that this line *can* be construed in various ways. Thecla enlightened women and men, or women alone, or even men alone, although the prior narrative of her instruction of Tryphaena and her female household mitigates against this last reading. For a woman to teach other women was not nearly as transgressive as a woman teacher of men. Read this way, the story of Thecla conforms more closely to the view of the Pastorals that Paul forbade women to teach or have authority over men, but not over other women.[92]

It may or may not be significant that although Paul tells Thecla to "go forth and teach the word of God,"[93] the verb *didaskein* (to teach) never otherwise occurs to describe Thecla's activity. Instead, she instructs (*katexesasa*) Tryphaena and her household, and enlightens (*photisasa*) many, all with the word of God. It is precisely to teach (*didaskein*) that the author of 1 Timothy, writing in Paul's name, does not allow women (2.12). One simple enough explanation is that all three verbs were construed as synonyms. Alternatively, however, the present text deliberately avoids using *didaskein* with regard to Thecla.[94]

Textual Issues and Gender

These observations raise the question of whether the material in our present manuscripts of Thecla was altered in antiquity to address precisely some of

---

92. Boughton 1991 used this observation to support a very different conclusion, namely that the ancient readers excoriated by Tertullian read badly, a view that Cooper 1996 shares, although to somewhat different ends.

93. *Thecla* 41. ὕπαγε καὶ δίδασκε τὸν λογὸν τοῦ θεοῦ. The use of ὕπάγω is somewhat interesting. Although it does sometimes mean to go forward, its primary semantic field involves leadership and bringing something or someone under one's control, LSJ s.v.

94. In one of the longer versions of Thecla, manuscript M, Thecla is "eager to teach the word of God that the city (of Seleucia) might believe." See later.

these issues. Scholars have long been somewhat puzzled by Tertullian's claim that people were using the example of Thecla to authorize women teaching and baptizing. In the story as we have it now, Paul's directive to Thecla to teach is clear enough, but as we have seen, the text may be read to depict Thecla as teaching only other women. Yet Tertullian's ire seems to require a more transgressive narrative.

Further, in the version we now have, Thecla explicitly baptizes only herself. Conceivably, however, Tertullian knew a version of the story in which Thecla explicitly taught men and women, and baptized others. Perhaps the story of Thecla's public career after chapter 43 been condensed down to the single line preferred by the late nineteenth-century editors of the text.[95] Hilhorst argues that Tertullian's critique requires the story of Thecla to "have contained unambiguous descriptions of baptizing by Thecla," because, if all Thecla had done was baptize herself, surely Tertullian would have pointed that out in support of his position. He also speculates that "Thecla's baptizing activities . . . have been eliminated to prevent their being used as an argument for baptizing by women."[96] If so, one might wonder why the same revisers didn't also remove Paul's authorization of Thecla's teaching, unless, as I suggested earlier, the present text was construed to mean that Thecla taught only other women.

It's also possible that the text as we have it was sufficient to support a reading of Thecla as baptizing others, in its use of the verb "enlighten" (*photizō*). This verb may allude to baptism already in Heb 6.4 and 10.32, although this is not definitive.[97] In the Latin translation of Thecla, *photizō* is rendered as *illuminare*, which itself sometimes connotes baptism.[98]

Differences between the Greek manuscripts of Thecla and those in Syriac, Armenian, and other languages demonstrate that the text underwent considerable alteration, apparently aimed at domesticating (re-feminizing?) the figure of Thecla. These would appear to be the work of the translators, but, not

95. Hilhorst 1996:162. As I suggest earlier, though, the text as we have it could easily have been read to make Thecla a teacher only of other women, which would have been more or less acceptable in numerous Christian circles. This assumes, furthermore, that the reconstruction of a text that ended at 43 sufficiently approximates its earliest form(s). Several of the extant and preferred Greek manuscripts do end at this point.

96. Hilhorst 1996:162–63.

97. φωτίζω occurs in 2 Kings 17.28 and Eph 3.9, and LSJ, s.v., cites these as support for its definition of φωτίζω as "to instruct or teach," although in both these cases, a somewhat subtler distinction may be at work. In accord with its more basic meaning, φωτίζω may here mean to enlighten (through instruction). But one needs to be careful here; according to LSJ, φωτίζω connotes baptism in Hebrews, but as Harry Attridge's notes in the Oxford Annotated edition of the NRSV indicate, this is by no means explicit or required by the sense (2257, note to 6.4).

98. Interestingly, in the Armenian *Life of Saint Eugenia*, when a virgin named Basilia becomes a Christian, she is baptized by a bishop, who came to her "and illumined her with holy baptism" (*Eugenia* 20, trans. Conybeare 1894).

inconceivably, they also reflect some alteration to the underlying Greek texts.[99] Beyond this, just how much revision the Thecla story may have undergone remains elusive.

Interestingly, in one longer ending,[100] having come to Seleucia, Thecla retreats to a cave, where some "well-born women" hear[101] about Thecla, come to her, learn the *logia*[102] of God, and even live an ascetic life with her. In this version of the story, Thecla is a miracle worker and model ascetic, who gathers a community of similarly minded female ascetics around her.[103] These women are said to learn (*emanthanon*), although Thecla is not explicitly said to teach. Paul's earlier instruction to her to go forth and teach the word of God remains, but it is subordinated to this other image, and nothing in the text represents Thecla teaching men. Her role as teacher is thus minimized, although perhaps not completely eliminated.

In another manuscript of this longer ending, the phrase *kai pollous photisasa*, and so forth, appears to be absent.[104] If this phrase generated or, at least, facilitated the view that Thecla had baptized persons other than herself, its absence (or removal) from this version would effectively negate or, at least, no longer support, such an understanding. In this manuscript, the claim that Thecla is anxious to teach the city of Seleucia, which contains many lawless "Hellenes" more or less replaces the phrase that "she enlightened many."

This question of alterations, although perhaps unresolvable, is not insignificant. Cooper's critique, for instance, presumes that the text of Thecla was not composed to support women's teaching and baptizing, regardless of its utility and usage in those debates. At the same time, her thesis provides little explanation for why, in this story, Paul explicitly directs Thecla to go forth and

99. See Haines-Eitzen 2000 for other changes in the Greek manuscript traditions: Shira Lander notes instances of this same tendency in the Armenian translation, in an unpublished seminar paper.

100. Codex G, Bodleian 180, apparently twelfth century.

101. Literally, learn (μαθοῦσαι).

102. Elliot's translation (which I used for this portion in *WRGRW* obscures the conformity with Paul's directive to Thecla to teach "τὸν λογὸν" of God.

103. On these endings, see Davis 2001:39–47. In the ending set in Seleucia, local physicians plot to rape Thecla because she is using her own virginity to usurp the power of Artemis. Depriving the saint of her virginity will thus deprive her of access to Artemis' healing, and restore the power of the physicians. Davis 2001:45–46 notes that this ending accomplishes several things the earlier story lacks. It provides a martyrdom, where Thecla is both protomartyr and apostle; it provides a site of martyrdom (the cave under Zeno's basilica), including a specific site of veneration within the shrine, namely, the rock itself where Thecla disappears; and it accounts for the shrine's lack of relics (since here Thecla chooses to disappear into the rock rather than be raped). The story of Thecla's subterranean journey to Rome serves to authorize a shrine there as well (Davis 2001:46–47).

104. καὶ πολλοὺς θωτίσασα: manuscript M, Vaticanus Graecus 1190, dated to 1542 (but erroneously identified as fourteenth century by Lipsius and Bonnet 1891, and then Vouaux [1913]). Lipsius's apparatus provides no reading for M at this point, presumably because it is absent altogether, but I have been unable to verify this. The printed reading occurs in manuscripts EFKL (d) ms; manuscripts ABC read ἐφώτισεν: G reads πολλοὺς θωτίζουσα τῷ λόγῳ τοῦ χριστοῦ.

teach the word of God, instruction that seems to have no particular function in a narration of power struggles between Christian males and their elite opponents and that is absent in all the otherwise somewhat similar tales in the *Acts of Andrew, Peter, Thomas,* and *John.* Such a directive does, however, make sense in a different power struggle, one between diverse Christian interpreters of Paul's teachings about gender and authority. Were the text to include a much lengthier description of Thecla's subsequent baptizing and teaching, it might be harder to argue that those elements do not, in fact, reflect something of the intentions of the story's formulators. Certainly, many scholars think that such practices of textual alteration characterized the other side of this debate. The author of the Pastorals invoked Paul's authority to argue unambiguously that women could not teach, and someone, perhaps even the author of the Pastorals, may have inserted into 1 Corinthians the famous verses, 14:33b–36, attempting to restrict women's speech in the communal assembly.

Conclusions

Thirty-some-odd years after I first wrote about Thecla, it seems an infinitely more complex tale, confirming, of course, the insights of literary theorists that readers are always implicated in the meanings of texts. It is far more apparent to me that gender constructions play major roles in the structure and elements of the Thecla narrative that complicate, indeed compromise, our ability to read these texts as transparent verisimilitude. Cooper's critique is a significant corrective to earlier work on Thecla that paid insufficient attention to the rhetorical interests at work in the construction of the story. I and earlier scholars certainly initially neglected these lines of analysis, and even some more recent scholars continue to avoid them. The critiques of Boughton, Dunn, Schneemelcher, and others against Davies, MacDonald, and Burrus, focus on the narrower questions of female composition, authorship, and the possible existence of some ancient approximation of a modern feminist movement, and on the seemingly distorting bias of some contemporary scholars (not, of course, themselves), rather than on the rhetorical, ahistorical interests of the ancient texts themselves. These scholars still continue to treat ancient sources as historically useful, and their complaint here is merely that a "bad" history is being produced. Although refuting the views of Boughton and Dunn to some extent, Bremmer and some of his students still continue to work with similar methodological and theoretical frameworks. Matthews and Davis are more sophisticated in their understanding of the issues, particularly Matthews, but both conclude that Cooper's rejection of virtually any historical and social verisimilitude behind the texts is excessive. Davis responds somewhat briefly to Cooper and to Elizabeth Clark who, he thinks, "helpfully redirect our attention to the ways in which texts were used to negotiate power between social groups," but he finds their approaches "a bit too pessimistic about the historian's ability to read ancient narratives for insight in the social roles of early Christian women." He argues again for verisimilitude, and he cites interesting ethnographic studies showing that women storytellers incorporate details of their own lives into their stories.[105] For him, the important potential instances of verisimiltude are Thecla's asceticism, travel, and the relation of charismatic wandering women to settled local communities. Davis takes a middle ground on issues of authorship: he thinks that women storytellers may well have been responsible for the tales, but that they were assembled by Tertullian's presbyter.[106]

It now seems clear to me that what's being argued in *Thecla*, as in Justin Martyr's *Apology* (with which *Thecla* may have some indeterminate connection), is that Christians are the true bearers of morality and piety, as demonstrated in their women, who function generally in antiquity to index the presence or absence of these qualities in any particular social group. Gender reversal is here central to the critique leveled by the text. Christian women are the ultimate exemplars of masculine morality and piety, compared to whom even Christian men are deficient in this regard, or at least less impressive. And elite polytheist men, presumed by the dominant culture of the second and third centuries to be the most suitable exemplars of morality and piety are, on the contrary, demonstrably the least virtuous, in all senses of the word.

With Davis and Matthews, I concur that Cooper's pessimism about historical reconstruction is excessive, although my reasons for thinking so and my interests in the project as a whole are somewhat different. In my view, Cooper's position is compromised for a variety of reasons. In part, as I argued earlier, it is because she focuses too much on the intentions of the author, having failed to see that the text we have does not afford us that access for various reasons; in part because of the circularity of her argument about function; and in part because she does not allow for the very real possibility that the surviving text(s) has been already altered, excising precisely the portions that point, at least hypothetically, to a different function and, therefore, intention on the part of whoever is responsible for the formulation of the story of *Thecla*.

I continue to think that there is some verisimilitude here, although perhaps not as much as I initially assumed thirty-some years ago. I am probably

---

105. Davis 2001:18–19.

106. Davis 2001:14–18: his argument relies, in part, on Tertullian's use of the verbs "contruere" (put together), and "cumulare" (amassing it). See also Davis 2000.

less confident in my initial reading that the descriptions of Thecla, Maximilla, Drusiana, and others as elite, childless, and so forth tell us something of the demographics of women who would have found ascetic forms of Christianity appealing, although I continue to think that the use of anthropological analogies for such movements and their adherents is worth pursuing, if from a better database.

Still, I remain convinced that actual social circumstances and debates underlie the story of Thecla particularly, and the stories of other celibate, ascetic women in the various apocryphal *Acts*. It presently seems to me that in some early Christian communities, including those of the second and third centuries C.E., probably in Asia Minor, North Africa, and perhaps elsewhere, the question of women's prerogative to baptize, teach, and exercise authority, self-control, and control over others, activities that were clearly construed as "masculine" prerogatives in the thinking of many ancient persons, was a real issue.

Part of my assessment here relies on the specific element of the Thecla narrative in which Paul commissions Thecla to go forth and teach the word of God. Cooper's thesis of these narratives as vehicles for male exploration of competing claims of masculinity simply does not explain why Paul would do so, or more precisely, why someone would fashion and/or transmit a story in which the apostle does so. Cooper presumes that the relationship between this element of the story and any actual practice or argument was expedient, at best; "misreaders" of the story drew on the Thecla tale to license a practice the author had no intention of authorizing.

At most, I suppose one might argue that Paul's commissioning of Thecla is the final demonstration of her transformation into the perfect masculinity that exemplifies Christianity. (Celibate) Christians are so virtuous that even their women can exercise masculine authority over others, or perhaps, put differently: celibate Christians, even women, are all male. Yet even this does not explain why the text chooses to demonstrate Thecla's masculinity in this particular form, especially when none of the other comparable stories does so.[107] The visibility of the other side of this argument, in 1 Tim 2.12, points further to a live debate, and not merely a fantastical imagining of gender reversal, despite the utility of narratives of women exercising masculine authority for the expression of social inversion and disorder, as has been argued, for instance, in the Greek narratives of Amazon women.

Women's teaching and baptism, as well as their more general exercise of authority over others appears closely linked with celibacy, both socially and

---

107. Although the account of Mariamme in the *Acts of Philip* (Bovon, Bouvier, and Amsler 1999), probably fourth/fifth century, may be another such instance.

theoretically. This is, at many levels, highly unsurprising.[108] In the ancient Mediterranean (and indeed in many cultures), women's lack of autonomy and authority over others is directly correlated with heterosexual intercourse. Women (perhaps by definition)[109] are liable to be penetrated by men, with or without consent. This fundamental passivity was seen to be inconsistent with the exercise of active authority. These associations are particularly visible in ancient ideas about female prophecy. Women prophets are virtually always celibate, apparently on the cultural logic that a woman who is penetrated by a man, and under his authority, cannot be the conduit for divine speech. Here again, analogies between the vagina and the mouth; between heterosexual intercourse and divine possession/prophecy, are very much at work.[110] A woman whose sexuality is controlled by a man, particularly a man with whom she is liable for sexual intercourse, cannot exercise authority over men; however, apparently, a celibate woman could, both because she was not under male authority, and also because her abstinence from the defining act of female submission and subordination, sexual penetration, perhaps allowed her to be constructed as sufficiently male/masculine.

Like the fictional Thecla, then, real celibate women had the actual freedom to travel, teach, baptize, and so forth, a freedom available (if also contested) precisely because they were not constrained by the responsibilities of marriage, childbearing, and domestic tasks. Similarly, like the fictional Thecla, real celibate women escaped to some extent, an underlying ideological system of gender relations that subordinates women to men, female to male, and so forth. It is this point that I particularly did not see, at least in anything like this framework, over thirty years ago. Nevertheless, my use of Burridge's idea of measures of prestige to develop the notion of specific "measures of a [wo]man"[111] is

108. See, e.g., Kitch 1989. For a more problematic case, see Gutschow 2004.

109. See Parker 1997.

110. In a fine seminar paper several years ago, Jesse Goodman (Brown '04) argued that in Aeschylus' *Oresteia*, Cassandra's role as prophet relies on ideas about prophecy as sexuality. True prophecy is wifely fidelity: the male god inseminates his prophet with his true words as the husband inseminates his wife with his own seed. Underlying this is also a notion of conception as solely the result of male action, a theory that Apollo himself articulates in the play. Thus, prophecy comes only from the male god, and the female prophet is simply the passive receptacle and deliverer, as the wife is of legitimate children. And as legitimate children are validated by public acceptance of them as such, so legitimate prophecy must be validated by public acceptance of the truth of the god's words. Furthermore, then, the female prophet must have the same fundamental characteristics as the faithful wife: her fidelity must be unassailable. This may illuminate some of the anxiety ancient Christian writers have about female prophets, both Christian and otherwise, even while they concede that God can choose to prophesy through a woman if God so chooses. The "orthodox" example they often cite—that of the prophesy of Mary in Luke—that "henceforth all women shall call me blessed," raises precisely some of these problems, since Mary is herself pregnant with the true male child of the true God. One of Origen's objections to the Greek oracle, the Pythia, was precisely that she was female, and not a male through whom God speaks on account of male virtue (*Against Celsus* 7.5–6).

111. Burridge 1969, esp. 42–48.

clearly relevant, still, if inadequately expressed. That is, Burridge certainly didn't think in terms of gender systems (although he did note the appeal of millenarian movements to women), but it's probably still true that certain kinds of social movements do, whether intentionally or otherwise, address, critique, and transform ideologies of gender.

Although the associations of celibacy and female autonomy are already visible in philosophical circles, they may also have their basis in ancient Jewish and Christian speculation on Genesis, as I have argued for the Therapeutae, and has been argued for the *Gospel of Thomas* and various "gnostic" texts, 1 Corinthians and others.[112] Being in Christ abolishes the state of "*arsen kai thelu*" (Gen 1.26; Gal 3.28)[113] that characterized the primordial human, and reverses the actions of Adam and Eve, undoing gender and gender distinctions. With the abolition of gender distinction went human sexuality (or perhaps vice versa), but in either case, the practical ramifications would have been quite similar: celibate women could do what men did, however contested the practice and the theory might have been in some quarters.

If, then, the story of *Thecla* in particular does still point both to actual ancient Christian women baptizing, teaching, and exercising authority in various other forms, as well as contestations over those practices, is it necessary to return to the question of at least some female participation in the formulation and transmission of these stories? In his recent study of the ancient cult of *Thecla*, Davis invokes ethnographic studies of women storytellers to support the possibility that ancient Christian women actively engaged in story formulation and wove details of their own experiences into the tales they told.[114] Yet it is important to remember that we should presume no easy correlation between the sex of the storytellers and the concepts of gender to which they subscribed. Male adherents to particular interpretations of Genesis, and of the "word of God" could surely have envisioned Thecla. And yet, I do sometimes wonder whether the extensive articulation of loving female relationships in *Thecla* is at least consistent with the possibility of female formulation, particularly if, as I suggested earlier, it is difficult to think of a compelling (male) interest behind those aspects of the story.

If it is also true that texts in antiquity are, by their very nature an exercise of authority, what, exactly, is the text of *Thecla* doing? I now think that *Thecla* is in some respects quite subversive, even while it continues to reinforce certain dominant values, arrogating them to Christians. Compared to various

---

112. Davies 1992.
113. Interestingly, though, this pair "male and female" is absent in the version of this saying in Col 3.11.
114. Davis 2001.

early Christian writings such as Acts, or the Pastoral epistles (with which it seems to be entangled) this text is *not* arguing that Christians are exemplars of Roman family values.[115] Rather, it reconfigures social and familial relations, at most arguing that (certain, ascetic) Christians are exemplars of some but not all such values. They are exemplars of traditional philosophical virtues of self-control; truthfulness, and so forth, even while in their renunciation of marriage, sexuality, and childbearing, they are not exemplars of traditional social values.

So, too, *Thecla* challenges gender constructions to some degree, or at least gender constraints, in asserting quite explicitly that (virgin) females may teach, act autonomously, and so forth. At the same time, it also relies on those constructions for the logic of the story: Christians are constructed as "female" yet are ultimately the true exemplars of masculinity; their opponents are constructed as "male" but are ultimately the true exemplars of femininity. *Thecla* does not, actually, propose an alternative system of gender, nor challenge the assumptions of feminine weakness or masculine strength. Rather, it continues to map those onto the Self and the Other.

The location of the "text" within the broader structure or framework of the *Acts of Paul* probably functions to subordinate some of the critique of Thecla to other interests: that is, to domesticate it somewhat, and certainly to rehabilitate Paul, whose presentation in *Thecla* is not terribly flattering, Tertullian's claims about its author's intentions notwithstanding. In fact, Tertullian's claims are themselves the earliest demonstrable attempt to respond to the challenges posed by the story.

Three decades ago, scholars like Davies and Burrus saw contemporary utility in the possibility that women were responsible for the story of Thecla. Such a thesis provided both real women authors to interrogate, at least through their creations, and historical precedents for contemporary (Christian) women in search of legitimation for their leadership roles in contemporary Christian churches. When I first began my scholarly work on women's religions in antiquity, real women to interrogate were highly appealing; historical precedents for women leaders intriguing but not personally compelling. I thought then, and think now, that it is both unwise and unnecessary to rely on historical precedent to authorize contemporary women's rights. I no longer think, if I ever did, that it is terribly useful to posit female authors, and then explicate those texts as windows into the thoughts and experiences of ancient women; on the contrary, I think it is generally inadvisable to do so, except perhaps as a self-conscious thought experiment.

---

115. On which, see D'Angelo 2003a; 2003b.

Ultimately, then, it really doesn't matter whether the story comes from women. The arguments both of MacDonald and now Davis are plausible, namely, that there would have been women storytellers and that this might have been a story they would tell, although one might argue that MacDonald's arguments are primarily based on literary allusions that are themselves likely to be rhetorical (in the Pastorals particularly). Davis's analogies from modern ethnography are a somewhat different kind of argument, and interesting, if ultimately unresolvable. But in the end, I think it matters less who formulates the story and more what possibilities the story licenses in antiquity. What its formulators intended is also intriguing but, again, inaccessible, although I continue to think it plausible that the formulators of the Thecla story really did intend to legitimate certain alternative roles for women. This may call for caution; not inconceivably, Paul's commissioning of Thecla, which comes at the very end of the tale, could have been appended to an already circulating story that does not end with the martyrdom of either Thecla or Paul. At the very least, whoever is responsible for the element of Paul's commissioning of Thecla, and her going forth to teach the word of God, and illumine/baptize many, really does mean to legitimate women. Who that might have been remains beyond the limits of our present knowledge.

5

Artemisia of Minorca

Gender and the Conversion of the Jews
in the Fifth Century

Introduction

Various late antique Christian sources report that in the early
fifth century C.E., the bones of the first century martyr, St. Stephen,[1]
were discovered in the holy land.[2] Numerous miracles were said to
attend the distribution of the relics across the Mediterranean.[3]
Most striking among these is a Latin narrative describing how
the entire Jewish[4] community of Minorca converted to Christianity
shortly after some of the bones of Stephen were brought to the
tiny island off the coast of Spain. Known as the *Letter on the
Conversion of the Jews*, the narrative claims to be written by one
Severus of Minorca, recently appointed the island's orthodox

This chapter also appears as Kraemer 2009, with the knowledge of the editors of *JECS*.

1. Acts 6.8–7.60.

2. According to the *Revelation of Saint Stephen* (PL 41.807–81, as the *Epistula Luciani*), a
Christian priest named Lucianus had a dream in which the first-century rabbi, Gamaliel, appeared
to him and revealed the location of his bones, those of Stephen, and two others: Vanderlinden
1946; see Jacobs 2003:29–32.

3. E.g., Evodius, *On the Miracles of the Protomartyr, Saint Stephen*, PL 41:833–54; *The Passion
of St. Stephen*, translated in van Esbroeck, 1984:101–5. See Bradbury 1996:16–25. Particularly
interesting are the accounts in Augustine, *City of God* 22.8 (CCSL 48:815–27) of miracles effected at
shrines of St. Stephen in North Africa almost a decade after the events of the *Letter* of Severus. For
discussion, see Lander 2002.

4. By the fifth century C.E., the translation "Jewish," rather than "Judean," seems more
appropriate, and I use it throughout this chapter. For further discussion, see the Introduction and
chapter 7.

bishop.[5] The *Letter* is striking for many reasons, not the least of which is its apparent unique description of a late antique Latin-speaking diaspora Jewish community, and of their extensive social relationships with Minorcan Christians. Particularly fascinating, though, is its representation of several elite Jewish women as the last to convert, after all their male relatives and compatriots had accepted Christianity.

Because it is a text few have studied, I will provide a summary of the *Letter*, which highlights the gaps and evasions I will explore further later. I will then consider issues of authenticity, historicity, artifice, and power relations in the construction of the letter, before turning to a detailed analysis of the accounts of these women, who serve as the ultimate exemplars of Jewish stubbornness in the face of the reasonableness and truth of Christianity. I will argue that the uses of gender in these narratives, particularly the representation of women as the last to convert, suggests alternative explanations for both the stories and their prominent location at the conclusion of the *Letter* that in turn call into question their historicity.

Summary of the *Letter*

According to the *Letter*, shortly after an unnamed priest[6] brought the relics to the church in one of Minorca's two towns, Magona (modern-day Mahon), the local Christian community was seized by a desire to convert the substantial and influential Jewish community there. The author is highly evasive about what, precisely, the Christians did to effect their desire, but apparently, the two communities had agreed to a public debate (6.6). Previously cordial relations between individual Christians and Jews were ruptured as a result of Christian pressures (5.1).

In relatively short order, word was sent to the head of the Jewish community, a man named Theodorus, who had left Minorca to attend to estate business on the larger island of Majorca. Again somewhat evasively, the author indicates that Theodorus returned quickly and temporarily restrained the

---

5. Critical edition, lengthy introduction, translation, and brief notes now in Bradbury 1996; also Amengual i Batle 1991. For additional references to earlier editions, see Bradbury 1996:72–77. A fuller title occurs in some manuscripts—*Epistula Severi episcopi de conversione Iudaeorum apud Minorciam insulam meritis sancti Stephani facta*: "The Letter of Bishop Severus on the Conversion of the Jews on the island of Minorca accomplished by the merit of St. Stephen."

6. The priest, however, is known to have been Paul Orosius; see Bradbury 1996:20–25, who dates Orosius's visit to Minorca to late summer or perhaps fall, 416 C.E., a year and a half before the events narrated by Severus. Bradbury thus thinks that Severus had been endeavoring for some time to pressure the Minorcan Jewish community (Bradbury 1996:25).

Christians (7.2). Nevertheless, both sides continued to gird for battle. The Jews not only consulted their scriptures but apparently amassed weapons in the synagogue, fearing physical attack by the Christians (8.5). The Christians' preparation is cloaked in elusive language, but the author suggests that the Jews' weaponry would be of no avail, because the Christian battle line was defended by the power of the holy Spirit.[7]

The coming events were, the author maintains, prefigured in several dreams whose similarity the author offers as evidence of their divine origins and trustworthiness. A dedicated Christian virgin named Theodora, and Severus himself, both dreamed that an elite widow begged Severus to sow all her fields (10.1–4). The author is explicit that the widow symbolizes the synagogue, widowed by her own impious murder of Christ (10.4–5) and now repentant. Seemingly aware that claiming such dreams after the fact is suspicious, the author insists that he had this dream thirty days prior to its fulfillment, and recounted it publicly without understanding its meaning at the time (10.6). The Jewish leader Theodorus had a different dream, which the author claims Theodorus, too, recounted publicly before its fulfillment. On his way to the synagogue, twelve men barred his path, warning him of a lion in the synagogue. Frightened, Theodorus nevertheless managed to peer into the synagogue, where he saw monks singing terribly sweetly.[8] The sight of monks in the synagogue terrified him even more, and he ran first to the house of a Jew named Reuben, then to an unnamed female relative (*mater propinqua*),[9] who soothed him and rescued him from his terror (11.6).

Inspired by the power of Stephen, Christians from Jamona, the other town on Minorca, now travel the thirty miles to Magona. Upon their arrival, Severus invites the Jews to come to the church, apparently for a disputation on the Law (12.6). The Jews, however, refuse, claiming that to do so would violate the Sabbath. Severus scoffs, pointing out that the Jews were hardly being forced into "menial labor on the Sabbath," but rather being invited to a calm debate. Suggesting that their refusal is a ruse to avoid the debate altogether, Severus even challenges the Jews to show "the rule by which it was prohibited for them to engage in discussion on a holy day."[10]

---

7. *Letter* 8.5: *Ut Christianorum aciem virtute Sancti Spiritus praemunitam.*

8. *Letter* 11.4: *monachos illic mira suavitate psallentes.*

9. *Letter* 11.5. Severus is explicit that the *propinqua* is explicitly the church: she is "that one of whom it is written, 'una est propinqua mea,'" although Bradbury notes that there is no such line in the Vulgate, although he thinks it's similar to Song 6.8: *una est columba mea perfecta mea*, Bradbury 1996:127 n. 10. The figure of the otherwise unidentified *propinqua* thus represents the orthodox church as a female relative who clasps Theodorus to her bosom and provides him complete solace, contributing to Severus's representation of the synagoge and church as close kin.

10. *Letter* 12.6: *praeceptum quo in die festo sermonem his conferre prohibitum sit.*

Whatever ultimately compelled them to do so, the Jews show up at the house where Severus is staying in Magona. Rather than begin a disputation, he immediately asks them why they have stored up weapons in the synagogue? The Christians, he says, have brought books to instruct; the Jews weapons to commit murder. You, he says, "thirst for our blood; we for your salvation."[11] The Jews deny this is the case, and offer an oath, but Severus brushes them off, pointing out that an oath is pointless when the truth can be easily discerned by going to the synagogue itself.

En route to the synagogue, a particularly strange scene ensues. The Christians chant Ps. 9.7–8, "Their memory has perished with a crash, and the Lord endures forever."[12] Although this is obviously a pointed refrain whose referent is understood (by both the author and his Christian readers) to be the Jews, they also join the singing, with "a wondrous sweetness" (13.2: *mira iucunditate*).

While they are walking, violence breaks out. Once again the author is evasive, particularly on the culpability of the Christians. The instigators are allegedly "certain Jewish women" (13.3: *quaedam Iudaeae mulieres*), who throw down stones on the Christians from some higher vantage point. God, the author claims, used the women as a vehicle to rouse the Christians from their so far gentle behavior (*lenitas*). The Christians then pick up the stones to throw at the Jews, although the author distances himself from their behavior, and suggests that they were motivated more by zeal for Christ than by (inappropriate) anger. Just as, miraculously, none of the stones thrown by the women hurt anyone, so, too, none of the Jews is hurt, nor do any even pretend that they have been so, although they might have been expected to feign injury to stir up ill will (13.7). Severus concedes, however, that one man among the Christians did throw a stone. Although that man had intended to hit a Jew, in fact, he hit the slave of one of the Christians, who had come, not out of love of Christ, but out of greed for plunder. An episode of Jewish women who throw stones and Christian men who restrain their (natural?) desire to reciprocate seems particularly telling in a narrative that begins by evoking the stoned protomartyr, Stephen.

The story of the greedy slave serves as the context (or, perhaps, the pretext) for one of the text's most evasive passages. Hit on the head, the slave recalled his true head, Christ, and "put fear in everyone lest they lapse in a similar way. Therefore, after the Jews had retreated and we had gained control of the synagogue" (13.11–12), the author relates, no one stole or looted anything. However, what caused the Jews to retreat and how the Christians gained control of the synagogue is glossed over quickly in those six words: *posteaquam Iudaeis*

---

11. *Letter* 12.10: *Vos vero . . . sititis nostrum sanguinem, nos vestram salutem.*

12. *Letter* 13.2: *Periit memoria eorum cum strepitu et Dominus in aeternum permanet.*

cedentibus synagoga potiti sumus (13.12). With similar brevity and avoidance of agency, human or otherwise, the author tells us that "fire consumed the synagogue itself" and all its ornaments. Who set or what caused the fire passes unremarked. All that survived was the silver, which the Christians dutifully returned to the Jews, lest they be accused of taking spoils, and the sacred books, which the Christians kept to prevent the Jews from harming them.[13] With the Jews now in shock at the devastation of the synagogue, the Christians retreat to the church and pray for the conversion of the Jews. The very next day, part of Theodorus's dream is fulfilled: a Jew named Reuben does indeed accept Christ.

Although the author does not remark on the significance of the interval, three days then pass while the Christians prayed and the Jews "persevered in faithlessness" (16.2: *in perfidia perstiterunt*). Theodorus then comes with his supporters to the ruins of the synagogue, where he offers various arguments that the Christians are unable to refute on their own, leading them to pray to God for assistance. What Severus represents as a miracle then occurs. The Christians shout aloud, "Theodorus, believe in Christ" (16.4: *Theodore, credas in Christum*). Miraculously, though, the Jews mishear this as "Theodorus has believed in Christ" (16.7: *Theodorus in Christum credidit*) and, although the author insists they have no cause for fear, they nevertheless become terrified.

For the second time in the narrative, Jewish women are now distinguished in their response from the men. "Racing together" in a state of disarray, they shriek, "Theodorus, what have you done" (16.8). Some of the men seek to hide in town, while others flee to the groves and mountains. Now more of Theodorus's dream is fulfilled. Finding himself abandoned by his companions, he, too, seeks refuge, standing on the very spot where, in his dream, he had been terrified by the thought of the Lion in the synagogue. As in his dream, Reuben appears and comforts him, inviting him to accept Christ. Ultimately, Theodorus agrees, but asks for time to address his people, and bring them with him (16.16).

At the news of Theodorus's acceptance of Christ, the Christians are overjoyed. In a somewhat remarkable scene, "Some ran to him affectionately and caressed his face and neck with kisses, others embraced him in gentle arms, while still others longed to join right hands with him or to engage him in conversation."[14] Still apparently following the outline of Theodorus's dream, Severus relates that Theodorus set out for his own home, not completely calmed by Reuben, for he had yet to come to the house of the female relative

---

13. This is a particularly peculiar claim that might be grounded in the Christian theory that the Jews altered their copies of scripture to delete or revise readings favorable to Christian interpretation.

14. Letter 16.18: *Alii in eum amabiliter irruentes, os ipsius osculis et colla mulcebant; alii eum ulnis mollibus complectebantur; alii autem dexteram dexterae adiungere aut sermonen conserere gestiebant.*

who would completely free him from all confusion and fear. The Christians, however, set out for the church again singing hymns, a concatenation of 2 Cor 1.3 and Jer 9.1. Coming out after services, they find a large group of (gender unspecified) Jews, asking for "the symbol of Christ," so Severus returns inside the church and "marked the sign of salvation on their foreheads" (17.3).

At this point, Severus returns to those men who had fled the town earlier. Remarking that each person has his own individual conversion story (18.1), he offers just a few examples, whose authenticity is guaranteed by the trustworthiness and character of his sources (18.3). First, he tells the story of two leading Jewish men, Theodorus's own brother, named Meletius, and one Innocentius, a refugee from the recent barbarian invasions of Spain. Although they initially hide out in the rocky areas above the town, a series of minor miraculous events compels them to accept Christ and return to Magona, where, contrary to their expectations, they find Theodorus safe and sound and still a Jew (although not for very much longer). Then he narrates the experiences of several Jews who resist Theodorus's plan to bring the Jews to Christ himself, because they have themselves already felt the divine call to conversion. These include a young man conveniently named Galilaeus,[15] an elder named Caecilianus, and his brother, Florianus, both *patres synagogae*, who collectively urge their fellow Jews to "abandon the error of our misguided way, if it can be done, and unite together in the faith of the church." Even if they cannot persuade others, they themselves, together with their households, "will join in alliance with the faithful ranks of the Christians" (19.8–9).

The author then narrates several miracles evocative of the Exodus from Egypt, which he proffers as evidence that the Jews were now making an exodus from the Egypt and slavery of their unbelief (20.15), under divine guidance. First, two monks lying in a field outside the church saw a ball of brilliant light. The same sight was also seen from an upper story by several Jewish women who had not yet converted, including Meletius's wife. Shortly before this, a fine dusting, redolent of honey, had fallen on the island, prompting the people to draw an explicit connection to the manna God provided the true Israel, and the fiery column that accompanied them out of Egypt (20.15–21).

On the day that Theodorus was expected to fulfill his promise to convert and to bring the remaining unconverted Minorcan Jews with him, he again demurred, this time because his wife was still back on Majorca, and he feared that "if she learned that her husband had converted without her agreement," she would "remain firm in her faithlessness, as usually happens" (21.2). Continuing with his representation of the Christians as ever fair and conciliatory,

---

15. Bradbury 1996:37, finds it somewhat odd that a Jew in the early fifth century C.E. would have been given a name long associated with Christians.

the author claims that the Christians were willing, but those Jews already con-verted acted contrarily. The final part of Theodorus's dream is now fulfilled, as "he flew swiftly to the bosom of his kinswoman," now explicitly identified as the church (21.3). He was followed by the whole synagogue, whose abandon-ment of disputation the author takes as marvelous, if not miraculous (*mirum dictu*). Even some Jews who had just stopped on the island while waiting for favorable winds to resume their journey, and were completely free to go, chose, the author claims, to become Christians (23).

The author thus saves for the final portion of the narrative the conversion accounts of three Jewish women, who held out until the very end. The first of these was Artemisia, wife of Meletius. The two other hold-outs were the wife of Innocentius, the refugee from Spain who accompanied Meletius during his brief flight, and her sister, "a widow of excellent reputation." (26.1: *sorore sua venerabili, sicut fama testis est, vidua*). Under circumstances that I'll consider in detail later, all three women ultimately accept Christ, and the conversion of the Jews of Minorca is complete.

Severus's narrative ends with a few details and summations. Five hundred and forty Jews, he claims, were added to the church. As proof of the fruits of righteousness produced by their conversion, the Jews are now bearing the expense, not only of leveling what remained of their synagogue, but also the expense of building a new basilica, whose stones they even carry on their own shoulders (30.2). Yet again, Severus says nothing about just how these events came about. He closes with an exhortation to his reader(s) to "take up Christ's zeal against the Jews, but do so for the sake of their eternal salvation." For perhaps, he writes, the fullness of the Gentiles and the salvation of all Israel predicted by the apostle (Paul) has finally come (31.2–3).

Authenticity and Historicity of the *Letter*

Given the *Letter's* potential utility for reconstructing both an otherwise undocu-mented diaspora Jewish community, and its transformation into Christianity, it is essential to consider both the authenticity of its authorship, and the probable degree of its historical reliability. The relationship between authenticity and historicity is, of course, quite complex: that the *Letter* is the "authentic" work of Severus, bishop of Minorca, in the early fifth century C.E. does not, of course, guarantee its reliable presentation of particular persons and events. Conversely (if less likely), its pseudonymous composition would not inherently signal the complete invention of the events it relates, but it would certainly warrant extreme caution, if not complete skepticism.

Various earlier scholars, especially B. Blumenkranz, argued that it was not, in fact, a contemporaneous composition by a fifth century Minorcan bishop but a later fabrication.[16] More recent scholars have argued, however, that the *Letter* is definitely authentic, citing in particular the relatively recent discovery and publication, in 1981, of two letters to Augustine from another Minorcan Christian named Consentius, one of which explicitly refers to "certain miraculous things" recounted in some narrative by Severus.[17] Bradbury argues at some length that certain details in the letter, particularly the author's accurate knowledge of early fifth century festal dates, make it unlikely that the work could be the production of a much later forger, as some earlier scholars had argued.[18]

Beyond these arguments, certain elements of the letter seem to me to provide additional support for the position that the letter is a genuine work of Severus of Minorca in response to a mass conversion of Jews on Minorca in 418 C.E. following (although not necessarily immediately) the arrival of what were taken to be relics of St. Stephen. Bradbury is well-aware of the anti-Jewish character of the *Letter*, and he notes that it claims to be accompanied by a tract of arguments to be used in disputes with Jews, although no such tract has been transmitted with it in the manuscript tradition.[19] Yet when compared with the invective of other late antique anti-Jewish writing, such as Chrysostom's *Against Judaizing Christians*, or Tertullian's *Against the Jews*, the anti-Jewish rhetoric in the *Letter*

16. E.g., Blumenkranz 1960: for details and additional references, see Bradbury 1996:9–14.

17. E.g., Hunt 1982; Wankenne and Hambenne 1987; Fontaine 1991:120; Bradbury 1996:15; see also Amengual i Batle 2001. Reviewers of Bradbury are routinely accepting of his detailed arguments refuting Blumenthal. The letters of Consentius may be found in Divjak 1981; English translation in Eno 1989. In *Letter* *12, Consentius claims that he himself had sworn off writing, so that he could devote himself to reading scripture. Severus, however, apparently prevailed on Consentius to write something of these events, which Severus then incorporated into his own letter: "he [Severus] borrowed from me [Consentius] words alone in order that he himself might write a letter containing a narrative of the events" (*ut epistolam quae rei gestae ordinem contineret ipse conscriberet, sola a me verba mutuatus est*), *Letter* 12*13.3–6, in Bradbury 1996:59. The precise literary relationship between whatever Consentius wrote and the present *Letter* is unclear. Bradbury critiques scholars who have suggested that Consentius actually intended to write his own narrative, but was pre-empted by Severus (Bradbury 1996:58 n. 153). Fontaine 1991 argues that Severus reworked Consentius's version, intentionally using a simpler style that functioned to critique the larger literary culture of which Consentius was a representative. After a detailed discussion of Consentius *Letter* *11, where Consentius argues, against Augustine, for a coercive response to Priscillianists in Tarragona, Bradbury concludes that "the similarities between the accounts of events on Minorca and in Tarragona raise the possibility that Consentius was more deeply involved in the composition of the *Epistula Severi* than we had suspected," Bradbury 1996:69. J. N. Hillgarth 1994:730 supports the thesis that Consentius "must at least have been responsible for the organization of the circular, if he was not in fact its real author."

18. The author claims (*Letter* 12.4) that he arrived in Magona on February 2, which was the Jewish Sabbath: in 418 C.E. February 2 was, indeed, a Saturday. He also claims that these events occurred before Lent: in 418 C.E., the first Sunday of Lent fell on February 24; Bradbury argues that no seventh-century forger would have known these details accurately (Bradbury 1996:12).

19. Bradbury notes the thesis of Seguí Vidal that the missing tract might be the well-known *De altercatione ecclesiae et synagogae dialogus* (PL 42:1131–39) (Bradbury 1996:127 n. 8).

seems mild. This restraint seems quite consistent with the historical and social situations both explicit and implicit in the work. That is, if Severus wrote as the bishop of a church that now included a significant number of wealthy and influential former Jews, who continued to hold civic offices and exercise civil and social authority (as the author claims is the case for Theodorus, who remains *patronus*, and Caecilianus, who is now *defensor*, 19.6), he might well find it advantageous to exercise restraint in his use of anti-Jewish language. This restraint could conceivably simply be explained as the subtle strategy of a particularly sophisticated author, but it seems to suggest an author quite sensitive to the actual dynamics of relations between Christians and newly converted influential Jews.

Two other features of the *Letter* are germane to the question of authenticity. Many other ancient Christian anti-Jewish tracts are characterized by an apparent absence of knowledge of actual contemporaneous Jews, and the representations of Jews and Judaism in those texts often strike modern scholars as drawn entirely from biblical texts, whether Jewish or Christian. The representation of Minorcan Jews in the *Letter* contains numerous details that could not have been derived from the "Old" and "New" Testaments, and that are, further, consistent with the limited epigraphical evidence for late antique diaspora Jewish communities, particularly those of the Latin west. Elite Jewish men holding various known civic offices are epigraphically attested in places like Venosa in the fifth/sixth centuries, and the title Severus gives to Theodorus, the transliterated Greek *pater pateron*, occurs also in a roughly contemporaneous inscription from Venosa.[20] Just as the attestation of the title "rabbi" is extremely rare in diaspora Jewish inscriptions before the sixth century, so, too, the title is conspicuously

---

20. *JIWE* 1.114 = *CIJ* I² 619b; dated, with no real certainty, to the fourth or fifth century C.E. Bradbury offers this inscription as another instance of the Jewish usage of the ltitle πατὴρ πατέρων (transliterated in Severus as pater pateron), although it's not entirely clear that the inscription is Jewish, since the title *pater patrum* has numerous attestations in Mithraic inscriptions (see *JIWE* 1, p. 146). Bradbury also cites several other Venosan inscriptions, *JIWE* 1.85 = *CIJ* 1.² 607; *JIWE* 1.68 = *CIJ* I² 610; *JIWE* 1.90 = *CIJ* I² 614, as instances of *pater patrum*. These Latin inscriptions actually contain the abbreviation PP, which earlier epigraphers took as P(rae)p(ositus); it is precisely the explicit Greek title of πατὴρ πατέρων in *JIWE* 1.114 that has been used to read the Latin abbreviation as *pater patrum* (see *JIWE* 1, p. 91; see also Bradbury 1996:32 n. 76). In a somewhat circular fashion, Noy actually cites the occurrence of the title *pater pateron* in Severus to support his interpretation of the abbreviation PP, whereas Bradbury points to the inscription as additional evidence for the probable accuracy of the title. Although the term πατὴρ συναγωγῆς occurs in numerous Jewish inscriptions from Rome and elsewhere (e.g., *JIWE* 2.209, 210, 288, 540, 544, 560, 576, 578, 579, 584), the title πατὴρ πατέρων as a demonstrably Jewish communal title is not attested in other late antique diaspora communities.

The somewhat derogatory designation of Theodorus as "high priest of that faithless people" (*summus sacerdos perfidi populi*: *Letter* 11.2) raises other issues. Severus's use of it is clearly inflammatory and could have been derived from biblical representations, but then again, it might also raise questions about the continuing usage of priestly titles, themselves attested epigraphically (e.g., Samoe of Sardis, *IJO* 2.63); for a discussion of other instances, see Brooten 1982:95–99. Theodorus is also called *legis doctor* (6.2), a phrase that also occurs in Matt 22.35 (Vulgate), referring to the Pharisees, and in Acts 5.34, where it applies to Gamaliel. This last is mildly interesting, since Gamaliel was associated with the burial and rediscovery of the bones of Stephen. See Irshai 2010.

absent from Severus's account.[21] The patterns of names of Minorcan Jews are consistent with the prosopography garnered from western Mediterranean inscriptions, a mixture of Greek (Theodorus; Artemisia), Latin names (Caecilianus, Innocentius, Florianus), and perhaps Hebrew (Reuben). Severus appears to exhibit a relatively sophisticated understanding of the principles of Jewish Sabbath observance that seems difficult to derive from biblical passages alone. When the Jews decline his invitation to come to the church for a disputation because it's the Sabbath, Severus implies that their objections are not consistent with their own laws (12.5–6). He understands that "menial labor" is forbidden, and concedes that entering a church on the Sabbath *might* even be considered a violation of purity regulations. But all he is proposing (or, at least, all he admits to proposing) is a calm discussion of scripture, which is surely not forbidden by Jewish law; he even implies that the Jews would be unable to produce a text (of what sort he doesn't say) that would support such a view.

Taken together with the other evidence Bradbury adduces, I am inclined to think that the *Letter* does refer to the conversion of Minorcan Jews in 418 C.E. and is probably the work of Severus, even if he draws substantially in some way from Consentius. Severus is, in any case, the authorial voice of the narrative, and I will subsequently refer to the author as Severus.

Yet assuming that Severus is the author of the *Letter* still leaves a multitude of issues unresolved. Authenticity of authorship is, by itself, no guarantor that the text conveys accurate historical data. However ancient readers might have read it, to a contemporary reader, Severus appears at the very least disingenuous. His representation of the Christians as uniformly kind, loving, and joyously welcoming of the new Jewish converts stands in tension with his own descriptions of the great fear and anxiety that overcame many of the Jews, a tension heightened by his insistence that their fears were completely ungrounded.[22] Severus omits several key pieces of information that one might have expected him to divulge, such as whether weapons were, in fact, found in the synagogue.[23] He deftly sidesteps the issue of who causes the fire that destroys the synagogue and provides no explanation for how it was that former Jews

---

21. See, e.g., Cohen 1981.

22. It also stands in tension with the long tradition of ancient Christian anti-Jewish rhetoric and violence, but that's not necessarily relevant here, since his portrait of previously amicable relations between Christians and Jews might conceivably be a more reliable representation of the situation on Minorca, where, if Severus's description is viable, the local Jewish community was socially more prominent and powerful than the orthodox Christians.

23. Earlier, Severus simply states that the Jews were amassing weapons in the synagogue, so perhaps the reader is expected to presume their discovery, but it is nevertheless somewhat surprising that he neglects the opportunity to drive home this point when he describes the combined mass of Christians and Jews proceeding to the synagogue to investigate the charge and its refutation.

shouldered (apparently both literally and figuratively) the burden of dismantling the synagogue walls and erecting a new basilica.[24]

Conceivably, some of this relates to the author's awareness of various
imperial legislation prohibiting violence against Jews, the burning of synagogues, and the misappropriation of synagogue property. In 393 C.E., Theodosius (with Arcadius and Honorius) authorized the protection of synagogues from
destruction and despoiling.[25] In 397 C.E., Arcadius (with Honorius) ordered the
Prefect of Illyricum to protect Jews and their synagogues from attacks.[26] Much
closer to the Minorcan events, in 412 C.E., Honorius (with Theodosius II) decreed
that synagogues were not to be damaged or seized, probably a response to the
very recent seizure of a synagogue in Edessa and its conversion to a church.[27]

Whether Severus is likely to have known edicts promulgated in the East is
unclear. Nevertheless, it's particularly interesting that the edict of 412 C.E.
explicitly prohibits summoning Jews on the Sabbath, for any reason whatsoever, "for that day of their religion must not be perturbed by any legal accusation."[28] Further, several edicts issued in the years immediately following the

24. Bradbury 1996:130, takes this to mean on the site of the old synagogue, which is possible, but not
definitive. Nothing in the text conclusively identifies the location of the synagogue, although it and the church
seem to be at some distance from one another. Remains of four early Christian basilicas have been found on
Minorca, some of whose mosaics have been seen as similar to those of various Jewish synagogues in late antiquity (e.g., de Palol 1967a; 1967b: see now also Blázquez 1998, who does not cite Bradbury, and may not have seen
it at the time. The mosaic floor of the basilica of Es Fornás de Torelló, said to date to the sixth century, and thus
apparently too late to be the basilica mentioned in Severus, contains elements particularly frequent in late
antique Jewish decorative programs from the land of Israel as well as from a synagogue floor from Hamman Lif
in North Africa, including lions, peacocks, and the tree of life. De Palol actually took the position that this and
other Minorcan basilicas had been built by former Minorcan Jews (in Blázquez 1998:169). Although some
scholars have argued that these mosaic programs reflect contact with North Africa (citing most notably Hamman
Lif), others, including Blázquez, argue for Palestinian models, either through craftsmen or pattern books. In any
case, the most intriguing basilica is that southwest of the present town of Mahon, in Son Bou, on the beach. In
the 1950s, Seguí Vidal and Hillgarth argued that this basilica is the site of the former synagogue, although de
Palol disagreed (see Bradbury 1996:16 n. 32). Bradbury himself is fairly dismissive of this possibility, even while
he notes that the foundation of the Son Bou basilica could be as early as late fourth century, which would certainly
make it a feasible candidate for the synagogue, were it not so far from Mahon. Bradbury does not discuss the
mosaic programs, nor cite the more detailed article of de Palol: Blázquez's article appeared after Bradbury's book.
Finally, Severus claims that the fire left the walls of the synagogue still standing, and that the Jews subsequently
pulled down the walls and carried its stones for the building of the basilica (*Letter* 30.2). Although this might
suggest that the basilica is not on the same site, if it were, it would suggest that an earlier mosaic floor might have
remained. I hope to explore these issues further in a subsequent article.

25. The sources of these edicts are complex. Although some are preserved only in one source, such as the
Theodotion Code, others are preserved in various sources, often abridged, edited, and otherwise altered. Hence, all
references to imperial legislation here are taken from the extremely helpful edition of Linder 1987. This edict is
Linder 1987: no. 21, pp. 189–91.

26. Linder 1987: no. 25, pp. 197–98.

27. Linder 1987: no. 40; pp. 262–67; esp. 263. As Robert Doran points out in personal communication,
the evidence for the destruction of the synagogue in Edessa comes from the Syriac *Edessene Chronicle*, where its
precise date is unclear.

28. Linder 1987: p. 265.

Minorcan episode and the apparent composition and dissemination of Sever-us' *Letter* (420 C.E.; 423 C.E.) explicitly prohibit the burning of synagogues, the occupation of synagogue property, and other offenses against Jews.[29] The edict of June 423 C.E. is explicit that Christians shall not "raise their hands" against "peaceful Jews and Pagans who are not attempting anything seditious or unlawful."[30] Linder thinks these edicts represent not only a late imperial response to the attacks in Edessa, and in Alexandria in 414 C.E., but also to the more recent rampages of the Syrian monk Bar-Sauma in 419–422 C.E.[31] Whether they also respond to the Minorcan account is unclear, but certainly they would have been quite germane.

All this suggests that Severus's evasive account is a pre-emptive defense against any claims that the actions of the Minorcan Christians were in any way illegal.[32] The Jews were not summoned on the Sabbath, but merely invited for a friendly exchange; the synagogue just happened to burn; the Christians stole nothing and only took certain valuables from the synagogue for their protection. No Jews were ever physically harmed or even at risk. Instead, the only violent perpetrators appear to be Jews, and Jewish women at that, and in any case, the Christians had reason to believe that the Jews were stockpiling weapons, an unresolved charge that could easily have been construed as seditious or unlawful, or, at least, as evidence of their intent to commit crimes against the peaceful Christians. Most scholars presume that the actual events underlying the *Letter*, while perceptible to some degree, were quite different; the Jews were compelled to convert by a combination of pressures including actual physical violence, the threat of violence, and various forms of intimidation, including but not limited to the burning of the synagogue and the confiscation of copies of Jewish scriptures.[33]

Women, Religion, and Gender in the *Letter*

For those with interests in the study of women, religion, gender and history, the representations of women in the *Letter* and its uses of gender are especially vexing. Narratives about potentially historical individual Jewish women from

29. Linder 1987: no. 46 (420 C.E.), pp. 283–86; no. 47 (February, 423 C.E.), pp. 287–89; no. 48 (April, 423 C.E.), pp. 289–95; no. 49 (June, 423 C.E.), 295–301.

30. Linder 1987: p. 299.

31. Linder 1987: p. 263; 288.

32. Bradbury summarizes these edicts in his survey of religious coercion in the fourth and fifth centuries (1996:53–57), but he does not comment on the consonance between the imperial prohibitions and the *Letter*.

33. For a critique of how Peter Brown in particular minimized the "human costs" of these events, see Ginzburg 1996:207.

this period are virtually nonexistent, and an historian could easily be forgiven for wishing that some portion of Severus's accounts of women might be true, however distorted. One can easily sympathize with Bradbury's acceptance of this element of the *Letter* as historically reliable, and his admiration for the courage of the women who clung to their ancestral religion in the face of extraordinary pressure. Yet close analysis suggests that not only do rhetorical strategies dictate much of the rest of the *Letter* as a whole, so, too, what Severus says about women has more to do with the uses of gender in the narrative than it does with actual Minorcan Jewish women. The women who continue to resist conversion serve as the ultimate exemplars of Jewish stubbornness in the face of the reasonableness and truth of Christianity. Gendered as female, this stubbornness is itself configured as feminine insubordination and resistance to divinely licensed masculine authority generally. In several instances, Severus constructs women's resistance to Christianity as marital insubordination and their ultimate acceptance of Christianity as appropriate female submission to marital, ecclesiastical, and divine male authority. Nevertheless, groups of unnamed women, as well as more individually identified women, appear at several interesting points in the narrative. Apart from the Christian Theodora, all the women explicitly present in the text are, in fact, Jewish women.

Groups of Unnamed Women

Severus claims that as the crowd of Christians and Jews was traveling to the synagogue, certain Jewish women (*quaedam Iudaeae mulieres*) "acted recklessly" and threw the first stones that would have triggered a riot, had a minor miracle not intervened to bring the Christians to their senses.[34] He claims that the women threw from some elevated location (*ex superiori loco*), which seems to imply that the women are not traveling with the crowd. Their apparent high vantage point is consonant with the location of women's quarters on the upper stories of ancient houses, as well as with both the image and the reality that women used the flat roofs of houses as a platform from which to view local happenings.[35]

In a different episode, Severus recounts the response of Jewish women upon hearing the (erroneous) news that Theodorus had converted. "Racing together with disheveled hair and wild howling, their women assailed Theodorus

---

34. *Letter* 13.3–12: here 13.3: *audaciam praesumentes.* I think this may mean something more like "presumed to act with audacity."

35. It's also consonant with the topography of parts of Magona (modern Mahon), an issue I plan to explore in a subsequent article on the possible location of the synagogue.

with repeated cries, "Theodorus, what have you done?"[36] The use of *concurrentes* ("racing together") may imply, here as well, that the women are not present at the synagogue disputation but come running at the news. The characterization of the women as "theirs" (*mulieres eorum*) also contributes, if unsurprisingly, to the construction of the "Jews" as really "Jewish men."

In a third instance, Severus claims that the miraculous ball of fire seen by monks in a field outside the church was also seen by several Jewish women who had not yet converted, "as they were looking out of an upper storey."[37] Yet again, this location of the women may contribute to the perception that women are removed from the sphere of much ordinary social male interaction, and reflect a fairly ordinary fact of women's residence in ancient Mediterranean towns. Here, however, it may also provide a convenient vantage point from which the miraculous light could have been seen.

Severus thus deploys gender in various ways. Blaming the women for almost starting a riot maps irrationality, lack of self-control and gender-inappropriate audacity onto women. This entire episode is puzzling. Clearly, it provides an explanation for the events Severus subsequently (and perhaps somewhat defensively) describes, namely, Christian restraint during and after the (unexplained) synagogue fire. It is somewhat hard to imagine why Severus would have constructed this sequence of events in this particular way, given how strained it all seems, and it is tempting to suggest that it reflects, in a vastly duplicitous and apologetic way, some underlying historical realities. Blaming women for throwing the first stones might function to deflect responsibility not only from Christians, who may really have initiated whatever violence took place (culminating in the burning of the synagogue), but also from the Jewish men who, according to Severus, remain in considerable power even after their conversion. It also represents the entire Christian entourage as demonstrating great (masculine?) self-restraint (and perhaps also not violating imperial legislation).

The women's response to Theodorus's apparent (and actually vowed) conversion heightens the representation of Jews as inappropriately and irrationally terrified. Ancient readers may have associated the description of the women with disheveled hair (*sparsis crinibus*) and shrieking wildly (*cum ferali ululatu*) with women's mourning practices. Alternatively, it might suggest that the women thought the situation so dire that they rushed out in public with their hair inappropriately loose, screaming animal-like noises. Either contributes to the representation of the women as undisciplined and without appropriate self-control and

---

36. *Letter* 16.8: *Mulieres eorum sparsis crinibus concurrentes cum ferali ululatu nomen Theodori repetitis vocibus accusabant dicentes, "O Theodore, quid fecisti?"*

37. *Letter* 20.11: *de cenaculo prospicientes.*

perhaps even without modesty (in that they rush out in public, inappropriately groomed), as well as irrational and lacking discernment, since, after all, Theodorus has not (yet) converted, and in any case, their negative perception of this is, from Severus's perspective, deeply misguided. It's also interesting to note that Jewish women behaving like this in similar conditions and circumstances is a trope that signals the gravity of the offense against the Jews.[38] Here, significantly, it serves to highlight, not the offense against the Jews (except perhaps ironically, to a highly resistant reader of Severus), but their ignorance and irrationality.

Attributing a sighting of the miraculous ball of fire to Jewish women is somewhat more difficult to assess. Certainly, it is useful for Severus to claim that Jews as well as Christians saw the miraculous light, but attributing the experience to Jewish men would have served him at least equally well. Conceivably, it is the vantage point of an upper story that leads him to attribute the sighting to women, rather than men, but this is simply impossible to determine. Interestingly, the women's testimony is given no less credence than that of the male monks, but it's difficult to know what, if anything, to conclude from this. Although contemporary scholars of early Christianity have sometimes focused on rabbinic proscription of women's legal testimony, there is no particular reason to think that Severus or the Jewish community he describes knew of this. Severus would, after all, have been all too familiar with gospel traditions in which women reliably testify to the empty tomb and the resurrection.[39] Yet on the other hand, the author is cautious about the identification of the miraculous light: "Even now, it is still unclear whether this thing was an angel, or St. Stephen himself or what it really appeared to be."[40]

Women Identified More Individually

As Bradbury and others have remarked, Severus's account is notable for its emphasis on the resistance of four Jewish women, three of whose conversion accounts are narrated at the end of the *Letter*. For Bradbury, Severus has here

---

38. E.g., 3 Macc 1.18–20. Other instances might include Josephus's description of Berenice appearance in Jerusalem, with shaven head, barefoot, performing a Nazarite vow to protest the cruelties of Florus, *War* 2.309–14; Philo's image of sequestered Jewish women exposed to the eyes of Roman soldiers, *Against Flaccus* 89, although here the women are violated by the incursion of soldiers in their homes, rather than voluntarily leaving their homes. This trope applies to women far more broadly: in 3 Macc 1.4, Queen Arsinoe exhorts the troops against the Jews with wailing and tears, her hair all disheveled; by contrast, in the Christian *Martyrdom of Saints Perpetua and Felicitas* 20, Perpetua exhibits a striking concern for a decorum of dress and hair, despite her imminent death.

39. Although for what it's worth, the only gospel Severus actually seems to quote is Luke, the one canonical gospel where the women's testimony goes unbelieved (Luke 24.11) until the male disciples see evidence for themselves.

40. *Letter* 20.12: Bradbury's translation, modified, of *Verum hoc, utrum angelus an ipse sanctus Stephanus an vere id quod visum est fuerit, incertum etiam nunc est.*

accurately conveyed the resistance of the women, as he writes: "The independence and courage of these women in the face of Christian intimidation are very conspicuous, but it is unclear why they were less susceptible to the application of terror than their male kin."[41]

All four women are described as members of the elite classes (24.1, *nobilissimas Iudeorum*), and three are the wives of powerful, prestigious men: Theodorus; his younger brother Meletius; and the Spanish refugee, Innocentius. Interestingly, Severus provides the name of only one woman, Meletius's wife, Artemisia, whose name seems to have some relation to the tale told about her conversion, as I will discuss later. The other women remain anonymous. In an earlier period, one might be tempted to attribute this to a reluctance to name women in public, particularly the wives of elite men. By the fifth century, literary and epigraphical sources alike suggest this deference seems to have waned considerably and there are any number of additional plausible explanations for the omission of their names, from Severus's own ignorance, to the possibility that he, or Consentius, or someone else, has manufactured these narratives together with the persons to whom they are attached.[42]

According to Severus, although Theodorus agreed to convert to Christianity on the day of the confrontation between the Christians and the Jews, he deferred any formal action until he could assemble the synagogue congregation and persuade them to join him. When, however, the Christians pressure him to make good on his promise, he offers a new rationale for a further postponement. He fears that if his wife, who is still back on Majorca, "learned that her husband had converted without her agreement," she would "remain firm in her faithlessness, as usually happens. Further, she might become confused in her judgment and, at the instigation of her mother in particular, who was still alive, abandon both the marriage and the religion."[43]

Modern readers might be tempted to conclude that on both occasions, Theodorus was stalling for time.[44] Nevertheless, the story of Theodorus's wife is actually much more complicated than Bradbury's reading of it, and of the subsequent narratives, as demonstrations of the greater fortitude of the women in the face of Christian pressure. First, unlike the women whose conversions are later narrated, Theodorus's wife is not on Minorca and might, conceivably, have

---

41. Bradbury 1996:130 n. 23.

42. Although manufacturing them still doesn't explain why names aren't provided for them. Here, too, the thesis that Severus writes shortly after the actual events, while there are still numerous persons alive to contradict his account, might be factored in here.

43. *Letter* 21.2. I have slightly altered Bradbury's translation of *et a coniugio et a religione discederet*, which reads "abandon both the marriage and her husband's religion" (Bradbury, *Severus*, 115).

44. E.g., Bradbury 1996:8.

been safe from Christian pressures on Majorca (where Severus remarks they had an estate). Severus's precise language, "that first he [Theodorus] wanted to bring his wife here [Minorca]" suggests that his wife might not yet be enroute, and could, conceivably, remain safely where she was. In fact, Theodorus converts immediately after he asks for this delay, and there is no indication in the text that his wife ever returned or ever converted. Severus's silence on the fate of Theodorus's wife might even suggest that, if the story contains some truthful elements, she remained on Majorca and did not convert.

Further, despite Bradbury's admiration, this vignette may equally be seen as a critique of both Theodorus and his wife. Theodorus is presented as believing that he must consult first with his wife in order to secure her assent to the conversion. Otherwise, she "may remain firm in her faithlessness, *as usually happens*" (emphasis mine). In placing this speech in Theodorus's mouth, Severus may intend to insult him or, at least, accuse him, indirectly, of dissembling. Earlier, Severus represents the two synagogue leaders, Caecilianus and Innocentius, as committing both themselves and their entire households to Christ, in a speech that presumes the assent or, perhaps, the submission of those households, including their wives. Yet here, Theodorus seems to lack the ability to compel his wife's assent to his decisions.

Although Bradbury construes this as evidence of the women's fortitude,[45] claiming that the wives of Jewish men have independent views, and expect to be consulted, was unlikely to have been construed as an indication that the women were intelligent, autonomous, courageous persons. Rather, it implies that these women are insufficiently subordinate to their husbands, and, at least in the case of Theodorus's wife, inappropriately influenced by their mothers. Theodorus, it seems, and perhaps, by extension, other Jewish men are not, in fact, able to control their wives as they should (and as Christian scripture itself requires, although Severus never explicitly raises any of this). This is a serious challenge to the honor of a man who held the position of patron of the community and head of the synagogue, as well as an insult to his wife, casting her as insubordinate to the authority of her husband.

Further, implicit in the account of Theodorus's wife is the widely held ancient notion that without appropriate masculine guidance, women (and here perhaps more specifically Jewish women) generally lack the capacity to discern the truth, and rather hold stubbornly to their own erroneous beliefs.[46] Portraying Jewish women as more devoted to Judaism is highly unlikely to be, for

---

45. And his reviewers do not challenge this assessment.

46. That again recalls the accusations in the 2 Tim 3.6–7 about women who will listen to all sorts of false teachers and lack discernment.

Severus, a compliment; rather, it may cohere with ancient associations of women and femininity with superstition, irrationality, inappropriate submission to divinely ordained authority, and so forth. The idea that Theodorus needs to consult his wife thus functions at least as much to insult each of them as it does to describe any actual resistance on the part of some Jewish women.

Although it may not be true in all cases, Kate Cooper's assessment that, in many late antique narratives, the presence of a woman signals the critique of a key male figure may be applicable here.[47] Additionally, it's possible that this scene invokes the ancient shared Jewish and Christian stereotype of the man who listens to his detriment to the voice of a woman/his wife, most explicitly in the story of Adam and Eve, but also in service of the defamation of numerous powerful men.[48]

Severus is actually fairly explicit that the three women who hold out until the very end are exemplars of Jewish "hardheartedness of belief" (*duritia perfidiae*, 24.1). Consider first the conversion of Artemisia, the wife of Theodorus's brother Meletius. Their story exhibits a considerable degree of literary artifice, some of which appears to revolve around their names. Her husband's name, Meletius, could easily be read as the Greek Melitios (from *meli/melitos*; honey),[49] meaning "of, or belonging to, honey,"[50] a supposition that seems reasonable given the number of Jews in the story who have Greek names. Artemisia's name is, on the one hand, a theophoric ("belonging to the goddess Artemis"), but it also has some associations with water.[51] After Meletius converts to Christianity as a result of his trying encounter in the hills outside Magona with Innocentius, his "distraught" wife[52] flees their house and takes refuge in a vineyard that Severus interprets as a demonstration of Luke 5.37: "the Jews have received the 'must' of the New Testament not like 'old wineskins', but like 'new winevats'" (24.4). She takes with her a small group of women: an otherwise unidentified female friend, a nurse, and a few female servants. For two days she remains in the vineyard, implacable and furious at her husband.[53]

Artemisia's actual conversion is prompted by a minor miracle. On the morning of the third day, she orders one of her servants to draw water for her

---

47. "[W]henever a woman is mentioned, a man's character is being judged," Cooper 1996:19.

48. E.g., Josephus's critique of Herod Antipas and Herodias, *Antiquities* 18.255.

49. LSJ, s.v. μέλι, 1097.

50. The Latin for honey is also "mel."

51. The nymphs of Artemis were said to be the daughters of Okeanos, and associated with streams, water, and perhaps also clouds, e.g., Apollonius of Rhodes, *Argonautica* 3.876–83; Ovid, *Metamorphoses* 3.163–72.

52. *Letter* 24.2: *coniugis sui Meletii conversione commota*. Bradbury's translation may be a bit strong: *commotus* has a wide range of connotations: "moved," "excited," "disturbed," "roused," "shaken," "outraged," "provoked," "unbalanced," "unsettled," Lewis and Short, s.v., 383.

53. *Letter* 24.5: *a viro suo offensa inexorabilis permansisset*.

to wash her face. The water that the servant brings her from a wine-vat tastes and smells like honey; in fact, the entire water supply has turned into the sweetest honey. The miraculous transformation of ordinary water into something terribly sweet (itself evocative, but not identical, to Jesus's transformation of the water into wine at the wedding at Cana) impels her conversion. The author is quite explicit that he sees the conversion of the Jews through a typological reading of the Exodus narrative and that various aspects of Exodus signs conform to those of the converting Jews (e.g., 20.15–19). He writes that "Meletius' wife was compelled by the honey to cast away the bitterness of her unbelief," which may be understood to mean that the wife is compelled by the husband; he also construes this event as a type of the transformation of the biblical bitter waters associated with the Exodus story.[54]

Artemisia's resistance is constructed particularly in terms of opposition to her husband. That Artemisia was initially furious at her husband and unwilling to be placated, equates resistance to Christianity with wifely resistance to her husband, a resistance that is itself represented in terms of a lack of emotional self-control. This is evident, not only in her anger, but in the poor judgment she exercised by taking with her other presumably vulnerable women, all but one (the *amica*) of whom are her servants and/or slaves, ignoring the risk that their frailty[55] poses in such circumstances.

Artemisia's response to the transformed water heightens the representation of her as irrational; she becomes angry and interrogates the hapless servant "indignantly" (*indignans*, 22.5). When the miraculous honey sweetens not only the women's tastebuds but Artemisia's disposition as well, she returns to the town and her husband, properly submissive. No longer resistant, she is now the dutiful wife who submits to her husband's decision and accepts Christ.[56]

Although Severus never explicitly makes reference to the Pauline traditions subordinating wives to husbands, or the household codes in various New Testament epistles, this association of faith in Christ with wifely submission accords closely with those passages. As in 1 Cor 11, for instance, the husband is the head of the wife as Christ is the head of the church, so here Artemisia as a Jewish woman resists her husband (and Christ); as a Christian woman, she is obedient to both.

54. Exod 15.23–25; which follows on the Miriam story and which may or may not be significant here. It's also intriguing that rabbinic exegesis of roughly the same period emphasized the sweetness of the food God provided to the Israelites during their journey (an observation I owe to Jordan Rosenblum).

55. *Letter* 24.2: *oblita femineae infirmitatis*, which Bradbury translates as "without any thought for feminine frailty." Perhaps one might translate "oblita" as *disregard*. This, too, can be seen both as a compliment, but also an insult, i.e., Artemisia *should* have known better, but was so *commota* that she didn't.

56. *Letter* 24.10: *ad fidem Christi sine reluctatione consensit.*

It is through this lens that we might then analyze Severus's claim that Artemisia does not herself relate her miraculous experiences to a wider audience, but rather does so through her husband (*per eum omnibus indicavit*, 24.10). This small detail enhances the representation of Artemisia as a subordinate wife, who does not even speak in public, but rather through her husband. It further contributes to my earlier argument about the absence of women. Whether there is here a subtle allusion to 1 Cor 14.33b–36 is possible but not definitive. What is clear, though, is that Artemisia does not speak to the *ecclesia*, but rather tells her husband privately. He then speaks for her in public.[57]

Although there is no way to know why there are virtually no Christian women explicitly mentioned in the *Letter*, it is interesting that this representation of women's speech is consistent throughout. The only Christian woman explicitly identified in the text is the consecrated virgin, Theodora, who had the prophetic dream identical to that of Severus. Somehow, obviously, the content of Theodora's dream reaches Severus, but he never actually describes who Theodora told and by what means, and her speech remains implicit at best.[58] At several points in the narrative, Jewish women do speak (and act) in public, but both their speech and their acts may be indicative of their lack of self-control and appropriate submission to masculine authority.

The two remaining women who resist conversion are the unnamed wife of Innocentius and her unnamed sister. The conversion of the wife of Innocentius is similarly constructed in terms of resistance and submission to her husband. She does not flee her husband's house, but, on the contrary, appears to be confined there for "nearly four days" with her husband and "the whole crowd of the brethren" (*fraternitatis multitudo*) gathered at their house, dismayed that "so great an abundance of happiness was being opposed by a single woman" (27.1–3). Like Artemisia, Innocentius's wife remains stubborn and unmoved by the pressures applied to her. She is "overwhelmed by the incurable sickness of her unbelief" (27.2), and she refuses the "medicine" offered by the Christians, a description that may draw on a notion of women as more susceptible to disease.[59] In his typical fashion, Severus is somewhat oblique about

57. This notion of men speaking for women in public appears in the (perhaps fourth-century C.E.) *Debate Between a Montanist and an Orthodox*, where it is explicitly connected to Pauline teachings about women's head-coverings, praying or prophesying in the public assembly and not exercising authority over men: Heine 1989:124–26, using the text of Ficker 1905:446–63.

58. The figure of Theodora merits additional consideration. It is reminiscent of Tertullian's description of the visions of the female prophet in *On the Soul* 9, which Severus might well have known, at least partly because it is in Latin. Other female figures in Latin Christian traditions have prefigurative dreams, including Perpetua; but one might also think of 1 Cor 11.3–11, which allows for women prophets to prophesy in the ἐκκλησία; and also of distinctions made in some Christian circles between what "women" could do and what "virgins" could do (even if Tertullian resists this).

59. For the possibility of this view in Philo, see Szesnat 1998:102.

precisely what transpires during those four days. Innocentius appears to try everything from threats to tears to prayers to move his resistant wife, who remains unmoved by the torrent of verbal pressures. Ultimately, the Christians resort to prayer, prostration and weeping, which finally works. Innocentius's wife confesses belief in Christ and her desire to become a Christian. Although this vignette does suggest that Christian men speak with the woman, and that she confesses her belief verbally to them, it is important to note that the entire scene takes place within her husband's house, where, presumably, she remains protected from any suspicion of impropriety, particularly since her husband appears to be present the entire time.

The final conversion is that of Innocentius's widowed sister-in-law. Perhaps because she is a "venerable widow," her conversion lacks the components of resistance to spousal authority. Severus claims that on hearing of her brother-in-law's conversion, she boards a ship to leave Minorca. He adds that the Christians not only allowed, but encouraged her to do so, in the face of her resistance to either miracles or verbal arguments (thus perhaps, again, presenting her as stereotypically irrational). This statement, of course, belies Severus's general representation of the Christians as applying only moral suasion; that they allow her to leave makes clear that they could have prevented her. If Bradbury is correct that a February passage was somewhat hazardous, the Christians' encouragement of the journey is even more disingenuous than it appears.[60]

On the eighth day, as the Christians are preparing to return to Jamona, having apparently converted the entire Jewish population of Minorca, Innocentius's sister-in-law is blown back to the island. How she comes to find herself at Severus's feet is unclear, but he claims that she "wrapped herself about my knees and begged with tears for the assistance of our faith." Lacking, perhaps, a husband through whom to submit, the widow subordinates herself instead to the male bishop. The longest direct speech of any woman is put into her mouth, consistent, perhaps with her depiction as presently unmarried, and thus perhaps more able to speak directly with men, or at least with a bishop.[61] Why, he asks her, did she wish to abandon her brothers, an inquiry that may still construct her actions as a kind of resistance to male authority.[62]

The woman's reply is quite fascinating. She portrays herself as Jonah, who also fled God (on a ship, as did she), and was forced to abandon the ship and

---

60. Bradbury 1996:130. Still, such a crossing is related to, and perhaps even required by the Jonah story that provides the paradigm for her experience.

61. For the question of speech between (Jewish) married women and men who are not their husbands, see Kraemer 1999:38–41.

62. *Deserere*: the same verb is used of Artemisia's departure from Meletius.

obey the will of God, after a divinely orchestrated storm. (The biblical Jonah, however, actually abandoned the ship in order to save his innocent Gentile shipmates). Were this to reflect her actual response, it would be tantalizing evidence of the knowledge of a Jewish woman of scriptural traditions,[63] and the ability and desire to interpret particular human experiences through such a lens. However, the Christian identification of Jonah as a type of Christ, particularly for his three days in the belly of the fish, raises questions about the plausibility that a new (and probably traumatized) convert would spontaneously proffer the story of Jonah without prompting. It might, however, suggest that Severus thought his audience would find this either plausible or suitably miraculous. The question remains, though, whether the Jonah paradigm dictates the form of the story or whether some actual events/conditions prompt the choice of Jonah as a suitable frame. In either case, she begs Severus to accept both her and her two young twin daughters, which he happily agrees to do.

Conclusions

Although Severus's representation of Jewish women (and indeed, of the Jewish community in Minorca; and its relations with the local orthodox Christian community) is quite fascinating, in the end, it is difficult to say what if any historical and social data might be extracted from his narrative. As Severus deploys them, Jewish women repeatedly serve as representations of Jewish stubborness in the face of the reasonableness and truth of Christianity. This representation is reinforced by the depiction of both the church (*ecclesia*) and synagogue as female; the church as a prophetic virgin and the synagogue as a bereft widow in Severus's dream, even if this last is undercut a little by the description of two of the three women who ultimately convert as *matronae*, as respectable married women. The representation of their stubborness as marital insubordination and their conversion as marital subordination (and subordination to male/divine authority) is significant.

Yet, Severus's actual descriptions of Jewish women, even when scrutinized carefully, yield relatively little that is remarkable, apart from the portrait of them as "brave resistors," which I have called into question. The only women described are the wives or relatives of elite men. What Severus says about them is consistent with fairly conservative ancient notions: the women appear mostly removed from the public eye; good women stay home and submit to masculine

---

63. *Letter* 28.5: *Et Ionas propheta a facie Dominie fugere voluit, et tamen voluntatem Domini licet invitus implevit.* Bradbury here cites Jonah 1.1–4, but Severus's telling is not an exact quotation of this.

authority; resistant women listen instead to (the bad advice of) their mothers. The names of these women are not uttered in the text, apart from that of Artemisia (whose mention may have something to do with the fame of her father, apparently a civic leader named Litorius known from several external sources).[64] Women don't actually appear to speak in public; they are not explicitly present in the synagogue (although they *might* be so implicitly) and may not be part of the singers enroute to the synagogue. Elite women may appear to be educated, if that is what we may conclude from Innocentius's wife's response to Severus, but that would hardly be startling at this point. Interestingly, the one person said to be learned in Greek and Latin literature as well as Jewish law is her husband, Innocentius (18.15). The entire authority structure of the Jewish community appears to be male; despite the attestation of the title *mater synagogae* elsewhere in the Mediterranean diaspora,[65] there appear to be none on Minorca. Only men are *doctores legis*. The roles of a few elite women are hinted at, but hard to interpret, such as the elusive *propinqua* to whom Theodorus allegedly confides his dream. Significantly, Severus avers that he knows this not from the woman herself, but because Theodorus has reported it to him (in keeping with Severus's apparent view that respectable married women do not speak for themselves in public).

A few details in the text are somewhat more difficult to explain as the products of rhetorical interests and constructions, such as the "fact" that Innocentius's wife has two twin daughters, or the description of one of the women accompanying Artemisia as a nurse (which Bradbury takes to mean that Artemisia had a baby, although it could equally as easily be construed as Artemisia's own nurse, still living with her). Not inconceivably, of course, these are, in fact, glimpses of actuality, but there seems to be no way to know. Just as easily, these are the details of verisimilitude that, as literary theorists have explored, function to create a persuasive narrative world.[66]

What appeared, then, at first blush, to be descriptions of Jewish women, here resisting Christianity, throwing rocks, and refusing to convert, turns out to be the deployment of female characters for rhetorical purposes, relying on gender

---

64. See Bradbury 1996:34–37. That her father is well attested doesn't actually resolve much, because, not inconceivably, Severus knows there is such a woman, but he gives her name on the assumption that others don't know it either; on the other hand, it could have been her name, despite its theophoric associations. Actually, the issues here are quite complex. Apart from the *Letter*, nothing in the extant data about Litorius would lead a contemporary scholar to identify him as a Jew. Bradbury notes that he could conceivably have been a pagan, a Jew, or even possibly a Christian, or a convert to Christianity (although I think this last less likely, since it would serve Severus' interests to note that, if he knew it), Bradbury 1996:36–37; Artemisia, then, could have been a non-Jew who became one, either to marry Meletius, or for other reasons; she could also have been born Jewish.

65. For women called mother of the synagogue, see Brooten 1982:57–72.

66. See, e.g., Clark 1994; 1998b; 2004; see also the Introduction.

stereotypes and associations for various effects, including a subtle critique of Jewish men (and women) and the promotion of (Christian) gender roles and values.

This, then, may provide us with an explanation for Severus's representation of Jewish women as the last to convert, that calls into question the historicity of his account on this point (as on many). As I have demonstrated, Severus repeatedly deploys women as exemplars of wifely disobedience. To do so, however, requires that the men convert first, so that the women's failure to do so can be constructed as disobedience to their now Christian husbands. A narrative in which the women converted first, and the men resisted, would not be nearly as useful. Women who converted while their husbands remained Jewish would still have been disobedient, but their disobedience would have posed Severus a dilemma. For now, the women's marital insubordination could have been, at least theoretically, commendable, since it was an insubordination undertaken for a higher reason, acceptance of Christ. Because Severus repeatedly demonstrates that acceptance of Christ makes women appropriately submissive and accepting of male authority, his needs were best met by depicting Jewish women as converting last. Then and only then could their initial refusal of Christ best exemplify Jewish stubborness and wifely insubordination, and their acceptance of Christ best exemplify the proper submission of Christian women.

Finally, Severus's use of gender throughout the text, particularly his feminization of Jews in general, but Jewish men in particular, and his subsequent remasculination of Jewish men, once they become Christian, may relate to various power contests that underlie the text. Severus's artful account unquestionably masks a whole host of ancient competitions for prestige and power. The convenient recovery and display of the relics of Stephen appear to have been deployed as a major Christian weapon in the cooptation of the prestige of the Maccabean martyrs for Christian consumption, a competition that had apparently heated up considerably in Syrian Antioch in the late fourth century.[67] The synagogue where the Maccabean relics were allegedly preserved was taken over by Christians in c. 380 C.E. The Emperor stripped Gamaliel VI of the title *praefectus honorarius*, on October 20, 415, with the office itself disappearing soon thereafter.[68] Ginsburg proposes that there is a direct connection between the Jewish proselytism and synagogue construction that prompted the dismantling of the patriarchate and the discovery of Stephen's relics shortly thereafter, which was accompanied by the tale that Gamaliel I, himself a crypto-Christian, had appeared to a priest named Lucian, and led him to the grave containing his bones, those of Stephen, those of Jesus's disciple Nicodemus, and Nicodemus's

---

67. Rutgers 2009.
68. Linder 1987: no. 41, pp. 267–70; Ginzburg 1996:214.

son, Abibas).[69] It is tempting to suggest that the role assigned by Christians to Gamaliel I on the heels of the deposition of Gamaliel VI is not coincidental.[70]

The importation of Stephen's relics appears to have offered Christians on Minorca an opportunity to reconfigure the existing power relations between Christians and Jews. Severus's account represents Jews as holding the major positions of civil authority and social prestige. Regardless of whether Severus was a key player in these events or whether others, including Consentius, orchestrated them, Christians appear to avail themselves of the opportunity to attack that authority and prestige by subordinating elite Jews to the authority of the Christian bishop. The power balance on Minorca between Christians and Jews has been irrevocably inverted. Where Christians were once subject to the theologically inexplicable domination of the Jews, they are now firmly in control, solving, in the process, the theological dilemma posed by their cognitive dissonance: Christianity supplanted Judaism, yet the Jews of Minorca continued to flourish and even dominate, at least socially, civically, and economically, in the local Christian community.

That such a move is at work is implied in the final section, in which Severus claims that the former Jews now willingly demolish their own synagogue and pay for a new church, even carrying the stones on their own backs. They thus are seen to submit to the authority of the bishop and the church. As the work of Andrew Jacobs suggests, this scene of Jewish willing demolition of their former synagogue may constitute a paradigmatic example of colonial powers fantasizing about the Other who desires to be subordinated.[71]

That social dynamics between Jewish and Christian communities on Minorca are very much at issue is also implicit in a scene between Reuben and Theodorus, in *Letter* 16. When Theodorus encounters Reuben, the latter says, "What do you fear, Lord Theodorus? If you truly wish to be safe and honoured and wealthy, believe in Christ, just as I too have believed. Right now you are standing and I am seated with bishops; if you should believe, you will be seated and I will be standing before you" (16.14–15). It is this speech, arguing that only conversion to Christianity will preserve Theodorus's power within the ancient Minorcan social order that ultimately appears to persuade Theodorus. Although in *Letter* 12.10, Severus insists that the Christians desire the salvation (*salutis*) of the Jews, Reuben makes no such pitch to Theodorus; his argument is couched entirely in the language of worldly prestige, even if, perhaps, it is intended to

---

69. For a brief but telling analysis of this story, see Jacobs 2003b:29–32.

70. Ginsburg makes the connection between the deposing of Gamaliel and the finding of Stephen's relics, but doesn't develop the connection between the two Gamaliels, Ginzburg 1996:214. For a recent dissection of these connections, see Irshai 2010.

71. See Jacobs 2003a; 2003b.

be construed in terms of "spiritual" safety, honor, and wealth. Theodorus's expressed intention to convert is met with a host of actions that signal both dominance and subordination in the ancient systems of benefaction and patronage. Christians "caress his face and neck with kisses," "embrace him in gentle arms," long to join "right hands" with him or converse with him. Whether such actions also represent Christian fantasizing here, about their own desires and behaviors, remains an open question.

Bradbury suggests that something more complicated is transpiring, for Severus allows that even now, Theodorus continues to be *patronus*, and Caecilianius is still so eminent among the Minorcans that "even now he has been elected *defensor*" (19.6). That is, the continuing influence and prestige of the Jews, even after their conversion, constrains Severus.

It is also highly likely that the *Letter* plays some significant role in the contestations between Severus and other Christian claimants to authority, a dynamic that may be visible now and again, as in Severus's aside, at *Letter* 8.2, that the accompanying (but now missing) tract of anti-Jewish arguments was prepared "not for anyone's edification. . . . (for in that we are utterly deficient and hope rather to acquire it from your Blessedness) but that it might be noticed that we showed considerable concern, in so far as our abilities allowed, for the struggle that had been engaged." Nevertheless, he goes on, it was Christ who "achieved everything with His own forces and without us even uttering a word." Whether this is modesty, or its rhetorical mask, by taking limited credit for these events, while ceding other credit to St. Stephen, Christ, and God, Severus constructs himself as the instrument of the saint, and of Christ, and as an effective mediator. And throughout the text, a struggle for civic, economic, and political power is cast in theological (and perhaps even, as Bradbury suggests, millenarian) terms.

To the extent, then, that Severus represents Jewish men as female, by subordinating their wives to them, he may also re-masculinize them to some degree, once they become Christian. More generally, perhaps, Severus feminizes Jews and presents their gender relations as disordered; only when they become Christians do their gender relations become properly ordered. This is rhetorically effective, but, not inconceivably, it also points to the real underlying power dynamic on Minorca. Severus has taken on the Jewish power elite and subordinated and humiliated the men, particularly Theodorus, a process that is then unsurprisingly represented in gendered imagery. Yet as we have seen, the *Letter* claims that Severus continues his relations with these men, now reconfigured and somewhat inverted. They now bow to his authority. Thus, his representation of gender relations repairs to some extent the damage he has done to their reputation and perhaps contributes actually to their collective ability to function in this re-aligned power dynamic.

6

Veturia of Rome and Rufina of Smyrna as Counterbalance

Women Office Holders in Ancient Synagogues and Gentile Adopters of Judean Practices

Rufina, *Ioudaia*, *archisynagōgos*, built this tomb for her freed slaves and the slaves raised in her house. No one else has the right to bury anyone (here). Anyone who dares to do (so), will pay 1500 denaria to the sacred treasury and 1000 denaria to the Judean *ethnos*. A copy of this inscription has been placed in the (public) archives.

—*IJO* 2.43 = *CIJ* 2.741

Veturia Paulla. . . . placed in her eternal home, who lived 86 years, 6 months, a proselyte of 16 years under the name of Sarah, mother of the synagogues of Campus and Volumnius. In peace (be) her sleep.

—*JIWE* 2.577 = *CIJ* 1.523

Introduction

Some time in the second, or perhaps the third, century C.E., a woman named Rufina designated a burial area for her freedpersons and household slaves, in the ancient city of Smyrna on the Aegean

All inscriptions are here identified by their numbers in either the Cambridge series (*JIGRE* for Egypt and *JIWE* for western Europe) or the Mohr Siebeck series (*IJO*, for eastern Europe and Asia Minor), as well as their older numbering in *CIJ*, as appropriate (see below, n. 75, with bibliography). In addition to the discussions in those volumes, see also Brooten 1982; Kraemer 1992:106–27; Kraemer 1998a. The second epigraph also appears in Brooten 1982:57–59. The translation here follows Noy.

coast of Asia Minor. The relatively brief inscription, above, which Rufina commissioned has been the subject of considerable interest in the last thirty years particularly because Rufina explicitly describes herself as *archisynagōgos*, a term often translated as ruler, or head, of a synagogue.[1] Rufina also calls herself by a term, *Ioudaia*, usually translated simply as "Jewish." Here, however, I prefer the term "Judeans/Judean," rather than the more conventional "Jews/Jewish," following the important arguments of Steve Mason that for much of the period under discussion in this study, the most appropriate classification is an ethnic one (understood in terms of ancient constructions of ethnicity), rather than the modern and somewhat anachronistic category of religion, understood to be separable from ethnicity.[2] Very few Judeans explicitly identify themselves on Greco-Roman inscriptions with the term *Ioudaia* or the masculine *Ioudaios*, and I have argued elsewhere that it may be intended to indicate that Rufina was also not born to Judean parents, but rather at some point became *Ioudaia*.[3]

Although most heads of synagogues attested in ancient inscriptions are men,[4] Rufina's inscription is not the only instance of a woman head of the synagogue. Two others are attested elsewhere in Asia Minor (Theopempte in Caria, perhaps in the fourth or fifth century C.E. and a woman whose name is not preserved, from Göre in Cappadocia in the same period).[5] Another, Sophia, is attested from Gortyn, on Crete, again in the fourth or perhaps fifth century C.E. Seven other inscriptions appear to designate women as members of the councils of elders associated with some ancient synagogues.[6] Nor, if Rufina did adopt Judean practices at some point in her life, would she be the only woman recognized as such in an inscription. Several women are explicitly identified as proselytes in Greco-Roman inscriptions that seem securely Judean, including Veturia Paulla (above), and a woman called Felicitas, both from Rome, as well

---

1. For a thorough consideration of the term and its ancient connotations, see Rajak and Noy 1993.

2. Mason 2007; see also Elliott 2007, whose publication overlaps with that of Mason. For the view that religion emerges as a salient category much earlier, see Cohen 1999:109–39; for a somewhat different argument that it emerges in late antiquity, see Boyarin 2004; 2006; for the thesis that it only emerges as a salient category in the early modern West, see Asad 1993. For ancient views of ethnicity, in contradistinction to the modern category, Mason particularly commends the work of Konstan 1997, especially his view of ethnicity as discourse, rather than "fact," in Mason 2007:483 n. 57. For the question of when the translation "Jew, Jews, Jewish" becomes more appropriate, and my translation choices in this study, see the Introduction.

3. Kraemer 1989b; 1992:121–22.

4. Brooten 1982:83–92 details over thirty such inscriptions. At the time she was unaware of *IJO* 2.255, which adds another woman to the mix, and probably also of Scheiber 1983: no. 10 (a male ἀρχισυνάγωγος named Ioses). In *WRGRW* 86, *IJO* 2.255 is identified as unpublished: I was unaware at the time that it was forthcoming in this volume, which was also published in 2004. Interesting, the ratio of 10 percent women is roughly comparable to the ratio of women generally in these inscriptions.

5. *WRGRW* 85 and 86.

6. *JIWE* 2.24 = *CIJ* 1.400; *JIWE* 1.59 = *CIJ* 1.581; *JIWE* 1.62 = *CIJ* 1.590; *JIWE* 1.71 = *CIJ* 1.597; *IJO* 1 Thr3 = *CIJ* 1.692; *SEG* 27 (1977), 1201; Kraemer 1985; all in *WRGRW* 88.

as a young woman called Sara, from Cyrene.[7] In addition, a variety of other inscriptions may be indirect evidence of non-Judean women adopting Judean practices, something I will define more precisely later.

No women synagogue officers are attested in ancient literary sources, although this may not be all that surprising, because the late antique (second to fifth century C.E.) Judean diaspora communities, from which all the epigraphical evidence for such women comes, appear to have left no surviving literary sources, although some relevant accounts are found in non-Judean writers, both Christian and non-Christian.[8] No writings are known, for instance, by Judeans living in Asia Minor, or Rome, from the second to the fifth centuries C.E.[9] However, several literary sources describe an interest in Judean cultic practices on the part of non-Judean women. The writings of Josephus in particular contain several such accounts. He devotes a considerable portion of his *Antiquities* book 20 to an account of how Helena, Queen of Adiabene, adopted Judean practices, together with her entire household.[10] Elsewhere, he juxtaposes two stories of the gullibility of aristocratic Roman women, that of Paulina, a devotee of Isis lured into having extramarital sex with a suitor disguised as the god Anubis, and that of Fulvia, a high-ranking woman whose adoption of Judean devotions Josephus claims ultimately had dire results for Judeans in Rome.[11] In yet another instance, he claims that plotters against the Judeans in Damascus concealed their plans from their wives, virtually all of whom were devotees of Judean practices.[12] Josephus also claims that Poppaea Sabina, wife of emperor Nero, pleaded the cause of a Judean embassy from Jerusalem because she was God-revering (*theosebēs*), a description that has occasioned considerable debate.[13]

These accounts, however, are not entirely limited to Josephus. The Roman historian Dio Cassius claimed that the emperor Domitian exiled his relative, Flavia Domitilla, because of her Judean practices in the late first century, although Christian traditions will later remember her as a convert to

7. *JIWE* 2.62 = *CIJ* 1.462.

8. On this, see Kraemer 1998; also Rutgers 2000.

9. Rutgers 2000 has argued for the Jewish authorship of two anonymous/pseudonymous works; see now Jacobs 2006. Josephus may also be writing from Rome at the very beginning of the second century, but that doesn't contradict my basic point. Conceivably, quite a few of the works classed as pseudepigrapha might come from such authors. My point here is merely that none are either explicitly identified as such, nor demonstrably so.

10. *Antiquities* 20.17–53; 92–96; *WRGRW* 103.

11. *Antiquities* 18.81–84; *WRGRW* 111.

12. *War* 2.559–61, *WRGRW* 104A. See also later, n. 21.

13. *Antiquities* 20.189–98; *WRGRW* 104B; on the meaning of θεοσεβής, see later; see also Kraemer 1998:132–35; 272–73; *WRGRW*, p. 281. On Poppaea, see Smallwood 1959; Williams 1988.

Christianity.[14] In an account highly reminiscent of the stories about Poppaea, a narrative of conflicts between Judeans and their neighbors in Alexandria claims that when Judean envoys traveled to Rome to counter charges made before the emperor Trajan, his wife, Pompeia Plotina intervened effectively on their behalf both with members of the Senate and with the Emperor himself.[15] There has been some scholarly speculation that a woman named Pomponia Graecina, said by Tacitus to have been tried for "superstitio externa" during the reign of Nero, was actually tried for Judean practices.[16] In the fourth century, John Chrysostom will decry the interest of some Christian women in festivals and other observances of the local synagogue.[17]

It was also for many years a commonplace, at least in some circles, to claim that the majority of converts to Judaism (the usual phrasing) in the Roman period were women. (Similar claims have been made about women's interest in Christianity, beginning as early as the author of Luke-Acts' repeated claims that elite women were regularly attracted to Christianity, as well as the accusation of the second-century Christian antagonist Celsus, but still argued in modernity by Adolf von Harnack, and much more recently by Rodney Stark).[18] The

---

14. Dio Cassius, *Roman History* 67.14.1–2. According to Dio, her husband, Flavius Clemens, also a relative, was executed. For later remembrances of Domitilla as Christian see Jerome, *Letter* 108, to Eustochium (the Life of Paula), 7, where he claims that Paula venerated Domitilla, whom, he says, had confessed herself a Christian and was exiled to Pontia; *WRGRW* 71. Domitilla and Clemens are said to have been just two of many executed or deprived of their property on the charge of atheism, which Dio says was leveled against "many others who drifted into Judean ways" (ἐς τὰ τῶν Ἰουδαίων ἤθη ἐξοκέλλοντες). Matthews erroneously claims that Domitilla was also executed (2001:16). See also Lampe 2003:198–205.

15. *P. Oxy.* 1242, the "Acta Hermaisci," in Musurillo 1954:44–48. Musurillo thought that although the earlier accounts of Poppaea's support of Jewish envoys to Nero might here have been projected onto Pompeia Plotina, it was also possible that this reflected actual second-century events, 162–63. See also Matthews 2001; D'Angelo 2003.

16. Tacitus, *Annals* 13.32, argued by Mommsen 1907: vol. 2:278. See also Goodman 1989. She has also been taken for a Christian (e.g., Mierow 1939). For a brief but judicious discussion that recognizes that this description could refer to any number of foreign practices, see Lampe 2003:196–97, with additional references to others who have argued that it was Christianity (196 n. 3). According to Tacitus, Pomponia was referred to her husband, Aulus Plautius, for punishment. On the advice of relatives, he acquitted her.

17. John Chrysostom, *Against Judaizing Christians* 2.3.3–6; and 4.7.3, where Chrysostom cautions his male congregants not to allow their wives or slaves to attend the theater, let alone the synagogue (*WRGRW* 41).

18. Celsus, *Aletheis Logos*, cited in Origen, *Against Celsus*; Harnack 1908:ii.64–84, especially 73, where he argues that the apocryphal *Acts* are "untrustworthy" in their details, but "express correctly enough in general the truth that Christianity was laid hold of by women in particular, and also that the percentage of Christian women, especially among the upper classes, was larger than that of Christian men." In his discussion of the spread of Christianity to Spain, he writes: "It is noticeable that the female sex in Spain, as elsewhere, appears to have taken a keener interest in Christianity than did the men" (ii. 305 n. 1). Lieu 1998 notes rightly that many people just repeat Harnack's assertions. Nevertheless, it's worth noting that Harnack's assemblage of the pertinent texts was quite impressive. For a more recent argument, see Stark 1996, with extensive critiques and a response by Stark in *JECS* 6.2 (1998). Stark 2001:233 also claims that "religious movements typically overrecruit women," based on various contemporary studies. For the possibility that Acts responds to the kinds of charges made by Celsus, see Kraemer 1992:128–29; on Acts' accounts, see Kraemer 2000a; 2000b; 2000c; see also MacDonald 1996.

assertion of George Foote Moore in his classic and often-cited *Judaism in the First Centuries of the Christian Era: The Age of the Tannaim* is representative of widely held views: "Women in general had only their fathers or husbands to reckon with; and partly from excess of religiousness, partly because they had no public religious duties, women were in the large majority among [Gentile] adherents of Judaism, and a still larger proportion, doubtless, of the proselytes."[19]

The evidence for this view included everything from the several examples in Josephus surveyed earlier and to which I will return, to the limited epigraphical evidence for proselytes, surveyed later, to an unexamined assumption that, because male conversion required circumcision and female conversion did not, it was far easier for women to become Jews, and thus far more likely.[20] (The view that Josephus ascribes to one of the Judean merchants advising the household of Helena of Adiabene, that it was not necessary for men to be circumcised [considered more later], is conveniently ignored in these discussions). The interest of Gentile, particularly Roman, women in Judean practices was sometimes seen as part of the broader interest of Roman women in non-Roman religions.

19. Moore 1927:1.326. This same excess of religiousness and lack of public religious duties is never offered as explanation for, say, Jewish women's interest in non-Jewish practices. Other examples include Leon 1960:256 and Goldstein 1965:10. Lieu 1998 also cites Blumenkranz, and claims that Bernadette Brooten still assumed "that women were a majority among full converts" (citing Brooten 1982:144–47). It is also asserted by van der Horst 1991:109–10, and Zabin 1996:279, citing van der Horst 1991 and Brooten 1982 for support. Zabin suggests that the opportunity to hold offices might account for the predominance of female converts. See also Shaye J. D. Cohen's brief treatment of "women's Judaism" (2006:73), where he makes the somewhat more moderate claim that "[a]mong the converts to Judaism in antiquity, a fair number were women," citing especially Josephus's account of the women of Damascus (*War* 2.20.2). Here he worries only whether Josephus here means "conversion" or "sympathizing." Feldman, too, takes these and other claims more or less at face value, e.g., 1993:438 on the women of Damascus, whose interest in Judaism he attributes to "the relatively more elevated position of women in Judaism and . . . the fact that they did not have to undergo excision." Here he also takes Josephus's story of Helena of Adiabene as an instance of the "particular impact [of the proselytizing movement] on women, although, as I discuss later, all Josephus actually says is that the women of the king's harem took up Judean practices, as did Helena herself. Elsewhere, Feldman attributes the special interest of Gentile women in Judaism to the observance of Jewish holidays, here more or less just reproducing the claims of John Chrysostom, 1993:376. Zilm 2008 avoids claiming that women were the majority of converts, but considers the various narratives in Josephus and other sources sufficiently historical, despite the cautions of Lieu 1998, discussed later. Her argument that Gentile women found rituals of menstrual purity particularly appealing seems far too optimistic, on many fronts.

20. Goldstein 1965:15. These views continue to be repeated in more recent scholarship (e.g., van der Horst 1991:109): "As a matter of fact we know from literary sources that there were more female than male proselytes and Godfearers, probably because [it was easier for women to convert]" since they didn't have to be circumcised. Van der Horst here approvingly quotes Leon, 1960:256. Although we don't really *know* any such thing, it is true that Roman imperial legislation outlaws the circumcision of Roman citizens (*cives Romani*) already in the late third century C.E. (e.g., Linder 1989, no. 6). The history of Roman prohibition of circumcision (either of Judeans, or non-Judeans, or some permutation thereof) is complex, as are questions about their enforcement: for some discussion, see Linder.

In her now-classic study of women leaders in ancient synagogues, Bernadette Brooten argued that the inscriptions of Rufina and other heads of synagogues, as well as those inscriptions for women called mother of the synagogue,
elder, and other titles associated with synagogue offices, demonstrated beyond
reasonable doubt that at least a small number of women did function in official, formal capacities in some diaspora communities. No inscriptions have yet
been found for women synagogue officials in the synagogues of the land of
Israel (and very few women donors are attested in those synagogues).[21]
Although Brooten's work has persuaded the vast majority of scholars in the
field, it has also been subject to ongoing critique, both by scholars who continue to advocate the older view assaulted by Brooten herself that women's
titles were honorary, and by those who dissent from the larger implications
Brooten drew from this evidence concerning women's public presence and
participation in ancient synagogues.

Further, in a hard-hitting article published in 1998, Judith Lieu challenged
the view that literary accounts supported the thesis that Gentile women were a
majority of converts either to Judaism or to Christianity.[22] Proffering brief discussions of Livy's account of the suppression of the Bacchanalia and the oft-
cited claim of Celsus, the second century C.E. critic, that Christianity appealed
primarily to women, slaves, and little children, she argues that "the discourse
concerning the conversion of women serves a political and propagandistic end
of characterizing the religion concerned and its relationship with the norms of
society: it also provides justification for (re-)asserting control."[23] Commenting
on the alleged prominence of women among "heretical" Christian groups, she
argues that "what we are dealing with is a rhetoric which identifies women with
non-normative or marginalized religion," and finds it somewhat incredulous,
literally, that scholars, including myself, might mistake this rhetoric, in John
Chrysostom and others, as evidence of women's interest in Judaism.[24] In Lieu's
reading, "much of the supposed evidence of the significance of women in early
Christianity. . . . is rather of women as a topic of concern in the early Church.
This does not point to the numerical dominance of women so much as
to women as a problem, and particularly as a symbol of the tension between

---

21. E.g., a Greek votive from Ascalon from Lifshitz 1967: no. 70, (also *CIJ* 2.964) by Kura Domna, dated
quite late, to 604 C.E. This inscription is significant in that it lists her first as a joint donor, together with another
person whom Lifshitz took to be a man called (Ku)r(os) Mari(on), but this is not entirely clear: only the rho of
Kuros is visible, and the person's name appears to be Mari(n), which is well attested as a woman's name, at least
earlier, in Egypt. The remainder of votive offerings in this list are by men. There are some votives from families,
including husbands and wives, but it's not clear that these involve women as active donors.

22. Earlier, n. 20.

23. Lieu 1998:13.

24. Lieu 1998:14 n. 42, citing Kraemer 1992:108 and Feldman 1993:376.

separate identity and social respectability which is characteristic of early Christian literature."[25] Thus Lieu concludes pessimistically, "the evidence often cited for the attraction of women to Judaism or Christianity is not this: they are sources for different political agendas. . . . The gendering of conversion is a matter of rhetorical and not statistical analysis. The move from rhetoric to social experience must remain hazardous."[26]

Not long after Lieu's article appeared, Shelly Matthews published a detailed study of accounts of elite women's proclivity for foreign religions in the early imperial period, focusing particularly on Josephus and Acts. Matthews argues persuasively that Josephus's intertwined accounts of Fulvia and Paulina rely heavily on "common Roman tropes and stereotypes concerning the prominence of noble women in foreign religions," in order to argue that other foreign religions, particularly the Isis cult favored by the Roman emperor, Domitian, himself, challenge the Roman social order, promoting unchastity, gender disorder, and confusion of class distinctions. Judean practices, by contrast, at least in Josephus's representation, did no such things.[27] Matthews, however, does not here make Lieu's move to disregard these narratives as productive for women's history; on the contrary, while acknowledging that her reading "displaces a reading of the narrative as a transcript of events in the lives of actual historical women," she nevertheless insists that these stories serve as "a springboard into a reconstruction of women as historical agents, actively participating in 'foreign' religious cults in Rome."[28] Although her work is acutely sensitive to problems of rhetoric in the depictions of women's interest in foreign religions, Matthews does, in fact, think that Roman women, at least in the early imperial period, *were* quite interested in a variety of non-Roman religions, including but hardly limited to that of Judeans.

Although I have written about much of this material previously, in this chapter I revisit the available evidence and prior scholarly arguments both for Gentile women's interest in Judean practices and for women holding offices in ancient synagogues. In part, I am interested in whether epigraphical evidence

---

25. Lieu 1998:15.

26. Lieu 1998:20.

27. Matthews 2001. Matthews argues that "Josephus's demonstration that Isis religion violates the chastity of Roman women is his indictment of Rome's tolerance of this religion and an assertion of Judaism's superiority over the Isis cult," Matthews 2001:20. Matthews does not appear to have read Lieu 1998, which may have appeared in the interval between the completion of Matthew's dissertation and its publication as this book.

28. Matthews 2001:25. Matthews may prefer this reading because it serves (conservative yet feminist) Christian rhetorical interests, namely, to demonstrate the active roles played by women in Christian missions. She may wish not to suggest that it is only Christian women who do so. I think this is visible in her argument that Romans 16, which she takes as written to Rome, "suggests the involvement of women slaves, freedpersons, and possibly even citizens in shaping and sustaining religious practice among minority religions in Rome," 2001:25–26.

offers us any less fraught access to women's actual practices, and how much ancient constraints of gender are implicated in the discussions of both of these topics. My arguments and conclusions differ to some extent both in substance and in theory from my earlier views and from those of other scholars.

In particular, I will argue that the debates about both conversion and leadership have been the wrong debates. Although I continue to think that the evidence suggests that at least a few women held offices in some ancient synagogues that entailed the performance of some communal responsibilities beyond the contribution of funds, more important than whether women's titles were functional or honorary is how women's office titles were embedded in ancient theories of gender relations, as well as in actual social practices. In my earlier work, I explored some, but not all, aspects of this, particularly in my consideration of the construction of civic office holding and benefaction as the appropriate responsibilities of the most elite families toward their larger family, the city itself.

Similarly, my review of the evidence for the gender distribution of Gentiles drawn to Judean practices will suggest that it is difficult to generalize from the thin available data, both epigraphic and literary. More important than whether women were disproportionately attracted to the veneration of "other people's deities" is how such claims (and perhaps practices) are, again, embedded in ancient theories of gender relations.

In my view, the long-standing scholarly distinction between *conversion* and *God-fearing* or *partial adherence* to Judaism (something, interestingly, no one claims for Christianity)[29] has been poorly theorized by scholars in the past. I will argue that what is usually called conversion often centrally entails, at least in antiquity, a change in ethnicity, effected particularly through the construction of new kinship relations.[30] This itself relies on a notion of ethnicity (and kinship) as changeable, rather than fixed, contrary to our present western notions of ethnicity as genetic and immutable (and in many present circles, functioning as a stand-in for race).[31] By contrast, the veneration of the gods of

29. Although Constantine's initial patronage of the Christian god while he continued to venerate other deities might be a fine example of a Gentile Christian "God-fearer."

30. In this regard, I am also quite intrigued by the recent revised dissertation of Zeba A. Crook (Crook 2004), who argues for conversion as a change of patronage, loyalty, and benefaction, rather than as a change in some psychological or emotive state. I intentionally avoid the language of "fictive" kinship here, partly out of awareness of anthropological arguments that all kinship is to some extent a social construction, and thus "fictive." Nevertheless, it seems clear that old kinship relations are here dismantled, and replaced with new ones. For a brief overview of "fictive kinship," see Shipton 1997. I thank my colleague Saul Olyan for this reference.

31. For recent analyses of ancient thinking about ethnicity, and its implications for changing cultic devotions, see especially the revised Brown doctoral dissertation of Hodge 2007, and Buell 2005, as well as the review by Stowers 2007. I thank my daughter, Jordan Kraemer, presently a doctoral candidate in anthropology, for calling to my attention the point about ethnicity as a stand-in for race, in one of our many helpful conversations about this and other projects.

others, what is usually described as "God-fearing" when non-Judeans venerate the Judean deity, does not require this change in ethnicity and kinship, and probably also relies on a polytheist cosmology; it is thus a very different cultural practice.

Whether the ancient evidence conforms to distinctions between conversion and the veneration of the gods of others is not entirely clear. The category of "conversion," particularly when applied to antiquity, is itself problematic, grounded as it is in notions of religious exclusivity.[32] As we shall see, much of what is proffered as evidence for "God-fearing" may sometimes simply be ordinary acts of piety; while some, if not many, donations and other acts of benefaction toward Judeans by Gentiles may well be an ordinary ancient polytheist practice of benefactive exchanges, which authors like Josephus and perhaps Luke then "misrecognize" as acceptance of Judean practices and even identity because it serves their apologetic interests to do so.

My present assessment of the epigraphical evidence for, and the literary accounts of, Gentile women's attraction to Judean practices in the Roman period will cohere in some respects with that of Lieu, at least to the extent that I think rhetorical concerns motivate the representation of women's devotions in the literary texts, and certainly make it difficult to discern gendered patterns. Unlike Lieu, I will here explore in more depth the relationships between ancient constructions of gender and those particular ancient religious practices usually designated as conversion. I will argue that thinking about conversion as reconfigured kinship illuminates the elements of the surviving inscriptions and literary evidence. And unlike Lieu, I am somewhat more willing to think that nonliterary sources like inscriptions and, occasionally, even literary sources give us some (admittedly limited) entry in ancient social realities.[33]

---

32. The secondary literature on the subject of "conversion" in antiquity is substantial, and often focused on the paradigmatic conversions of Paul on the one hand and Augustine on the other. The work of A. D. Nock (Nock 1933) long played a role in these discussions, including his much-critiqued hierarchical distinction between conversion on the one hand and adhesion on the other. For some recent studies, see, e.g., Goldstein 1965; Gager 1975; Segal 1990; Goodman 1991; 1994; Sievers 1996; McKnight 2002; Mills and Grafton 2003. There is also an extensive literature on contemporary studies of religious conversion and change by sociologists and anthropologists, often but not always focused on New Religious Movements: see, e.g., Buckser and Glazier 2003. This work clearly has implications for the study of antiquity, even though the actual data for antiquity, especially literary narratives, makes the topic particularly thorny. The sociologist Rodney Stark attempts to apply contemporary methods to the data for antiquity, with mixed critical reviews (Stark 1996). Working in the opposite direction, scholars of antiquity have also attempted to apply contemporary theories to ancient data (e.g., Gager 1975; Segal 1990; Crook 2004).

33. Many of the materials that Lieu treats briefly in her article are considered in much greater depth throughout this book, from Livy's account of the origins and suppression of the Bacchanalia, to Thecla and others. It's also unfortunate that Lieu's article and my *When Aseneth Met Joseph* (Kraemer 1998) appeared within a few months of each other, since my analysis there of the role of gender in conversion narratives is more consonant with Lieu's work than she knew or might have anticipated, and her overview discussion of *Aseneth* does not engage my arguments about other aspects of the text as well.

Gentile Engagement with Judean Practices: Methodological and Theoretical Considerations

Any discussion of Gentile attraction to Judean practices in antiquity needs to begin with some definitions, itself a vexed issue. Juvenal's much-quoted satire of the Roman man whose father revered the Sabbath and abstained from eating pork, and who himself becomes circumcised has often been taken to reflect an ancient distinction between those Gentiles who observed some Judean practices, and those Gentiles who fully adopted a Judean identity and way of life, including an acceptance of Judean practices (and related beliefs), a rejection of prior practices and associated beliefs, and incorporation into at least a local Judean community sufficient to allow for marriage to (other) Judeans, meals with (other) Judeans, burial with other Judeans, and other aspects of communal life.[34] Rabbinic references that appear to make a similar distinction are frequently offered as further support of this thesis.[35] So, too, are references in the Acts of the Apostles to Gentiles whose reverence for the God of Israel makes them particularly interested in early Christian preaching. Luke's story of the Roman centurion, Cornelius, who had made frequent donations to the synagogue in Caesarea (Acts 10), is regularly cited in this context.

Yet whether and how much such distinctions correspond to ancient social realities, and, more specifically, whether such "sympathizers" are designated by particular Greek, Latin, and Hebrew terms remains much disputed. Juvenal's designation of the Sabbath-observing father as "metuentem sabbata patrem," has long been the basis of an argument for a technical use for terms of "fearing" God, particularly when read in concert with the various references in Luke-Acts to those Gentiles who feared (*sebomenos/phoboumenos*) God. Persons called by this term, whether in literary references or epigraphical attestation, could be

---

34. Juvenal, *Satire* 14.96–99. The bibliography on this distinction is extensive: see, e.g., Cohen 1989. This particular formulation is my own. Of course, many ancient Judeans, from the Pharisees to the Qumran covenantors to the Therapeutae to devotees of Jesus to the rabbis, had rules about all of these (e.g., meals, marriages, motherhood, and mortuary rites), whose function, if not also intention, was to delineate narrower understandings of community and identification.

35. See Feldman 1950. In this judicious article early in his career, Feldman argued against the earlier views of Jean Juster that the Greek terms θεοσεβὴς, σεβούμενον τὸν θεόν and φοβούμενος τὸν θεόν; and the Latin *metuens* (*domini*) all referred to such sympathizers. In Feldman's view, only the rabbinic phrase *yirei hashamayim*, heaven-fearers, clearly designated such persons. All other phrases are inherently ambiguous, even though some might in fact designate "sympathizers." Feldman did not, however, question the larger distinction, only its indicators. Feldman 1993:342–69 revisits these issues at length. Although he continues to recognize that not all usages of the term are unambiguous, he very much thinks there is such a technical category as a God-fearer, relying particularly on the Aphrodisias stele, and its third-century date (since refuted). Feldman's views on this issue are very much affected by his desire to refute a lachrymose model of Jewish history by emphasizing the success of Jewish proselytizing, and the appeal of Jewish practices to non-Jews. See also Feldman 1989.

assumed, in the absence of further evidence, to be Gentile devotees of the God of Israel.[36]

That all usages of the debated Greek and Latin terms designate Gentiles who observed some aspects of ancient Judean practice is, of course, patently absurd. Louis Feldman dispatched this argument with a few choice examples in a brief early article that many scholars cite but, perhaps, have failed to read. In support of Feldman's view that "[these] terms . . . are not at all uncommon in the general sense of 'religious' or 'pious'" may be added a much longer list of uses of these terms, both literary and epigraphical, that corroborate his findings.[37] The Greek term *theosebēs* in particular, to which I will return later, is used, among many other instances, by the fourth-century polytheist Roman emperor, Julian, as a term for polytheist piety;[38] as the name of a Christian woman donor to a church in Aquileia in the late fifth or early sixth century;[39] and as a descriptor both for the patriarch Joseph and for his eventual wife, Aseneth, in *(Joseph and) Aseneth*.[40]

36. For a history of this debate, see Koch 2006; Kraabel 1981. See also Moore 1927–30:1.254; MacLennan and Kraabel 1986 and below, nn. 44 and 52. Interestingly, far less invoked in these debates are the several instances of late Roman imperial legislation against persons called "heaven-fearers" (*Caelicolari*), whom Linder renders sometimes as "heaven-fearers" (especially in his translation of the actual legislation) and sometimes as "God-fearers" (especially in his discussions). See, e.g., Linder 1987: no. 35, Honorius, with Arcadius and Theodosius II, 25 Nov 407 and no. 39, Honorius with Theodosius II, 1 April 409. Honorius calls the *Caelicolari* those "who have meetings of a new doctrine, unknown to me (*qui nescui cuius dogmatis novi conventus habent*)," and language similar to this is repeated in various other versions of this law, e.g., *Codex Justinianus* 1:9:12: "A new crime of superstition claimed somehow the unheard name of Heaven-Fearers (*Caelicolarum nomen inauditum quodammodo novum crimen superstitionis vindicavit*). . . ." Linder comments that since there is extensive evidence for God-fearers previously (and here he assumes that these are all the same), what must be new about these God-fearers is that they seem to be Christians. That they do seem to be Christians is clear from the *Justinian Code*, which orders these Heaven-Fearers to return to God's law and Christian veneration or be subject to the penalties of heretics. But if this is true, then it's not clear to me that these Caelicolari are, in fact, those called θεοσεβεῖς in inscriptions, and the relationship between these particular persons (assuming they are real) and other persons designated θεοσεβεῖς, seems less obvious than Linder presumes.

37. Feldman 1950:204.

38. Julian uses this language in a letter to Atarbius (*Letter* 37) to designate pious pagans with no Judean associations whatsoever; as a designation for Alexander (*Letter* 111.21) and Diogenes (*Against Heraclius the Cynic* 8.26).

39. *AE* 1975: no. 410, a list of donors to a church mosaic, with a woman donor named Theosebes: "Victorinus et Theosebes cum filiis suis f(ecerunt) p(edes) CC." Victorinus and Theosebes, with their sons [or perhaps children] paid for two hundred feet (of mosaic).

40. For its occurrence in *Aseneth*, see Kraemer 1998:132–35; 272–73; 291–92. It occurs in *The Letter of Aristeas* 179.3 and the *Testament of Naphtali* 1.10; in the Gospel of John 9.31: "We know that God does not hear sinners, but does hear one who reveres God (τις θεοσεβὴς) and does the will of God" (translation mine; cf. the NRSV "[God] does listen to one who worships him and obeys his will"). Herodotus uses it to designate the piety of the Egyptians: 2.37; 1.86. Trebilco catalogues occurrences of θεοσεβὴς in classical Greek authors, and in a number of other inscriptions: 1991:146–47 with notes on 246–47. In addition to those instances, Strabo (*Geography* 7.3.3) reports that according to Poseidonius, the Mysians are called θεοσεβεῖς on account of their religiously motivated vegetarianism. θεοσεβὴς occurs in the Greek magical papyri (*PGM* 4.685), where the petitioner describes (him)self as ευσεβὴς και θεοσεβὴς: "you send to me, who am pious (ευσεβεῖ) and God-revering (θεοσεβεῖ), health and soundness of body"). θεοσεβὴς and closely related forms are prevalent in numerous Christian sources. The apostle Andrew is described as ἀνήρ θεοσεβὴς in the *Acts of Andrew* 60.7; Thecla is called

For Feldman, the issue was primarily semantic. He had no doubts that the category itself was reasonable, in light of numerous ancient literary depictions of such persons, and rabbinic references in particular. It bothered neither Feldman nor many of the scholars who have written on this, either previously or subsequently, that such a distinction relied heavily upon an unarticulated and unexamined assumption about normative Judean practices, themselves presumed to be largely identical with rabbinic standards of observance. That is, to distinguish between the "partial" practice of Gentile "sympathizers" and the "full" observance of Gentile converts or proselytes is to presume that Judeans themselves had a consistent level of "full" practice against which to measure Gentile engagement. Yet we know, of course, that this is at best an ancient rabbinic fantasy, and that the range of Judean practice in the Roman period was considerable, even as its precise contours continue to elude us. Nevertheless, as I shall argue later, it is possible that some meaningful distinctions, if somewhat different, may be made between *conversion* and *veneration*.

Further critique of this thesis was offered by A. T. Kraabel, whose seminal article argued that Luke's God-fearers were the evangelist's own literary creation and said nothing about the existence or interests of such persons in the first century C.E. They functioned to account for the transition of nascent Christianity from Jews to Gentiles via Gentiles already interested in Judaism, and disappeared from Luke's literary scene once they had served their purpose.[41] Although some scholars found Kraabel's assessment of Luke's God-fearers persuasive, others did not, or continued to maintain that, regardless of Luke, the basic model was sound.[42]

In 1975, excavators at Aphrodisias in Caria (modern Turkey) found a large inscribed stele that seemed for many scholars to resolve whether *theosebēs* was

---

θεοσεβὴς in the *Acts of (Paul and) Thecla* 38; so, too, Andronicus, "who formerly was not the god-fearing (θεοσεβὴς) man he is now . . .," in the *Acts of John* 63 and the converted Callimachus in the *Acts of John* 76. In the *Pseudo-Clementine Homilies* 11.16, a θεοσεβὴς is one who truly performs the law: although the ethnicity of such a person is perhaps ambiguous here, it does not seem to mean a non-Judean who practices some limited portion of Judean law. θεοσεβὴς also appears in Eusebius's quotation from Melito's book to Antoninus Verus (Marcus Aurelius): "It has never before happened . . . that the race of the religious (τὸ τῶν θεοσεβῶν γένος) should be persecuted . . ." (*Ecclesiastical History* 4.26.5, translation Lake in the LCL). Here, though Melito obviously intends a reference to the persecution of Christians, the term itself may be construed broadly.

41. Kraabel 1981; see also R. S. MacLennan and A. T. Kraabel 1986. Kraabel argued that there was no definitive epigraphical evidence for "God-fearers" as a category of partial adherence. The publication of the Aphrodisias inscriptions, discussed immediately after this, led many scholars to argue that such evidence was now both clear, and relevant to the interpretation of other inscriptions, but as I indicate later, neither is quite so self-evident. Levinskaya's far-ranging discussion of the relevant inscriptions was intended in part to refute Kraabel's claim, but in fact, her largely sober and judicious evaluations suggest, in the end, that the epigraphical evidence remains ambiguous at best.

42. Bernays 1885; Feldman 1950; 1986; 1989; Smallwood 1959; Bellen 1965–66; Lifshitz 1970; Seigert 1973; Finn 1985.

a technical term for Gentiles who affiliated partially with Judaism (as the question has usually been phrased). The stele inscriptions, which circulated in a kind of samizdat form before their formal publication in 1987, comprised two distinct faces.[43]

The dating of both faces has been much debated. The initial editors took both faces to be one related inscription and vacillated between an early date, around the third century C.E., and a much later date of fifth or even sixth century C.E., ultimately proposing the former. Subsequent scholarship, though, has both demonstrated that the two inscriptions are separate, perhaps of substantially different date, and are in any case both relatively late.[44]

The inscription on face *a*, sometimes mischaracterized as a synagogue inscription,[45] and now thought to be the later inscription (fifth century C.E.), appears to recognize donors to a charitable organization of some sort (the options range from the more plausible burial society to the less likely soup kitchen proposed by the initial editors).[46] Interestingly, the patron of the organization, named Iael, may well be a woman.[47] The remaining donors, all men, have names often associated with Jews, such as Theodotos, Samouel, Benjamin, Ioudas, and Sabbatios. Of particular interest is that several of these men are identified either as "proselyte" or as *theosebēs*, assuming that these are the correct completions of the abbreviations, respectively, *proselu*, *prose*, and *theoseb*.[48]

It was face *b*, however, that had the greater impact. This face, now re-dated to the fourth century C.E., contains two lists. The first of these has no header, but is a list of approximately fifty men, some of whose biblical names suggest

43. Reynolds and Tannenbaum 1987. The inscription has since been designated *IAph* 11.55; it is also catalogued as *IJO* 2.14. The Aphrodisias inscriptions are now available on an extensive web site: *IAph: Inscriptions of Aphrodisias*: at http://insaph.kcl.ac.uk/iaph2007/index.html.

44. On issues of dating, see especially Bonz 1994 and Chaniotis 2002; see also Botermann 1993. For a critique of the view that the organization on face *a* is a soup kitchen, see Williams 1992, whose title is a slight misnomer, since Jews are never explicitly identified as such in the inscription; see also most recently Gilbert 2004 and Koch 2006.

45. Whether it is from a physical synagogue cannot be determined, but it is not necessary and perhaps contrary to the association mentioned on face *a*.

46. I argued for the probability of a burial association at a session on the inscription at the annual meeting of the Society of Biblical Literature in 1989. Williams 1992 makes a similar argument.

47. Brooten 1991. The problem, briefly, is that the biblical name Iael is clearly that of a woman (Judg 4–5), and is unattested as a man's name in the onomastica for Judeans, yet the title used here is in the masculine form. Brooten takes the name as dispositive, especially given the demonstrable use of grammatically masculine titles for women elsewhere. For a survey of readings of the name Iael as both masculine and feminine, see the discussion to *IJO* 2.14, pp. 92–93, with detailed bibliographic references.

48. The term θεοσεβέστατη (most reverent or pious one) is given in Sophocles, s.v., as an epithet for Christian bishops (noted in Noy's discussion of *JIWE* 2.364, which has itself sometimes been reconstructed as (θεο)σεβέστατη). It occurs, inter alia, in a Christian inscription from the Golan Heights, perhaps fifth century C.E. (Gregg and Urman 1996: Fig 22 [p. 31]). It has also been offered as the expansion of θεοσεβ in *IJO* 2.27, the offering of Capitolina (e.g., Lifshitz 1967: no. 30, perhaps also Robert 1970:409–12) but the current editors prefer θεοσεβῆς.

that they are Jews: Joseph, son of Zenon, several named Ioudas, (including one whose father was named Paulos) and a few named Jacob.[49] The second list, also of about fifty men, does carry a header: it lists "those who are *theosebēs*." The first eight are identified as (city) councilors. None of these men have distinctively Jewish names, like Joseph or Ioudas or Jacob in the first list, although there is some overlap of names such as Zenon.

This list of fifty-some *theosebeis* (plural) was immediately seen by some scholars as dispositive evidence for the widespread technical meaning of the term. Despite these uncertainties about the identity of the donors on face *a*, the context of the lists on face *b*, the relationship of the faces to one another, the nature of the organization recognized on face *a*, and the date of the inscriptions, many scholars have taken the Aphrodisias inscriptions to resolve definitively the debates about the meaning of *theosebēs* as an indication of partial adherence to Judaism.[50]

In my view, the claims made for these inscriptions are greatly inflated. The inscription on face *a*, designating several persons as proselytes and *theosebeis* (if these are the correct completions) may indeed indicate that in the fifth century—or at whatever date the inscription was made—in Aphrodisias, these terms had the connotation often imputed to them. I remain somewhat less persuaded that the inscription on face *b* is a list of some fifty Aphrodisian Gentile practitioners of Judaism (in the fourth century), partly because we simply do not know how the first list might have been headed (that is, to what category *theosebēs* is here opposed or juxtaposed).[51] The numerous late antique uses of *theosebēs* to denote general piety seem to me to challenge any simple reading of this inscription. Conceivably, this is a list of Gentiles who have contributed in some way to a communal enterprise whose donations themselves are understood to be an act of piety, with nothing further to be deduced about

49. That these names are also used by Christians in late antiquity has played little role in scholarly debates. The occurrence of the name Paulos might actually give one pause, but conversely, the multiple persons named Ioudas are often thought to demonstrate non-Christian identity, on the theory that Christians would not name a child after the arch-traitor Judas.

50. E.g., Levinskaya, "The importance of this inscription . . . lies in the fact that, once and for all, it has tipped the balance and shifted the onus of proof from those who believe in the existence of Luke's God-fearers to those who have either denied or had doubts about it," 1996:80; quoted also in Koch 2006: n. 8. The studies noted here for the most part take the evidence from Aphrodisias into account: Tannanbaum 1986; Goodman 1988; Williams 1988; Overman 1988; Cohen 1989; Feldman 1989; van der Horst 1989; Trebilco 1991:147–66; Murphy O'Connor 1992; Wander 1998. For additional discussion and bibliography, see Kraemer 1998:132–33; 272–73 (with detailed notes on 283–84).

51. Some scholars have proposed that it would have read ὅσοι Ἰουδαῖοι, e.g., Koch 2006:6. In my view, there is simply no way to tell what was the missing phrase, and I think this reconstruction relies on the construal of θεοσεβεῖς as a category of Gentile God worshippers, although Koch, who thinks it likely, does, also, share my view that here θεοσεβὴς is a term of praise applied to donors, rather than a demonstrable indication of their interest in the practice of Judaism: 2006:6–7.

their interest in Jewish practices.[52] I am further leery of attempts to extrapolate from local usage at Aphrodisias to communities far removed both geographically and chronologically. As a general method, I find this faulty, but it is even more troubling when the subject is Judeans or Jews and Judaism in antiquity, because it seems integrally related to faulty assumptions about the uniformity and homogeneity of Judeans or Jews and Judaism in the ancient world that themselves have a history and a utility in various debates.[53]

But more substantially, I am troubled by the degree to which these debates have lacked any grounding in social theory. Despite the extensive amount of attention paid to the question of whether there was a widespread, if not universal, category of "God-fearers," separate and distinct from another widespread, if not universal, category of "proselytes," there has been little attention to the underlying questions of theorizing the categories in the first place, and even less to how such categories might intersect with theories of gender.

As Steve Mason demonstrates, both insiders and outsiders thought that the *Ioudaioi* (Greek) or *Iudaei* (Latin) were unquestionably an *ethnos*, just as were the Egyptians, the Romans, the Syrians, and others. In antiquity, an *ethnos* was distinguished by a distinctive character, ancestral traditions, perceptions of shared kinship, charter stories, customs, conventions and laws, and political arrangements.[54] *Ethnē* also typically had their own distinctive deities and cult practices, both ancestral rites, often practiced domestically, and public rites involving priests, temples, and animal sacrifices. Still, Mason notes that, in the ancient Mediterranean, there was no "one-for-one match between a people and a single cultic system," citing both the presence of temples to numerous ethnic deities in the major cities, and the diverse quasi-private initiations into the cult of diverse deities such as Isis, Demeter, Mithras, and others.[55] Further, there may have been a significant distinction between venerating someone else's deity, for instance through votive offerings, or financial donations to their temples or shrines, and participating in animal sacrifices to that deity. Mason points out that Judean cult was, with a few notable exceptions, only performed at the temple in the mother city, Jerusalem, so that Judeans living outside the land of Israel "had no visible cultic expression," even while, presumably, they engaged in various other forms of devotion to their God,

---

52. In my more obstreperous moments I wonder whether θεοσεβὴς is not even here a donor category, analogous to contemporary uses of "angels" to designate the donors of particularly large gifts to charitable causes.

53. These surface to some extent in a fascinating article (Mitchell 2005), which considers a late antique Christian (probably Montanist) inscription that refers to a burial society called a δεκανία, led by a male προστάτης, which Mitchell argues has links to local Jewish communities.

54. Mason 2007:484.

55. Mason 2007:485.

such as synagogue attendance, Sabbath observance, food restrictions, and festival celebrations.[56]

The integral relationship between ethnicity and devotion to deities has substantial implications for questions about what is often termed religious conversion. In his collection of essays on what he terms "the beginning of Jewishness," Shaye Cohen argued that in the texts of the Hebrew Bible, there is neither a separate and distinct category of religion (Judaism), nor, correspondingly, any such thing as religious conversion. The biblical texts envision, and, perhaps, also reflect, social constructs in which different peoples are characterized, if not also defined, by birth (ancestry), language, connections to a homeland, and the veneration of ancestors and particular deities, in a complex that closely resembles the "ethnicity" elaborated by Mason, although Cohen doesn't use this particular formulation. In such an environment, a change of deities entails a change of ethnicity, something that can be effected at least through marriage, and perhaps also through other social mechanisms such as adoption.

The paradigmatic example here is, of course, that of Ruth, the grandmother of king David. In the biblical book that bears her name, Ruth is a young Moabite woman who initially marries an Israelite man (as does her sister, Orpah). After he dies without leaving her heirs, her mother-in-law, Naomi, tells Ruth and Orpah to return to their own families. Orpah agrees, but Ruth refuses, in a now-famous speech that highlights the connections between ethnicity, ancestry, territory, and veneration of the gods: "Do not press me to leave you or to turn back from following you. Where you go I will go, where you lodge, I will lodge; your people shall be my people, and your God my God. Where you die, I will die—there I will be buried."[57]

Cohen argues further that in the Hellenistic period, it becomes feasible to worship the Judean God without becoming a member of the Judean *ethnos*, effectively creating the Judean religion, or Judaism. In this model, of course, conversion becomes not, or no longer, the joining of the Judean *ethnos*, but the adoption of the specifically "religious" practices of that *ethnos*, its veneration of its particular god, perhaps while remaining a member of another *ethnos*. For Cohen, this is particularly important because his interest is in precisely this "beginning" of "Jewishness" as distinct from ethnic "Judean-ness." For Mason, by contrast, the fact that it is now possible to segregate out participation in someone's else *cultus* from membership in their *ethnos* does not create the

56. Mason 2007:485–86.
57. Ruth 1.16–17a.

category of religion, and so, correspondingly, doesn't create the category of Judaism as a religion, which he dates rather no earlier than the mid-second century C.E., and sees as a product of Christian theologizing.

Although I am fairly persuaded by much of Mason's argument here, my concern is more with the cultural logic, the constellation of cultural concepts, that underlie what is commonly called conversion. It is my argument that what is commonly characterized as "full" conversion to Judaism in antiquity is, in fact, precisely the change of ethnicity envisioned in biblical texts, even while merely venerating other people's deities is not (or at least, not necessarily). Although Cohen argues that veneration of the Judean God becomes a religion at this point precisely because it can be practiced by non-Judeans, non-Judeans *could* always have venerated the Judean God. As Mason's numerous instances make clear, in a polytheist cosmology, one *can* always venerate the deity or deities of another ethnicity, although perhaps one *should* not. Doing so does not deny the existence of one's own ethnic deities, although it can have all sorts of implications about those deities and one's relationship to them.

In a monotheist worldview, however, venerating someone else's deities is unacceptable by definition. From a Judean perspective, outsiders who wished to venerate the Judean god, for whatever reasons, were engaging in a somewhat incomprehensible or, at least, an ultimately paradigm-threatening activity (because their continued veneration of their own deities made clear that they did not accept the premise of Judeans that the Judean god was the only God). For those same outsiders, on the other hand, venerating the Judean god could be seen to be quite appropriate and comprehensible. One could do so without violating one's own veneration of non-Judean deities, although the Judeans themselves might complain, argue, or, for their own social and political reasons, they might be quite happy to accept such honor and veneration.

From the Hellenistic period on, it's not so much the possibility that has changed, as the actuality. It *may* be that, prior to the Hellenistic period, non-Judeans were less likely to have much interest in venerating the Judean god (or anyone else's god[s], for that matter). This might relate to the political implications of doing so: to worship someone else's gods is to affirm their power, including the political power of their kings and rulers over one's own. In the larger cultural climate of the Hellenistic world, which brought many people into proximate, intimate contact with the practices, shrines, and temples of others, however, devotion to the gods of others took on broader possibilities, some of which were personal, some of which continued to draw on such actions as representations of complex human social relations in which reciprocity and patron-client relationships might be expressed through mutual devotion to each other's deities, and so forth.[58]

The mechanisms through which one effected the transformation frequently called conversion unquestionably reflect ancient notions of ethnicity. Becoming a Judean and becoming a Christian in antiquity were very much about restructuring kinship: it is about making the non-Judean a member of the Judean *ethnos*, and making the non-Christian a member of the new Christian *ethnos*.[59] One can become a member of an *ethnos* through legitimate birth or legal adoption, and unsurprisingly, then, stories about converts regularly entail the use of one or both metaphors. By contrast, merely venerating "other people's" gods neither requires a change of ethnicity nor utilizes the attendant imagery.

Yet gender is a major qualifier here. To be born into an *ethnos* in antiquity was not merely to be, in our terms, the biological child of a mother and father already themselves members of such an *ethnos*. Rather, ancient ethnicity seems to be disproportionately a function of paternity. The Hebrew Bible understands an Israelite to be the son of a male Israelite, as is clear from the Hebrew expression that Israelite itself translates, "son of Israel," and that, of course, even the word Israel*ite* incorporates, although many English speakers will miss this. The daughter of an Israelite is not herself an Israelite, any more than the daughter of an Athenian citizen is herself an Athenian, even while the daughter of an Israelite is capable of transmitting the ethnicity of an Israelite man to his licit children. Ethnicity is thus fundamentally about fathers and sons. More generally, then, ethnicity is an attribute of men that applies secondarily to women by virtue only of their connections to men, so that women can easily, or more easily, lose their ethnicity, for instance through marriage.

Licitness is also crucial, as is one's status as free (or freed) or enslaved. Children born into slavery have no licit ethnicity,[60] while enslaved persons may

---

58. For recent discussion of the social dynamics of "conversion," see, e.g., Buckser and Glazier 2003. See also Hak 2006 for a recent dispute about whether structuralist-functionalist theories (associated especially with É. Durkheim) or rational choice theory (formulated particularly by Rodney Stark and collaborators) better explains why people convert to a new religion. Hak particularly engages Stark and Finke 2000 and their distinction between conversion (shifts across religious traditions) and re-affiliation (shifts within religious traditions). He argues for a modification of these distinctions (conversion as a shift in ideological views and/or the associated patterns of behavior: re-affiliation as the joining of an(other) ideological intermediate group (Hak 2006:299). Critiquing the deprivation explanations offered by rational choice theorists, he argues that conversion and reaffiliation can be *either* personal connections *or* ideological conviction, and that Durkheimian theory (of the lessening of cohesion as the real trigger) provides a better explanation than Stark and Finke for why this is the case (2006:303; see also 308). How much this may apply to ancient practices remains to be investigated.

59. As the work of both Hodge 2007 and Buell 2005 makes clear, becoming Christian may also have simultaneously involved, at least early on, the construction of a new *ethnos*, as well as incorporation into that *ethnos*.

60. Although they do seem to have some practical ethnic "connections," as in the description of a slave as "Egyptian" or "Judean."

lose their ethnicity, becoming blank slates of a sort, whose owners feel free to rename them—names being a function of freedom and licit paternity. These social processes and underlying cultural logic may be glimpsed in some of the extant manumission inscriptions. Women can impede the transmission of ethnicity and licitness: a child born to an enslaved woman and a free father does not bear the father's ethnicity and is not legitimate. But women cannot effect the transmission of ethnicity in and of themselves, the later rabbinic definition of a Jew as the child of a Jewish mother notwithstanding.[61] Men require women of appropriate status to bear children who are of their ethnicity and are their legal heirs, but it is the father whose participation is crucial.[62] Further, this participation is not identical to the sexual process of reproduction. In Greek and Roman practice, paternity and, therefore, ethnicity only became a social fact when the father formally and publicly accepted the newborn child as his own.[63]

This suggests that metaphors and rites of adoption will be particularly relevant for male conversion, but less so for women.[64] Although licit birth and adoption are the means by which males become members of a *familia*, and more broadly an *ethnos*, and licit birth the means by which females attain whatever status they have within these gendered constructions of family and ethnicity, marriage is also the means by which women routinely move into a new ethnicity. For women, marriage seems, in and of itself, to effect the necessary transformation. For men, marriage might occasionally be the impetus to join a new ethnos, but this seems to have been highly unusual, and, in any case, to require him to perform acts of rebirth and/or adoption not required of women.[65]

This offers, perhaps, a better explanation of the distinction between partial and full proselytes that one finds perhaps in rabbinic literature, and certainly in contemporary scholarly literature, and that may correspond to some degree to

61. Cohen 1985 has shown that this is a rabbinic innovation; it is clearly not the general cultural principle of ancient understandings of ethnicity and identity.

62. Based on her fieldwork in a rural Turkish village in the 1980s, Delaney 1991 argues that cultural theories of conception themselves tend to support and replicate these ideas. She alludes to similar ideas in ancient thought (on which see also DuBois 1988).

63. See, e.g., Hanson 1999.

64. It seems that it was difficult to adopt girls under Roman law, which actually utilized two different forms of adoption, one for persons under the power of another, and one, *adrogatio*, for persons who were *sui iuris* at the time. Women could not be adopted by *adrogatio*; see, e.g., Gardner 1991:8–9, who points out that there would have been little point to adopting a woman through *adrogatio*, since women could neither have direct legal heirs nor found a new *familia*. As Gardner points out, adoption was about removing a person (usually a male) from one *familia*, and inserting that person into another *familia* (Gardner 1998:117). For a more detailed treatment, see Gardner 1998:114–208. In this regard, the story of Tryphaena and Thecla in the *Acts of Thecla* is an interesting example of a wealthy woman with no heirs, her own daughter being dead, who seems to make Thecla her heir, although no legal process is discernible in the text. The difficulty adopting daughters or the infrequency of such adoptions may be related to the underlying cultural logic I have articulated here.

65. Foreign royalty who wished to marry women of the Herodian family were apparently expected to undergo rites of incorporation, on which see n. 68.

ancient patterns of practice. That is, some Gentiles in antiquity, both men and women, venerated the Judean god, for all sorts of reasons, and under all sorts of circumstances—political, social, and personal. Gentile benefactors made donations to local synagogues; individuals prayed to the Judean god for personal benefits; foreign rulers gave substantial gifts for the functioning of the temple in Jerusalem.[66] Interestingly, non-Judeans sacrificing to the Judean God in the temple in Jerusalem seems largely unheard of, partly, of course, because much of the evidence for non-Judean veneration postdates the fall of the Temple in 70 C.E., and partly because Gentiles were forbidden to enter the inner precincts of the Temple.

Others chose, for whatever reasons, to join the Judean *ethnos*, engaging in what we have come to call conversion. We have only a limited knowledge of what they did to do so, but we have some glimpses, all of which are consistent with the thesis that new kinship is being constructed. As my detailed discussion of the inscriptions will make clear, proselytes appear to have changed their names: Veturia to Sarah, Felicitas to Peregrina (although this particular instance is less clear), many men to Judah, the first-born son of the patriarch Jacob and the eponymous ancestor of the Judean *ethnos*. There is also some evidence that proselytes no longer considered themselves the children of their fathers. Rabbinic sources claim this, and the small corpus of proselyte inscriptions is consistent with this: virtually no proselyte is identified by the name of a father (with the possible exception of one particularly vexing exception that I will discuss later, the epitaph of Eirene, and where I now think it's quite possible that *proselyte* there actually applies to the father, not the deceased child).

That male proselytes generally underwent circumcision makes perfect sense within this model of conversion as re-configured kinship. Israelite males were circumcised at birth as the quintessential external sign of their kinship. If circumcision is how Israelite and later, Jewish, men "make" Jewishness and Jewish masculinity (and, in Nancy Jay's argument, actually construct lines of male kinship that intentionally exclude or at least obscure the role of women in the actual biological process of producing sons), it seems particularly appropriate that a man who now wishes to be incorporated into the Judean *ethnos* must also be circumcised.[67] That this sometimes posed significant difficulties (as in, for instance, the debate Josephus includes in his discussion of the household of

---

66. E.g., Antiochus III, c. 200 B.C.E., who, according to Josephus (*Antiquities* 12.137–44) gave extensive gifts for the sacrificial cult. For discussion of this passage and other instances, as well as a fairly thorough overview of debates about the authenticity and reliability of these decrees in Josephus, see Schwartz 2001:52–55. Conversely, Judeans made donations in honor of rulers. In addition to inscriptions by Judeans for various Ptolemaic rulers from Egypt, see, e.g., Scheiber 1983: no. 3, an inscription by Cosmius, ἀρχισυνάγωγος of the Judeans in Spondilla, for Severus Alexander and his mother, Julia Mamaea, obviously dated to Severus' reign, 222–235 C.E.

67. Analyzed in depth by Eilberg-Schwartz 1990; Jay 1992; see also Cohen 2005.

Adiabene, or the occasional reluctance of prospective Gentile husbands of Herodian women to be circumcised, also from Josephus) doesn't make the underlying cultural logic any less the case.[68]

Despite the extensive scholarly ink spilled on this question, the issue isn't whether women were more likely to be proselytes because they didn't have to be circumcised, whereas men were more likely to be "God-fearers." If it is true that women were disproportionately proselytes (which, as we shall see, the evidence does not permit us to determine), it is unlikely to be because men were reluctant to put a knife to their penises, something that I suspect relates more to contemporary male scholarly anxiety than to ancient realities.[69] Rather, as I have suggested earlier, the fact that females do not have the same degree of incorporation into ethnic identity as males may mean that it is culturally easier for them to leave one ethnicity and move into another, with less attendant ritual transformation. In rabbinic law, for instance, a woman converts merely through an act of immersion in water, which is often construed as ritual cleansing (of her prior Gentile impurity?), but which may also be construed as an act of ritual death and rebirth into the new *ethnos*, or at least into it as much as is possible for females. This makes eminent cultural sense, for all females are born, even if they are rarely adopted.

Because much of the evidence for Gentile interest in Judean practice in the Roman period comes, not from explicit references to proselytes or other

---

68. On Helena, see later; see also Josephus, *Antiquities* 20.139, where Drusilla's first betrothal falls through after Antiochus's son Epiphanes μὴ βουληθεὶς τὰ Ἰουδαίων ἔθη μεταλαβεῖν, perhaps translated as "did not wish to take part in Judean customs," or "participate in Judean customs," or even "adopt" Judean customs, all of which are attested meanings of μεταλαμβάνω, and more ambiguous than Feldman's "convert to the Jewish religion." Since Azizus of Emesa was willing to be circumcised to marry Drusilla, it seems that this was the determinative issue, although Josephus does not explicitly say this. (She ultimately ends up married to the Roman procurator of Judea, Felix, who is not said to undergo circumcision). Further, this makes sense of Paul's denial of circumcision, in a manner that shifts the discussion away from questions of Paul's loyalty to Torah, although it may have other components as well. At the very least, if circumcision makes a male a member of the Judean *ethnos*, and Paul has in mind a wholly new *ethnos*, circumcision would not be the rite imposed on new "sons," even as it would not bar those who had been previously circumcised. This is precisely what Paul says repeatedly: neither circumcision nor uncircumcision is anything: e.g., Gal 5.6; 6.15; 1 Cor 7.18–19. Rom 4.11 argues that Abraham was circumcised to make him the ancestor of those who, while uncircumcised, still trust in God's promise to Abraham. For Paul, the new rites of incorporation center on death and rebirth, marked particularly by baptism and metaphors of rebirth, as well as by metaphors of adoption, themselves reinforcing the gendered nature of this system, and themselves, perhaps, appealing to traditions that understood the sonship of Jesus in analogous ways, as the chosen, adopted son of God. The absence of virgin birth traditions in Paul and any real references to Jesus's biological mother (or father) is quite consistent with this, as is Paul's seemingly unself-conscious reference to James as the brother of the Lord (Gal 1.19).

69. 1 Macc 1.15 suggests that Judean men were quite willing to undergo the pain of epispasis to remove the effects of earlier circumcision; conversely, Josephus claims, in his account of the "conversion" of the household of Adiabene, that the debate over circumcision had to do with the political consequences, and not the personal discomforts entailed. Paul's circumcision of Timothy in Acts 16.3 (itself a somewhat odd story) contains no hint that Timothy might have resisted out of concern for the pain!

language designating converts, but to the more amorphous references that scholars have seen as evidence of something other than conversion (or what I have re-described earlier as joining the Judean *ethnos*), in the survey that follows, I will attend to evidence for both: Gentile women who appear to have become part of the Judean *ethnos*, to the extent that women could, in fact, do so, as well as instances of Gentile women who may have, at least at certain points in their lives, engaged in various Judean practices, without a corresponding change of ethnicity. References to women called *theosebēs*, or *metuentes*, and comparable terms will only be relevant if it seems reasonable to think that the term does in fact signal Gentile interest in Judean practice. If it signals only commended piety or if it is impossible to tell, it will be obviously of less force for any arguments one might then make both about the interest of Gentile women in Judean practice, and the explanations for such interest.

Epigraphical Evidence

Proselyte Inscriptions

Persons designated on inscriptions as proselytes (either in Greek or Latin) have generally been presumed to be converts to Judaism, defined along the lines I suggested earlier, although without the attendant theoretical framework. Scholars have occasionally noted that even the term *proselyte* is potentially ambiguous: Justin Martyr, for instance, uses it at least once to refer to devotees of Christ,[70] and Martin Goodman has suggested that in Matt 23.15 it refers to taking up association with a particular Judean group.[71] The term also designates a few persons on ossuaries from the *Dominus Flevit* ("the Lord wept") cemetery in Jerusalem. Some scholars consider these to be converts to Judaism, but others consider them converts to Christianity.[72] If they do here

---

70. Justin refers to "Christ and his proselytes" (τὸν χριστόν και τοὺς προσηλύτους αὐτοῦ), *Dialogue with Trypho* 122.5; although generally Justin does use the term to refer to those who adopt Judean practices (e.g., *Trypho* 122.1–123.2; 23.3). Here I have relied on Sievers 1996.

71. Goodman 1991:60–63, cited in Sievers 1996:36 n. 11.

72. See Sievers 1996:36, with details in nn. 7 and 8. Two inscriptions (rm. 79, nos. 13 and 21 use the Greek; a third, no. 31, is in Aramaic. It seems that Christian scholars (B. Bagatti and E. Testa) read these ossuaries as Christian, whereas Figueras 1983 (who wrote his doctoral dissertation at Hebrew University in 1974 on decorated Jewish ossuaries) reads them as Jewish. The editors of *IJO* 3 consider one of the Greek inscriptions (*Syr 9*) Jewish (*IJO* 3: pp.15–17). In fact, these inscriptions raise numerous problems. On the inside of the ossuary lid, in very poorly executed letters, *IJO* 3 Syr9 seems to commemorate one "Ioudan" as a proselyte, and the editors write: "Someone buried in an ossuary with a name derived from Judah and described as a proselyte can hardly be anything other than a Jew ..." (*IJO* 3: p. 17). However, there is a charcoal mark on the side of the ossuary that seems to resemble closely a *chi rho*, for which multiple explanations have been proposed, including everything from a marker of Judean Christian identity, to a merchandising mark. The editors tentatively date the ossuary to the first

designate persons who have become devotees of Jesus, this might support Goodman's proposal that, at least in the first century, the term *proselyte* designates persons who come over from one Judean community to another.[73]

Setting aside these interpretive problems for the moment, the total number of Greek and Latin inscriptions that may designate persons as proselytes is quite small: Sievers's most inclusive list is approximately twenty-eight, although my own count of those in Greek and Latin is fourteen.[74] The precise number of extant Judean inscriptions from antiquity is a moving target that depends in part on how one identifies a Judean inscription, as well as continuing new finds. However one counts, the total number of inscriptions in Greek and Latin through perhaps the sixth century is on the order of perhaps 1600, with by far the largest percentage coming from catacombs in Rome (on the order of 600, well over a third).[75]

Scholarly discussions tend to obscure the fact that the proselyte inscriptions are sparse not only in number, but also in distribution and date. No one area has yielded more than a handful of inscriptions: seven are from Rome, with one possible additional inscription whose reading is uncertain; another one is from elsewhere in Italy. Dating these inscriptions is difficult,

century C.E. but note that earlier editors took it to be fourth century C.E. (SEG 17 [1960], 785). See also Donaldson 2000, who notes that in the other Dominus Flevit inscriptions, the deceased are identified by their filiation, and thus proposes that the term *proselyte* functions as a marker of familial incorporation that appears consistent with the model I propose here (2000:384). Two other Aramaic inscriptions in this volume identify proselytes: *IJO 3 Syr72* from Jerusalem, for a man named Judah, which they date to first B.C.E.–C.E., and *IJO 3 Syr84*, a donor plaque from Dura Europos in the third century C.E. for an unidentified male.

73. This is my language: he would just say they have moved from one form of Judaism into another. Although I am not intentionally equating the two terms (proselyte and convert), the use of proselyte for what I here describe as "conversion" might support my theory, given the connotations of *prosēlutos* as one who has arrived a (new, foreign) place, and thus has come over from one place to another (LSJ, s.v. προσηλύτευσις). The Dominus Flevit inscriptions could still be understood to entail movement into a new *ethnos* (see also Donaldson 2000); whether, as Goodman proposes, becoming a Pharisee could be construed similarly is a more difficult issue, in need of consideration. Rosenblum 2010 suggests that the rabbis are constructing a new *ethnos* of sorts, one marked by reconfigured (rabbinic) kinship (rabbinic lineages), marriage rules, rites of adoption, sonship language, restrictive meal practices, and so forth.

74. See below, n. 78, for a detailed list.

75. For my earlier consideration of these issues, see Kraemer 1991. Also helpful is van der Horst 1991. For many years, the primary collection of ancient Jewish inscriptions was *CIJ* (Frey 1936) itself only partial. Volume I (western Europe, including Rome) was reprinted in 1975, with an extensive prolegomenon by B. Lifshitz. Inscriptions found only in that edition are cited as *CIJ* I². Inscriptions cited as *CIJ* I are found both in the 1936 edition and the 1975 edition. The study of such inscriptions has been much improved in recent years with the publication of half a dozen volumes, all but one with English translations, notes, and bibliography: for Egypt, *JIGRE* (Horbury and Noy 1992); for western Europe excluding Rome, *JIWE* I (Noy 1993); for the city of Rome and environs, *JIWE* 2 (Noy 1995); for Eastern Europe, *IJO* I (Noy, Panayotov, and Bloedhorn 2004); for Asia Minor, *IJO* 2 (Ameling 2004); for Syria and Cyprus, *IJO* 3 (Noy and Bloedhorn 2004). These volumes classify approximately 1458 inscriptions as Jewish: *JIGRE*, 134; *JIWE* I, 192; *JIWE* 2, 600; *IJO* I, 98; *IJO* 2, 258; *IJO* 3, 176. This does not include inscriptions from Cyrene or North Africa (on which see Le Bohec 1981 and Stern 2008). A project to collate and publish Jewish inscriptions from the land of Israel is ongoing.

but generally the Roman inscriptions appear to be second to fourth century C.E. The earliest appears to be an inscription from Masada, securely dated to the early 70s, at the end of the first revolt. One other inscription, from Cyrene, is dated first to second century C.E. The latest is apparently face *a* of the Aphrodisias stele, from the fifth century C.E., which appears to designate three men as proselytes. Thus the bulk of these inscriptions are late (third to fifth centuries C.E.), with just a few earlier instances.

To draw anything in the way of general observations from this data seems close to futile.[76] The proselyte inscriptions constitute no more than 2 percent of the extant inscriptional corpus, and probably somewhat less, whereas that corpus itself testifies to only a tiny fraction of Judeans who lived in the Greco-Roman Mediterranean. The Judeans buried in Roman catacombs, for instance, average out to no more than a few persons a year over the several centuries the catacombs appear to have been in use, assuming that all these persons were, in fact, Judeans. Even if one envisions a far smaller time period for the use of the catacombs, it seems incomprehensible that more than a small fraction of Judeans living in Rome are buried there.[77]

Nevertheless, in my initial work on this material over twenty-five years ago, it did seem to me intriguing that a significant percentage of those persons identified as proselytes in these inscriptions are women. Sievers noted that of his twenty-eight possible epigraphical proselytes, half were female, half were male. Although he gives no gender count for his final list of fourteen clear references, the total appears to be six: five of the seven from Rome, and one from Cyrene. All the proselytes from Aphrodisias are male, as is the proselyte from Masada, and those in Greek from the Dominus Flevit cemetery in Jerusalem discussed earlier. Using a slightly different database, Judith Lieu identified nineteen proselytes, nine of whom she identified as female. Thus, both Sievers and Lieu calculated that roughly half of the proselytes mentioned epigraphically were female.

---

76. Still, the dating of these inscriptions may be significant; if the Roman inscriptions are properly dated, that there appear to be none later than the fourth century makes some sense. After this, various legal consequences for converting non-Jews appear in Roman imperial legislation: see, e.g., Linder 1987 no. 8 (Constantine, 18 Oct 329); no. 12 (Constantius II, 3 July 353); no. 16 (Gratian, 21 May 383). Although the enforcement of those laws was clearly not uniform, and may have been largely irrelevant in certain parts of the empire, in Rome itself, it is likely to have been significant, even when the imperial administration was in Constantinople. At the very least, conversion might not be something to advertise epigraphically. This might also explain why in the fifth century one can still find at least a few proselytes (on face *a* in Aphrodisias), something that might have been far less feasible elsewhere in the empire. The question of conversion to Judaism by either Christians or others after this is both complex and largely beyond the scope of this study.

77. This seems, however, roughly consistent with the data for Roman period burials generally: we have evidence for the burials of about 1.5 percent of the population for the 350-year period between 25 B.C.E. and 325 C.E. (Bodel 2008:242).

My own most recent calculations produce slightly but, perhaps, not significantly different results. Fourteen inscriptions identify a total of sixteen persons identified as proselytes, (accepting, with the editors of *IJO* 3, only one from Dominus Flevit, a male named Ioudan, as becoming Judean.[78] Since both Greek inscriptions from Dominus Flevit for proselytes are male, how many of these are included changes the percentage of female proselytes, but not their actual numbers).[79]

Excluding any data from Dominus Flevit, there are at most thirteen inscriptions identifying fifteen persons. Five are explicitly female: Veturia/Sarah, Felicitas/Peregrina, and Crysis, all of Rome; Sarah of Cyrene, and Aste(r) of Caesarea.[80] Eirene is clearly female, but whether she or her unnamed father is the proselyte is not entirely secure.[81] One highly fragmentary Greek inscription that appears to contain the feminine form [Io]udea, has often been read to designate the deceased as prose[lutos] and possibly also [th]eoseb(e)s, although there is considerable debate about all three readings, especially the last two.[82] A fifth-century Greek epitaph from Venosa contains the letters "pros. . . . it[i]" after the probably male Anastases. At most, then, there are eight female proselytes, out of a total of between fifteen and seventeen persons (if one included back in the two male proselytes in Greek inscriptions from Dominus Flevit).

One might initially be tempted to point out that all these calculations suggest a relatively equitable distribution that, in turn, implies that women and

---

78. 1. *JIWE* 2.62 = *CIJ* 1.462 (Felicitas); 2. *JIWE* 2.218 = *CIJ* 1.256 (Nicetas); 3. *JIWE* 2.224 = *CIJ* 1.222 (Chrysis); 4. *JIWE* 2.392 = *CIJ* 1.202 (name lacking; see also later on whether προσήλυτος actually occurs); 5. *JIWE* 2.489 = *CIJ* 1.21 (deceased is Eirene); 6. *JIWE* 2.491 = *CIJ* 1.68 (Crescens); 7. *JIWE* 2.577 = *CIJ* 1.523 (Veturia Paulla); 8. *CIJ* 1.576 (Anastases); 9. Luderitz, *Cyrene* 12, (Sara); 10. *IJO* 2.14 (Samuel, Joses, Joseph); 11. Masada 1989 (male name, lacking); 12. *IJO* 3, Syr9 (Ioudas); 13. Lifshitz 1961:115–16, no. 2 (Aste[r]); 14. *CIJ* 2.1385. This last is a little puzzling: in Greek it reads Ιουδατος Λαγανιωνος προσηλυτου. Frey's French translation is ambiguous; it's unclear whether he takes the proselyte to be Ioudas, son of Laganion, or to be Laganion (*CIJ* 2, p. 318). As I note later (e.g., n. 88) proselytes are not identified in the inscriptions by a patronymic, presumably because becoming Judean nullified their patrilineage, so it seems more likely that the proselyte is Laganion or that this is a geographic of some sort. Ioudas is a well-attested name for male proselytes. In any case, the list by van der Horst 1991:71–72, is comparable in scale, with some differences, to my own. He counts sixteen inscriptions and eighteen persons, but he includes four inscriptions from Dominus Flevit, including one (rm. 79, no. 22) thought to be a forgery (see *IJO* 3, pp. 115–17); he does not have Sarah of Cyrene nor an inscription for an unnamed male proselyte from Masada, which might not have been available to him at the time.

79. The third possible proselyte inscription from Dominus Flevit, rm 79, no. 31 is Aramaic: the editors take it to read "Salome the proselyte." The feminine form, גיורתה, seems clear, whether or not the person's name is Salome (as opposed to just the word שלום).

80. The actual inscription reads "Aste," but Lifshitz construed it as Aster (and as a Grecized form of the Hebrew Esther), arguing that the dropped final rho is attested elsewhere (1961:116). Aster is attested in a Roman epitaph (*JIWE* 2.91 = *CIJ* 1.306, where Frey also comments that it is very probably a form of Esther: Asther also occurs in several relatively late inscriptions from Venosa.

81. See later.

82. *JIWE* 2.392 = *CIJ* 1.202. The editors tentatively reconstruct προσήλυτος relying on the epitaph of Eirene.

men were equally likely to become Judeans, and that there is, thus, no basis for the repeated assertions that women were the majority of converts. It is important, however, to keep in mind that on the whole, women are significantly underrepresented in the corpus of ancient inscriptions. Inscriptions for women (and girls) constitute approximately 40 percent of the surviving epitaphs, both Jewish and non-Jewish,[83] whereas women donors constitute a considerably smaller proportion,[84] and the number of named women is an even smaller percentage of named men (perhaps on the order of 10 percent). Thus an even distribution of males and females in any given sample may well be a disproportionate percentage of females.[85] This is particular true in the case of the Roman inscriptions where, of the seven proselytes, five are female. Still, the sample is sufficiently small that we should not extrapolate on the basis of this data alone. In my view, it is far more helpful to discuss the particular inscriptions to see what they suggest, rather than to try to generalize from the statistics at hand.

By far the richest and most significant inscription for a female proselyte is the epitaph of a woman called Veturia Paula which opens this chapter. Incised on a sarcophagos, the inscription was seen and transcribed by several antiquarian scholars in the seventeenth century, but its whereabouts, as well as its provenance, have been unknown for a long time. Its clear reference to two synagogues, one attested in inscriptions from the Monteverde catacomb, and the other in inscriptions from the Vigna Randanini catacomb strongly supports the view that Veturia lived in Rome for at least some period of time.[86]

83. Zabin 1996 cites Hopkins 1985:118, table 1, for general figures. She counts 291 males (57 percent) commemorated in Jewish burial inscriptions from Rome and 221 females (43 percent). She relied, however, on *CIJ* 1 and the appendix of inscriptions in Leon 1960, because, as noted earlier, she did not have access to *JIWE* 2. This might prompt some recalculation, but I have not attempted to do that here. See also the calculations and discussion in Rutgers 2000 who rightly critiques some of my preliminary calculations (Kraemer 1986, reprinted without my knowledge or permission in Juschka 2001).

84. Kron 1996 found that donations by women were on the order of one-tenth of those by men, cited in Cole 2004:114, with cautions about the data.

85. Citing Kraemer 1986, Matthews makes a similar point about these very inscriptions (2001:26). Still, in adducing these inscriptions as context for her otherwise carefully nuanced discussion of Roman practice in the first and second centuries C.E., Matthews, too, amalgamates evidence that may chronologically be much later, and thus not necessarily relevant. Van der Horst also makes a similar argument (1991:109).

86. The synagogue of the Volumnesians is attested in several inscriptions found in the Monteverde catacomb, (*JIWE* 2.100 = *CIJ* 1.402, a child μελλάρχων; *JIWE* 2.163 = *CIJ* 1.417, the epitaph of Flavius Sabinus, an officer for life (?) of the synagogue; *JIWE* 2.167 = *CIJ* 1.343, the inscription of Hilarus, archon of the synagogue). The synagogue of the Campesians (perhaps deriving from a location near the Campus Martius—see *JIWE* 2, p. 250) is attested in two other inscriptions: *JIWE* 2.288 = *CIJ* 1.88, from the Vigna Randanini catacomb, the epitaph of a young archon, aged 8, the son of Julianus, called "father of the synagogue of the Campesians"; and *JIWE* 2.560 = *CIJ* 1.319, a marble plaque of uncertain provenance, the epitaph of Irene, the virginal bride of Clodius. Either Clodius, or perhaps Irene herself, was the sibling of Quintus Claudius Synesius, father of the synagogue of the Campesians. All these inscriptions are tentatively dated to the third to fourth centuries. As Brooten noted in her initial study, the majority of titles associated with these two synagogues are father and mother of the synagogue.

Remembered for being the "mother" of two separate synagogues, Veturia Paula is said to have been 70 when she became a proselyte, taking the name of the quintessentially illustrious Jewish mother, the matriarch Sarah. (Whether these two data are related is unknowable). That she did so at an age that was, in antiquity, quite old, and lived another 16 years, has some interesting implications for arguments often made about Gentile women's interest in Judean practices. Veturia/Sarah is unlikely to have become a Judean in order to marry one, for several reasons. Although it is not impossible that she married (surely not a first marriage) at this late age, it would be highly unusual.[87] The absence of any mention of a husband, himself presumably prominent in the local communities, also suggests otherwise. Nor is there any indication that she undertook this change together with a husband, which, again, we might expect to find noted in her epitaph.

As Brooten explored in depth in her study, Veturia/Sarah is also highly unlikely to have derived her titles of office from her relationships with male relatives. Her Gentile father is unlikely to have been the basis on which she was given the title "mother of the synagogue" in two separate congregations, because, as a Gentile, he is unlikely to have held office in either congregation (even if one wants to imagine that he might have been a supporter of one or more congregations). Nor is it worth meaningful speculation that her conversion might have followed his, since the odds of Veturia's father being alive when she was 70 are vanishingly small, given ancient demographic patterns. And in both cases, one might expect some mention of the father under these highly unusual circumstances. As is typical of proselyte inscriptions, Veturia/Sarah's claims no filiation, either paternal or maternal.[88] More demographically feasible is the possibility that Veturia/Sarah followed a son into Jewish practice, but this seems even less plausible, given the absence of any mention of children in the inscription. On the contrary, Veturia/Sarah's inscription suggests that at the time of her death, she either had no immediate living family, whether husband or children, or she had severed her ties with them in the course of her new ethnic identification. It is tempting to imagine, based particularly on her age, that Veturia/Sarah's conversion was facilitated by the autonomy that comes to women who outlive their husbands and perhaps also

---

87. Frier 1999:93 suggests that women were highly unlikely to contract additional marriages after about 35.

88. Although see the discussion of Eirene, the child proselyte whose parents commemorate her in *JIWE* 2.489 = *CIJ* 1.21; and note also *JIWE* 2.491 = *CIJ* 1.58, the epitaph of Crescens Sincerius Judeus, whose mother erects the memorial (but does not identify Crescens' father). I have noted elsewhere the (remote) possibility that Crescens is called proselyte for his conversion to Christianity, despite the designation Judeus, but most scholars consider this unambiguously Jewish, and that is the most likely reading (Kraemer 1989b).

their adult sons, especially if they have sufficient economic resources at their disposal. Veturia's title of "mother of the synagogue" strongly suggests that she had and used such resources for the benefit of these two congregations, whether the title designates an office with particular functions (as discussed earlier) or whether, as some scholars have argued, "mother of the synagogue" was a title bestowed on certain benefactors for their largesse, without pointing to what Horbury calls "governing" functions.

A second inscription that may also hint at underlying social realities is that of the woman called Felicitas.[89] A Latin epitaph on a marble plaque originally found in 1906 in the Monteverde catacomb, and now on display in the Pio Christiano Museum at the Vatican, it commemorates a forty-seven-year-old woman explicitly designated a proselyte. The dedicator of the inscription is Felicitas's unnamed male patron. Like most inscriptions from this catacomb, it has been dated to the third or fourth centuries.

Although this inscription is quite easy to read, there has been considerable puzzlement over the meaning of the letters VINUENN in line 2, as well as the referent of Peregrina in line 3. The most likely, but by no means definitive, reading seems to be "Felicitas, a proselyte for six years under the name Pereg-rina, who lived forty-seven years. Her patron (had this made) for the one well deserving."[90]

If this reading is correct, Felicitas, like Veturia, became Judean relatively late in life, although obviously at a meaningfully younger age. Like Veturia, Felicitas would seem to have taken a second name, Peregrina, perhaps designating her status as a "stranger." That both inscriptions retain the woman's earlier name may be an acknowledgment that some persons continued to relate to them by their prior names.

Although not all clients had previously been slaves of their patrons, Felicitas is usually taken to have been the freedwoman of her unnamed male patron, perhaps partly on the basis of her name, which is well attested for slaves.[91] Some scholars have speculated that this patron, presumed to be Judean himself, was somehow involved in her conversion.[92] There is considerable evidence that Judean slaveholders facilitated, if not required, Judean practices of their slaves, although by the fourth century, it became increasingly problematic to do

89. *JIWE* 2.62 = *CIJ* 1.462.
90. Noy notes that ANNVI might also be read Annu I, meaning a proselyte for a year, but he thinks this less likely than the reading given here: *JIWE* 2, p. 55. Frey, the editor of *CIJ*, read the garbled letters NUENN as "by the name of Naomi," influenced, no doubt, by the apparent appropriateness of the name Naomi for a convert.
91. Perpetua's female co-martyr, Felicitas, is identified as a slave in the *Martyrdom of Saints Perpetua and Felicitas* 2, the editorial frame, but nowhere else in the narrative.
92. E.g., Noy, *JIWE* 2, p. 55.

so, as Christian emperors legislated against it.[93] One other Latin proselyte inscription is explicitly the dedication of a female patron named Dionysia to her client, Nicetas.[94] It is still in the Vigna Randanini catacomb, incised with a seven-branched menorah, and tentatively dated, as are most of these, to the third or fourth centuries. As with the epitaph of Felicitas, whether Nicetas had previously been Dionysia's slave is conceivable but not demonstrable.

There is also evidence that male slaveowners freed female slaves with whom they wished to contract a more licit relationship (including, presumably, one that led to the production of licit heirs).[95] Based partly on rabbinic rulings that require the conversion of the slave in such situations,[96] inscriptions like this have sometimes been read as suggesting that marriage was the impetus for conversion. In this particular case, such a scenario is not impossible, but it is perhaps improbable. Felicitas was at least forty-one when she became a proselyte, if not older.[97] Such age does not, of course, make it impossible that marriage was the impetus, but it does make it unlikely that marriage aimed at the production of licit heirs was, given the demographic reality, both in antiquity and in modernity, that few women are still fertile in their forties.[98]

Still, the combination of Felicitas's age and her likely prior status as a slave, raise important questions. If it is the case that Judeans felt obligated, or at least pressured, to manumit slaves who adopted Judean practices (which would cohere with the logic of conversion as joining the Judean *ethnos*), Judean slave owners had economic incentives for not encouraging their slaves to convert, or at least not until the point when they might have sold them anyway (when, for instance, they were no longer able to perform the physical labors for which they had originally been acquired or raised). Felicitas's age might suggest that she was no longer capable of bearing children who could either provide labor for their owner or be sold for income; alternatively (and not mutually exclusively) she might no longer have been able to serve as a wet-nurse, a function attested

93. See, e.g., Hezser 2005, especially 35–36, on rabbinic arguments for immersing and circumcising (male) slaves before using them in rabbinic households; see also prohibitions against converting slaves to Judean practices in Linder, no. 11 (Constantine II, 13 Aug 339) [pp.144–50]; no. 17 (Gratian with Valentinian II and Theodosius, Sept 384) [pp.174–77].

94. *JIWE* 2.218 = *CIJ* 1.256.

95. See, e.g., Treggiari 1991:120; 123.

96. See, e.g., the discussion of Hezser 2003:415ff. Hezser notes that Josephus expands the Levitical categories of marriage partners forbidden to priests to include slaves and female prisoners of war (*Antiquities* 3.276), which is particularly interesting because, in his *Life* 414, Josephus, who claims priestly descent, says that he was married to a slave while himself enslaved to Vespasian, a marriage that was terminated (apparently by the wife) after they were freed.

97. If, as Noy considers (earlier, n. 90), she was only a proselyte for one year, she would have been forty-six at the time.

98. Frier 1999:94–100, esp. 96.

for both slaves and poorer free persons.[99] These scenarios themselves depend partly, although not entirely, on whether we imagine that Felicitas had been born and raised a slave, or whether she had become enslaved as an adult.

Further, that Felicitas was at some point enslaved and then freed raises questions about whether her conversion was an autonomous choice, or something coerced. In the case of Veturia/Sarah, it was tempting to suggest that the autonomy of advanced age played a role in her new affiliation, but in the case of Felicitas, older age might not necessarily point to autonomous choice. Although nothing in the inscription enables us to answer this question, it is easy enough to imagine that slaves might well find accepting membership in the Judean *ethnos* in exchange for manumission highly preferable to remaining enslaved. Several manumission contracts from the Greco-Roman period point to such connections between manumission and conversion (or at least service to the Judean god), although none come from Rome in this period.[100] Thus, while Veturia/Sarah may point to the possibility of older, elite women choosing a new religious association, and the privileges and social rewards that come with benefaction, that of Felicitas may point to a more complex and, to contemporary sensibilities, more disturbing dynamic underlying the adoption of new religious practices.

A third inscription from Rome provides considerably less information, but may still illustrate some of the social dynamics involved. This is yet another Latin epitaph from the Vigna Randanini catacomb, dated to the third/fourth centuries, a short inscription set up by Mannacius for his "sweetest" sister, Crysis.[101] As a printed photograph indicates,[102] the word *proselyte* comes below the main inscription in smaller letters, perhaps suggesting that it was an addition, correction, or afterthought of some sort.

Epitaphs erected by siblings are not unknown, but are relatively rare, a reflection of the general commemorative practices of antiquity in which dedications to wives by their husbands are most frequent, followed by dedications of wives to their husbands, for those inscriptions in which the dedicator is known. That a woman would be memorialized only by her brother generally suggests that, at the time, she had neither a living husband nor living parents (nor living children). Because, however, Crysis is called a proselyte, it is possible but of course not demonstrable that this change resulted in severed ties with

---

99. For a (probably) Judean wetnurse contract, see *CPJ* 1.146 (*WRGRW* 51); on wet nursing in the Roman period, see Hopkins 1986.

100. E.g., *CIRB* 70, 71, 73: see Gibson 1999.

101. *JIWE* 2.224 = *CIJ* 1.222. I read *sister* here to denote a biological sibling, but it does have alternate connotations in antiquity, including, of course, its use as a term for Christians, itself relying on constructions of Christians as an *ethnos*.

102. *CIJ* 1.159.

whatever living relatives she may have had. The failure to identify her, not only by the name of a husband (which presumably she does not currently have), but also by the name of her father, suggests that he was not Judean, although it might also mean that Crysis had been a slave at birth and, so, had no legal father. Hypothetically, the parents of the two siblings might have become Judeans after Crysis was born, but before Mannacius' birth. In such a case, though, we might expect some indication of filiation. The fact that Mannacius paid for his sister's plaque in a catacomb containing many other Judean burials[103] (where the inscription may still be) suggests, at least, that he acquiesced in some way to her conversion, if he was not also himself a proselyte.

The remaining proselyte inscriptions for women afford little additional insight into why and how women became proselytes, although the epitaph of Sara of Cyrene, age eighteen, might conceivably point to marriage as the impetus, and the name Sara is evocative of Veturia's new name, several centuries later in a different locale. One other inscription, though, requires reconsideration, the Greek epitaph on a marble plaque from the Villa Torlonia catacomb in Rome, for a three-year-old female child, dated to the same period as the rest of the Roman proselyte inscriptions.[104] I wrote about this inscription extensively some years ago, where my interest was primarily to consider the possibility that the terms *Ioudaios, Ioudaia, Iudeus, Iudea* in Greek and Latin inscriptions frequently indicate that the person was a convert. I will not initially attempt to translate the first part of the inscription, but rather provide a slightly annotated transcription that indicates the interpretive dilemmas it poses:

> *Eirēnē trezptē* (=*threptē?*) *prosēlutos patros* (father) and *mētros* (mother)
> *eioudea is(d)raēlits*
> She lived three years, seven months, one day

The only unambiguous part of the inscription is the deceased's age at death. The name Eirene means peace, and the phrase "in peace," or more frequently "in peace (be) her sleep" occurs regularly in Roman Judean epitaphs, usually at the end. Hypothetically, one might translate "Peace to (the) *threptē*, (she) of a proselyte father and a Judean, Israelite, mother."[105] All recent interpretations of the inscription, however, take Eirene to be the child's name, an

---

103. John Bodel (2008) argues that Roman catacombs were not as homogenous as they have often been presumed, an argument that has considerable implications for assessing the co-called Jewish catacombs, and for accounting for those burials that lack distinctive Judean markers.

104. *JIWE* 2.489 = *CIJ* 1.21; with extensive bibliography in *JIWE* 2.

105. This was not one of the translations I considered previously.

interpretation supported by its occurrence at the beginning of the inscription. All interpretations have also taken *threptē* to apply to the deceased, this term generally designating a person born into slavery and raised in the slaveholder's household, often for household duties, although it can also sometimes designate a person abandoned at birth, rescued, and then raised as a slave.[106] A *threptē* (masc. *threptos*) of the first sort did not, by definition, have a licit father, which might suggest that Eirene is a *threptē* of the second sort—a rescued foundling, although as we shall see, this creates some interesting interpretive dilemmas. It is not even entirely clear that *threptē* is the intended reading: the spelling, *trezpte*, is unique, and although no one has suggested that this might represent the deceased's name, it might be possible (if highly unlikely) to read the first two words of the inscription as "peace to Trezpte."

It is the remainder of the inscription that has occasioned the most scholarly discussion.[107] At issue have been to whom the terms *proselyte*, *Eioudea*, and *Is(d)raelites* apply, and what, precisely, they were intended to signify. The apparent grammatical forms of these terms have contributed to the confusion. The term *proselyte* is here masculine. The use of masculine forms to describe women is well attested in general, but the number of Greek proselyte inscriptions is so small that there are no other comparable instances. All of the Latin proselyte inscriptions from the Roman catacombs use appropriately gendered forms. Thus it might seem that proselyte here refers to the father, something I now think quite possible. However, proselyte occurs here in nominative form, whereas *patros* is the genitive for the Greek *father*. The term *matros* (mother), is also genitive. Eioudea, perhaps a misspelling for Ioudaia, appears to be a feminine nominative, which, if grammatically accurate, should describe the deceased, leaving aside the question of what, precisely, it intends to signify.[108] The term *Is(d)raelites* is particularly problematic. Although modern readers might not be surprised to see a Jew described as an Israelite, the term never occurs in ancient Jewish inscriptions, Roman or otherwise, and has been found so far only in Samaritan Greek inscriptions of a much earlier date.[109] Its ending (in *ēs*) could be read as a nominative masculine applying to the father, if we privilege

---

106. For references, see Kraemer 1989b:39 n. 10.

107. In addition to the discussion in Noy, *JIWE* 2, see also Kraemer 1989b:38–41, and van der Horst 1991:110–11, who favors applying all the descriptors to the deceased: Eirene, a *threptē*, proselyte, Jew, Israelite. See also now Hezser 2005:132, where she follows the translation in Noy and considers Eirene to be the proselyte, and an abandoned child raised by Jews.

108. This spelling does not occur elsewhere in the Roman inscriptions, but is found quite a few times in Asia Minor, e.g. *IJO* 2.179; 190; 241; and *IJO* 2.37 (*CIJ* 2.748), the seat plaque in the Miletus theatre. The spelling Eiodaios also occurs in *IJO* 1. Ach40: Demetrios Demetriou Eiodaios.

109. *IJO* 1. Ach66; Ach67.

agreement of gender over agreement of case. If we privilege agreement of case, it could apply to the deceased, as some scholars have read it. Alternatively, it is a feminine genitive applying to the mother."[110] Although I and others have noted the Samaritan use of *Israelites*, no one has yet taken that seriously and suggested that the phrase *Judean Israelite* might mean a Samaritan from Judea.

Part of the ambiguity with this inscription lies, of course, in the problems with its spelling, declensions, and even, perhaps, word order. But it also exemplifies a larger problem of theory and method. Scholars who have written about this inscription appear to assume that whoever commissioned it knew the identity markers of all of the persons involved, as well as the relations between those persons. They also appear to assume that these meanings were generally fixed in antiquity, so that the interpretive problems are here a function of the idiosyncracies of this particular inscription and not the larger problems of interpretation.

Yet on the contrary, this inscription exemplifies the larger hermeneutical issues. We have no way of knowing whether whoever commissioned the inscription was in fact a competent actor. Conceivably, the parents commissioned the inscription. Most readers would assume that those parents would have known what they were doing, and what they intended to put on the inscription. Although plausible, we cannot know this, and it is not impossible to imagine any number of scenarios that might produce an ambiguous, if not incoherent, inscription. Hypothetically, but yet consistent with what we know about the process of inscriptions in general, the inscriber made mistakes the parents were unable to recognize, being illiterate (as most persons were). Then we modern interpreters are trying to find coherence and significance where something different was intended by the dedicators. How would we know whether the dedicators used these various terms with meanings no longer accessible to us? How would we know whether these terms had taken on particular, idiosyncratic meanings for a particular social group? It is the practice of epigraphers to utilize methods that seem, on the one hand, quite reasonable: to look for parallel usages in other inscriptions, to identify names attested elsewhere, including in literary sources, or alternatively to note names, phrases, and features that appear to be unique. These practices are grounded in theories of the probability of meanings in general, and particular meanings in specific. Scholars tend to presume that a set of social facts is reliably represented in an inscription, and that our problem is merely to discern those facts. Although it's true that, if an

---

110. In Kraemer 1989b I said that the only argument no one had made, understandably, was precisely this—that *Israelite* applies to the father.

inscription is entirely idiosyncratic and ascribes meanings to particular terms that are restricted to a very small circle of persons, we have no hope of being able to understand those meanings, it's also true that our methods tend to ignore precisely such possibilities. In the case of this child's inscription, imagining a different dedicator—one less knowledgeable about the child's circumstances—might produce a different reading.

It is, then, actually impossible to determine the social situation that underlies this inscription, not only because of the ambiguities of the inscription itself but also because we cannot know what correspondence exists between the inscription and some set of social facts. The discussion that follows, then, is largely hypothetical, whose aim is simply to explore the possible but by no means necessary or even probable ramifications of this inscription.

If it is the three-year-old deceased girl who is in fact a proselyte, and assuming that *threptē* is what the dedicators intended, several scenarios may be envisioned: The child was either a foundling (more likely, I think), or a household slave raised in her owner's home. The dedicators are either the child's foster parents, or her biological parents. The term *foster parents* is probably a better English translation than *adoptive parents*, because calling them adoptive parents could be construed to signal some legal process that seems unlikely here in light of the child's probable designation as a *threptē*. If her foster parents, they were either Judeans or proselytes themselves (one or both) who, then, incorporate the child. Conceivably, the mother was a proselyte, and the father was not, although the reverse is possible. It is less likely, but not impossible that one parent (perhaps the father) was Judean, the other (perhaps the mother) Samaritan, if that is what the term *Israelites* was intended to signal. If the dedicators are her foster parents, and themselves proselytes, this inscription testifies indirectly to yet another Gentile Roman woman who became Judean, which might also be true if only the father was Judean by birth.

Alternatively, the parents are Eirene's actual birth parents, who reclaim her at death. But if so, under what circumstances did the child become a proselyte? That she is buried in a catacomb with numerous Judean burials certainly strengthens the argument that either she is, in fact, a proselyte, or the natural child of presently Judean parents, although this would imply that those parents had once abandoned her and then reclaimed her for burial. One might imagine all sorts of scenarios here, for instance, Gentile parents who abandon a baby (perhaps even one born illicitly), become Judean, regret abandoning the baby, and reclaim her for burial in a Judean site at death (or even reclaim her before her death). Her mother might have been an enslaved Judean whose child was taken from her (as regularly happened to enslaved mothers). The mother could then have been freed, married a proselyte, reclaimed the child, and converted the child as well. Yet another scenario could involve an enslaved mother owned by a master who subsequently became a proselyte, and retrieved the child (who might easily have been his own daughter, given the regular sexual use of slaves by their owners). In any case, if the child is a proselyte, this inscription points to another dynamic of conversion, one that entailed no choice on the part of the child. But in the end, the problems both of data and of theory make any resolution more a function of what we find plausible than of the actual social reality. Someone in this inscription was a proselyte, but who and how that factors into a consideration of women who became Judean remains elusive.

The proselyte inscriptions, thus, do not allow us to draw reliable conclusions about the degree to which women were over- or underrepresented among those ancient Gentiles who became members of the Judean *ethnos*. The data neither confirm nor disprove older theses that women predominated among proselytes, even while it would be a mistake to read these numbers as a reliable representation of the gender distribution of converts. Yet, as we have seen, several of the specific inscriptions allude to important social processes by which women might have been incorporated into the Judean *ethnos*, including autonomous choice (Veturia/Sarah, in all likelihood, and perhaps Crysis), and perhaps something more complex, such as coercion related to manumission or marriage (Felicitas/Peregrina), or even, perhaps, the incorporation of a child (Eirene).[111] These inscriptions are also consistent with a model of conversion as a change in ethnicity brought about through processes of reconfigured kinship, which may have been subtly but significantly different for females.

"God-Fearers" in Greek and Latin Inscriptions: Venerators of the Judean God?

THE LATIN INSCRIPTIONS. The designation of individuals as either *metuens* (*deum*), in Latin, or *theosebēs*, in Greek, occurs on the same order, if not precisely the same number, as proselyte inscriptions. Interestingly, although the author of Luke-Acts repeatedly describes people as *seboumenos ton theon*, this language is unattested epigraphically. Despite Juvenal's reference to a "sabbath-revering" father (*metuetem sabbata patrem*), only six Latin inscriptions designate individuals with some form of the verb *metuo* (to fear) whose object appears to be religious. Although five of these were considered in Frey's

---

111. One might speculate that marriage played some role in the designation of both Sarah of Cyrene and Aste(r) of Caesarea as proselytes, but the inscriptions themselves provide no real support for this. Aste(r)'s inscription also names one Paregorius, whom Sievers seems to take as her husband, but the inscription is hardly explicit on this point.

collection, Noy rejects four of these five as having no demonstrable association with Jews and Judaism.[112]

Of these six inscriptions, one clearly commemorates a young man, aged fifteen.[113] Four clearly designate women, of which Noy rejects three.[114] The sixth, an inscription from North Africa whose reading of *metuens* is itself a reconstruction, lacks definitive indicators of sex.[115] Thus, although it may have no statistical significance of any kind, the majority of these inscriptions, unlike Juvenal, characterize women.

Noy included only one inscription, from Pola in Aquileia, whose language compels some Judean association. It reads:

> Aur(elius) Soter et Aur(elius) Stephanus
> Aur(eliae) Soteriae Matri Pientissimae
> Religioni Iudeicae Metuenti
> F(ilii) P(osuerunt).

> Aurelius Soter and Aurelius Stephanus
> to Aurelia Soteria, mother, most pious,
> of the religion of the Judeans, [God]-revering
> [or: revering the *religiones* of the Judeans]
> Her sons placed this.

By itself, this inscription raises intriguing issues. Like the epitaph of Veturia, it is known only from early antiquarian reports, which claim it was once in the church of St. Vito in Pola. It is impossible to date with any certainty, although the prominence of Aurelian names supports a date after the early third century, and perhaps as late as the fifth century. That the sons of Aurelia Soteria erected her epitaph is clear enough, but the remainder of the inscription is troubling.

Scholars have differed in their view of whether *pientissima* simply describes Aurelia Soteria, or whether it modifies her devotion to Judean

---

112. Noy prints them all as *JIWE* 2.626, in an appendix of non-Jewish inscriptions. These were *CIJ* 1.5; 285; 524; and 529. He notes that recent scholarly opinion has favored his judgment, relying particularly on the example adduced by Feldman 1950, *CIL* 6.390, and writes, "There is no reason to connect with Judaism someone merely described at Rome as metuens." Leon 1960 also excluded them from his catalogue of Jewish inscriptions from Rome.

113. *JIWE* 2.626 i = *CIJ* 1.5, for Aemilius Valens, found in the Vigna del Pino.

114. *JIWE* 2.626 ii, for Larcia Quadrillata, found in San Sebastian, in Rome; *JIWE* 2.626 iii for Maiania Homeris, of unknown provenance (and which Noy thinks may be Christian, *JIWE* 2, p. 509); and *JIWE* 2.626 iv, for an unknown person, apparently female. Noy notes that the second portion of the inscription (*hic sita e[st]*) was inscribed over an erasure.

115. *CIL* 8.4321: Le Bohec 1981:191 Nr. 72. In the sixteenth century drawing reproduced in *CIL*, only the letters "METUI", preceded by the letters "IS" are legible. Frey 1930 initially included it, but he never produced a section or volume on Jewish inscriptions from North Africa, which, to date, still have never been systematically collected and edited. For a thorough assessment of the data, see Stern 2008 (her revised Brown doctoral dissertation).

religion. Interestingly, all contemporary interpreters presume that *pientissima* has some religious connotation (at least judging by the frequent translation of "most devout" or "most pious"), despite the fact that *pietas* regularly connoted familial devotion.[116] Most of the debate, however, has centered on what it might have meant to call Aurelia Soteria *"religioni Iudeicae metuenti."* Does describing her as *metuenti* imply that *pientissima* really does connote maternal devotion, while *metuenti* signals her particular degree of piety towards the divine? Is she simply a Judean mother commended for her exceptional piety? But if so, this language is highly unusual, in fact unique so far in the corpus of Judean inscriptions. Is she perhaps a Judean convert, or is this that rare instance of a more obvious technical usage of *metuens*, in which the deceased was in fact a "fearer" of the Judean religion, some particular category of affiliation?

The interpretation of this inscription is complicated somewhat by another inscription from Pola, whose only apparent connection to Judeans is that it was made by a woman also named Aurelia Soteria.[117] It, too, is known only from antiquarian manuscripts of the eighteenth century and later. In it, Aurelia Soteria commemorates a twenty-seven-year-old woman named Aurelia Rufina, whom she describes as an *alumna*, a Latin term that frequently had the same connotations as *threptē* in Greek. Unlike the epitaph of Aurelia Soteria by her sons, this one begins with the common Latin abbreviation DM, for the phrase, *Dis Manibus*, a dedication to deities of the dead translated in numerous ways by modern interpreters.[118] Whether the two women are one and the same seems, like many similar issues, impossible to resolve on the present evidence. The name seems common enough that they could be two different women (including perhaps relatives).[119] That this Aurelia Soteria describes Aurelia Rufina as *pientissima*, applied by the sons to the Aurelia Soteria of the first inscription is intriguing, if hardly determinative. Here, too, whether it connotes devotion to the gods or Rufina's service to her mistress is incertain. Elsewhere in the inscription, Aurelia Soteria proclaims that Aurelia Rufina was *fide cognita* and *memor obsequii eius*, which Noy translates as "Her faithfulness was known and she was mindful of her duty." Surely, this is a plausible translation, and yet

---

116. See, e.g., Scheiber 1984: no. 4, *Pulchra uxor pientissima*. (although this actually reads *fuentissa*). Zabin 1996:275 argues that in the Roman world, women's *pietas* was particularly associated with the fulfillment of private, familial obligations, whereas male *pietas* regularly had connotations of public duty. Based on her analysis of the Roman Judean burial inscriptions, however, she argues that this distinction was less true for Jewish women, who are regularly praised for their devotion to the law, and so forth. I think this is an optimistic reading.

117. *JIWE* 1.202 = *CIJ* 1.641. Noy includes it in an appendix of inscriptions "not considered Jewish."

118. See Kraemer 1991; Rutgers 2000:269–72 (an appendix on *Dis Manibus* inscriptions) from Goodenough 1953: vol. 2:137–40.

119. For instances of related names, see Noy, *JIWE* I, p. 17, who notes, though, that the more common feminine form is Soteris: he doesn't actually cite any other instances of the form Soteria; see also his discussion of the second inscription on p. 287.

itself somewhat ambiguous, perhaps intentionally. It is unclear whether Rufina was faithful to her mistress, or to some other power here unspecified, in which case one might expect the less ambiguous "her faith was known."[120] If, as other scholars have recognized, both inscriptions refer to the same woman, various scenarios are possible. Some scholars think that if they are the same, this strengthens the reading of Aurelia Soteria as some sort of partial adherent to Judaism, on the assumption that a "full" Jew or a "full" convert would not dedicate a burial inscription to the *Dii Manes*. Alternatively, of course, it might simply mean that Aurelia Soteria, herself Judean, had an alumna who was not Judean, whom she honored in death with an appropriate burial inscription.

As intriguing as these few inscriptions are, in the end, they remain sufficiently ambiguous that we can draw no conclusions about whether Gentile women or men were disproportionately likely to be engaged in some limited form of participation in Judean practices, at least in the communities from which these inscriptions come.

THE GREEK *THEOSEBES* INSCRIPTIONS. The situation is far more complex when we consider the corpus of Greek *theosebēs* inscriptions. If for the moment, we set aside face *b* of the Aphrodisias stele, with its list of about fifty men designated *theosebeis*, there are at most eighteen inscriptions designating an individual as *theosebēs*. The term also occurs, somewhat ambiguously, in two inscriptions from the theatre at Miletus, in situ, designating particular seating areas.[121] One of these is a Roman inscription whose reading of *theosebēs* is very much in doubt, leaving a corpus of seventeen inscriptions. Two transliterate the Greek term in Latin,[122] but the remainder are all Greek. Six of these are

120. Noy translates *fides* simply as "faith," in a late trilingual Greek, Hebrew, and Latin inscription from Tarragona, Spain (*JIWE* 1.185).

121. *IJO* 2.37, in situ and seen by the author in 2000, is a much discussed plaque, which reads: τοπος Ειουδεων των και θεοεεβιον, which the editors emend to τόπος Ειουδέων τῶν καὶ θεοσεβίον, dated anywhere from the second century C.E. through the fifth century C.E. (see Ameling, *IJO* 2 p. 169). There has been considerable discussion of the seemingly odd order of the words τῶν καὶ (the genitive plural article, and the Greek conjunctive "and"), and its implications for translation. Is this the place of two groups (presumably related in some manner): the *Ioudaioi* and the "*theosebeis*," which would support the view that θεοσεβεῖς here indicates a category of Gentile participants in Judean (or Jewish?) practices, or does θεοσεβεῖς here modify *Ioudaioi* (e.g., "place of the *Ioudaioi*, the ones who [also] are θεοσεβεῖς" and if so, why?). For a summary of some alternatives, see Trebilco 1991:159–62; cf. Levinskaya 1996:63–65. Elsewhere in the theater, and often less noted (Trebilco, for instance, does not mention it), is an inscription that only reads θε[οσ?]εβίον, *IJO* 2.38, and another, *IJO* 2.39, which refers to the "Blue" Jews (the Blues were a circus faction in late antiquity). The first inscription, *IJO* 2.38, is usually dated to the second/third century, but the Blues inscription is probably to be dated quite late, in the mid-fifth century C.E. or after. See, e.g., Alan Cameron 1976:194–96, cited in Rouché 1995:38 n. 2. Rouché suggests that at Miletus, the inscriptions designating seat areas appear to have been made at the same time, in contrast to those at the theater in Aphrodisias, which were regularly scratched out and re-done. If this is correct, then *IJO* 2.37 is likely to be much later, perhaps consistent with the use of θεοσεβής on face *b* at Aphrodisias.

122. *JIWE* 2.207 = *CIJ* 1.228 (Eparchia).

epitaphs, two from Rome, one from Venosa, one from the island of Rhodes, one from Cos, and one whose provenance is unknown, although it has features common to inscriptions from Asia Minor. Debates continue about whether some of these demonstrate any relationship to Judaism, including the epitaph of Agrippas, apparently from Rome, that of Euphrosyne, from Rhodes, that of Epitherses, of unknown provenance,[123] and even that of Marcus, from Venosa.[124] The remainder are all votive and/or donative inscriptions from several sites in Asia Minor: Philadelphia, Sardis, Aphrodisias, and Tralles. Most of these appear dated to the fourth/fifth centuries C.E., and most, but not all, have some clear association with Jews.[125]

Women constitute, at best, only a quarter (four) of these inscriptions. Only one is unquestionably associated with Judeans, the epitaph of Eparchia, age fifty-five, from the Randanini catacomb in Rome, dated perhaps to the third/fourth centuries.[126] All the others are among the inscriptions whose relationship to Judeans or Jews is debated. Lifshitz included the epitaph of Euphrosyne, found on a black marble altar from Rhodes, in his revision of Frey's corpus of Jewish inscriptions, based perhaps on the judgment of the great epigrapher, Louis Robert, who thought it either Jewish or "judaizing." Ameling has excluded it from *IJO* 2.[127] Here he appears to take this inscription as an instance of *theosebēs* as a marker of piety unrelated to Judeans, although there is no way to resolve the dispute definitively. The epitaph of Eirene from Cos poses almost identical problems of classification.[128] It is identical in formulae to that of Euphrosyne: both give the name of the deceased, followed by the words "*theosebēs*, worthy, farewell."[129] The only conceivable difference is the name, Eirene, which is well-attested for Judeans throughout the ancient Mediterranean, but this really seems an insufficient reason to include the inscription of Eirene, while excluding that of Euphrosyne.

---

123. Published in Pfuhl and Mobius 1979 no. 1697, plate 248. Levinskaya 1996:67–68 comments that the inscription, which depicts "a man lying on a couch, a seated woman, and a boy pouring a libation on an altar . . . would look perfectly at home in a pagan context." Conceivably, here θεοσεβής simply designates Epitherses' well-known piety, but Levinskaya notes that it might also here indicate a "Jewish sympathizer in a pagan family." There seems to be no way to be sure, but if this inscription is not that of someone interested in Judean practices, it demonstrates, conversely, that θεοσεβής is sometimes if not often simply a marker of commendable piety. The circularity of the evidence is often exceedingly aggravating.

124. *JIWE* 2.627i= *CIJ* 1.500; which Noy includes only in an appendix of inscriptions considered not Jewish; *CIJ* 1² 731e, which Ameling excludes from *IJO* 2, discussing it only in a footnote (58 n. 72 [incorrectly listed in the index]; *JIWE* 1.113 = *CIJ* 1² 619a.

125. The exceptions are Capitolina, *IJO* 2.27; not in *CIJ*, although it is included in Lifshitz 1967: no. 30; and Eustathios, *IJO* 2.49 = *CIJ* 2.754 (Lifshitz 1967: no. 28).

126. *JIWE* 2.207 = *CIJ* 1.228.

127. Levinskaya writes: "Either option [of Robert's 1937:441 n. 5] is equally tenable" (1996:62), with reference in n. 43.

128. *IJO* 2.6; not in *CIJ*: Paton and Hicks 1891: no. 278.

129. θεοσεβὴς χρηστὴ [χρηστὰ] χαῖρε.

Most problematic is the donor inscription made by a woman named Capitolina, from Tralles in Caria (as is Aphrodisias) dated to the mid-third century C.E.,[130] a donor inscription which reads:

> (I), Capitolina, esteemed and "God-revering,"
> have made the whole *bathro[n]*
> and have decorated the stairs with mosaic
> in fulfilment of a vow on my behalf,
> and that of my children and grandchildren.
> Blessings.

Numerous aspects of the inscription are ambiguous. The first is the term *theosebēs* itself, which is actually abbreviated in the inscription as *theoseb* (as is true of the persons so designated on face *a* of the Aphrodisias inscription; the term for "esteemed," is similarly abbreviated). Other readers of the inscription have suggested that these should be taken as superlatives (most esteemed; most God-revering), but to the best of my knowledge, there is little if any attestation of the form *theosebēstatē* except in Christian inscriptions (which this inscription was initially taken to be), and Ameling prefers *theosebēs*. It is also not clear what *bathron* designates, which is why I have here left it untranslated.[131]

Whether the building that Capitolina has funded is a synagogue remains uncertain and cannot be determined from the inscription itself. That it is a religious site of some sort is strongly suggested by the votive nature of the inscription: having made a vow (to an unidentified deity), Capitolina has fulfilled it with these gifts. Such language is common in, but by no means unique to, late antique synagogues. The phrase at the end, *eulogia*, blessings, is again well attested in Jewish contexts, but also in Christian contexts, although rare in demonstrably non-Jewish, non-Christian inscriptions.[132]

As Trebilco discusses, a woman named Claudia Capitolina is attested in another inscription from Tralles. This Claudia came from a prominent Asian

---

130. *IJO* 2.27. The dating relies partly on *IGR* 4.1340, discussed later, concerning a woman, also named Capitolina, and partly on seeing the term ἀχιολογωτάτη (most esteemed), as characteristically third century C.E.

131. Trebilco translates βάθρο[ν] as "platform" (1991:252 n.53) and proposes that it is a Torah or menorah platform, or perhaps a bema used for reading of scripture, all translations that rely on the thesis that this is a synagogue inscription. According to LSJ, s.v., it is generally anything on which something stands, but can specifically designate a bench or a seat (which would invalidate Trebilco's interpretation), as well as steps and even a throne. Because the inscription speaks also of a staircase, steps are an interesting alternative, but there need not be any connection between the two elements of the building Capitolina funded. Lampe defines βάθρον as a base, foundation or pavement, or even a church bench (as in Eusebius, *Ecclesiastical History* 10.4.44). It is exceedingly common in Christian church inscriptions, usually with verbs of building, and seeming to mean just built "from its foundations."

132. E.g., Goodenough 1953:2.115–16 for its Jewish and Christian usages. Trebilco also cites Robert 1964:54 n. 1, that the phrase "ὑπὲρ εὐχῆς" is rare in "pagan" inscriptions.

family: her father was proconsul of Asia, and her husband a Roman senator and priest for life of Zeus Larasios in Tralles, with an illustrious pedigree of his own.[133] Although Trebilco seems certain that the two women are to be identified, others are more cautious.[134] If this inscription refers to the same woman, and commemorates donations to a synagogue, it is obviously significant evidence for a non-Judean woman's benefactions to the local Judean community, analogous, perhaps, to those of Julia Severa of Akmonia in the first century.[135] But like the gift of Julia Severa, whether it testifies to a specific attachment to Judean practice, itself alluded to, if not indicated by the term *theosebēs*, cannot be determined.[136] It might simply indicate that gifts to a Judean synagogue could be construed as a general form of piety (again remembering that for Gentiles, the Judean god was still a god).

Thus it appears that the vast majority of those persons designated as *theosebēs* in both Greek inscriptions and the few Latin transliterations are men, a proportion that increases exponentially if we factor in the list of *theosebeis* on face *b* of the Aphrodisias inscription. Some scholars have seen data of this sort as evidence for the thesis noted earlier that women were more likely to convert "fully" to "Judaism," whereas men were more likely to resist, perhaps because doing so involved circumcision.

Yet at least on the basis of the epigraphic evidence, this argument remains inconclusive, at best. As we have seen, the proselyte inscriptions do not allow us to reach any meaningful conclusions about the actual distribution of men and women among proselytes, particularly given the fact that we lack epigraphical evidence for most Judeans, let alone most proselytes. Several arguments also undermine our ability to draw conclusions from the *theosebēs* inscriptions.

First, as many scholars have repeatedly pointed out, while it is possible that in some inscriptions, *theosebēs* identifies a Gentile who engages in some limited Judean practices and remains on some social fence between Judeans and non-Judeans, in most cases, the inscriptions remain ambiguous. A case in point is a third-century inscription from Deliler, near Philadelphia. It records the donation of a wash-basin by a man named Eustatios to the "most holy synagogue of

---

133. *IGR* 4.1340 according to Trebilco 1991, who also cites Groag 1907.

134. As Levinskaya notes, Groag 1907 thought that the inscription was Christian, and thus that Capitolina could not be this same Claudia Capitolina, although he thought she was of the same family. Levinskaya herself is more cautious, rightly in my view: 199: 65–66.

135. Lifshitz 1967:33 = *MAMA* 6.264; *IJO* 2.168; Kraemer 1992:119–21.

136. Again, Levinskaya 1996 takes a similar position, concluding that this inscription in no way resolves questions about the use of θεοσεβὴς as a technical category. In my view, the use of θεοσεβὴς together with ἁγιόλογος, particularly given the use of και to link them, suggests that piety is at issue, not a technical term of affiliation with the local Judean community.

the Hebrews," in memory of his brother, Hermophilos, a donation made together with a woman named Athanasia, who is probably Eustatios's sister-in-law (his brother's wife).[137] Were it not for the fact that Eustatios designates himself but neither his brother nor Athanasia, as "the *theosebēs*," the inscription would probably simply be read as a memorial donation by a Judean to a local synagogue.[138] Scholars have taken Eustatios to be a "God-fearer," a proselyte, or just a devout Jew. But as Levinskaya concedes at the close of her analysis favoring the first option, "it is impossible to say for sure."[139] If reasonable, although not dispositive, arguments can be made that Eustatios intended "the *theosebēs*" to signify both his Gentile birth and his formal but partial affiliation with a local Judean community, other inscriptions are even more resistant to classification.

In fact, of the inscriptions that call individuals *theosebēs*, none, apart from face *b* on the stele from Aphrodisias, <u>must</u> be read to have some technical meaning beyond devotion to the divine. Although *theosebeis* at Aphrodisias clearly intends some particular meaning, what that is continues to elude us, particularly in the absence of the corresponding term for the list of those many names that are well attested for Judeans. Even if at Aphrodisias in the fourth century (the present most reasonable date for face *b*), *theosebeis* had some very particular meaning, we can neither know nor assume that it had the identical meaning elsewhere, and at other times.

If *theosebēs* is not, generally, a term that connotes a particular level of ancient piety somewhere between polytheism and exclusive devotion to the Judean god, then the highly skewed gender distribution of persons called *theosebēs* can hardly be explained by the thesis that women were more likely to convert but men were more likely to remain in this more liminal but still formal category of God-fearers. Yet the disparity certainly invites explanation. As I

---

137. She is called νύμφη, which can mean bride, but particularly in Asia Minor, is also used for sister-in-law, which certainly fits the context.

138. Why the synagogue is called "of the Hebrews" is another issue: whether it is simply the local (and conceivably quite late) phrase for what elsewhere is called "of the Judeans" (as in the dedication of Tation), or whether it refers to a particular synagogue to be distinguished from some other local synagogue is, again, unclear. Levinskaya (1996:61 n. 40), notes the possibility that it connotes speakers of Hebrew or Aramaic, although she doesn't advocate or defend such a reading, and a Greek inscription for such a synagogue seems somewhat incongruous, apart from the general lack of evidence for such congregations in Asia Minor.

139. Levinskaya 1996:61–62. She rebuts Trebilco's (1991) argument that if Eustatios was a "God-fearer," Hermogenes should have been one, too, because, otherwise, why would Eustatios make a donation in his memory in an institution to which he had no connections. Hence Trebilco concluded that Eustatios was simply a Jew advertising his own piety. In Levinskaya's view, even in ancient Asia Minor, people might make donations to institutions dear to them on behalf of others with little or no connections to those institutions, noting especially Gentile gifts and offerings to the Temple, and Jewish offerings on behalf of emperors and others who clearly had no affiliation with the Temple or with particular synagogues, with references from Schürer 1987:2.309–13. Part of the problem here, of course, is that any explanation requires us to imagine the intentions of a man about whom we know nothing other than this inscription.

noted earlier, among the *theosebēs* epitaphs, at least half are for women. Yet the majority (eleven) of the *theosebēs* inscriptions are either votive offerings or donor inscriptions (or both),[140] and virtually all these persons are men. Nine of the eleven, for instance, come either from face *a* of the Aphrodisias stele, or from the complex at Sardis (six), where women are never the primary donors in any inscriptions, although they are sometimes attested as donating with their husbands. It is at least worth noting that all these inscriptions may be roughly contemporaneous (fourth/fifth century).[141] For whatever reasons, the Aphrodisias inscriptions together mention at best only one woman, Iael, *prostatēs* of the association of the Lovers of Learning, and even the identification of Iael as female has been disputed.[142] If the organizations from which these inscriptions are drawn are largely those of men, it is perhaps not particularly surprising that virtually all the *theosebeis* are also men. In other words, here the gender distribution is a function of some other qualities of this particular corpus of inscriptions, and provides us with no useful information about the degree to which Gentile women were or were not likely to adopt some intermediate degree of Judean practice that itself is less than securely attested epigraphically. And finally, were it to be the case that women were disproportionately proselytes, this might be less a function of male reluctance to be circumcised, and more a function of the fact that women were seen, in antiquity, to be more loosely incorporated into any particular ethnicity, and thus able to move more easily from one to another, to the extent that women were even seen to have ethnicity.

Women Proselytes and Theosebeis in Literary Accounts

The literary evidence for Gentile women's apparent interest in things Judean is well known, as I surveyed at the outset. Josephus's account of the adoption of Judean practices by the whole royal household of Adiabene, including Queen Helena, is usually represented by contemporary scholars as conversion, which appears to envision the process of ethnic transition I have discussed earlier. In fact, though, Josephus's language is more ambiguous than many

---

140. The distinction between a donative and a votive inscription can be subtle. Votive inscriptions are all, in some sense, donatives, since generally, people vowed to make a gift if the condition of the vow was fulfilled (recovery from illness, safe travels, and many other such concerns). But donatives might not have been associated with vows (unless, perhaps, one "vowed" in advance to make a donation, analogous to the modern practice of pledging a gift, and then subsequently making the actual payment).

141. For an intriguing argument that the last stage of the Sardis synagogue is probably to be dated to the fifth century, rather than somewhat earlier, see Magness 2005.

142. Brooten 1991; see the discussion to *IJO* 2.14; see also Gilbert 2004, who seems to accept Brooten's view.

scholarly discussions acknowledge.[143] Others appear to be claims of Gentile women's actual veneration of the Judean god. These include the stories about Domitian's relative, Flavia Domitilla, noted earlier; the various references in Acts,[144] perhaps including Luke's representation of Lydia and her circle of women celebrating the Sabbath on the riverbank outside Antioch;[145] and perhaps also John Chrysostom's railings about his women parishioners' fondness for attending synagogue in Antioch.[146] Interestingly, though, several of these accounts may more properly describe elite women's patronage of Judeans and Judean causes, without regard to their own veneration of the Judean god, such as Josephus's accounts of the intercessions of Poppaea on behalf of various Judeans, including himself,[147] and his claim that he was the recipient of continuous benefactions from Domitia, wife of the emperor Domitian.[148] Further evidence for such patronage may also be found in several important and much discussed inscriptions, particularly that of Capitolina of Tralles and the inscription from Akmonia occasioned by the restoration of a synagogue originally built by Julia Severa.

The account that has received perhaps the most scholarly scrutiny has been Josephus's claim that Nero's wife, Poppaea, intervened on behalf of an embassy from Jerusalem because, he says, she was *theosebēs*.[149] This description has occasioned substantial scholarly debate over whether Josephus is here saying that Poppaea was a formal "God-fearer," itself providing affirmation of the existence of the category in the first-century, or whether Josephus is "merely" saying that Poppaea was motivated to help the Jerusalem envoys out of some general sense of piety.[150]

---

143. *Antiquities* 20.17–53; 92–96; *WRGRW* 103. What Josephus actually says is that the Judean Ananias, going to see the wives/women of the king, ἐδίδασκεν αὐτὰς τὸν θεὸν σέβειν ὡς Ἰουδαίοις πάτριον ἦν, that is, "he taught them to fear [or revere] God following the Judean ancestral practice." Feldman's translation of "to worship God after the manner of the Jewish tradition" obscures the use of language often associated with "God-fearers" rather than "converts." In the debates that then ensue about whether Helena's son, Izates, now ruling as king, should be circumcised, Ananias says that Izates can τὸν θεῖον σέβειν, that is, he can "fear [or venerate] the divine," without being circumcised, as long as he was "zealous" for τὰ πάτρια τῶν Ἰουδαίων, the ancestral practices of the Judeans. Feldman translates as "if indeed he had fully decided to be a devoted adherent of Judaism," which here suggests more of the fuzzy language of "adherence" construed in opposition to "conversion." It's interesting that, although Josephus claims that Izates adopted Judean practices, the majority of persons who do so appear to be the women of the royal household. See also later, on Helena.

144. E.g., Acts 13.50; 17.4; 17.12.

145. Acts 16.13.

146. *Against Judaizing Christians* 2.3.3–2.3.6; 4.7.3; *WRGRW* 41.

147. *Life*, 13–16.

148. *Life*, 429.

149. *Antiquities* 20.189–98.

150. E.g., Feldman 1950: see also Feldman's notes to the LCL edition of Josephus; Smallwood 1959; Williams 1988: Matthews 2001.

Shelley Matthews's revised Harvard dissertation illuminates many of the difficulties with this narrative. Matthews positions Josephus (and to some extent Luke) somewhere between the pole of pure rhetoric on the one end and positivist history on the other. Although she shares the view of Cooper, Clark, Lieu, and others that accusing men, in general, and elite men, in particular, of being subject to "womanly influence" can be a form of criticism against such men, it can sometimes have positive rhetorical effect. This is precisely what she thinks both Josephus and Luke are doing: deploying "high-standing Gentile" women "for positive rhetorical effect." Somewhat less pessimistically than Clark and others, Matthews thinks that some history can be extracted from all this: "the rhetorical presentation of high-standing women benefactors in these literary sources is congruent with the historical phenomenon of noblewomen's benefaction in Greco-Roman antiquity."[151] This doesn't mean, for her, that any particular story is reliable. Rather, rhetorical representations depend for their force on an underlying reality.

Matthews argues that in Josephus, the support of such women, often the wives of the emperors, is adduced as (indirect) evidence of the worthiness of (Judean) causes. In the *Antiquities*, she sees it as "part of a larger narrative pattern . . . that repeatedly characterizes Gentile noblewomen as saviors and benefactors of the Jewish people."[152] More specifically, Matthews proposes that in casting the support of women like Poppaea in terms of piety, Josephus somewhat masks the more nakedly political, or power, aspects of this: the "rhetorical effect [of assigning religious motive to the emperor's wife] is to mask the politically subversive implications of Poppaea's actions."[153] As for whether Josephus intends to portray Poppaea as a technical "God-fearer" or simply as motivated by piety, Matthews sides with Margaret Williams: "it is best to read the text as scripting Poppaea with a pious attachment to Judaism somewhere between the two extremes of a proselyte's devotion and a pagan's nonspecific 'superstition.' "[154] Her point seems more to be that this is what Josephus is trying to do, rather than providing us any access to what motives Poppaea might herself have had. This distinction has often been blurred in scholarly discussions, on the assumption that Josephus's depiction is largely accurate, and that the dilemma is primarily what *theosebēs* meant in the first century. Matthews herself claims that Josephus regularly uses *theosebēs* to signal attachment to "the Jewish religion in some manner," suggesting that some intermediate level of interest in Judaism is what Josephus intends to signal.[155]

---

151. Matthews 2001:50.
152. Matthews 2001:30.
153. Matthews 2001:35.
154. Matthews 2001:35.
155. Matthews 2001:35.

But there is another way to read this that relates to the specifics of the position Poppaea advocated. According to Josephus, Agrippa II expanded his palace to afford himself an excellent view of everything that transpired in the Jerusalem temple.[156] Unspecified elite men of Jerusalem, incensed at Agrippa's actions, countered by erecting a wall on the temple perimeter that blocked not only Agrippa's view but also that of the Roman guards charged with security during festivals. Siding with Agrippa, the Roman procurator, Festus ordered the wall taken down. The protesters asked to send an embassy to Nero to adjudicate the dispute, to which Festus agreed.

Here, Josephus sides with the temple supporters, not with Agrippa or the Romans, support that could easily be construed (by his Roman readers in the late first century) as anti-Roman. So, too, could Poppaea's advocacy on their behalf be (mis)construed. By casting her support as the consequence of her piety, her *theosebeia*, Josephus *might* be saying that Poppaea sides with the opponents of the wall because she sees this as a general issue of piety, not because she was specifically attached to the Judean god. Josephus has made it clear that it was not Judean custom for the goings on in the temple to be spied upon, let alone the actual sacrifices.[157] Josephus may here cast Poppaea as defending a larger Roman value, namely, the integrity of a temple to a deity, even a foreign deity. After all, from the Roman perspective, foreign deities were still deities, and deserved respect, even if they were lesser deities; it was only the Judeans and Samaritans, and the handful of Christians (and the random skeptic or two) who thought otherwise.

As we have already seen in the discussion of *theosebēs* inscriptions, most scholars have tied themselves up in knots over what, exactly, "*theosebēs*" meant, as though it had a fixed, singular meaning shared by those who used it and those who heard it, and which we have only to discover through careful research. They have then agonized over what this does or doesn't say, about Poppaea's personal piety and possible attachment to Judaism, and about how this figures into some larger portrait of Gentile interest in Judaism. That the meaning of *theosebēs* was fluid, ambiguous, and deeply dependent on contextual clues that we in the twenty-first century now lack, seems to elude many if not most modern readers. That is, Josephus clearly had something in mind when he attributed Poppaea's support to her being *theosebēs*. If in fact, Poppaea did intervene on behalf of the temple party, she had reasons for doing so, some of which were probably self-conscious, whereas others may not have been. Whether anything Josephus says gives us access to those reasons is not

---

156. *Antiquities* 20.189–90.
157. *Antiquities* 20.191.

clear. Not inconceivably, it was precisely the ambiguity of the term *theosebēs* that Josephus found efficacious. Judean audiences could understand this as a veiled reference to her true affinity for their views, whereas his Roman patrons could construe her actions as a general laudable piety that overrode the otherwise troubling lack of support for a client ruler, the Roman procurator, and the Roman military. Or Josephus might, in fact, have intended something fairly fixed, which still would not have prevented his various audiences from interpreting him in diverse ways, as indeed modern scholars have done for decades, if not longer.

Another episode that has occasioned much commentary is Josephus's narrative of Fulvia, a high-ranking Roman matron swindled by unscrupulous Judean men who solicited contributions from her for the temple and then used those contributions for their own benefit. Josephus claims that when this became known, Tiberius ordered all the Jews expelled from Rome.[158]

Josephus says of Fulvia that she was "of the most worthy women" and had come over to the Judean laws or customs: *nomimois proselēluthuian tois Ioudaikois*. Feldman translates this less ambiguously as "a woman of high rank who had become a Jewish proselyte." Although I have enormous respect for Feldman's knowledge of Greek, I think this translation is governed by unsubstantiated assumptions.[159] The phrase "come over to the Judean *nomima*" is not so clear, at least from this remove (perhaps to Josephus' intended and actual readers, it was not ambiguous): *ta nomima* are usages and customs.[160] Despite the generous gifts that she allegedly gave for the temple, and despite Josephus's wording, Fulvia does not appear to fall into the category of one who has changed ethnicity, since she is apparently still very much functioning as the wife of Saturninus, a "friend" of the emperor Tiberius. According to Josephus, it is Fulvia, herself, presumably incensed at the realization that she had been defrauded, who prompted her husband to seek redress from the Emperor. Josephus says nothing about whether Fulvia continued her Judean practices. Surely she could no longer associate with the swindlers, and it would be difficult for us to envision her continuing to associate with Judeans, if, as Josephus suggests, they had all been expelled from Rome. One wonders, further, whether a woman could become a Judean and still be married to a Roman aristocratic male with imperial connections. My point, though, is not to reconstruct what Fulvia did, to which I think we have no access, but rather to analyze Josephus's representation of her. In fact, yet another reading of this narrative

158. *Antiquities* 18.81–84.
159. Although perhaps what Feldman intends by the phrase "Jewish proselyte" is more ambiguous than I give him credit for.
160. See, e.g., Mason 2007:484.

is that Josephus does "intend" to represent Fulvia as a "convert," but that this representation is his artifice, and casts Fulvia's actual and more minimal engagement as something more substantial than it was.

I have not devoted much discussion so far to the extensive narrative in Josephus about a foreign woman of high rank who adopts Judean practices, Queen Helena of Adiabene, but a few observations are worth making here. Much of the narrative about Helena focuses on her views in the debate about whether her son, Izates, can effectively rule the kingdom of Adiabene if he is circumcised, which she opposed. In many ways, Helena conforms to the type of virtuous foreign woman whom Josephus represents as patrons of the Judeans at the same time as she also operates effectively in the public sphere. Her initial adoption of Judean practices appears to take place within the appropriate confines of the women's quarters.[161] Helena's new practices are affirmed by her son, Izates, and everything she does continues to be seemly. Although she opposes Izates's circumcision, she ultimately accedes to it, and her resistance is entirely politically pragmatic. Eventually, desiring to worship[162] at the temple of God, and to bring thanksgiving offerings,[163] she travels to Jerusalem, where she alleviates a famine by paying for massive amounts of food for the starving populace. (Rabbinic traditions will remember her more cultically specific donations of a gold candelabra and a plaque bearing the portions of Leviticus concerning the Sotah—the woman accused of adultery). She doesn't make this journey, or give these enormous donations, until after the death of her husband, and with, it seems, the consent of her son. In Josephus, then, Helena, as mother, exerts appropriate and (from Josephus's perspective) positive influence on her son, facilitating his adoption of Judean (i.e., better) piety.[164]

Particularly salient is Matthew's observation that Josephus's description of these relationships relies upon basic norms of benefaction, including

---

161. Although what, exactly, Judean merchants are doing in the women's quarters of the royal Adiabene household is not clear.

162. Or perhaps prostrate herself—προσκυνῆσαι.

163. χαριστηρίους θυσίας. I do wonder what Helena would have had to do, if anything, to prostrate herself at the temple, and bring those gifts. According to Josephus, ritually pure Judean women were restricted to a special courtyard of the temple (War 5.198–200). In Against Apion 2.102–4, he offers a somewhat different representation: Gentile men and (ritually pure) Gentile women could enter an outermost court: a second court was restricted to Judean men and their ritually pure Judean wives/women. A third inner courtyard was restricted to ritually pure Judean men, a fourth to properly garbed Judean priests, and the sanctuary itself only to the properly garbed high priest. Where, in these schemata, might Helena have been able to worship the Judean god?

164. Still, Josephus does seem to obfuscate on how Monobazus, Helena's husband and brother, felt about any of this. Monobazus the elder is still alive when both Izates and Helena learn (from different teachers) about Judean piety (Antiquities 20.34–35), and Ananias, Izates's initial teacher, accompanies Izates to see his father, although Josephus says nothing about Monobazus's response.

reciprocal exchange of goods and services; personal ties of some duration, as opposed to commercial connections; and asymmetry, that is, lack of friendship between patron and client.[165] This model suggests that, although some women who provide patronage to Judeans may have been interested in Judean practices and ideas, this was by no means necessary as an explanation for their support.[166] Matthews herself notes that there's somewhat of a contradiction here between Roman norms of *matronae* as confined to domesticity and numerous instances of their engagement in public life and power relations.[167] Josephus, she argues, presents Gentile women "as effective historical agents with great political acumen, neither constrained by the Roman propagandistic ideal of the virtuous matron as a homebound spinner of wool, nor condemned as transgressors of proper social roles."[168] Although she finds Hillard's thesis that attributing political power to a woman served primarily to feminize the man or men allegedly under her influence to account for some representations, she points out that it does not explain Josephus's representations here.[169] Noting that elite Gentile women in Josephus use their influence with men to support those Judeans whom Josephus himself supports, she argues: "It would be difficult to read these stories both as affirmation for these women's intercessions on behalf of the Jews and as insinuations against the men who succumb to womanly wiles."[170] Here she appeals to another aspect of Kate Cooper's work—that the allegation of womanly influence could have a positive dimension: "The positive version dwelt on a man's licit relationships with female family members, whose soothing charm would ideally restore him to order when he had strayed and persuade him to hear the voice of reason. A man represented as being in harmony with his legitimate wife was thus symbolically anchored to duty and to the cause of the

165. Matthews 2001:42 here draws on the work of Saller 1982.

166. Or, to draw here on the larger model of Bourdieu, these women are to some extent playing the game generally played by men, which elite women were able to play, in somewhat constrained fashion, by virtue of their wealth and family connections.

167. Citing Hillard 1992, who, noting that most indications of women's political influence come in legal and political oratory, concluded that "the allegation that a woman wielded political power was made primarily for the purposes of effeminizing the male who was purportedly under her influence" (Matthews 2001:44). This is a more specific version of Kate Cooper's argument discussed earlier in chapter 4, as Matthews notes (2001:46). Matthews also notes the work of Fischler 1989, who saw a contrast between the total exclusion of women from political power under the Republic, and the increased possibilities for imperial women, which she associates with monarchy by its very nature. For Fischler, these negative accounts are a response to the anxiety that this new access to power produced, a reading that sees historicity behind the rhetoric: Matthews 2001:44–45.

168. Matthews 2001:45.

169. Although it might explain his representation of women and men like Herodias and Herod, on which see, inter alia, Kraemer 2006.

170. Matthews 2001:46.

common good."[171] Consistent rather with these ideas, "Josephus employs the figure of a Gentile (Roman) woman as one who provides a voice of reason to the men with whom she is involved."[172]

I think, though, that it may not be this simple. If it's true that depicting a man as subject to womanly influence can be read either as a critique of his masculinity, or as an affirmation of his familial and civic devotion, those who craft such depictions run the risk of having them misconstrued, intentionally or otherwise. Josephus in particular runs the risk of being heard quite differently than he may have intended. As Matthews observes, Josephus claims that he himself was the recipient of benefactions and intercessions by several imperial wives. In 64 C.E., obtaining an introduction through a Judean actor he knew, he successfully sought Poppaea's assistance in gaining the release of priests who had been brought in chains to Rome. Years later, he claims, Domitia, wife of the emperor Domitian, was his patron.[173]

Given the complex meanings attributed to such representations, claiming that prominent women plead Josephus's cause can easily be heard to mean that prominent men who support his cause are themselves effeminate, because they are (inappropriately) influenced by women. Josephus needs to argue that the women's influence is appropriate. Matthew's solution is to distinguish between Josephus's location as an insider and his location as an outsider. As an insider, Josephus levels such accusations against Judean men he wishes to impugn, such as Herod Antipas. When writing as an outsider who seeks acceptability, she claims, his point is that having Gentile noblewomen advocates demonstrates the legitimacy of the outsiders.

Matthews is well aware that "the standing of Jewish clients before their patrons was much more precarious than Josephus will allow" and that his representations are optimistic, intended to obtain favorable treatment for Judeans by demonstrating such treatment to have long-standing precedent.[174] To some extent, his stories about the support of elite Roman women for Judean causes, and even their more general interest in Judean practices, serve these purposes.

Yet surely it would have served his interests even better to tell numerous stories of elite Roman men as the patrons and supporters of Judean causes. Josephus does, of course, claim to have been enslaved and then freed by Vespasian, and to have been the recipient of many subsequent benefactions from his imperial patron and former owner (if only briefly). But his representation of

171. Cooper 1992:153, cited in Matthews 2001:46.

172. Matthews 2001:47.

173. *Life*, 429.

174. Matthews 2001:49. She offers a particularly nice demonstration of this in the two different versions of Claudius's edict: the one reported by Josephus, and an Alexandrian papyrus copy.

himself as the client, not only of Poppaea, but far more recently of Domitia, raises a different possibility. Is what's really at stake Josephus's own legitimacy, which is impugned or at least vulnerable *precisely* because of his female patrons? If so, Josephus's real goal in these depictions is to legitimize that patronage, because it may, itself, be used to criticize (and femininize) him, and his having been enslaved, even to the emperor, cannot have helped him. Perhaps it may also be the best access to power he (presently) has.

This results, then, in a tension between his own interests and prevailing understandings of imperial female patronage. Ironically, his need for such patrons itself may affirm his outsider status: insiders have far more direct access to male power networks. This may be all the more interesting if Josephus is writing specifically with Domitia in mind (she was empress from 81 C.E. to 96 C.E.). If so, he may be saying that her patronage of him, and her support for Judeans generally, is consistent with the behavior of a long line of illustrious, virtuous empresses and other imperial women, including Antonia, Agrippina the Younger, wife of Claudius, and Poppaea.

This examination of Josephus suggests several things. First, it makes clear that to cast elite Roman women as the patrons of Judeans does not actually tell us anything about whether they might, themselves, have had some interest in the practice of Judean devotions, even when, as in the case of Josephus's representation of Poppaea, their patronage is explained in terms that could be construed as devotion to the Judean god. Hints of elite Roman women venerating the Judean god may be found in the reports that the charges of atheism lodged against Flavia Domitilla and others during the reign of Domitian were due to their adoption of Judean practices, but there is really no way to assess this. Conceivably, the story of Fulvia is similar evidence. Matthew's analysis of this as Josephus's attempt to argue that Judaism posed no threat to Roman social order and values (in contrast to the Isis cult favored by Domitian),[175] however, raises the possibility that the episode says little about the piety of Fulvia, even though, as Matthews argues more generally, it might rely on Roman beliefs that such things were possible, if not exactly frequent. Even the case of Helena becomes troublesome for its conformity to these issues.

One other fictive narrative of a Gentile woman who adopts Judean practices occurs in the romance of "Clement" and his family, known as the Pseudo-Clementines.[176] According to both versions of the Pseudo-Clementines, the

175. Earlier, pp. 225–26.
176. Rehm 1994; Lagarde 1966 [1865].

Recognitions and the *Homilies*, the narrator's twin brothers, called Faustinus and Faustinianus, were separated from their family as young boys, and sold into slavery. They were bought by a "very respectable" woman, who ultimately adopted them and gave them a comprehensive Greek education. Called Justa, this woman appears to be the unnamed Canaanite woman of Matt 15.22–28, whose daughter Jesus heals of demon-induced illness (and who here acquires the name of Berenike). In the preferred reading of the *Recognitions*, Justa is simply a Judean woman: "*Iudaeae, honestae admodum feminae, Iustae nomine.*"[177] In others, however, she is called not *Iudaeae* (or *Iudae*), but *viduae*, a widow. Only in the Greek *Homilies* is Justa called a proselyte of the Judeans.[178]

In both Matthew and Mark 7.24–30, a Gentile woman (a Syro-Phoenician in Mark) comes to Jesus and asks him to heal her daughter. Jesus demurs, saying that "it is not right [or fair: *kalos*] to take the children's bread and throw it to the dogs," equating Gentiles with dogs, and the Judeans with the children. The woman responds that "even the dogs beneath the table eat from the children's crumbs."[179] In the Markan version of the story, Jesus agrees to heal the daughter "for this saying," that is, apparently, for the persuasiveness of her answer, and sends the woman home. There is no indication that she subsequently becomes a follower of Jesus or a practitioner of Judean cult, although later Christian readers certainly construed her as the latter. Only in the Matthean version (itself probably responding to the Markan characterization) does the woman acknowledge Jesus as son of David, and does Jesus say that he heals the daughter on account of her mother's faith or trust.

Conceivably, the designation of Justa as a proselyte in the *Homilies* is a response to exegetical concerns based in the divergent gospel accounts. The characterization of her as a Judean in the *Recognitions* is, in fact, somewhat at odds with both gospel accounts, which construe her either as a Gentile whose acceptance of Jesus is at best deeply implicit (Mark), or a Gentile who trusts in Jesus and recognizes his Davidic status (Matthew). For the author and some readers of the Pseudo-Clementines, this last might have made her a Judean, producing the reading in the *Recognitions*. The variant *widow* might then respond to concerns that in the gospels, the woman isn't a Judean, or perhaps the concerns of some readers that she shouldn't be a Judean. The characterization of her as a proselyte of the Judeans in the *Homilies* might attempt to answer

---

177. *Recognitions* 7.32.2–4. I thank my former students, Dr. Curtis Hutt, and Jonathan Aronchick (Brown 2009) for bringing this to my attention.

178. *Homilies* 13.7.4. Theissen 1991:69–71 translates this more carefully as "Now the woman who bought us was a proselyte of the Jews . . ." compared to the English translation in *NTA* 2:527, which describes her as "a convert to Judaism."

179. Mark 7.28, my translation.

the question of how the Gentile woman become a Judean, by casting her as a proselyte.

In either case, it would seem unwise to adduce this story as useful evidence for Gentile women's interest in Judean practices. Interestingly, in that she appears to be autonomous, with considerable financial resources, the figure of Justa is in some ways more consistent with the few women proselytes in epigraphical sources, than with the married elite women who populate Josephus's narratives. Her autonomy (presumably as a widow), however, is almost certainly a product of the canonical accounts, and her substantial wealth serves the interests of the Pseudo-Clementine narrative. Justa facilitates the education of the twins, who, together with Clement himself, as Kelley points out, collectively become experts in the totality of Greek philosophy and knowledge, thus making them uniquely able to dispute any claims contrary to (Christian) knowledge.[180]

Some Preliminary Conclusions

In the end, we are left with strikingly little reliable data about Gentile women's engagement with Judeans, whether in the form of ethnic transformation, or some veneration of the Judean god, or even simply patronage of Judeans for any number of complex and only partially accessible motivations. It seems fair to say that the often-repeated claims about the proportions of women proselytes and women God-fearers do not hold up under careful scrutiny of both the inscriptional evidence and the literary evidence, although this is less because these claims are false and more because we simply do not know. Much of what passes for evidence of such disproportions is simply not what it has been taken to be.

As has been the case in much of this study, literary accounts of women's religious proclivities often turn out to be something other than they seem. The many stories of Roman matrons' Judean devotions, which come from Josephus (as most of these do), appear to be part of Josephus's complex rhetorical strategies that point more to Roman women's involvement in the peddling of influence and patronage in the imperial environment than they do to personal religious proclivities. The Clementine Justa seems mostly a product of exegetical constraints and narrative needs. The minimal epigraphical evidence, if not always subject to the same liabilities, nevertheless has numerous ambiguities and uncertainties of its own. Occasionally, though, it does suggest that women did sometimes undertake such transformations or adopt such practices, and

---

180. Kelley 2006:44–45.

provides hints of the social processes and gendered cultural logic underlying such practices.

Women Office Holders in Ancient Jewish Synagogues, Revisited

What then, of the epigraphical evidence for women office holders in ancient synagogues? Are we on any firmer ground here? That a small number of women, like Rufina, are explicitly called by the titles of synagogue officers is unquestionable. As I noted at the beginning of this chapter, at least four women are called *archisynagōgos* (head of the synagogue), one of whom is also called "elder."[181] Another seven "elders" are attested.[182] One woman bears a title that might connote an office, Peristeria, called *archēgissa*.[183] As I noted earlier, the association called a *dekania* at Aphrodisias may have had a woman patron, called *prostatēs*. This is probably not a reference to a synagogue official, although it *may* refer to a Judean association of some sort. Like Veturia Paula, renamed Sarah, various women in Rome and Venosa are called "mother of the synagogue," a title whose masculine equivalent, "father of the synagogue," is also well attested in those same (and other) synagogues.[184]

Although older generations of scholars paid little attention to these inscriptions, generally dismissing them out of hand as honorifics granted to the female relatives of male synagogue officers and benefactors, Brooten's Harvard dissertation re-opened the question of what these titles say about women's participation in the organizational structures of ancient synagogues.[185] I do not mean to discount the ramifications of the historical issues

---

181. Sophia of Gortyn (*CIJ* 1² 731c = *IJO* 1.Cre3).

182. From Venosa: Beronike (*CIJ* 581 = *JIWE* 1.59); Mannine (*CIJ* 590 = *JIWE* 1.62); Faustina (*CIJ* 597 = *JIWE* 1.71); also Rebeka (*CIJ* 692 = *IJO* 1 Thr3); Makaria (SEG 27 [1977]1201); Eulogia (*JIWE* 1.163). Another from Noccere, near Pompeii, was unknown to me in 1992, and perhaps also to Noy, *JIWE* 1, which lacks it. The excavator, M. Conticello de'Spagnolis, shared it with Bernadette Brooten, who told me.

183. Brooten 1982:35–39 (*CIJ* 1² 696b = *IJO* 1.Ach3).

184. Four women are actually called "mother of the synagogue," including Veturia/Sarah and two others from Rome, *JIWE* 2. 251, 542, 577 and one from Brescia; *JIWE* 1.5. One inscription from Venosa, *JIWE* 1.63 = *CIJ* 1. .606, calls a woman *pateressa*, whereas a second (*JIWE* 1.116 = *CIJ* 1² 619d) calls Faustina μήτηρ. Because her husband is also πάτηρ and πάτρονος τῆς πόλεως, it seems more likely that this is a title, not an indication of maternity. On the title "father of the synagogue," see, e.g., Levine 2000:404–6. See also Noy's mention of women called *mater* in trade group honors (*JIWE* 1. p. 148).

185. Brooten 1982 herself lays out the history of these views prior to her dissertation, but they continue to assert themselves. Particularly interesting is the discussion of Linder to the exemptions of priests, *archisynagogoi*, fathers of the synagogue and others who serve synagogues: he writes that the term *pater synagogae* "was probably purely honorific, devoid of any effective function, although our law seems to indicate such functions." (Linder 1987:137 n. 11). He gives no explanation for why the law (Linder 1987: no. 9, Constantine, 29 Nov–1 Dec 330) is wrong on this point.

here. Trying to determine with as much certainty as the sources allow what women actually did in ancient Judean communities (and others) is highly significant, at the very least for the production of better histories, and both my own work and that of others has focused in the past on these problems.[186] Yet I have come to think that the debates that such work has prompted have often been misguided, and have been far too pre-occupied with whether these titles were "honorary" or "functional."

In part, early arguments about these titles as "honorary" served, I think, to deflect any attempt to use these inscriptions as precedent for contemporary practice: whether this was intentional, in some manner, on the part of scholars who argued this position is a historiographic project beyond the scope of this study. It also may have served to guard against claims or implications that ancient Judaism was heteropraxic, if not heterodox, given modern orthodox opposition to women's full and equal participation in contemporary synagogue life.[187] To call women's titles "honorary" was code language for "insignificant," or even "meaningless." Women's titles did not threaten the implicit system of hierarchical gendered order that was part of many scholars' deeply embedded notion of Jewish life in antiquity as standing in a more or less seamless continuity with subsequent rabbinic orthodoxy.

In this light, the recent arguments of four scholars, Tessa Rajak, David Noy, William Horbury, and Lee Levine, concerning women office holders, are quite fascinating.[188] In a brief treatment published in 1992, Rajak argued, against Brooten, that all ancient synagogue titles were essentially honorary, since they were conferred, not only on women, but also occasionally on young children, proof dispositive for her that they cannot have entailed the performance of any substantial responsibilities.[189] Rajak also criticized Brooten for failing to situate "the honorands of the synagogue inscriptions" within the larger world of inscriptions honoring holders of various civic offices. Further,

---

186. E.g., Kraemer 1992:106–27; Zabin 1996:262–82. Zabin did not have access to *JIWE* 2, inscriptions from the city of Rome, whose 1995 publication probably overlapped with the production of her article.

187. This is itself a complicated issue: orthodox rabbis and institutions have generally opposed the ordination of women rabbis and resisted women reading Torah in front of men, although there are occasional exceptions.

188. Tessa Rajak 1992:22–24 (subtitled "Women Benefactors and Community Practices"); Rajak and Noy 1993; Horbury 1999, esp. 388–401, subtitled "Women in Office;" Levine 2000:470–90 (titled "Women in the Synagogue").

189. Rajak 1992:23, citing what is now *JIWE* 1.53, an epitaph from Venosa for a three-year-old boy who appears to be called ἀρχισυνάγωγος. The inscription is known only from nineteenth-century transcriptions, and there appear to be some doubts about its authenticity (*JIWE* 1, p. 74). Noy notes several other children with office titles: *JIWE* 2.288 = *CIJ* 1.88, a child *archon*; and a twelve-year-old *grammateus* and *mellarchon* (*JIWE* 2.547 = *CIJ* 1. 284). It's also interesting that both synagogues associated with Rufina had young male children either slated to become *archon*, Siculus Sabinus, or just called *archon*, Annianus, son of Julianos. Conceivably, designating a child *archon*, as in the case of Annianus, might in fact be an honor for a deceased child slated for future office, rather than an indication of actual child offices. I don't think it ever occurs for a living child.

in Brooten's representation of women *archisynagōgoi* as what Rajak called "dedicated female rabbis of progressive persuasion," she "vastly overestimates the amount of administrative activity that would have surrounded an ancient institution."[190]

In a jointly authored article published only a year later, Rajak and Noy offer a more tempered critique of Brooten's work, as part of a detailed analysis of the title *archisynagōgos*. They argue, with considerable persuasion, that the portrait of *archisynagōgos*, and other offices is at least sometimes derived from polemical Christian references; is amalgamated from very disparate evidence; presumes an imaginary homogeneity and constancy of ancient Jewish practice; and functions on occasion to reproduce rabbinic categories on evidence for diaspora communities (something they suggest Brooten did as well). Against the prevailing thesis that *archisynagōgos* is simply the Greek equivalent of the Hebrew *rosh ha-knesset*, they find equally if not more plausible the alternative thesis that the Hebrew has been derived from prior usage of the Greek.[191] Thus it would appear that they lack commitments to the older constructions of ancient Judaism better served by the thesis that women did not actually hold offices in Jewish synagogues.

Despite this, their careful analysis of these ancient office titles as local, variable in meaning, and rooted in ancient practices of benefaction does not seem to extend to considerations of gender. They concede, on the basis of relatively abundant evidence and analogues from the larger cultural contexts, that Judean women were probably "owners of wealth in their own right, who gain titles and honours because they are able to be benefactors."[192] On the question of whether women actually did anything beyond provide funding and prestige, they suggest, in rather elusive language, that "Brooten's claim of functional equality is acceptable (though perhaps less so in the case of the small children), but the synagogue service is not the correct setting for that equality, and the contribution of women, just as that of men, must be envisaged as patronal and perhaps ceremonial rather than religious."[193] What distinction precisely, they envision between patronal, ceremonial, and religious remains implicit. Finally, they conclude that "the public behaviour of these women, like that of the benefactors of Asia Minor, 'was still defined and constrained by the . . . traditional ideology,'" appealing to the judgment of Riet van Bremen.[194]

190. Rajak 1992:23.
191. Rajak and Noy 1993:87.
192. Rajak and Noy 1993:87.
193. Rajak and Noy 1993:87.
194. Van Bremen 1985:236, with fuller study in van Bremen 1996.

Horbury's treatment, published several years later (1999), takes a more moderate position. Horbury's work demonstrates, in various respects, the problems Rajak and Noy identify in many treatments of Jews in late antiquity, exemplified for instance in the homogenizing, static title of his chapter, "Women in *the* Synagogue" (emphasis mine), the same title of Lee Levine's chapter in *The Ancient Synagogue*, which appeared the following year.[195] Horbury resists what he sees as an artificial distinction between "functional" and "honorific" titles, partly because, like Rajak and Noy, he sees these titles as embedded within ancient systems of patronage and benefaction. He argues that an office like that of *archisynagōgos* "would have entailed, for incumbents of either sex, the vital communal function of financial subsidy, and it would have been esteemed by either sex, like other offices, as an honour."[196] For Horbury, *archisynagōgos*, for instance, is functional because the provision of financial resources was "a vital communal function," and it was honorary because people who made such benefactions received honors in return (if not also provided such benefactions in response to public honors). He then considers what particular functions women might have performed for these various offices. Yet he introduces a distinction of "governing" function, which he thinks women were unlikely to have performed.[197] Horbury is unimpressed with the argument from children office holders that figures prominently in Rajak's analysis: "in view of ancient custom with regard to honours the phenomenon is no guide to the nature of the offices concerned."[198] Yet in the end, his argument isn't really all that different from that of Rajak and Noy in many respects.

Levine, by comparison, argues much more strongly for the possibility that women *archisynagogoi* and perhaps other office holders did more than donate and receive honors.[199] Part of his argument here rests on his response to Rajak and Noy in his chapter on synagogue offices, where he argues that *archisynagogoi* in general were neither simply nor necessarily donors. Although some *archisynagogoi* clearly did provide major financial support to particular communities, the two were not inextricably linked.[200] Much of Rajak and Noy's argument against women as actual "leaders" rests on their view that *archisynagōgos* is integrally related to benefaction (that women could do), and not the exercise of authority that women (in their view, apparently) could not do. There is a serious circularity in

195. Levine 2000:470–90.

196. Horbury 1999:391; restated in similar language on 397. Perhaps there is some relationship between these arguments and British scholars' greater familiarity with a culture of public honors.

197. E.g., Horbury 1999:390.

198. Horbury 1999:397 n. 119.

199. Levine 2000:483. "There is a possibility that most, if not all, the titles that appear in over a score of Diaspora inscriptions are those of functioning women officials."

200. Levine 2000:399.

the argument of Rajak and Noy: it is precisely because women (and perhaps occasionally children) hold the title of *archisynagōgos* that they are so persuaded it must reflect benefaction and social honor, rather than communal activity. Levine's separation of benefaction and the office of *archisynagōgos* in any case facilitates his view that women office-holders could have exercised some authority.

What I find troubling about many of these arguments is partly their assumption that we can and do know what transpired in ancient synagogues. Horbury, for instance, thinks that a woman *archisynagōgos* "could perhaps have participated in the appointment of readers," but appeals to some amorphous and apparently uniform "current convention" that might have prevented this, "as it certainly would have made it unlikely that she should herself read or teach."[201] A curious combination of the Pastoral epistles and the rabbis seems to be calling in the background. He also seems confident that some amorphous social process called "contemporary feeling" would have prohibited women from participating in any synagogue council, even while their donations would have been welcomed, together with other unspecified "burdens of office."[202] As I noted, he distinguishes between what he calls "governmental functions," which he thinks women could not have performed, unless perhaps with regard solely to other women, and liturgical functions, which he thinks women could have had, at least with regard to hymnody and prayer. It's not clear, however, whether this just means he thinks women sang and prayed aloud in synagogue services.[203]

Levine, on the other hand, thinks it unlikely that women had "any kind of active leadership in or responsibility for congregational worship in general," on the basis of "women's generally inferior status in antiquity," a broad and unexamined argument comparable in some ways to Horbury's invocation of "contemporary feeling" as social explanation.[204] Where Horbury seems to envision

201. Horbury 1999:397.

202. Horbury 1999:396–97, 399.

203. On the gender associations of these practices, see chapter 2.

204. Levine 2000:478; repeated on 490. He then devotes considerable discussion to *t. Megillah* 3.11–12, which appears first to allow women to read from the Torah on the Sabbath, and then to forbid it, concluding that what appear in the Tosefta as contiguous and thus somewhat contradictory views were initially "separate and independent pericopae," 479. Levine's approach throughout this discussion is to amalgamate evidence from all ancient Jewish sources, from diverse locations and dates, an approach consistent with the singular title of the book, *The Ancient Synagogue*. Nevertheless, Levine does allow at times for a diversity of practice, as in his argument that when it comes to "Women as benefactors and as synagogue officials, some very clear geographical distinctions can be made," 2000:484. Levine attributes this diversity to influence from the cultural practices of the surrounding communities, an old argument clothed in slightly new dress: "when such a phenomenon [of women holding defined communal positions] occurs, it clearly is due to synchronic forces impacting on the local Jewish communities," because this is clearly, in his view, a departure from earlier Jewish practice (Levine 2000:488). Although I appreciate Levine's generous references to my own work throughout his chapter, his approach, like Horbury 1999, exemplifies the issues Rajak and Noy identified in their article, which is cited in his bibliography, but doesn't seem to filter into his discussion of women *archisynagogoi*.

women participating in (and perhaps leading?) some aspects of synagogue liturgy, namely, singing hymns and praying, Levine seems more dubious, and notes that all the liturgical titles attested, both from literary sources (including rabbinic sources) and inscriptions, apply only to men.[205]

Other aspects of these discussions trouble me even more. The frequent framing of ancient practices in terms of leadership, while understandable, has perhaps been misleading.[206] The term *leadership* is in many ways a modern one, even while it corresponds to some degree to ancient ideas about the exercise of authority over others. It has been used somewhat loosely to cover everything from the holding of priestly offices in ancient temples, including the Judean temple in Jerusalem, to patrons of ancient religious associations, to women functioning in various capacities in early Christian groups as missionaries, prophets, teachers, heads of house churches, and so forth. Amalgamating these diverse instances of social practices obscures the underlying ancient association of authority with masculinity and maleness, particularly through associations of masculinity and maleness with activity as opposed to passivity; with domination as opposed to subordination; and with the various capacities themselves associated with leading, ruling, and control of others: rationality, self-control, and so forth. Conflicts over women's performance of certain social roles depended, in my view, precisely on these associations.

Thus the question of whether these titles were "honorific" or "functional" attends insufficiently to the underlying logic of gender arrangements. Implicit in many of the debates seems to be the assumption that "functional" outranks "honorific," and that, at least from our twenty-first century vantage point, a world where women did actually "function" in such offices would be "better" than one in which they did not. It's possible that Rajak and Noy are actually arguing, against this view, that benefaction was more highly valued in antiquity than tasks that we might call administrative or management, so that excluding women from the performance of such tasks has no negative implications. On the contrary, it could be argued that what is really at stake is a class distinction. The kinds of administrative tasks that Brooten envisions for Rufina and other

---

205. Levine 2000:484.

206. Brooten's study is entitled "Women Leaders in the Ancient Synagogue," a category that receives little social theorizing, although Brooten is exhaustive in her analysis of the evidence for these particular offices and her consideration of what women and men might have done to fulfill their responsibilities. Interestingly, Eisen's collection of epigraphic and literary evidence for Christian women holding church offices, for which Brooten's study was explicitly the impetus, is entitled, perhaps more carefully, *Women Officeholders in Early Christianity: Epigraphical and Literary Studies*, itself a translation of the original German, *Amtsträgerinnen im früen Christentum: epigraphische und literarische Studien* (Eisen 2000). Levine's chapter on synagogue offices is entitled "Leadership," 2000:387–428. It contains no definition of leadership, or theorizing of the category.

female synagogue officers might, conceivably, have had far less prestige in antiquity than Brooten's reconstruction imagines.

Yet if this is Rajak and Noy's view, it is not particularly apparent. Their insistence that women's synagogue titles must be construed within ancient systems of benefaction (with which I generally concur) and do not point to women's active engagement in the management of synagogue affairs (about which I am less certain) does seem to suggest that the latter have more ancient cultural value than the former, if for no other reason than in Rajak's and Noy's view, apparently, women were ultimately excluded from the most prestigious cultural activities. These questions, however, deserve more exploration than we have given them. Not inconceivably, it is precisely benefaction that is the more valued than administration, although this still leaves unanswered why, then, administration should be off-limits to women. Then again, perhaps the simple answer is that it wasn't, which is, of course, another way to read these same inscriptions.

Apologetic concerns may underlie some, if not all, of these treatments. At the end of Horbury's survey he writes, "Women in the synagogue, therefore, were indeed subject to repressive tendencies, but they were not in a wholly unfavourable position by comparison with their forebears or their Christian contemporaries."[207] For Horbury, at least, construing synagogue offices as the honors attendant on patronage and benefaction may somehow blunt the impact of the inescapable reality that women were still restricted in antiquity from exercising the same authority as men. In her own piece, Rajak presents herself as the guardian of "unbiased" scholarship, able to see through what she takes to be Brooten's projection of a 1980s feminist perspective onto the data of antiquity. In the piece co-authored with Noy, these views are somewhat tempered. Still, for all their nuanced arguments about the diversity and variability of ancient Jewish communities and organizations, and their critique of much scholarship on ancient Judaism, with regard to women and gender, they largely affirm older conservative views.

All these authors also fail to articulate the degree to which honor itself, in antiquity, is highly gendered. Thus, ironically, to insist that these offices are indications of honor, not function, and that's why women can hold them not only seems to rank "function" above "honor"; it also ignores the degree to which honor was itself usually gendered as masculine, and was disproportionately an attribute of elite men. Further, honors accorded to men affirmed

---

207. Horbury 1999:401. This conclusion is strikingly reminiscent of the arguments made by classicists like A. W. Gomme in his (once) famous piece, "The Position of Women in Athens in the Fifth and Fourth Centuries B.C." (Gomme 1925).

the performance of ideal(ized) masculinity, whereas those accorded to women appear to have affirmed the performance of ideal(ized) femininity. Thus the really interesting question is not whether women held such offices. This seems apparent on its face, and also historically unremarkable, at least in particular locations like Asia Minor, given the abundant evidence for women office holders in numerous cities and cults. Rather, it is whether such office holding was in any way transgressive, and if not, how it fit into particular systems of gender in antiquity.

With Rajak and Noy, I concur that Riet van Bremen was on the right track in her argument that women held offices within the constraints of ancient gender ideologies. My own view continues to be that women could hold offices, including that of *archisynagōgos* (whatever, precisely, it entailed) so long as their doing so could be expressed in terms and images of social relations that themselves accorded with notions of gender hierarchy and did not, in practice, involve the violation of hierarchical relations. The work of many scholars, especially R. A. Kearsley and subsequently Steven Friesen on women office holders in Asia Minor,[208] has demonstrated that the construction of public benefaction and the holding of cultic offices (which themselves involved substantial acts of such benefaction) as an extension of familial responsibilities was instrumental in women's ability to hold such offices. Although such actions *might* have been read, in some social systems, as women inappropriately exercising authority over men, it seems abundantly clear from the public honors accorded such women, often and perhaps unsurprisingly couched in familial language, that this simply was not the case.

The question remains just how much access we have to how women's performance of particular acts would have been construed, either by them or those around them. Although we generally lack the evidence to determine whether, in practice, the responsibilities of such offices entailed particular women exercising authority over men, it does seem interesting that those women designated *archisynagōgos* in ancient inscriptions are never explicitly identified as married. This suggests several things. First, at the social level, it may suggest that unmarried women of sufficient age could exercise some "masculine" authority because they were not, themselves, subject to familial male authority in the form of either a father, or a current husband. This may be particularly true for widows, women previously married, whose marriages terminated honorably in death, not divorce, and who may thus have had both financial resources and some control over those resources. As I have argued

---

208. Kearsley 1986; 1990; 1994; 2006; Friesen 1999; see also van Bremen 1996.

earlier, it may well be that women are most likely to hold such offices when they are either relatively autonomous, or of sufficiently elite status, or sufficiently wealthy that these override the cultural disabilities of gender.

Second, at the theoretical level, the question remains whether such offices were constructed as inherently masculine and, thus, whether women holding such offices was inevitably contradictory, at least implicitly. As we saw in chapter 4 on Thecla, this was certainly the view expressed explicitly by Tertullian with regard to the Christian priesthood and the practices of baptism, teaching, eucharist, and others; they are inherently male actions whose performance by women is thus illogical and transgressive. Such offices may well have been presumed, on the whole, to be gendered, and to require certain masculine characteristics of activity, self-control, exercise of authority over subordinates, and the like. Yet since the epigraphical evidence for women with such titles is incontrovertible, we must consider how their having done so relates to these general cultural frameworks. My argument is that there is some elasticity in these cultural connections that either muted the implications of authority and hierarchy associated with these offices or constructed the women who held them as sufficiently male, or at least, not female, perhaps by virtue of their being older, widows, wealthy, and the like. And although Tertullian certainly provides no access to the *habitus* (to borrow here explicitly from Bourdieu) of diaspora Judean communities in the late second and early third centuries C.E., it is perhaps instructive that he worries, explicitly, that some women might, in fact, escape the disabilities of gender through virginity and be considered exempt from the constraints on "women."[209]

I am not arguing here that women office holders in Judean congregations relied on distinctions between sexually inviolate women and women subject to male penetration for the legitimacy of their claims to office, if only because there seems to be no need to do so. Elite married women in Roman Asia Minor were regularly able to hold and perform the functions of numerous offices and priesthoods. Still, in those cases, their ability to do so seems integrally linked to the construction of those benefactions as the extension of the familial obligations of the extremely wealthy to the cities as a whole, overriding other potential cultural meanings. Women office holders in Judean synagogues might conceivably have been understood in similar ways, particularly for those synagogues in the same cultural milieu of Roman Asia Minor, from which all but one of the known women *archisynagōgoi* come. Yet it seems also not inconceivable that this other dynamic is at work, and even that both could be operative at the same time.

---

209. *On the Veiling of Virgins*: see earlier, ch. 3.

As the discussion of Thecla and early Christian women's activities makes clear, these are not easy matters to resolve, and there is, at least on the Christian side, ample evidence of challenges to these constraints. This may mean that such challenges might have been posed by Jewish women as well, or even just alternatively that in some communities, women's performance of any number of activities might have been construed as appropriate, even though we now lack access to those social realities.

7

Rethinking Gender, History, and Women's Religions in the Greco-Roman Mediterranean

Introduction

My goal for this study was to explore and theorize the relationships between religion and ancient constructions of gender, and more specifically, between such constructions and women's religious practices, that is, women's devotion to or engagement with imagined divine beings.[1] Yet such a project is immediately compromised by the fact that the evidence for women's religious practices, primarily ancient literary accounts, but also documentary and epigraphical evidence, is itself enmeshed in naturalizing constructions of gender.

The preceding chapters have explored this problem through diverse examples. Women's affinity for Bacchic rites in republican Italy and Rome turns out to be Livy's polemical characterization that affords us little useful access to women's practice and intentions. Rabbinic debates about Judean women studying Torah, as well as other representations of women, dissolve into rabbinic anxieties and fantasies. A resurrected woman's report of the gender-specific punishments in the afterlife in the *Acts of Thomas* constructs a female figure as the guarantor of a divinely authorized gendered ethic. Justin Martyr uses the figure of an elite Roman matron who sought to live a life of self-disciplined Christian asceticism to represent Christians as

---

1. For discussion of this terminology and its underpinnings, see the Introduction.

the truest exemplars of the righteous philosophical life. Philo's Therapeutic women philosophers look more and more like a working out of his idealized philosophic community, generated in significant degree by his exegesis of the deliverance of Israel from slavery in Egypt as the soul's liberation from the passions, and more specifically of Exodus 15 (the Israelite Song-by-the-Sea) as paradigmatic. As did Justin's matron, so, too, Paul's fictive disciple Thecla, from the *Acts of (Paul and) Thecla* offers a narrative of Christians as the ultimate exemplars of ascetic and philosophical virtues. Severus of Minorca casts Jewish women as the last hold-outs against Christian pressure to convert, not to show us their courage and faithfulness, but rather so that he can depict Christians as models of proper gender relations (with women submissive to men, male bishops, Christ and God), and Jews as paradigms of gender dis-order (with disobedient women, still the daughters of Eve, whose husbands are unable to control them). Ancient literary claims and modern scholarly assertions that Gentile women were disproportionately interested in adopting either Judean or Christian practices turn out to be the use of gender in service to various polemical debates, both in antiquity and in modernity, affording us little access into either the actual demographic realities of the adoption of new religious practices, or the interests and motivations of such persons. Contemporary scholarly debates about the epigraphical evidence for women holding offices in Diaspora Judean synagogues generally fail to recognize the extent to which women could only have done so in Judean communities that constructed those offices themselves as gender appropriate.

These diverse instances by no means constitute an exhaustive catalogue, so it is worth noting, at least briefly, other instances that, had I enough time and space, could doubtless also be pursued. As various scholars have shown, representations of female martyrs (both Christian and Judean), draw extensively on ideas of femininity as passivity and suffering.[2] This raises the strong possibility that narratives of female martyrs are fictions that are compelling precisely because of their exploitation of these associations. If so, we are left with little evidence for real women martyrs such as Potamiena, Blandina and other women among the martyrs of Lyon and Viennes,[3] and especially Perpetua,[4] whose authorship of the first-person portion of her martyrdom I seriously doubt, and whose historicity itself may be uncertain.[5] Over a decade ago, I

2. See, e.g., Perkins 1995; 2007; Shaw 1996; Castelli 2004; Cobb 2008.

3. Eusebius, *Ecclesiastical History* 6.5.1–7; 5.1.3–63, in *WRGRW* 115 and 113.

4. *The Martyrdom of Saints Perpetua and Felicitas*, in *WRGRW* 114.

5. For my earlier views of Perpetua, see Kraemer 1992:159–63; for my more recent views, see Kraemer and Lander 2000. Judith Perkins told me some years ago, in personal conversation, that she no longer thinks Perpetua was a historical figure: for her discussion of this in print, see now Perkins 2007. Others (continue to) consider Perpetua as such (Shaw 1993; Bremmer 2003).

argued that the transformation of the biblical Joseph's wife Aseneth from an Egyptian idolater to a devoted worshipper of the God of Joseph relies upon gender as a key element in the logic of transformation, affording us no meaningful access to the transformation practices of actual women.[6]

Much also might be done with the numerous accounts of women practitioners of what is sometimes called "magic." Theorists of religion have long debated whether a distinction between religion and magic is anything other than a distinction between Self and Other (we practice religion; they practice magic).[7] The work of Elizabeth Pollard has shown that although women are routinely represented as practicing *artes magicae*, or *mageia* in ancient literary works, the epigraphic and legal evidence suggests that it is actually men who are the major specialists and experts in *artes magicae*, and that the depiction of *artes magicae* as predominantly women's practice is grounded more in the feminization of such activities than in access to women's activities.[8] Michael Satlow and others have made similar arguments with regard to rabbinic depictions of women as practitioners of "magic."[9]

Still, I have argued in these chapters that some aspects of women's practices (their activities, if not ordinarily their intentions and self-understandings) remain perceptible. I think that women's authority to baptize, preach, teach, and travel really was hotly debated in some Christian circles in the mid-late second century and the early third century C.E., as evidenced by the various formulations (and textual problems) of the story of Thecla, Tertullian's critique of it, and the debates about the New Prophecy from the late second century on. I think that some Christian women did adopt ascetic practices that triggered complex social responses and consequences. I'm less convinced that Alexandrian Judean women did so in Philo's lifetime, although it's certainly not impossible. I think that at least a small number of women did hold offices in some Judean diaspora communities, offices that would have been construed

---

6. Initially, I included in this book a slightly updated and reworked version of my chapter "Why Is Aseneth a Woman? The Use and Significance of Gender in the Aseneth Stories," in Kraemer 1998:191–221. Ultimately, I decided that it wasn't necessary to repeat it here, even with some modest revisions.

7. Durkheim, for instance, famously argued that religion was social, whereas magic was individual; there is, he wrote, no "church of magic" (Durkheim 1915:43). The work of cognitive theorists of religion may suggest that there might be a useful practical distinction: if religion is defined as the "concatenation of human activities centered" on gods, and gods are defined as "non-human agents, with intentions, who interact with humans, and who have certain counter-intuitive properties, namely omnipotence, omniscience, immortality, and so forth," then, possibly, "magic" differs primarily in the characteristics of the nonhuman agents whose interaction is presumed. For references, see the Introduction. For the difficulties with the category "magic," see Smith 2004a. Notwithstanding this, scholars of antiquity use the category regularly, e.g., Graf 1997; Schäfer and Kippenberg 1997; Meyer 1999; Faraone 2001; Janowitz 2001; Mirecki and Meyer 2002; Luck 2006.

8. Pollard 2001.

9. Satlow 2002; see also Fishbane 2007.

within prevailing gender norms. But perhaps most importantly, I think that intersections between ideologies of gender and religious practices, as well as representations of such practices, are visible in these sources, which I have tried to extricate and analyze throughout this study. In this final chapter, then, I wish to pursue some of these issues a little further.

Intersections of Religion and Gender

As I illustrated in *Her Share of the Blessings*, and as numerous studies have continued to demonstrate,[10] in the ancient Mediterranean, much religion was gender specific. Many festivals (some Dionysian rites, the Adonia, the Matralia, the Thesmophoria) were celebrated primarily, if not exclusively by one sex or the other, as suggested not only by accounts in literary sources, but also to some degree by extant inscriptions.[11] Animal sacrifice was generally the domain of men, although women could sometimes eat the meat.[12] The Hebrew Bible mandates only the participation of adult men in the key festivals of Pesach, Sukkoth and Shavuot.[13] Elsewhere, biblical authors envisioned and/or required the presence of women as well. Accounts in Judean authors like Josephus and Philo suggest that, in practice, some women may have attended these festivals as well, although the extent of their participation, especially in the sacrifices, is less clear. Rites performed on behalf of the body politic were particularly the domain of men, although the converse is not as true as many might think: domestic religion was similarly the domain of men, even though women's devotions were frequently focused on the health and welfare of the more immediate family and household.[14]

Even festivals and rites incumbent on all persons, or at least all free adults, frequently had gendered dimensions. In domestic religion, male heads of families performed sacrifices on behalf of the whole household, whereas women might perform daily devotions whose very ordinariness contributed to their construction as lesser (and feminized). Gender-differentiated rites contribute to the making of women and men, females and males, and affirm the rightness

---

10. See, e.g., Staples 1998; Dillon 2002; Cole 2004; Goff 2004; Connolly 2007; Takács 2007.

11. Cole 1992; 2004.

12. Cole 2004:93–104 provides a detailed assessment of the epigraphical evidence for women's participation in feasts and sacrifices, including at least occasional evidence for women dining alone on sacrificial meat; see also 117–18. See also Jay 1992:53.

13. Exod 23.14; 23.17; Deut 16.16 (see also 1 Kings 9.25, where Solomon offers up burnt offerings and sacrifices three years a year).

14. Cole 2004:95; see also Bodel and Olyan 2008.

of those categories. As Goff illuminates, women's cult practices not only make good citizen wives and mothers, they also create other social categories of "not-wives," including slaves, prostitutes, and other marginalized categories, or what Margaret Atwood so brilliantly envisioned as "un-women" in the dystopic Republic of Gilead, together with wives and handmaids.[15]

Yet virtually alone among the religions of the late ancient Mediterranean, Christian ritual practice does not appear to differ for women and for men, with the significant exception of the eventual explicit exclusion of women from priestly offices. Ordinary and festival devotions and sacraments were not, at least in idealized form, gender specific, but were incumbent on women and men alike: (catechumenal) instruction, baptism, communal and individual prayer, hymning, prophecy, consumption of the eucharist, charity, as well as many ascetic practices, and so forth. There are hints, occasionally, of gender-specific practices, such as Epiphanius's well-known account of Marian devotion on the part of women he calls Kollyridians, although the reliability of this is, like the accounts of many women's practices in this book, deeply problematic.[16] And, of course, as I have considered briefly in the previous chapter, there are sometimes claims that women are disproportionately attracted to Christianity, or to so-called heretical practices (always by their opponents, of course).

The earliest depictions of Christ devotees, in the letters of Paul, provides little explicit evidence of gender-differentiated practices, despite Paul's famous insistence in 1 Cor 11.3–16 that women who pray and prophesy in the communal assembly should cover their heads while doing so, whereas men should not. However, I will consider the gendered nature of the practices Paul commends in this letter shortly. Similarly, the outsider description of Christian practices little more than a half-century later, by Pliny the Younger, then Governor of Pontus and Bythnia in Asia Minor, seems to suggest no distinction by gender. Writing to the Emperor Trajan to ask whether his response to those accused of being Christians is correct, Pliny notes that persons of both sexes are involved. Indeed, he claims to get his information about them particularly by torturing two female slaves (*ancillae*) called *ministrae* (usually translated as deaconesses).[17] All Pliny gets from his (former) Christian witnesses is that they met regularly on a fixed day before day, sang hymns responsively to Christ, as to a god, and bound themselves by an oath "not to commit fraud, theft, or

---

15. Goff writes: "Adult women's rituals are thus best understood within a model of gender ideology. . . . [T]he rituals aim at producing women who are equipped to perform successfully their roles within a patriarchal order and who have internalized a version of themselves that is useful to others." 2004:123; Atwood 1986.

16. Epiphanius, *Panarion* 78.23; *WRGRW* 38. For the argument that the Kollyridians are Epiphanius's imagining, see Ullucci 2005.

17. See, e.g., Kraemer 1992:182.

adultery, not falsify their trust, nor to refuse to return a trust when called upon to do so." They also assembled for a communal meal.[18]

Yet when scrutinized carefully, these same practices still routinely turn out to encode and affirm ideas about gender. It's worth a brief digression to make this point, with regard to prayer, prophecy, singing hymns of divine praise, being baptized, and baptizing others.

Prayer

One might expect prayer to be the least gendered of early Christian devotional forms. It is seen to be a universal human practice before the divine, fitting for both men and women, and numerous ancient narratives in all religious traditions depict women as praying, and often narrate their actual prayers.[19] Yet prayer may be seen to be appropriate for women precisely because it entails some degree of petition and subordination and constructs the petitioner as female in relation to the gods. To the degree that subordination is inevitably coded as feminine, prayer always has a feminine dimension to it. Even though it has the capacity to feminize, prayer is still regularly seen to be appropriate even for the most masculine men with tremendous amounts of authority, such as a high priest or the Roman emperor. Still, because prayer in antiquity is largely performed aloud and in public, it intersects with the gendered associations of speech, which is regularly constructed as masculine. This doesn't mean that women didn't pray aloud, particularly because silent prayer had other negative associations, which I explore elsewhere in my work on *Aseneth*, but it might lead us to expect to find fewer representations of women praying aloud in public and more representations of women's prayers performed in private, and/or in the company of other women.[20]

Interestingly, one of the most common roles of Christian female saints will be intercessory prayer, like the prayer of Thecla for Tryphaena's deceased daughter, Falconilla; or the well-known prayer of Perpetua for her deceased young brother, who died without knowledge of Christ, and whom she sees in a

---

18. Pliny, *Letters* 10.96–97. It's highly relevant that Pliny characterizes these practices with feminized language: "depraved, excessive superstition [*superstitionem pravam et immodicam*]."

19. For an overview of the prayers attributed to women in Jewish sources, see McDowell 2006. The author's lack of theoretical perspective and analysis detracts from the usefulness of his work. Women's prayers are found at numerous points in ancient Greek novels: e.g., the prayers of Callirhoe to Aphrodite, Chariton, *Chareas and Callirhoe* 2.2, 7.5, 8.8 (in *WRGRW* 23); the prayers of Anthia to Isis and Apis, in Xenophon of Ephesos, *Ephesian Tale of Anthia and Habrocomes* 4.3 and 5.4 (*WRGRW* 26). Interestingly, though, many of these prayers are performed without audiences: Callirhoe and Anthia both beseech the gods in their temples privately. This is true of Aseneth's prayers as well. Thecla's prayers, though, are increasingly performed in public.

20. *Aseneth* 15.7–8; see Kraemer 1998:26; 61–62.

vision, first suffering from the traditional thirst of the dead; and then, after her successful intercession, cleansed and refreshed in a Christian heaven; or that of the divine daughter of God, Metanoia, on behalf of "all those who repent" in *Aseneth*.[21] All three constitute instances of an acceptable female role where virtuous females intercede with (powerful) men on behalf of others, while lacking the ability to grant favors on their own.

Prophecy

As I considered in my earlier discussion of Thecla, prophecy itself can be seen as a fundamentally gendered category, that relies on the notion of penetration of a human by a divine agent, and casts the prophet into the role of the passive, penetrated, god-possessed female, even when the prophet is, as is usually the case, male.[22] A more complex set of analogies involving speech and seed, knowledge and fertility, may be at work here: the god is to the prophet as the husband is to the wife, and the words of the god are to the prophet as the husband's seed is to his wife.[23] Although the vast majority of the prophets in the Hebrew Bible are clearly men, the handful of female examples were sufficiently well-known in antiquity—especially Miriam the sister of Moses and Aaron—to

21. In offering this example, I still desist from concluding that *Aseneth* is the work of a Christian author, but if it is, then Metanoia is a type of Mary. For a recent argument that *Aseneth* is authored by a Christian, see Nir 2009.

22. The rarer case of the male prophet of the female deity probably still relies on gendered models, even if the gender of the prophet and the deity are then somewhat reversed. A refutation of the Montanists (the New Prophecy) by an author named Apollonius contained the following: "It is necessary to test all the fruits of a prophet. Tell me, does a prophet dye his hair? Does he line his eyelids? Does he love adornment?" Eusebius, *Ecclesiastical History* 5.18.11. Clearly, effeminate behavior disqualified a true Christian prophet. Another relevant example may be the priests of Cybele, the Galli, whose service to her is clearly related to their castration, an act that emasculates them, and to some degree necessarily feminizes them, although it may also make them some third gender (Ringrose 2003).

23. I owe this argument to Jesse Goodman, Brown 2004, whose fine seminar paper in spring 2004 argued that in Aeschylus's *Oresteia*, Cassandra's role as prophet relies on ideas about prophecy as sexuality. True prophecy is wifely fidelity—the male god inseminates his prophet with his true words as the husband inseminates his wife with his own seed. Underlying this is also a notion of conception as solely the result of male action—a theory that Apollo himself articulates in the play. Thus, prophecy comes only from the male god, and the female prophet is simply the passive receptacle and deliverer, as the wife is of legitimate children. And as legitimate children are validated by public acceptance of them as such, so legitimate prophecy must be validated by public acceptance of the truth of the god's words. Furthermore, then, the female prophet must have the same fundamental characteristics as the faithful wife: her fidelity must be unassailable. This may illuminate some of the anxiety ancient Christian writers have about female prophets, both Christian and otherwise, even though they concede that God can choose to prophesy through a woman if God so chooses. The "orthodox" example they often cite—that of the prophesy of Mary in Luke—that "henceforth all women shall call me blessed"—raises precisely some of these problems, because Mary is herself pregnant with the true male child of the true God. One of Origen's objections to the Greek oracle, the Pythia, was precisely that she was female, and not a male through whom God speaks on account of male virtue (*Against Celsus* 7.5–6).

authorize and legitimize women prophets in the Jesus movement.[24] The only other Judean evidence for women prophets in an ancient Judean movement is Philo's depiction of the Therapeutrides as "enthused" (that is, "god-possessed"). Apart from this, the evidence for Judean women prophets in Greco-Roman antiquity is more or less nonexistent.[25]

The attributes of women prophets in various early Christian sources tend to confirm these associations, for such prophets are generally (if not universally) represented as celibate or chaste. Not being penetrated by human husbands or other male authorities, they are available to be penetrated by the male deity. Interestingly, in the canonical gospels, only Luke mentions women prophets: the eighty-four-year-old widow, Anna, whom he locates in the temple in Jerusalem (Acts 2.36–37), something I find difficult to imagine as anything other than a fantasy, probably the author's; the four unmarried daughters of Philip in Acts 21.9; and of course the virgin Mary herself, who in Luke's birth narrative responds to the angel Gabriel by saying, "henceforth all generations will call me blessed" (Lk 1.48), giving rise to the characterization of Mary as a prophet. Perhaps best known are the Corinthian women prophets behind Paul's arguments in 1 Corinthians, who appear to be practicing celibacy, and to be the targets of Paul's admonitions to submit to marital relations, a topic about which there has been extensive discussion.[26]

Singing Hymns

Although early Christian literature actually says little about singing hymns, it says enough to support the conjecture that this was a common practice (shared with both Judean and non-Judean liturgies),[27] and that specifically Christian hymns were composed relatively early. Later Christian composition of hymns is, of course, easily demonstrable. As I noted earlier, it is one of the things Pliny reports to Trajan in the early second century. Already in 1 Cor 14.26, Paul writes "when you come together, each one (m.sing) has a psalm, a teaching, a revelation,

---

24. Miriam (Exod 15.20), Deborah (Judg 4.4), Huldah (2 Kings 22.4), an anonymous woman prophet in Isa 8.2, and No'adiah (Neh 6.14): also three passages mentioning women as or among prophetic groups (Ezek 13.17–23; Joel 3.1–2; and 1 Chr 25.1–8) (see Gafney 2008).

25. It's not at all clear what to do here with Juvenal's description of a Judean woman purveying access to the divine, *Satire* 6.542–47 (*WRGRW* 18).

26. E.g., Schüssler Fiorenza 1983; Wire 1990; Mitchell 1993; Martin 1995; MacDonald 1999; see also the various entries in *WIS*.

27. A wall painting from Herculaneum appears to depict a double chorus of male and female singers at a rite devoted to Isis: in Tinh 1971, reproduction, pl. xxvii; discussion, pp. 85–86.

a tongue, or an interpretation."[28] The language of some of these psalms may even be visible in Paul's letters, the Gospel of John, and other early texts.

Paul's phrasing in I Corinthians is actually quite instructive. That he uses the masculine singular *hekastos* need not, of course, demonstrate that he envisions the one who brings these as necessarily male, but it might.[29] Significantly, several, if not all, of these—the revelation, the speaking in tongues, the interpretation, and perhaps also the teaching[30]—may be construed as instances of divine inspiration, which each person then brings to share in the communal assembly. Women may be the recipients of such inspiration, but the question is whether they may speak or sing them in public. In one of the most famous verses in I Cor 14:33b–36, the letter prohibits women from speaking (*lalein*) in the *ekklesia*, and admonishes them to ask any questions they may have at home, to their "men." Many scholars, I among them, have taken this to be an interpolation into the text of I Corinthians by a later author intent on silencing women prophets, partly because these verses seem in direct conflict with I Corinthians 11, where Paul attempts to regulate the headcoverings of women prophets when they pray and prophesy in the assembly. Other scholars have argued that this seeming contradiction is what itself requires explication, and that resorting to interpolation as the explanation fails to consider how one author might have written all these verses and still have been relatively coherent and consistent. (This of course implies a theory of the consistent author, which may not, in fact, correspond to actual authors, myself included[31]). But if they are right (something we cannot, in fact, determine with any certainty on the available evidence), it may be that despite what he says in I Corinthians 11, Paul envisions these activities as something that women should not do in public, even though they may be the recipients of divine revelations and prophecies, particularly if they are celibate.

All these activities rely on a gendered paradigm of receptivity, passivity, and so forth, which is, on the one hand, natural to women, and, on the other hand, troubling, because it makes women the potential vehicles of authoritative knowledge. Restricting them to celibate women not only coheres with the sexualized metaphors of inspiration, but also, perhaps, solves the challenge to male hierarchy and authority posed if allegedly subordinate women receive such knowledge and transmit it to men: virgins, at least, may not count as

---

28. Translation mine: the NRSV translates the Greek ψαλμός as hymn, although in Philo, the term is regularly ὕμνος.

29. The immediate antecedent here is the masculine plural ἀδελφοί, whose inclusive translation is not necessarily warranted (Kraemer and Eyl forthcoming).

30. The NRSV translation of διδαχή as a "lesson" obscures the associations with inspiration.

31. John Marshall offers an intriguing analysis of Paul's diverse views in Romans 13, which might be equally applicable here (Marshall 2008).

"subordinate" women. The characterization of women as passive transmittors of this knowledge, as opposed to active teachers, may further assuage the difficulties inherent in women's mediation of such knowledge, as strongly seems to be implicit in Tertullian's later account of a female prophet in his New Prophecy church. She made sure to clear all her revelations with the appropriate (and presumably male) authorities before sharing them with a wider public.[32]

In any case, what 1 Cor 14.26 makes clear is that the composition of psalms, if not also their performance, is seen to be the product of divine agency, rather than an act of human volition and creativity. This same view is even more explicit in Philo's description of the Therapeutic composition of hymns, which, as I have discussed in that chapter, he clearly takes to be a form of inspiration. Thus, as with prophecy, the composition and performance of hymns may draw not only on the notion that God can possess whom God will (and to argue otherwise is to constrain the power of God), but also and importantly, on the gendering of the human prophet and hymnist as passive, receptive, open, and, thus, feminine in relation to a masculine deity.

Baptizing and Being Baptized

As for baptism, unquestionably, being baptized was seen as a universally available experience, not limited by social factors of gender, enslavement, and perhaps not even age (although this last will later become a matter of debate).[33] Still, even baptism itself is enmeshed in systems of hierarchy and prestige. This is apparent in the Matthean version of Jesus's baptism by John the baptizer (Matthew 3). There, when Jesus comes to be baptized, John initially demurs, claiming that he is in need of being baptized by Jesus, and not vice versa (Matt 3.14). Only when Jesus insists that his baptism is the fulfillment of "righteousness," does John do so (Matt 3.15). It may also account for the awkward treatment of Jesus's baptism in the Gospel of John, where John is never explicitly said to baptize Jesus (something that is also true of Luke). All may be baptized, but not all may do the baptizing.

This suggests that baptizing is also seen as masculine, in that it is active, rather than passive, and entails the exercise of authority, encoding hierarchy. Unquestionably, whether women may baptize becomes a subject of contention among early Christian groups. Tertullian, almost two centuries later, will make precisely this claim: that baptism and other priestly offices are properly

---

32. Tertullian, *On the Soul* 9; in *WRGRW* 93.
33. See, e.g., O'Donnell 2005:205–6.

masculine and may not be performed by women.[34] The view that women may not baptize, or may, at best, baptize other women is rooted not in issues of modesty (another instance, perhaps, of misrecognition) but in a cultural logic in which the baptizer is superior to the baptized, so that women baptizing men subverts the equation of superiority with masculinity, whereas women baptizing other women, although perhaps still problematic, at least does not fundamentally invert the implicit hierarchy. One might propose that it is no different from men baptizing other men, but I think that the logic of baptism may still require a person to exercise authority over another, and to the extent that women can rarely, if ever, signify authority, this could still be problematic.

Ancient Christian devotions to God were thus generally if not entirely gendered, even when they were practiced by both women and men. Further, the mere presence of apparently gender-neutral religious devotions does not make for a gender egalitarian system. Other major Christian activities, particularly those associated with Jesus himself, and with those who most closely imitated him, such as his male disciples, do differentiate between women and men, with certain key activities disproportionately performed by men, such as healing the sick, exorcising demons, and traveling for the purpose of seeking converts. These, too, are worth the short digression.

Healing the Sick and Exorcising Demons

Although both healing and the exorcism of demons are frequent activities of Jesus in the gospels, and of his male apostles in Acts especially, I can think of no instances in early Christian narratives where women are said to do either of these. Later hagiographical literature will, however, impute cures and exorcisms to female saints, such as the fifth-century *Life and Miracles of St. Thecla*.[35] These two activities may well be connected, with illness frequently understood to be a result of demonic possession. To the extent that ridding a person of a demon is an act of exercising authority ("to exorcise" literally means "to order [someone to get] out") it may well have been understood to be a distinctly masculine exercise of power and authority unavailable to, or at least inappropriate for, women.[36]

---

34. See earlier (ch. 4).

35. Dagron 1978; Johnson 2006.

36. A similar logic may also undergird ancient anxieties about women's performance of so-called magic, which itself involves the exercise of power and (il)licit authority. See earlier.

Travel

In early Christian narratives, especially gospels and acts, both canonical and apocryphal, Jesus and his male disciples travel extensively, and their itinerancy has been the subject of considerable scholarly scrutiny.[37] Occasionally, these narratives depict women as traveling with the men, most famously in Luke's claim that several women, including Mary of Magdala, came with Jesus from the Galilee and provided financial support for him and his male companions.[38] In the last several decades, scholars have debated how central such itinerancy was to early Jesus movements, and whether it extended to women and men equally.[39] Some Christian feminist apologists have, I think, wished to see women's itinerancy as another indication of the ways in which Jesus and early Christianity were "good" for women.

The mere representation of women as travelers is neither surprising nor inherently transgressive. Women in antiquity traveled for numerous reasons: to conduct business, including commerce, to visit family, to attend religious festivals, to seek cures, and various other reasons. Nevertheless, their doing so seems to be a site of considerable anxiety. For free women to travel is to leave the safety, both actual and cultural, of the domestic realm, where threats to their chastity, including opportunities for voluntary transgressions, are seen to loom large. Numerous perils befall traveling women in the Hellenistic novels, and in the apocryphal *Acts*, including Thecla. Precisely when she travels outside the family compound after her marriage to Joseph, our Aseneth is attacked by Pharaoh's son, who hopes to satisfy his lust for her. Further, the very act of traveling might suggest that a woman was abandoning her gendered responsibilities, including care of the home, and of her husband, children and larger household.

The canonical gospels and Acts promulgate neither the idea nor the image of the itinerant wandering single female preacher (although, as just noted, Luke highlights the presence of several women in the retinue that traveled with Jesus from Galilee). In early Christian sources, such as Paul's letters, canonical gospels, and Acts, women are represented as traveling in such a way as to avoid "scandalous" implications: often in pairs, with male "guardians" or "companions."[40] Travel for women may be related to representations of celibacy and asceticism. A celibate woman who travels is perhaps less

---

37. E.g., Theissen 1978.
38. Luke 8.1–3.
39. E.g., Schüssler Fiorenza 1983; D'Angelo 1990.
40. D'Angelo 1990.

vulnerable to voluntary sexual transgressions, and is less likely to be accused of abandoning her gendered obligations to husband, children, and household. Nevertheless, as we saw in the discussion of Thecla, even a celibate itinerant Christian woman could be portrayed as vulnerable and susceptible.

Spatial Considerations

Implicit in the discussion of travel are issues of spatial differentiation and gender. In a somewhat converse instance, it has for some time been argued by scholars that the early Christian predilection for gathering in private houses, rather than in public cult centers, facilitated the participation of women, and that some of these "house-churches" even seem to have been located in households headed by women.[41] The household environment may have made it easier for women to engage in certain activities without violating, or at least being taken to violate, commonly held gender norms: teaching, speaking to an assembled group, and so forth. Recent scholarship, such as that by Andrew Wallace-Hadrill, has argued that the division of public and private does not pertain so easily to Roman houses in particular, which were often open to public access, with interiors visible to the street, and which were the site of numerous social interactions throughout the day. Wallace-Hadrill has suggested that the gendering of such space was more a function of time than of space itself, as opposed to hellenic houses, where gender was mapped more rigidly onto space.[42] Nevertheless, the Roman *domus* was still relatively more private, and, therefore, more associated with women and femaleness, than major public spaces such as the Forum. Furthermore, certain public spaces were available to women, and women's presence in those spaces was not construed as a violation of gender conformity. Those spaces included temples, shrines, and other "holy" sites, theaters and certain other public entertainments, and markets, even though shopping often seems to have been the province both of men and of servants of both genders.[43] Women's presence in courts of law was also permissible under certain circumstances, particularly when women were accompanied by guardians—who function, among other things, as symbolic guarantors of female acquiescence to male domination. (This last highlights the drastic nature of the Augustan legislation rewarding women who bore sufficient children with the ability to act without a guardian!) The papers belonging

---

41. E.g., Schüssler Fiorenza 1983; one of the more recent and thorough treatments of this is Osiek and MacDonald 2005.

42. Wallace-Hadrill 2003; see also Wallace-Hadrill 1996; Baker 2002.

43. In Theocritis, *Idyll* 15, women complain that husbands are terrible shoppers: sent to the market for one thing, they come home instead with another.

to a woman named Babatha, found in the Judean desert fifty years ago, attest her presence at the Roman court in Petra, where she was involved in various litigations over her personal and financial affairs, including the guardianship of her son.[44]

The complex intersections of gender and space are well-illustrated by two passages from Philo, whose vision of public spaces as male and private spaces as female seems more Greek than Roman. In a passage in the *Special Laws*, he claims that marketplaces, council halls, law courts, and other public places are properly the domain of men, whereas women "are best suited to the indoor life which never strays from the house."[45] Several other Judean texts, 2 Macc 3.19, and 3 Macc 1.18–20, claim that in response to threats to the integrity of the temple, women in Jerusalem, ordinarily secluded, rushed in distress into the public streets. Philo, too, associates the public presence of ordinarily secluded women with attacks on Judeans or threats to their integrity. In his narration of the sufferings of Alexandrian Judeans under Flaccus, he claims that the Judeans were particularly outraged by searches of their homes for illegal weapons, which exposed Judean women, normally secluded from all but their closest male relatives, to the eyes of strange and terrorizing soldiers.[46]

Yet, as with many examples in this study, here, too, gendered concerns impinge on the representation of social realia. Secluded women in disarray in public seems obviously a trope, which signals the larger social threat and disarray, while women at home, in their place, signals social order.[47] That this is something of a fantasy on Philo's part, however, is suggested in his subsequent account of a different outrage on Judean women. During that same reign of terror of the Roman governor Flaccus, Judean women in Alexandria, were seized, together with other women, "like captives not only in the market-place but also in the middle of the theatre and taken on to the stage. . . ." Those who were ultimately found not to be Judean were released, whereas Judean women were pressured to eat pig meat. Those who ate the meat were released, but those who desisted were subject to *aikias anēkestous*, perhaps a euphemism for rape.[48] Philo says nothing about what these women, whom he calls "in no way unrighteous" (*mēden adikein*), were doing in the marketplace and the theater in

---

44. Texts in Lewis, Yadin, and Greenfield 1989; Yadin, Greenfield, and Yardeni 1994; and selectively in *WRGRW* 62. These texts have generated considerable scholarly analysis, see, e.g., Kraemer 1999c; 2003; Cotton 1993; Cotton and Greenfield 1994.

45. *Special Laws* 3.169–75; in *WRGRW* 14.

46. *Against Flaccus* 89.

47. I make this point also in Kraemer 1999c:60–61.

48. The phrase is nonspecific, referring to egregious affront (Feldman's translation is "desperate ill-usage").

the first place. If Philo has fabricated the incident, one might read it as his not-so-subtle critique of women who violate gender expectations: women who leave their houses for the male marketplace and theater should expect to be ill-treated by Gentile men. But alternatively, Philo has here demonstrated that his rigid separation of the sexes was not actually Alexandrian practice, even for elite Judean matrons.[49]

Even many of the public sites where respectable women could be present nevertheless continue to map gender and other ancient status markers. Hierarchical seating, by gender and social status, is attested for some Christian assemblies and for ancient theatres.[50] Whether women's presence in Christian assemblies was consonant with gender expectations or somewhat transgressive, it has often been contrasted with women's perceived absence in ancient synagogues. Much has been made of Judean women's alleged exclusion from synagogue worship and other cultic performances, as the context for explaining on the one hand the apparently relative absence of women among Jesus's closest followers and the radical difference of his treatment of women on the other. Ironically, some of the best, if inadvertent, evidence for women's routine presence in first-century C.E. synagogues may come from the narrative gospels. In the Gospel of Mark 6.3, for instance, the sisters of Jesus appear to be among those who hear him preach in the synagogue in his hometown of Nazareth.[51]

Still, in gender systems that consistently and pervasively constructed women as subordinate, passive, and inferior, relative to men, the mere presence of women in synagogues doesn't necessarily argue for any assault on that system, nor, similarly, does the generally well-attested presence of women in Christian assemblies, so-called house churches or otherwise. Rather, the issue is whether synagogues and Christian assemblies functioned as yet another social institution in which gender difference was constructed and affirmed,

49. This account has one other fascinating implication for debates about Judean women's headcoverings (see also ch. 2). Because the Romans arrested Judean women and non-Judean women indiscriminately, and could only identify the Judean women through interrogation, they apparently could not tell them apart on the basis of their dress. Judean women, or so Philo envisions, dressed just like other Alexandrian women (presumably of similar class). Thus, if the Judean women covered their heads, so did the other women; alternatively, if the other women didn't cover their heads, neither did Judean women.

50. Kraemer 1992:106–7, with various references.

51. In my entries on the sisters of Jesus, I raise the possibility that Matthew's seemingly minor omission of the word *here* from Mark's "Are not his sisters here with us," together with Matthew's removal of the reference to the Sabbath may intentionally mute the implication in Mark that women are present in the synagogue on the Sabbath. If this is true, it is susceptible to various interpretations: the author of Matthew, more knowledgeable about actual Galilean practices, might be correcting Mark's erroneous impression that women would have been present in the synagogue; alternatively, the author of Matthew might have other reasons for wishing to modify the Markan narrative that we cannot either access or even imagine. Kraemer 2000d; Kraemer 2000e.

produced and reproduced, in which women's presence in synagogues continued to authorize a particular gender system. The issue is what practices and
symbols were employed in synagogue and Christian assembly liturgies and
other activities, and how these either participated in, or perhaps critiqued, prevailing gender constructions.

Because our knowledge of ancient synagogue practices is actually quite
thin, it's really not easy to answer this question. To the degree that women did
attend synagogues, their presence and any participation was probably subordinated to a system of gender conventions in which the differentiations between
male and female were continuously expressed and affirmed, especially to the
degree that these were seen to be divinely ordained. Gender differentiation and
ranking could easily have been expressed in synagogues in multiple ways that
are no longer easily discernible. Numerous scholars have noted that there is no
real archaeological evidence for seating women in special galleries or rooms
within ancient synagogues, either in the land of Israel, or in the Diaspora.[52]
Still, seating arrangements could have segregated women and men through
any number of devices: front and back, right and left, up and down; sitting
(men) versus standing (women, perhaps along the periphery). All of these various dualistic modalities could have been deployed to differentiate gender, of
which the opposition of men inside and women outside is only perhaps slightly
more powerful. All of this applies equally to Christian assembly practices.

Yet even if men and women sat together in ancient worship services, such
practices by themselves do not necessarily encode egalitarianism, or lack of
gender difference. Excluding women from synagogue services would certainly
be a strong way of expressing gender hierarchy in a system in which attending
such services is seen as prestigious, although in fact there is no evidence that
women were ever actually excluded. Rather, they were merely discouraged from
attending synagogue.[53] On the contrary, donative inscriptions and occasional
literary references, such as the narrative in Mark, suggest that some women did
attend synagogue services and participate in synagogue life.[54] Donor inscriptions, of course, are not definitive proof: conceivably women could have paid
for inscriptions they never saw, although I think this unlikely. I find it hard to
imagine, for instance, that Julia(na) of Naro paid for the large mosaic synagogue floor at Hamman Lif but never attended services and other events there,

52. Brooten 1982:103–38; Horbury 1999; Levine 2000.
53. Various rabbinic writings do explicitly *exempt* women from attending synagogue: see Wegner 1988;
Kraemer 1992:95–98; Ilan 1995; Horbury 1999; Levine 2000.
54. Kraemer 1992:106–7. The inscription from a Judean synagogue in Asia Minor honoring a woman
named Tation with the privilege of sitting in the seat of honor is a particularly instructive example: *IJO* 2.36 = *CIJ*
2.738, *WRGRW* 661.

but it's also true that we can't know this.[55] Conversely, however, the presence of women in synagogues need not, in any way, point to egalitarian gender arrangements. These would probably only be discernible when the presence of women is completely integrated, and when gender is not, in fact, mapped onto any practices: when women and men sit interchangeably in all those dual locations of up and down, left and right, top and bottom, front and back; when women and men are equally speakers; when women and men engage in the identical liturgical practices, wear identical liturgical garments, and the roles of practitioners are in no way gender dependent or gender disproportionate. All of these, of course, have become common in recent years in contemporary Jewish and Protestant Christian egalitarian congregations.

What many discussions, scholarly and otherwise, have missed here is whether, even were women to engage in first-century synagogue worship, it would in any way have undercut the systems of gender that constrained their lives in many ways. One of the best illustrations of this is the question of whether women could, or did, read Torah in public, which I considered at some length in chapter 2. The issue is not really whether some women did or did not study Torah or read Torah in public, any more than the issue is whether Christian women (some of whom were also Judean, at least in the first century C.E. or so) were present in a communal assembly (which they regularly seem to have been). Only if, in doing so, they not merely threatened, but actually altered the gender systems in which these practices were embedded and constructed could we see these practices as truly transgressive and significant.

Religion and the Production and Enforcement of Gender

In a dense and provocative analysis of gender and power written at the end of his career, Pierre Bourdieu attempted to formulate a theory of gender that did not itself defend the gender systems he saw both in the North African Kabyle and in his French contemporaries, whose social arrangements had formed the basis for much of his theorizing. *Masculine Domination* was written partly as a response to critics who thought his earlier discussions tended to essentialize gender and construe gender difference as inevitable, rather than as specific

---

55. *CIL* 8.12457a, treated at length in Stern 2008 (the revision of her Brown Ph.D. dissertation). The reconstruction of her name is debated (Julia or Juliana) although the inscription was actually quite clear. The mosaic is known primarily from two somewhat different nineteenth-century drawings; only a few fragments are currently known, some of which are in the Brooklyn Museum, which exhibited them a few years ago (Bleiberg 2005). Assuming that women were excluded from synagogues, E. R. Goodenough asserts that Julia(na) would have commissioned the inscription, but never actually seen it (Goodenough 1953–64: vol. 2.100).

historically contingent productions.[56] Here he offers a theory of gender differ-ence as itself a product of an economy of symbolic goods, which is then legiti-mated, in part, by being inscribed back onto biological difference, and defended as rooted in that difference, when it is not, in fact, but is social in "origins."

Bourdieu's social theory responds to, critiques, and grows out of both Marxist theory and structuralism. From Marxist theory, Bourdieu took the pre-mise that all social relations are grounded in economic relations. Particularly relevant is Marx's view that gender hierarchy is rooted in ideas about private property: that the need to transmit property in familial lines facilitates gen-dered divisions of labor and the use of women as tokens of exchange in such transmission. For Marx, the subordination of women was rooted in capitalist systems, and communist systems would obliterate such relations. Marxist the-ory also proposed that theories of the universe are themselves rooted in mate-rial conditions, which generate particular economic and social relations. These theories both serve to legitimize those relations, but also present themselves as natural, as inherent in the order of things, a move crucial to their ability to serve as legitimizing. This notion that "ideologies" conceal their origins and their legitimizing functions is extremely important, and that notion underlies Bourdieu's own use of the concept of "misrecognition."

The structuralist theory that grounds Bourdieu's work posited that the gen-eration of binary opposites is fundamental to human thought and social orga-nization. Initially a theory of linguistics,[57] structuralism gained considerable currency as a theory of cultural meanings, particularly through the work of Claude Levi-Strauss, who argued that underlying all structural binary opposi-tions was the divide between nature and culture. In two important essays, Sherry Ortner explored the possibility that the association of women with nature and men with culture accounted for the nearly universal devaluation of women relative to men, ultimately concluding that although these associations are substantial and in some cultures pervasive, they are insufficient to explain the hierarchical values humans impute to gender difference.[58]

Bourdieu's work regularly highlights the presence of such structural oppo-sitions in cultural arrangements and practices. But where Levi-Strauss argued for the opposition of culture and nature as primary, Bourdieu actually argues that it is gender division that is itself the foundation of all subsequent binary oppositions. Gender is the primary, socially constructed category, which is then projected onto biological, anatomical difference, which is itself then used as the

---

56. Bourdieu 2001:vii (preface to the English edition).

57. Saussure saw the dichotomy between *langue* and *parôle* (grammar and words; structure and content) as generating binary oppositions: Saussure 1976, with helpful overview in Clark 2004:44–47.

58. Ortner 1974; 1996.

justification for the social category of gender difference (and hierarchy, although he doesn't say this in the quotation that follows here).

> The social world constructs the body as a sexually defined reality and as the depository of sexually defining principles of vision and division. This embodied social programme of perception is applied to all the things of the world and firstly to the *body* itself. . . . It is this programme which constructs the difference between the biological sexes in conformity with the principles of a mythic division of the world rooted in the arbitrary relationship of domination of men over women, itself inscribed, with the division of labour, in the reality of the social order. The *biological* difference between the *sexes*, i.e., between the male and female bodies, and, in particular, the *anatomical* difference between the sex organs, can thus appear as the natural justification of the socially constructed difference between the *genders*, and in particular of the social division of labour. . . . **Because** the social principle of vision constructs the anatomical difference and **because** this socially constructed difference becomes the basis and **apparently natural** justification of the social vision which founds it, there is thus a relationship of circular causality which confines thought within the self-evidence of relations of domination inscribed both in objectivity . . . and in subjectivity . . ."[59]

The basis of the social principle of vision itself is not entirely clear. If ideas of gender are the product of particular social arrangements, what generates those arrangements and not others? In a move that seems derived from Marxist theory, Bourdieu seems to suggest, at one point, that kinship is critical:

> The explanation of the primacy granted to masculinity in social taxonomies lies in the logic of the economy of symbolic exchanges, and more precisely in the social construction of the relations of kinship and marriage alliance which assigns to women their social status as objects of exchange defined in accordance with male interests to help to reproduce the symbolic capital of men."[60]

This explanation is not entirely satisfactory, not the least because Bourdieu's argument seems premised on the universality of patrilineal systems, which produce very different results from matrilineal ones, at least with regard to the uses of women as tokens of symbolic capital, if that capital is equated with

59. Bourdieu 2001:11, bold emphases mine; italic emphases original.
60. Bourdieu 2001:43.

honor. Matrilineal societies are well known for their relative disinterest in women as evidence of family and male honor, and virginity, premarital, and extramarital sex are of much less concern. The reasons for this seem fairly obvious. The transmission of property and identity from men to other men (specifically from a man to his sister's sons) does not depend on paternity, and hence on female "chastity." Why most societies are patrilineal whereas only a few are matrilineal (and some are neither) is unclear. Nevertheless it may be that this initial kinship structure, whatever produces it, does then generate different systems of gender, to some extent.[61]

Relatively few gender theorists have focused on the relationships and intersections between religion and gender.[62] Bourdieu is not really an exception here, but he does offer several mostly incidental observations that are germane.[63] For Bourdieu, what he calls the "mythico-ritual" system "consecrates the established order, by bringing it to known, and recognized, official existence."[64] It is one of the many social institutions that "amplifies and ratifies" structures and oppositions, in particular, "[t]he principle of the inferiority and exclusion of women ... to the point of making it the principle of division of the whole universe. ..."[65]

For Bourdieu at least, the relationship between religion and gender is relatively straightforward. Gender difference is constituted independently of religion, and religion "ratifies and amplifies" it, but does not create it. The basic components of gender difference, as Bourdieu identifies them, would exist in the absence of religion, but "mythico-ritual" systems are part of the means by which gender is articulated and defended.[66] Religion thus inscribes gender in the very order of things, ascribing it to divine will, and thus naturalizing it, which in turn masks its true nature as the product of human social processes.

It presently seems to me that Bourdieu's basic view of the relationship between religion and gender is probably right, although I am less persuaded of the complex explanation he attempts to offer for the primacy of gender. What

61. I thank Carol Delaney for her insightful critique of Bourdieu, in numerous conversations; see also Delaney 1991.

62. There are several anthologies whose titles might suggest an interest in this project, but in fact, the essays in these anthologies generally do not engage these larger theoretical concerns, particularly in the way that I wish to frame them here (King 1995; Castelli 2001; Juschka 2001). The work of Susan Sered (1994; 1999) is a notable exception.

63. He suggests that "religious or ritual activities" contain similar oppositions between "public, discontinuous, extra-ordinary male exchanges" and "private, even secret, continuous, ordinary female exchanges," Bourdieu 2001:48.

64. Bourdieu 2001:8.

65. Bourdieu 2001:42.

66. Ideologies of gender in communist, officially atheist, Russia and China might be excellent testing grounds (see, e.g., Marsh 1996 and Wolchik 1998). I thank Diana Shifrina for these references.

cognitive science theories of religion may ultimately have to say about this is unclear; they might suggest that both religious thought and perceptions of sexual difference are simultaneous in human experience, with attendant social manifestations.[67] Yet for my purposes, regardless of whether he is right about origins is separable from his argument that gender is constantly reproduced in embodied dispositions (*habitus*), including but scarcely limited to bodily comportment, taste in all manner of things, and choice of daily activities, that pervade ancient and modern daily experience, much of it at a subliminal level, and ratified through claims to naturalness, divine will, and so forth.

Religion is then one of those many social practices that are both gendered and gendering, constructing and inscribing gender on human beings and human actions and ideas. Devotion to imagined divine beings relies upon both general and specific concepts of gender. Divine beings themselves possess gender, and often exemplify ideal gender traits. At the same time, such devotion inscribes gender constructions in humans and authorizes (ratifies) these, not as the human phenomenon they are, but, through the process of misrecognition, as either the direct desire or action of the divine (for which the creation accounts in Genesis 1–3 are the quintessential western instance) or as an inescapable element of the cosmos (I have in mind here Buddhist accounts of gender origins). Certainly, some religious texts, authorities and such deny that gender is truly a divine attribute (Jewish, Christian, and Muslim theologies all sometimes argue this even though regularly relying on complex gendered imagery for all God-representations and God-language), or assert that gender is a contingent characteristic of finite, mortal bodies, but not infinite, immortal souls, and thus subject to dissolution at some point in a cosmological scheme. This, too, may easily be seen as a form of misrecognition.

As I noted at the beginning of this study, in antiquity, as in many cultures, women's performance of "religion" (women's devotion to the gods) is both acceptable and encouraged, provided that such devotion conforms to the pervasive and prevailing ancient constructions of femininity as passive, embodied, emotive, and un/insufficiently controlled. Religion thus serves to affirm the rightness of these particular gender constructions. Doing those things makes the things themselves gendered and also genders the persons who do them.

Of course, religion was by no means wholly a feminine domain: it can easily be argued that religion was (and is) far more a male domain, the demographics of religious practice notwithstanding,[68] particularly if one scrutinizes the ways in which men deploy religious practices, including theologizing, for

67. See the Introduction.
68. Numerous studies have documented the disproportionate attendance of women at religious services.

myriad strategic purposes. But just as for women the proper practice of religion inscribed, encoded, and enforced gender norms, so, too, proper men's religion needed to inscribe, encode, and enforce ideals of masculinity. This is apparent, for instance, in Livy's critique of the feminizing Bacchanalia, and his praise for proper, masculine Roman rites, in Tertullian's construction of priesthood and other Christian offices as masculine, and in the early rabbis' configuration of Torah study as the ultimate form of masculinity.

Religious practices regularly effect the production of properly gendered persons, both women and men. Numerous instances of this may be adduced. As Barbara Goff elucidates, ancient Greek religion was particularly concerned with the production of citizen wives who conformed to gender expectations. Images of transgressive females (wild Bacchics, witches, and others) served more as counterpoints to ideal female figures than as instances of actual persons. They served as models for what good Greek women should not do. But as in the case of Thecla, such practices and expectations may boomerang. Once the images of transgressive women are available, they can be marshaled in service of all sorts of things, including critiques of prevailing gender norms.

One of the primary religious practices for the production of properly gendered persons was animal sacrifice. As Nancy Jay argued some years ago in the posthumous publication of her dissertation, animal sacrifice, a common feature of agricultural, urban societies, produces male lineages purged of women. These lineages, which also then bring about male community, were structured hierarchically. They were enacted in the killing, distribution, and consumption of meat, with the imagined participation of one or more divine beings, in a system of reciprocal but not identical gift-giving, a system in which women are generally themselves one kind of gift to be exchanged, and largely, although not entirely, excluded from engaging in such exchanges.[69] This system itself expresses, encodes, reinforces, and authorizes, not only gender in general, but particular attributes of gender: masculinity as active, exterior, superior, self-controlled, hard, meat-eating, knife-wielding, speaking, ruling, with femininity as the negative inversions of all these traits.

The production of compliant, submissive women seems envisioned in the rabbinic practices prescribed for women, or perhaps more accurately, rabbinic rationalizations for these practices clearly offer divinely authorized explanations for women's performance of rabbinic gender norms, at least through threats of divine retribution for women who deviate. Various rabbinic traditions assert that women die in childbirth for failing to observe these rabbinically

---

69. Jay 1992; 2001. For a lovely overview of animal sacrifice, including useful qualification of Jay's work, see Ullucci 2008; on women as exchange, see Rubin 1975; Strathern 1990.

mandated practices (candle lighting, separation of dough, menstrual purity), a classic instance, perhaps, of misrecognition.[70] Bourdieu proposes that men are assigned the qualities of externality and discontinuity, while internality and continuity are mapped onto women, which certainly seems consistent with these rabbinic views.[71] Yet as I have argued in earlier work, what women actually did, and how they themselves construed these practices, is all but unavailable to us, except, perhaps, through imaginative use of self-conscious speculation, grounded in demonstrable ethnographic analogies.

Although it is tempting to describe these functions as the aim or intention or purpose of such practices, such formulation may itself involve misrecognition. Practices cannot have aims and intentions or purposes, which require agents. Rather, aims, intentions, and purposes are those of humans, and in this case, particular humans whose interests are served by these particular productions. To ascribe them to inanimate practices is to misrecognize precisely these interests and consequences.

It might thus seem that feminized religion produces feminized persons, whereas masculinized religion produces masculinized persons. Yet the very nature of devotion to deities envisioned to possess all kinds of knowledge, power, authority, and abilities that ordinary humans lack, either in kind or in degree, creates a dilemma. All sorts of devotion to gods gender the human being as female and employ attendant language, imagery and postures. With respect to the divine, humans are passive, subordinate, inferior, powerless, weak, ignorant, defenseless, humble. Religious practices from petitionary prayer, prostrate on the ground, to constructions of sexualized, marital union with the divine, all rely upon the construction of the human as feminized and the deity as masculine, sometimes even going so far as to imagine divine impregnation of the human soul.[72] The underlying cultural logic of religious devotion thus lends itself easily to being construed as female, or at least feminizing, and thus inappropriate for men. Still, in practice, men do engage in religious acts, including the formulation of ideas, and devotion to gods, which requires that the performance of masculinity is properly the province of men, whether the proper devotion to Roman deities advocated by Livy, the masculine study of Torah promulgated by the ancient rabbis and those who claim to be their subsequent fictive heirs, or the masculine exercise of Christian priesthood articulated as early as Tertullian and Epiphanius and as recently as the current Roman Catholic pontificate on the nightly news in 2008.

---

70. *Genesis Rabbah* 17.7–8; for other references and discussion, see Kraemer 1992:95–105; see also Baskin 1984.

71. Bourdieu 2001:30.

72. See Harrison 1996 and above, ch. 4.

Religion and the Critique of Gender

Yet if religion regularly has the effect of authorizing gender difference, and the myriad social consequences of gender hierarchy, numerous historical and ethnographic examples demonstrate that religion is often also a venue for the critique of gender. In the past, I have argued that various ancient religious practices constituted attacks on gender assymetry and social imbalance, affording women opportunities to critique constraints of gender and experience the benefits of temporary, if not permanent communities of like-minded persons. As I remarked in the introduction to this study, my earlier work drew extensively on deprivation theory—that is, on models of human behavior that see at least some religion as compensation for various forms of deprivation, from lack of economic resources to lack of access more generally to the forms of prestige operative in a particular cultural situation (what Bourdieu would come to characterize as cultural capital). In *Her Share of the Blessings,* I considered in more depth the problem of such theories, particularly Mary Douglas's critique of deprivation theories as insufficiently cognizant of the correspondence between particular religious practices and cosmologies, and her own hypothesis that practices taken to be responses to deprivation were better explained as the correlates of (if not actually the products of) particular locations on her mapping of human social relations and constraints. Although I found (and to some extent continue to find) Douglas's model productive for analyzing which kinds of cosmologies and practices flourish under particular social conditions,[73] such a model does not require the wholesale rejection of aspects of religion as compensatory. Many recent ethnographic studies of women's religions point in this direction. To cite but a few salient instances, Lynn Davidman's study on Jewish women who adopt orthodox Jewish practices; Marie Griffith's work on the women who join the evangelical Christian women's organization, Aglow; and Kim Gutschow's ethnography of Buddhist nuns in the Himalayan region of Zangskar all examine the ways in which these practices respond to and, to some degree, ameliorate tensions women experience around gender expectations.[74]

---

73. A particularly intriguing instance of how cosmology, gender, and women's religious practices intersect may be found in Sered 1999.

74. Davidman 1991; Griffith 1997; for a more sanguine view of some of Griffith's material, see Ingersoll 2003; Gutschow 2004. Sered 1994 critiques the utility of deprivation theory as an explanation of women's religious choices, partly on the grounds that it proposes nonreligious explanations for religious choices. I concur that deprivation theory does indeed propose "nonreligious" explanations for religious behavior. However, where I dissent from Sered is in seeing this as a disqualification of the efficacy of the theory. That women (or men, for that matter) may see their own choices as religious, or motivated by religious concerns, does not mean that these choices are not (also) a response to various experienced deprivations, nor that particular religious practices do not, in fact, provide some compensation and redress. Mahmood 2004 also endeavors to critique this position.

In this study, I have tried to refine the nature of those arguments, through both a more nuanced reading of the ancient evidence, and a more developed consideration of the theoretical underpinnings. Still, in many ways my views have not changed all that much on some of these issues. It still seems to me that women's religious practices regularly affirm and replicate identity and social location (including, in antiquity, status categories of birth, citizenship, class and ethnicity) yet also afford opportunities for resistance and critique, often in the form of both practices and imagined consequences that compensate for or restructure gender asymmetry.

What has changed in my thinking is my awareness of the complexity of these issues, both as historical and theoretical problems. Thus, Philo's Therapeutrides, for instance, are not a simple example of what childless, educated Judean women might have done to redress the social deficiencies of their childlessness. Whereas earlier, I took their existence to be a largely unproblematic historical "fact," and Philo's description of them access to a previously ignored social reality, I now think that they may well be largely, if not entirely, the production of Philo's rich imagination. His creation of them relies extensively both on understandings of gender he shared with the wider elite philosophical culture of first century Alexandria and his exegesis of Exodus 15, all perhaps in service to a competition to present Judean philosophers as the truest exemplars of a common Hellenistic tradition. Similarly, although in *Her Share of the Blessings*, I saw the Greek tale of Joseph and Aseneth as a potential window into the actual conversion rites and concomitant cosmologies of some ancient "hellenistic" Jews, whatever correlations there may be between the heroine of that account and actual ancient women (including whether such women were more likely to be Judean than Christian) now seem to me incredibly elusive. Rather, as I argued a decade ago, I see Aseneth's gender as, in part, a function of the exegetical concerns of its authors, and, in part, a key element of narratives of transformation, in which female figures are much more appropriate models than males.[75]

Thecla remains, as I have explored at length here, a complicated case. I am no longer sure that it provides us with reliable social description of women who found the theology and practices of wandering ascetic male Christian teachers compelling in the second century C.E. Yet at the same time, considerable cross-cultural ethnographic data suggests that religiously authorized celibacy is often particularly appealing to women who resemble in striking ways the women of the apocryphal *Acts* (including Thecla): women who are childless, unmarried, resistant to marriage, unhappily married, and resistant to the

75. Kraemer 1998.

strong gendered norms of their cultures.[76] Although any genetic relationship between Justin's account and the Thecla story is undemonstrable (though by no means impossible), many of the themes in the Thecla narrative are echoed in the account in Justin Martyr, lacking, as I have noted, the elements of miraculous rescues and fantastic details such as sympathetic lionesses. Justin's account, I have argued, itself displays elements of artifice, and the use of gender to construct a tale of Christian excellence and resistance to imperial power. And, perhaps like that of Thecla, the success of Justin's tale depended in part on the assumption that his audience would find its skeletal form consonant with the realities they knew. Further, the strong female bonds evident throughout the Thecla story are both consistent with ethnographic data on the appeal of heightened community for women whose ordinary experience is one of insulation and isolation (to borrow from Douglas's description), and the theory that *some* religion is compensatory and does offer its practitioners alternative forms of community.

Yet as numerous scholars have explored, gender was regularly the site of ancient cultural contestation. Not only were there competing ancient theories of gender difference, but conflicting definitions of masculinity and femininity were deployed to wage social and cultural battles and to differentiate social identities.[77] The Judean evidence provides numerous instances. Satlow and Levinson have explored how early rabbis refashioned Roman ideals of masculinity.[78] They retained certain shared defining characteristics of masculinity, including mastery over both the self and subordinate others, and public oral contestation and debate as a primary form of masculine competition. At the same time, they differed in positioning their own very specialized practice of Torah study as the ultimate act of masculinity. In doing so, they differentiated themselves from Greek and Roman definitions of masculinity, which emphasized the deliberate, controlled exercise of physical strength, athletic abilities, military prowess, and the selective use of violence.

Further, rabbinic constructions of masculinity would appear to have been equally differentiated from those of numerous other Judeans: revolutionaries from the Maccabean fighters to the anti-Roman Sicarii, the various other

76. See, e.g., Kitch 1989 on the demographics of Shakers, Koreshans, and Sanctificationists; Gutschow 2004 on the demographics of nuns in Zangskar; Harvey 2001. Despite Sered's critiques of deprivation theory, illness, problems with fertility, and child mortality frequently recur in the biographies of women who found the new religious movements she examines, especially those with high degrees of female participants. This is true, for instance, of the Shakers Ann Lee and Rebecca Jackson, the founder of Christian Science, Mary Baker Eddy, the Korean shamans described in Harvey 2001, and many others.

77. See the Introduction.

78. Satlow 1996; Levinson 2000.

groups known particularly from Josephus, the men responsible for the early-second-century anti-Roman revolts in Cyrene and Palestine (including the Bar Kokhba forces).[79] How much rabbinic re-definition of masculinity as Torah study and debate, as opposed to myriad other forms of masculine performance, was a response to the massive failure of the several revolts is impossible to determine, although certainly tempting to argue. At the very least, advocating such practices made, literally, a virtue of necessity.

Interestingly, Severus's account gives little if any sense that Minorcan Jews held concepts of ideal masculinity comparable to those of rabbis, some of whom, at least, were probably roughly their contemporaries, although the rabbinic construction of Torah study as elite masculinity probably antedates Severus by a significant amount of time. Although some Jewish men are praised by Severus for their knowledge of Jewish law and tradition, including Theodorus himself, none seem to devote themselves primarily, let alone exclusively to study. Magona has a synagogue (an actual building, not merely an assembly or community), but it appears to have no other Jewish buildings such as a rabbinic house of study (nor other Jewish institutions, such as a rabbinic court). Jewish men on Minorca appear to engage in the same commercial and civic pursuits as their Christian co-islanders. Theodorus is allegedly absent from Minorca when Severus arrives in Magona with his band of zealous Jamonans because he is seeing to his commercial interests off-island on Majorca, where he and his wife have considerable property. Jewish men held various civic offices that they continue to hold after their acceptance of Christianity. As I noted earlier, Severus impugns their masculinity in a variety of subtle ways: by representing them as having insufficient control over their wives, by showing them to be irrationally fearful of the peaceful, well-intentioned Christians, by depicting some of them as foolish buffoons in their resistance to Christ, and so forth. Still, on the whole, the standards of masculinity to which Severus appears to hold Minorcan Jewish men seem to be those shared with elite men in late antiquity more generally, rather than rabbinic paradigms. Minorcan Jewish women, too, look pretty much like the women of late antique provincial elite society: they are, for instance, reasonably visible, both in the narrative and apparently in Minorcan life, have some degree of autonomy, access to financial resources, and even some degree of formal education, even though they play

---

79. Standards of masculinity themselves could be challenged and contested. Particularly applicable here is Kuefler's use of the work of Robert Connell for the distinction between "hegemonic masculinity" and "subordinated masculinity," that is, the difference between the standards of masculinity of those men in power, and the standards of some subordinate but recognizable group/community of other men. The standards of Roman male elites versus those of the Palestinian rabbis would be one such instance, whereas the diverse Judean views of masculinity would provide other cases (Connell 1987, cited in Kuefler 2001:4).

no formal roles in Minorcan public life. For those who do not expect Minorcan Jews to look like rabbinic Jews, this makes, of course, perfect sense, regardless of what one thinks of Severus's recourse to extensive artifice in this narrative.

To return to earlier evidence, other Judean constructions of masculinity are visible in Philo, particularly in his depictions of both the Essenes as the ideal practitioners of the active life, and the Therapeutae as ideal practitioners of the contemplative life. As I considered earlier, Philo's ideal(ized) Therapeutae exhibit classic traits of elite masculinity (self-mastery manifest in ascetic bodily discipline; responsible discharge of familial and communal obligations; pursuit of philosophical studies and mystical contemplation, itself accomplished through rigorous self-control), while apparently declining some of the more prevalent forms of masculine competition and contestation, both physical and intellectual.

The first-century Judean advocate of Jesus of Nazareth, Paul, himself repeatedly invoked metaphors of masculine contestation, athletic competitions in particular, in his exhortations. Yet at the same time, he regularly constructed himself as the inverse image of masculine norms: physically weak, a poor public speaker, a man who labored alongside women and slaves, and was subject to the authority of others (including beatings and lashings at the hands of other Judeans, and imprisonment by civic authorities).[80] Even his self-characterization as a prophet chosen by God has the feminizing implications I explored earlier. That this representation is ultimately intended as ironic does not detract from my point that Paul, too, reconfigures masculinity for his own purposes.

Particular understandings of masculinity also appear to be at work in the representation of the Judean teacher, Jesus of Nazareth, in early gospel narratives, as Jerome Neyrey illuminates.[81] In all four canonical gospels, Jesus speaks and debates publicly and responds effectively to verbal challenges to his authority. He generally operates in the public arena, in markets, synagogues, the temple, roads, the shore, and even the sea of Galilee itself. Jesus never engages in patently female household tasks, whether cooking, cleaning, or childcare, and spends much of his time doing what most other ancient, free males did: hanging out with other males. Even scenes that place Jesus in more domestic locations may reflect the ideas about gendered space, because, as I noted earlier, some aspects of houses, such as dining rooms and reception rooms were understood to be male, public domains, at least at certain times of the day and for certain purposes, such as the reception of guests or male-only meals.[82]

The Jesus of the canonical gospels also exemplifies masculine self-control in many respects. He is never shown to engage in sexual behavior or to

80. Clines 2003; Larson 2004.
81. Neyrey 2003.
82. See, e.g., Andrew Wallace-Hadrill 1996; 2003; Baker 2002.

experience sexual desire, although occasionally Jesus may be portrayed as giving in to anger, most notably, perhaps, in the story of the withered fig tree and the incident in the temple courtyard.[83] Interestingly, the narratives of Jesus's suffering and ignominious death may have posed a serious challenge to this understanding of Jesus's masculinity, given widespread ancient constructions of suffering as fundamentally feminine. In this light, the refashionings of Luke and John, who cast Jesus's suffering as his intentional submission, may negate and thus remedy to some extent these feminizing implications.

Astute readers may have noticed that I have considered the masculinity of Jesus within the larger framework of Judean examples. I have done so partly because Jesus was himself Judean, and some of the gospel writers were likely, in my view, to have been Judeans themselves, while others were probably not.[84] Nevertheless, there is a sufficiently common ideology of masculinity in the gospel representations that has little if anything that seems truly novel, which is the point of Neyrey's analysis.

Subsequently, however, Christian authors will repeatedly differentiate themselves from the larger culture by their refashioning of masculinity. As I have noted several times in this study, various scholars have effectively shown how Christians valorized martyrdom by configuring feminine passivity and suffering as the ultimate masculine virtues (another instance, perhaps, of making a virtue of necessity). Kuefler has even argued that contestations of gender played a major part in the success of "orthodox" Christianity. In late antiquity, he proposes, the success of Germanic invaders and challenges within the structures of the Roman empire posed challenges to the longstanding Roman elite paradigm of masculinity. Orthodox thinkers and writers responded with the articulation of a new paradigm of masculinity that effectively responded to these particular historical situations, which, in turn, contributed significantly to the appeal and efficacy of orthodox Christianity.[85]

Gender also served as a site of contestation in a somewhat different manner. Characterizing one's opponents as feminine, while arrogating masculinity to the self (whether the author or some larger community related to the author) is a regular feature of ancient polemic (not to mention modern polemic, both

83. Roberts 2010.

84. As noted in the Introduction, and in ch. 7, I use the term *Judean* here in the sense argued by Mason 2007. I do not intend it to indicate anything more precise about Jesus's geographic origins and area of activity (that is, the region of Judea as opposed to the Galilee). In my view, the author of the Gospel of Matthew may have been Judean, as well as the author of the Gospel of John (although I think it quite possible that the author of John was Samaritan). I think it unlikely, but of course not impossible that the author of Luke was Judean. If asked to vote on the author of Mark, I would probably abstain.

85. Kuefler 2001.

trivial and otherwise).[86] Such polemic usually presumes shared ideals of gender, which can then be assigned to the Self, and denied to the Other. This, as we have seen, is the logic of Livy's account of the origins of the Bacchanalia, where he is explicit that the Bacchanalia emasculate good Roman men. It is the logic of Philo's critique of the banqueting practices of Greeks and Italians as feminine, feminizing, and morally defective, and, centuries later, of John Chrysostom's characterization of Jews in Antioch (whose festivals and other practices his Christian parishioners seem to find too appealing).

A related form of polemic attacks the other for failing to conform to proper gender relations. This is the tactic taken by Severus of Minorca, in his representation of Jewish women as insubordinate wives while Jews, only to become perfectly subordinate wives once they accept Christ (and his male representative, the bishop Severus himself). In Severus's portrayal, Jews have disordered gender relations, Christians have ordered ones.

The identification of diverse forms of masculinity has serious implications for corresponding notions of femininity and women's practices. As the rabbinic paradigm of Torah study as ideal masculinity became extended to a much wider range of Jewish men, domains rejected or devalued by men became dissociated from masculinity, and come, correspondingly, to be seen as appropriate domains for women, such as commercial competition.[87] We lack the evidence to know how much this might have been the case in late antiquity, nor to know how much Jewish men were able to study Torah intensively while still providing their families with basic economic support. But historical analogy might suggest that the more Jewish men adopted rabbinic paradigms of masculinity that valued intensive Torah study over other traditional forms of masculine pursuits, including agriculture, artisanship, and commerce, the more Jewish women may have been compelled to take over these activities.

---

86. See, e.g., Kraemer 1994; see also Levinson 2000.

87. This is perhaps part of a larger phenomenon in which anything not valued as masculine defaults to being feminine. But this is also a very complicated issue: one could cite modern instances of the feminization of particular professions, and the corresponding devaluation of those professions—medicine is often cited as a primary contemporary instance, along with the ministry. Yet where modern patterns suggest that it's the very admission of women to prestigious male professions that causes their devaluation, we lack the evidence to determine whether, for instance, other factors enabled Judean women to participate in commercial endeavors that then led men to devalue those activities, or whether their devaluing precedes their availability to women. Certainly, as Christians gained control over more facets of ancient life, they implemented increasing restrictions on the ability of now Jewish men to participate in economic life, as numerous laws in Linder 1989 demonstrate. Bourdieu raises some of these issues with regard to Jews centuries later: "The construction of the traditional Jewish habitus in central Europe, in the late nineteenth century, can be seen as a kind of *perfect inversion* [emphasis original] of the process of construction of the male habitus described here: the explicit refusal of the cult of violence, even in its most ritualized forms, such as duelling or sport, led to a devaluing of physical exercises, especially the most violent ones, in favour of intellectual and spiritual exercises, favouring the development of gentle, 'peaceful' dispositions (confirmed by the rarity of rape and other crimes of violence)" (Bourdieu 2001:51 n. 81).

The relationship between forms of masculinity and forms of femininity, and their implications for women's religious practices is also exemplified in Kuefler's argument. The new form of masculinity that Christian orthodoxy advocated authorized a corresponding form of femininity that severely constrained women's roles within the now dominant "orthodox" church. Kuefler actually suggests that some of this was quite conscious on the part of Christian thinkers. In contrast to scholars who have argued that the decline of options for Christian women, and their ultimate exclusion from Christian offices, particularly the priesthood and the episcopate, is inevitable in the development of radical religious movements into mainstream institutions, Kuefler suggests that these constraints and exclusions were grounded in the very particular historical and social circumstances of the late Roman empire. "Christian intellectuals used the dissonance between classical ideals for men and late ancient realities to undermine the traditional masculine ideal and supplant it with their own. At the same time, they emphasized the aspects of the Christian ideal that they felt best suited the goal of making Christian belief seem manly, reshaping Christian ideology as a masculine ideology."[88]

When I was seventeen, I had the closest thing to a revelation I have ever experienced. (Readers anticipating something profound, let alone pious, will be greatly disappointed.) It was the summer before my freshman year at Smith, and I was out on a small motor boat in Long Island Sound, with a young man I barely knew, and about whom I can now recall virtually nothing more than this. I was lying back watching the sky, and thinking about my own already manifest interests in the study of antiquity, when an insight came to me (or at least it seemed an insight to a seventeen-year-old). We study the past because we really wish to know the future, and because we think that there is some useful relationship between the past and the present that is predictive of the relationship between the present and the future.

To cast it only a little more subtly, those of us who think the past is explanatory want to know the history of our own cultural arrangements and how much they constrain us. If the post-structuralists, like Bourdieu and many others, are right, it seems that they constrain us greatly, and far more than we realize. Masculine domination, indeed all domination, is embedded in *habitus*, even the very thought structures with which we attempt to think about all this, and change it. Yet Bourdieu proposed, perhaps because he felt he had to, that only attention to the history of gender and its construction (and misrecognition?) as natural, will enable us to recognize it for what it is, and move beyond it. The consequences

---

88. Kuefler 2001:11.

of the critiques of gender and massive social changes in the second half of the twentieth century, at least in much of Europe and North America would seem to bear this out. I am regularly stunned by the number of my Brown female undergraduates who know virtually nothing of the history of women's subordination in American law and culture, and who at least claim to have experienced no discrimination, no limitations of any kind as a consequence of being female. The mother in me, and the feminist in me (not that they are exactly separate) celebrates this: the historian in me is horrified. Yet at the same time, there is substantial and continuing resistance to such change, particularly by fundamentalists of various traditions (Jewish, Christian [including Mormons], Muslim), supported by precisely the arguments that gender arrangements are divinely authorized and, therefore, cannot be changed. To unmask the history, and thus the contingency, and the artifice, of gender threatens, also, to unmask the history, and thus the contingency and the artifice of religious claims as well.

How much all this is applicable to larger arguments about the relations between religion and gender elsewhere, and more generally is beyond the scope of this project, although as I have tried to note, there is considerable consonance between the arguments made here, and subsequent historical and ethnographic studies. I am intrigued by emerging cognitive science theory and its potential to illuminate these issues, even though this research is new enough that it has not yet had much impact on these questions. It may well be that some discernment of sexual difference is, in fact, cognitive, intuitive, and fundamental to survival, but the specifics of gender probably are cultural, in the same way that the specifics of religions are cultural. Still, the more or less universality of gender difference, like the more or less universality of religion, suggests some underlying cognitive, evolutionary explanation. Yet although cognitive theory explains the apparent universality of religious thought and its social form (religion), it does so without authorizing it. That is, inherent in this model is the recognition that with the understanding of these mechanisms comes the ability to reject claims about supernatural beings and their relations to humans. So, too, while ideas about gender may have a cognitive basis, and survival benefits, recognition of how they originate in the human mind allows us to refuse them, even as we understand why they are so deeply entrenched and persistent.

When I began this work, I was in my early twenties. In my early sixties, I'm feeling too old (or at least sufficiently old), not to mention too much of a scholar of Greco-Roman antiquity, to be able to answer these questions. Although I'm not sure that this book constitutes the end of my reflections on these issues, I also recognize that many of these questions will have to fall to another generation of scholars, including that of my many wonderful students, and perhaps even also my own anthropologist daughter.

Works Cited

Allen, D. (2005). "Phenomenology." Pages 182–207 in *The Routledge Companion to the Study of Religion*. Edited by J. Hinnells. London: Routledge.

Ameling, W. (2004). *Inscriptiones Judaicae Orientis. Vol. 2, Kleinasien*. Tübingen: Mohr Siebeck.

Amengual i Batle, J. (1991). *Origens del cristianisme a les Balears i el seu desenvolupament fins a l'època musulmana*. Palma de Mallorca: Universitat de les Illes Balears, Facultat de Filosofia i Lletres.

———. (2001). "Consentius/Severus de Menorca: Vint-i-Cinc Anys D'Estudis. 1975–2000." *Arxiu de Textos Catalans Antics* 20, 589–700.

Anson, J. (1974). "The Female Transvestite in Early Monasticism: The Origin and Development of a Motif." *Viator* 5, 1–32.

Arjava, A. (1996). *Women and Law in Late Antiquity*. Oxford: Clarendon.

Asad, T. (1993). *Geneaologies of Religion: Discipline and Reasons of Power in Christianity and Islam*. Baltimore: The Johns Hopkins University Press.

Atkindon, P. C. (1982). "The Montanist Interpretation of Joel 2:28, 29 (LXX 3:1,2)." *Studia Evangelica* 126.7, 11–15.

Atwood, M. (1986). *The Handmaid's Tale*. Boston: Houghton Mifflin.

Aubin, M. (1998). "Reversing Romance: The Acts of Thecla and the Ancient Novel." Pages 257–72 in *Ancient Fiction and Early Christian Narrative*. Edited by R. Hock, J. Chance, and J. Perkins. Atlanta: Scholars.

Aymer, M. (1997). "Hailstorms and Fireballs: Redaction, World Creation, and Resistance in the Acts of Paul and Thecla." Pages 45–61 in *Rhetorics of Resistance. A Colloquy on Early Christianity as Rhetorical Formation*. Edited by V. Wimbush. *Semeia* 79.

Baer, R. A. (1970). *Philo's Use of the Categories Male and Female.* Leiden: Brill.

Baker, C. (2002). *Rebuilding the House of Israel: Architectures of Gender in Jewish Antiquity.* Stanford: Stanford University Press.

Barnard, L. W. (ed.). (1997). *The First and Second Apologies: St. Justin Martyr.* ACW 56. New York: Paulist.

Barrier, J. W. (2009) *The Acts of Paul and Thecla: A Critical Edition and Commentary.* WUNT 2. Reihe 270. Tübingen: Mohr Siebeck.

Baskin, J. (1984). "The Separation of Women in Rabbinic Judaism." Pages 3–18 in *Women, Religion and Social Change.* Edited by E. Findly and Y. Haddad. Albany: State University of New York Press.

Beard, M. (1993). "What Are We Talking About When We Talk About Women? *Her Share of the Blessings*, by Ross Kraemer." In *The London Review of Books*, 13 May, 19.

———. 1995. "Re-reading Vestal Virginity." Pages 166–77 in *Women in Antiquity: New Assessments.* Edited by R. Hawley and B. Levick. London: Routledge.

Beavis, M. A. (2004). "Philo's Therapeutai: Philosopher's Dream or Utopian Construction." *JSP* 14.1, 30–42.

Bellen, H. (1965–66). "Συναγωγὴ τῶν Ἰουδαιῶν καὶ Θεοσεβῶν. Die Aussage einer bosporanischen Freilassungsinschrift (CIRB 71) zum Problem der 'Gottesfürchtigen.'" JAC 8/9:171–76.

Bernays, J. (1885). "Die Gottesfürchtigen bei Juvenal." In *Gesammelte Abhandlungen* 2:91–80. Edited by H. Usener. Repr. Hildesheim: Georg Olms, 1971.

Bertrand, D. (1987). *La vie grecque d'Adam et d'Eve: Introduction, texte, traduction et commentaire.* Recherches Intertestamentaires 1. Paris: Librairie Adrien Masonneuve.

Betz, O. (1999). "The Essenes." *CHJ* 3, 444–70.

Blázquez, J. M. (1998). "Relations Between Hispania and Palestine in the Late Roman Empire." *Assaph: Studies in Art History*: special issue, *East Meets West: Art in the Land of Israel*, 163–78.

Bleiberg, E. (2005). *Tree of Paradise. Jewish Mosaics from the Roman Empire.* New York: The Brooklyn Museum.

Blumenkranz, B. (1960). *Juifs et chrétiens dans le monde occidental, 430–1096.* Paris: La Haye.

Bodel, J. (2008). "From Columbaria to Catacombs: Collective Burial in Pagan and Christian Rome." Pages 177–242 in *Commemorating the Dead: Texts and Artifacts in Context: Studies of Roman, Jewish and Christian Burials.* Edited by L. Brink and D. Green. Berlin: De Gruyter.

———, and Saul M. Olyan (eds). (2008). *Household and Family Religion in Antiquity.* Oxford: Blackwell.

Bonz, M. P. (1994). "The Jewish Donor Inscriptions from Aphrodisias: Are They Both Third-Century, and Who Are the Theosebeis?" *HSCP* 96: 281–99.

Boswell, J. (1980). *Christianity, Social Tolerance and Homosexuality: Gay People in Western Europe from the Beginning of the Christian Era to the Fourteenth Century.* New Haven: Yale University Press.

Botermann, H. (1993). "Griechisch-jüdische Epigraphik: Zur Datierung der Aphrodisias Inschriften." *ZPE* 98:184–94.

Boughton, L. C. (1991). "From Pious Legend to Feminist Fantasy: Distinguishing Hagiographical License from Apostolic Practice in the *Acts of Paul/Acts of Thecla*." *Journal of Religion* 71.3, 362–83.

Bourdieu, P. (1993). "The Production of Belief: Contribution to an Economy of Symbolic Goods." Pages 74–111 in *The Field of Cultural Production: Essays in Art and Literature*. Edited by R. Johnson. New York: Columbia University Press. Originally published as "La production de la croyance: contribution á une économie des biens symboliques." In *Acts de la recherches sciences sociales* 13 (Feb 1977): 3–43.

———. (2001). *Masculine Domination*. Trans. Richard Nice. Stanford: Stanford University Press. Originally published as *Domination Masculine*. Paris: Seuil, 1998.

Bovon, F. (1999). "Editing the Apocryphal Acts of the Apostles." Pages 1–38 in *The Apocryphal Acts of the Apostles*, Harvard Divinity Studies. Edited by F. Bovon, A. Brock, and C. Matthews. Cambridge, Mass.: Harvard University Press.

———. (2003). "Canonical and Apocryphal Acts of Apostles." *JECS* 11.2: 165–94.

———, B. Bouvier, and F. Amsler (eds). (1999). *Acta Philippi*. Turnhout, Belgium: Brepols.

Bowie, E. (1994). "The Readership of Greek Novels in the Ancient World." Pages 435–59 in *The Search for the Ancient Novel*. Edited by J. Tatum. Baltimore: Johns Hopkins.

Boyarin, D. (1993). *Carnal Israel: Reading Sex in Talmud*. Berkeley: University of California Press.

———. (1995). "Are There Any Jews in 'The History of Sexuality'?" *Journal of the History of Sexuality* 5.3, 333–55.

———. (1998). "Gender." Pages 117–35 in *Critical Terms for Religious Studies*. Edited by M. C. Taylor. Chicago: University of Chicago Press.

———. (2004). "The Christian Invention of Judaism: The Theodosian Empire and the Rabbinic Refusal of Religion." *Representations* 85:21–57. Repr. in *Religion: Beyond a Concept*. Edited by H. de Vries. New York: Fordham University Press, 2008, 150–77.

———. (2006). *Border Lines: The Partition of Judaeo-Christianity*. Philadelphia: University of Pennsylvania Press.

Boyd, B. (2006). "Getting It All Wrong: Bioculture Critiques Cultural Critique." *American Scholar* 75, 18–30.

Boyer, P. (2001). *Explaining Religion: The Evolutionary Origins of Religious Thought*. New York: Basic Books.

Butler, R. (2006). *The New Prophecy & "New Visions": Evidence of Montanism in the Passion of Perpetua and Felicitas*. Washington, D.C.: Catholic University of America Press.

Bradbury, S. (1996). *Severus of Minorca: Letter on the Conversion of the Jews*. Oxford Early Christian Texts. Oxford: Oxford University Press.

Bremmer, J. N. (1996). "Magic, Martyrdom and Women's Liberation in the *Acts of Paul and Thecla*." Pages 36–59 in *The Apocryphal Acts of Paul and Thecla*. Studies on the Apocryphal Acts of the Apostles 2. Edited by J. Bremmer. Kampen: Kok Pharos.

———. (2003). "Perpetua and Her Diary: Authenticity, Family and Visions." Pages 77–120 in *Martyrs and Martyrologies: papers read at the 1992 Summer Meeting and the 1993 Winter Meeting of the Ecclesiastical History Society*. Edited by D. Wood. Oxford: Blackwell.

Brooke, G. J. (2005). "Men and Women as Angels in *Joseph and Aseneth*." *JSP* 14.2, 159–77.

Brooten, B. J. (1982). *Women Leaders in the Ancient Synagogue: Inscriptional Evidence and Background Issues*. Brown Judaic Studies 36. Chico: Scholars.

———. (1991). "Iael Prostates in the Jewish Donative Inscription from Aphrodisias." Pages 149–62 in *The Future of Early Christianity: Essays in Honor of Helmut Koester*. Edited by B. Pearson, in collaboration with A. T. Kraabel, G.W.E. Nickelsburg, and N. R. Petersen. Minneapolis: Fortress.

———. (1996). *Love Between Women: Early Christian Responses to Female Homoeroticism*. Chicago: University of Chicago Press.

———. (2000a). "Matt 19:3–9, Divorced Wife." In *WIS*, 414.

———. (2000b). "Matt 5:31–32, Divorced Wife." In *WIS*, 407–8.

———. (2000c). "Mark 10:2–12, Divorced Wife." In *WIS*, 428–30.

———. (2000d). "Luke 16:18, Divorced Wife." In *WIS*, 448.

Brown, P. (1988). *The Body and Society: Men, Women and Sexual Renunication in Early Christianity*. New York: Columbia University Press.

Buckser, A., and S. D. Glazier (eds). (2003). *The Anthropology of Religious Conversion*. Lanham, MD and Oxford: Rowan and Littlefield.

Buell, D. (2005). *Why This New Race? Ethnic Reasoning in Early Christianity*. New York: Columbia University Press.

Burridge, K. (1969). *New Heaven, New Earth: A Study of Millenarian Activities*. Oxford: Blackwell.

Burrus, C., and L. Van Rompay. (2002). "Thecla in Syriac Christianity: Preliminary Observations." *Hugoye: Journal of Syriac Studies* 5.2 (online at syrcom.cua.edu/Hugoye).

———. (2003). "Some Further Notes on Thecla in Syriac Christianity." *Hugoye: Journal of Syriac Studies* 6.2 (online at syrcom.cua.edu/Hugoye).

Burrus, V. (1987). *Chastity as Autonomy: Women in the Stories of Apocryphal Acts*. Studies in Women and Religion 23. Lewiston, New York: Edwin Mellen.

———. (1991). "The Heretical Woman as Symbol in Alexander, Athanasius, Epiphanius, and Jerome." *HTR* 84.3, 229–48.

———. (1994). "Word and Flesh: The Bodies and Sexuality of Ascetic Women in Christian Antiquity." *JFSR* 10.1, 27–51.

———. (1995). "Reading Agnes: The Rhetoric of Gender in Ambrose and Prudentius." *JECS* 3.1, 25–46.

———. (2000). *"Begotten, not made": Conceiving Manhood in Late Antiquity*. Stanford: Stanford University Press.

———. (2001). "Is Macrina a Woman? Gregory of Nyssa's Dialogue on the Soul and Resurrection." Pages 249–64 in *The Blackwell Companion to Postmodern Theology*. Edited by G. Ward. Oxford: Blackwell.

———. (2004). *The Sex Lives of Saints: An Erotics of Ancient Hagiography*. Philadelphia: University of Pennsylvania Press.

———. (2005). "Mimicking Virgins: Colonial Ambivalence and the Ancient Romance." *Arethusa* 38.1, 49–88.

Butler, J. (1990). *Gender Trouble: Feminism and the Subversion of Identity*. New York: Routledge.

———. (1993). *Bodies That Matter: On the Discursive Limits of "Sex."* New York: Routledge.

———. (2004). *Undoing Gender*. New York: Routledge.

Bynum, C. W., S. Harrell, and P. Richman (eds). (1986). *Gender and Religion: On the Complexity of Symbols*. Boston: Beacon.

Calzolari, V. (1996–97). "Un nouveau texte arménien sur sainte Thècle: les Prodiges de Thècle." *Revues des Études Arméniennes* 26, 249–71.

———. (1997). "De sainte Thècle à Anahit." Pages 39–49 in *Tenth Anniversary Conference* (=*Caucasus World*). Edited by N. Awde. Richmond: Curzon, 39–49.

Cameron, Averil. (1980). "Neither Male nor Female." *Greece and Rome* 27, 60–68.

———. (1989). "Virginity as Metaphor: Women and the Rhetoric of Early Christianity." Pages 181–205 in *History as Text: The Writing of Ancient History*. Edited by A. Cameron. Chapel Hill: University of North Carolina Press.

Cameron, Alan. (1976). *Circus Factions. Blues and Greens at Rome and Byzantium*. Oxford: Oxford University Press.

Cansdale, L. (1997). *Qumran and the Essenes: a Re-evaluation of the Evidence*. Tübingen: Mohr Siebeck.

Carson, A. (1990). "Putting Her in Her Place: Woman, Dirt and Desire." Pages 135–69 in *Before Sexuality: The Construction of Erotic Experience in the Ancient World*. Edited by D. M. Halperin, J. J. Winkler, and F. I. Zeitlin. Princeton: Princeton University Press.

Castelli, E. (2004). *Martyrdom and Memory: Early Christian Culture Making*. New York: Columbia University Press.

——— (ed.). (2001). *Women, Gender, Religion: A Reader*. New York: Palgrave.

Chaniotis, A. (2002). "The Jews of Aphrodisias: New Evidence and Old Problems." *Scripta Classica Israelica* 22, 209–42.

Christian, W. A. (1964) *Meaning and Truth in Religion*. Princeton: Princeton University Press.

Church, F. F. (1975). "Sex and Salvation in Tertullian." *HTR* 68.1, 83–101.

Clark, E. A. (1994). "Ideology, History, and the Construction of 'Woman' in Late Ancient Christianity." *JECS* 2.1, 155–84.

———. (1998a). "Holy Women, Holy Words: Early Christian Women, Social History, and the Linguistic Turn." *JECS* 6.3, 413–30.

———. (1998b). "The Lady Vanishes: Dilemmas of a Feminist Historian after the 'Linguistic Turn.'" *Church History* 67.1, 1–31.

———. (1998c). "Melania the Elder and the Origenist Controversy: The Status of the Body in a Late-Ancient Debate." Pages 117–27 in *Nova & vetera: patristic studies in honor of Thomas Patrick Halton*. Edited by J. Petroccione. Washington: Catholic University of America Press.

———. (1999). "Rewriting Early Christian History: Augustine's Representation of Monica." Pages 3–23 in *Portraits of Spiritual Authority*. Edited by J. W. Drijvers and J. W. Watt. Leiden: Brill.

———. (2000). "Women, Gender, and the Study of Christian History." *Church History* 70, 395–426.

———. (2004). *History, Theory, Text Historians and the Linguistic Turn*. Cambridge, Mass.: Harvard University Press.

Clines, D. J. A. (1995). "David the Man: The Construction of Masculinity in the Hebrew Bible." Pages 212–43 in *Interested Parties: The Ideology of Writers and Readers of the Hebrew Bible*. JSOTSup 205. Edited by D. J. A. Clines. Sheffield: Sheffield Academic.

———. (2003). "Paul: The Invisible Man." Pages 181–92 in *New Testament Masculinities*. Edited by S. D. Moore and J. C. Anderson. Atlanta: Society of Biblical Literature.

Cobb, S. (2008). *Dying to Be Men: Gender and Language in Early Christian Martyr Texts*. New York: Columbia University.

Cohen, S. J. D. (1981). "Epigraphical Rabbis." *Jewish Quarterly Review* 72, 1–17.

———. (1985). "The Origins of the Matrilineal Principle in Rabbinic Law." *Association for Jewish Studies Review* 10, 19–53. Repr. in Cohen 1999: 263–307.

———. (1989). "Crossing the Boundary and Becoming a Jew." *HTR* 82.1, 13–33. Repr. in Cohen 1999:140–74.

———. (1999). *The Beginnings of Jewishness: Boundaries, Varieties, Uncertainties*. Berkeley: University of California Press.

———. (2005). *Why Aren't Jewish Women Circumcised? Gender and Covenant in Judaism*. Berkeley: University of California Press.

———. (2006). *From the Maccabees to the Mishnah*. 2nd ed. Louisville, Ky: Westminster John Knox.

Cohn, L., and P. Wendland (eds.). (1896–1930). *Philonis Alexandrini Opera Quae Supersunt*. Berlin: Walter de Gruyter, repr. 1962.

Cole, S. G. (1980). "New Evidence for the Mysteries of Dionysos." *GRBS* 21, 223–38.

———. (1992). "*Gynaiki ou themis*: Gender Difference in the Greek *Leges Sacrae*." *Helios* 19, 104–22.

———. (2004). *Landscapes, Gender and Ritual Space: The Ancient Greek Experience*. Berkeley: University of California Press.

Colson, F. C., and G. H. Whittaker. (1967–87). *Philo*. 10 vols. LCL. Cambridge, Mass.; Harvard University Press.

Connell, R. (1987). *Gender and Power: Society, the Person and Sexual Politics*. Oxford: Blackwell.

Connelly, J. B. (2007). *Portrait of a Priestess: Women and Ritual in Ancient Greece*. Princeton: Princeton University Press.

Conybeare, F. C. (1894). "The Acts of Saint Eugenia." Pages 147–90 in *The Armenian Apology and Acts of Apollonius and Other Monuments of Early Christianity*. London: Swan Sonnenschein & Co.

———. (1895). *Philo: About the Contemplative Life, or the Fourth Book of the Treatise Concerning Virtues. Critically Edited with a Defense of Its Genuineness*. Oxford: Clarendon Press.

Cooper, K. (1992). "Insinuations of Womanly Influence: An Aspect of the Christianization of the Roman Aristocracy." *JRS* 82, 150–64.

———. (1996). *The Virgin and the Bride: Idealized Womanhood in Late Antiquity*. Cambridge, Mass.: Harvard University Press.

Corley, K. (1993). *Private Women, Public Meals: Social Conflict in the Synoptic Tradition*. Peabody, Mass.: Hendrickson.

Corrington, G. P. (1990). "Philo *On the Contemplative Life*: or, *On the Suppliants*." Pages 134–55 in *Ascetic Behavior in Greco-Roman Antiquity*. Edited by V. Wimbush. Minneapolis: Fortress.

Cotton, H. (1993). "The Guardianship of Jesus Son of Babatha: Roman and Local Law in the Province of Arabia." *JRS* 83: 94–108.

———, and J. C. Greenfield. (1994). "Babatha's Property and the Law of Succession in the Babatha Archive." *ZPE* 104, 211–24.

Crawford, S. W. (2003). "Not According to Rule: Women, The Dead Sea Scrolls and Qumran." Pages 127–50 in *Emanuel: Studies in Hebrew Bible, Septuagint and Dead Sea Scrolls in Honor of Emanuel Tov*. Edited by S. M. Paul, R. A. Kraft, L. H. Schiffman, and W. W. Fields. Leiden: Brill.

Crook, Z. A. (2004). *Reconceptualizing Conversion: Patronage, Loyalty, and Conversion in the Religions of the Ancient Mediterranean*. Beiheft zur Zeitschrift für die neutestamentliche Wissenschaft und die Kunde der älteren Kirche 130. Berlin: de Gruyter.

Dagron, G. (ed.). (1978). *Vie et Miracles de sainte Thècle: Texte grec, traduction et commentaire*. Brussels: Société des Bollandistes.

D'Angelo, M. R. (1990). "Women Partners in the New Testament." *JFSR* 6, 65–86.

———. (1995). "Veils, Virgins, and the Tongue of Men and Angels: Women's Heads in Early Christianity." Pages 131–64 in *Off With Her Head: The Denial of Women's Identity in Myth, Religion, and Culture*. Edited by W. Doniger and H. Eilberg-Schwartz. Berkeley: University of California Press.

———. (2003a). "'Knowing How to Preside Over His Own Household': Imperial Masculinity and Christian Asceticism in the Pastorals, Hermas, and Luke-Acts." Pages 265–96 in *New Testament Masculinities*. Edited by S. D. Moore and J. C. Anderson. Atlanta: Society of Biblical Literature.

———. (2003b). "Eusebeia: Roman Imperial Family Values and the Sexual Politics of 4 Maccabees and the Pastorals." *Biblical Interpretation* 11, 139–65.

Daumas, F., and P. Miquel (eds). (1963). *De Vita Contemplativa*. Les Oeuvres de Philon d'Alexandrie. Paris: Éditions du Cerf.

Davidman, L. (1991). *Tradition in A Rootless World: Women Turn to Orthodox Judaism*. Berkeley: University of California Press.

Davies, P. R., and J. E. Taylor. (1996). "On the Testimony of Women in 1QSa." *DSD* 3.3, 223–35.

Davies, S. L. (1980). *The Revolt of the Widows: The Social World of the Apocryphal Acts*. Carbondale: Southern Illinois University Press.

————. (1986). "Women, Tertullian and the Acts of Paul." *Semeia* 38, 139–43.

————. (1992). "The Christology and Protology of the Gospel of Thomas." *JBL* 111.4, 663–82.

Davis, S. J. (2000). "A Pauline Defense of Women's Right to Baptize? Intertextuality and Apostolic Authority in the *Acts of Paul.*" *JECS* 8.3, 453–59.

————. (2001). *The Cult of Saint Thecla: A Tradition of Women's Piety in Late Antiquity.* Oxford: Oxford University Press.

————. (2002). "Crossed Texts, Crossed Sex: Intertextuality and Gender in Early Christian Legends of Holy Women Disguised as Men." *JECS* 10.1, 1–36.

de Palol, P. (1967a). *Arqueología cristiana de la Espana Romana.* Siglos IV-VI. Madrid: Valladolid.

————. (1967b). "En torno a la iconografia de los mosaicos de las basilicas de las Baleares." *Primera Reunión nacional de arqueología Paleocristiana. Actas.* Vitoria, Spain: Publicaciones de la Caja de Ahorros Municipal de la Cuidad de Vitoria.

Delaney, C. (1991). *The Seed and the Soil: Gender and Cosmology in Turkish Village Society.* Berkeley: University of California Press.

Derrida, J. (1989). "Biodegradables: Seven Diary Fragments." Transl. P. Kamuf. *Critical Inquiry* 15.4, 812–73.

des Bouvrie, S. (1997). "Euripides' Bakkhai and Maenadism." *Classica et Mediaevalia* 48, 75–114.

Devreese, R. (1965). *Le Fonds Grecs de la Bibliothèque Vaticane des Origines à Paul V.* Città del Vaticano: Biblioteca Apostolica Vaticana.

Dillon, M. (2002). *Girls and Women in Classical Greek Religion.* New York: Routledge.

Divjak, J. (ed.). (1981). *Epistolae ex duobus codicibus nuper in lucem prolatae.* CSEL 88.

Dodds, E. R. (1951). *The Greeks and the Irrational.* Sather Classical Lectures 25. Berkeley: University of California Press.

Donaldson, T. L. (2000). "Jerusalem Ossuary Inscriptions and the Status of Jewish Proselytes." Pages 372–88 in *Text and Artifact in the Religions of Mediterranean Antiquity: Essays in Honour of Peter Richardson.* Edited by S. Wilson and M. Desjardins. Waterloo, Ont.: Wilfrid Laurier University Press.

Douglas, M. (1970). *Natural Symbols: Explorations in Cosmology.* New York: Pantheon. Repr. London: Routledge, 1996, 2003.

————. (1978). *Cultural Bias.* Occasional paper, Royal Anthropological Institute of Great Britain and Ireland, no. 35. London: Royal Anthropological Institute of Great Britain and Ireland.

DuBois, P. (1988). *Sowing the Body: Psychoanalysis and Ancient Representations of Women.* Chicago: University of Chicago Press.

Dunn, P. (1993). "Women's Liberation, the Acts of Paul, and Other Apocryphal Acts of the Apostles." *Apocrypha* 4, 245–61.

Durkheim, É. (1965). *The Elementary Forms of the Religious Life.* Transl. J. Swain. New York: The Free Press, 1965, originally published George Allen and Unwin, Ltd. 1915.

Ehrman, B. (2003). *The Apostolic Fathers.* 2 vols. LCL. Cambridge, Mass.: Harvard University Press.

Eilberg-Schwartz, H. (1990). *The Savage in Judaism: An Anthropology of Israelite Religion and Ancient Judaism*. Bloomington: Indiana University Press.

Eisen, U. (1996). *Women Officeholders in Early Christianity: Epigraphical and Literary Studies*. Collegeville, Minn.: Liturgical Press, 2000. Originally published as *Amtsträgerinnen im früen Christentum: epigraphische und literarische Studien*. Göttingen: Vandenhoeck & Ruprecht.

Elliott, J. H. (2007). "Jesus the Israelite Was Neither a 'Jew' Nor a 'Christian': On Correcting Misleading Nomenclature." *Journal for the Study of the Historical Jesus* 5.2, 119–54.

Elliott, J. K. (1993). *The Apocryphal New Testament: A Collection of Apocryphal Christian Literature in an English Translation*. Oxford: Clarendon.

Elm, S. (1994). "Montanist Oracles." Pages 131–38 in *Searching the Scripture, Vol. 2: A Feminist Commentary*. Edited by E. Schüssler Fiorenza. New York: Crossroad.

Engberg-Pedersen, T. (1999). "Philo's *De Vita Contemplativa* as a Philosopher's Dream." *JSJ* 30, 40–64.

Eno, R. B. (ed.). (1989). *Augustine's Letters*, Vol. VI (1*-29*). FC 81.

Evans, E. (1964). *Tertullian. De baptismo liber. Homily on Baptism*. London: SPCK.

Faraone, C. (2001). *Ancient Greek Love Magic*. Cambridge, Mass.: Harvard University Press.

———. (2002). "Agents and Victims: Constructions of Gender and Desire in Ancient Greek Love Magic." Pages 400–26 in *The Sleep of Reason: Experience and Sexual Ethics in Ancient Greece and Rome*. Edited by M. Nussbaum and J. Sihvola. Chicago: University of Chicago Press.

Feldman, L. (1950). "Jewish 'Sympathizers' in Classical Literature and Inscriptions." *Transactions of the American Philological Association* 81, 200–208.

———. (1965). Josephus, *Jewish Antiquities*, Book 20. LCL. Cambridge, Mass.: Harvard University Press, vol. 9.

———. (1986). "The Omnipresence of the God-fearers." *Biblical Archaeology Review* 12.5, 58–63.

———. (1986–87). "Philo's Views on Music." *Journal of Jewish Music and Liturgy* 9, 36–54. Repr. in *Studies in Hellenistic Judaism*. Leiden: Brill, 1996, 504–28.

———. (1989). "Proselytes and 'Sympathizers' in the Light of the New Inscriptions from Aphrodisias." *REJ* 148, 265–305.

———. (1993). *Jew and Gentile in the Ancient World: Attitudes and Interactions from Alexander to Justinian*. Princeton: Princeton University Press.

Ficker, G. (1905). "Widerlegung eines Montanisten." *Zeitschrift für Kirchengeschichte* 26, 446–63.

Figueras, P. (1983). *Decorated Jewish Ossuaries*. Documenta et Monumenta Orientis Antiqui 20. Leiden: Brill.

Finn, T. M. (1985). "The Godfearers Reconsidered." *CBQ* 47, 75–84.

Fischler, S. (1989). *The Public Position of Women in the Imperial Household in the Julio-Claudian Period*, Ph.D. Dissertation, Oxford University.

Fishbane, S. (2007). *Deviancy in Early Rabbinic Literature: A Collection of Socio-Anthropological Essays*. Leiden: Brill.

Foley, H. P. (ed.). (1994). *The Homeric Hymn to Demeter: Translation, Commentary, and Interpretive Essays*. Princeton: Princeton University Press.

Fontaine, J. (1991). "Une polémique stylistique instructive dans la "lettre encyclique" de Sévère de Minorque." In *Eulogia: Mélanges offerts à A. R. Bastiaensen à l'occasion de son soizante-cinquième anniversaire*. Steenbrugis: Abbatia S. Petri; The Hague: Nijhoff, 119–35.

Foucault, M. (1978–86). *The History of Sexuality*. 3 vols. Trans. R. Hurley. New York: Pantheon Books.

Frankenberry, N. K. (ed.). (2002). *Radical Interpretation in Religion*. Cambridge, UK: Cambridge University Press.

Frazer, J. (1922). *The Golden Bough: A Study in Magic and Religion*, abridged. London: Macmillan. Originally published 1890.

Frier, B. (1999). "Roman Demography." Pages 85–109 in *Life, Death and Entertainment in the Roman Empire*. Edited by D. S. Potter and D. J. Mattingly. Ann Arbor: University of Michigan Press.

Friesen, S. J. (1999). "Ephesian Women and Men in Public Religious Offices in the Roman Period." Pages 107–13 in *100 Jahre österreichische Forschungen in Ephesos: Akten des Symposions Wein 1995*. Edited by H. Friesinger and F. Krinzinger. Vienna: Austrian Archaeological Institute.

Frey, J. B. (1930). "Inscriptions inedites des catacombs juives de Rome." *Rivista Archaeologia Cristiana* 7, 235–60.

———. (ed.). (1936). *Corpus Inscriptionum Iudaicarum. Recueil des inscriptions juives qui vont du IIIe siècle avant Jésus-Christ au VIIe siècle de notre ère*. 2 vols. Città del Vaticano, Roma: Pontificio istituto di archeologia cristiana.

———. (ed.). (1975). *Corpus of Jewish Inscriptions*, Vol. 1. Revised and Reprinted with a Prolegomenon by B. Lifshitz. New York: KTAV.

Gafney, W. C. (2008). *Daughters of Miriam: Women Prophets in Ancient Israel*. Minneapolis: Fortress.

Gager, J. G. (1975). *Kingdom and Community: The Social World of Early Christianity*. Englewood, N.J.: Prentice-Hall.

Gamble, H. (1995). *Books and Readers in the Early Church: A History of Early Christian Texts*. New Haven: Yale University Press.

Gardner, J. F. (1986). *Women in Roman Law and Society*. Bloomington and Indianapolis: Indiana University Press.

———. (1998). *Family and Familia in Roman Law and Life*. Oxford: Oxford University Press.

Geerard, M. (1992). *Clavis Apocryphorum Novi Testamenti*. Turnhout, Belgium: Brepols.

Geertz, C. (1973). "Religion as a Cultural System." In *The Interpretation of Cultures: Selected Essays*. New York: Basic Books. Repr. in *Language Truth and Religious Belief: Studies in Twentieth-Century Theory and Method in Religion*. Edited by N. Frankenberry. Atlanta: Scholars Press, 176–217.

Gibson, E. L. (1999). *The Jewish Manumission Inscriptions of the Bosporus Kingdom*. TSAJ 75. Tübingen: Mohr Siebeck.

Gilbert, G. (2004). "Jews in Imperial Administration and Its Significance for Dating the Jewish Donor Inscription from Aphrodisias." *JSJ* 35.2, 169–84.

Ginzburg, C. (1996). "The Conversion of Minorcan Jews (417–418): An Experiment in History of Historiography." Pages 209–19 in *Christendom and its Discontents: Exclusion, Persecution and Rebellion, 1000–1500*. Edited by S. L. Waugh and P. D. Diehl. Cambridge, UK: Cambridge University Press.

Glancy, J. A. (2003). "Protocols of Masculinity in the Pastoral Epistles." Pages 235–64 in *New Testament Masculinities*. Edited by S. D. Moore and J. C. Anderson. Atlanta: Society of Biblical Literature.

———. (2002). *Slavery in Early Christianity*. New York: Oxford University Press.

Gleason, M. W. (1995). *Making Men: Sophists and Self-Presentation in Ancient Rome*. Princeton: Princeton University Press.

———. (1999). "Elite Male Identity in the Roman Empire." Pages 67–84 in *Life, Death and Entertainment in the Roman Empire*. Edited by D. S. Potter and D. J. Mattingly. Ann Arbor: University of Michigan Press.

Goff, B. (2004). *Citizen Bacchae: Women's Ritual Practice in Ancient Greece*. Berkeley: University of California Press.

Golb, N. (1995). *Who Wrote the Dead Sea Scrolls? The Search for the Secret of Qumran*. New York: Scribner's.

Goldhill, S. (1995). *Foucault's Virginity: Ancient Erotic Fiction and the History of Sexuality*. Cambridge, UK: Cambridge University Press.

Goldstein, A. S. (1965). "Conversion to Judaism in Bible Times." Pages 9–32 in *Conversion to Judaism: A History and Analysis*. Edited by David Max Einhorn. New York: KTAV.

Gomme, A. W. (1925). "The Position of Women in Athens in the Fifth and Fourth Centuries B. C." *Classical Philology* 20.1, 1–25. Repr. in A. W. Gomme, *Essays in Greek History and Literature*. Oxford: Blackwell, 1937, 89–115.

Goodenough, E. R. (1953–64). *Jewish Symbols in the Greco-Roman Period*. 13 vols. New York: Pantheon.

Goodman, M. (1988). "Review of Reynolds and Tannenbaum." *JRS* 78, 261–62.

———. (1989). "Nerva, the Fiscus Judaicus and Jewish Identity." *JRS* 79, 40–44.

———. (1991). "Jewish Proselytizing in the First Century." Pages 53–78 in *The Jews Among Pagans and Christians*. Edited by J. Lieu, J. North, and R. Rajak. London: Routledge.

———. (1994). *Mission and Conversion: Proselytizing in the Religious History of the Roman Empire*. New York: Oxford University Press.

Graf, F. (1997). *Magic in the Ancient World*. Cambridge, Mass.: Harvard University Press.

Grant, R. M. (1998). *Greek Apologists of the Second Century*. Philadelphia: Westminster.

———. (1985). "A Woman of Rome: The Matron in Justin, 2 *Apology* 2.1–9." *Church History* 54.4, 461–72.

Green, G. (2005). "Hermeneutics." Pages 392–406 in *The Routledge Companion to the Study of Religion*. Edited by J. R. Hinnells. London: Routledge.

Gregg, R., and D. Urman. (1996). *Jews, Pagans and Christians in the Golan Heights*. University of South Florida Studies in the History of Judaism 140. Atlanta: Scholars Press.

Griffith, R. M. (1997). *God's Daughters: Evangelical Women and the Power of Submission*. Berkeley: University of California Press.

Groag, E. (1907). "Notizen zur Geschichte kleinasiatischer Familien." *Jahreshefte des österreichischen archäologischen Instituts* 10, 282–99.

Grossman, M. L. (2004). "Reading for Gender in the Damascus Document." *DSD* 11.2, 212–39.

Grubbs, J. E. (1995). *Law and Family in Late Antiquity: The Emperor Constantine's Marriage Legislation.* Oxford: Clarendon Press.

Gunderson, E. (2000). *Staging Masculinity. The Rhetoric of Performance in the Roman World.* Ann Arbor: University of Michigan Press.

Guthrie, S. E. (1993). *Faces in the Clouds: A New Theory of Religion.* New York: Oxford University Press.

Gutschow, K. (2004). *Being a Buddhist Nun: The Struggle for Enlightment in the Himalayas.* Cambridge, Mass.: Harvard University Press.

Hague, L. (1994). "Thecla and the Church Fathers." *Vigiliae Christianae* 48, 209–18.

Haines-Eitzen, K. (2000). *Guardians of Letters. Literacy, Power and the Transmitters of Early Christian Literature.* New York: Oxford University Press.

Hak, D. (2007). "Stark and Finke or Durkheim on Conversion and (Re-)Affiliation: An Outline of A Structural Functionalist Rebuttal to Stark and Finke." *Social Compass* 54.2, 295–312.

Halperin, D. M. "Why Is Diotima a Woman." Pages 257–308 in *Before Sexuality: The Construction of Erotic Experience in the Ancient World.* Edited by D. M. Halperin, J. J. Winkler and F. I. Zeitlin. Princeton: Princeton University Press.

Hänninen, M.-L. (1998). "Conflicting Descriptions of Women's Religious Activity in Republican Rome: Augustan Narratives about the Arrival of Cybele and the Bacchanalia Scandal." Pages 111–26 in *Aspects of Women in Antiquity: Proceedings of the First Nordic Symposium on Women's Lives in Antiquity, Göteborg 12–15 June 1997.* Edited by L. L. Lovén and A. Strömberg. Jonsered, Sweden: P. Åströms Förlag.

Hanson, A. E. (1990). "The Medical Writer's Woman." Pages 309–38 in *Before Sexuality: The Construction of Erotic Experience in the Ancient Greek World.* Edited by D. Halperin, J. Winkler, and F. Zeitlin. Princeton: Princeton University Press.

———. (1999). "The Roman Family." Pages 19–66 in *Life, Death and Entertainment in the Roman Empire.* Edited by D. S. Potter and D. J. Mattingly. Ann Arbor: University of Michigan Press.

Harding, S. (1983). "Why Has the Sex/Gender System Become Visible Only Now?" Pages 283–310 in *Discovering Reality: Feminist Perspectives on Epistemology, Metaphysics, Methodology and Philosophy of Science.* Edited by S. Harding and M. Hintikka. Dordrecht, the Netherlands: Reidel.

Harnack, A. (1908). *The Mission and Expansion of Christianity in the First Three Centuries.* 2nd ed. Trans. and ed. J. Moffatt. New York: G. P. Putnam's Sons.

Harraway, D. (1991). "'Gender' for a Marxist Dictionary: The Sexual Politics of a Word." In *Simians, Cyborgs and Women: The Reinvention of Nature,* New York: Routledge. Repr. in E. Castelli (ed.), *Women, Gender, Religion: A Reader.* New York: Palgrave, 2000, 49–75.

Harrison, V. (1996). "The Allegorization of Gender: Plato and Philo on Spiritual Childbearing." Pages 520–34 in *Asceticism*. Edited by V. Wimbush and R. Valantasis. New York: Oxford University Press.

Harvey, Y. K. (2000). "Possession Sickness and Women Shamans in Korea." Pages 59–65 in *Unspoken Worlds: Women's Religious Lives*, 3rd ed. Edited by N. A. Falk and R. Gross. Belmont, Calif.: Watson/Thomson Learning.

Hauptman, J. (1998). *Rereading the Rabbis: A Woman's Voice*. Boulder, CO: Westview Press.

Hay, D. M. (1992). "Things Philo Said and Did Not Say about the Therapeutae." *SBLSP* 31, 673–83.

———. (2003). "Foils for the Therapeutae: References to Other Texts and Persons in Philo's '*De Vita Contemplativa.*'" Pages 330–48 in *Neotestamentica et Philonica*. Edited by P. Borgen. Leiden: Brill.

———. (2004). "Philo's Anthopology, the Spiritual Regimen of the Theraputae, and a Possible Connection with Corinth." Pages 127–42 in *Philo und das Neue Testament*. Edited by R. Deines and K.- W. Niebuhr. Tübingen: Mohr Siebeck.

Heine, R. (ed.). (1989). *The Montanist Oracles and Testimonia*. Macon, Ga.: Mercer University Press.

Hengel, M. (1971). "Proseuche und Synagoge: Jüdische Gemeinde, Gotteshaus und Gottesdienst in der Diaspora und in Palästina." Pages 157–84 in *Tradition und Glaube. Das frühe Christentum in seiner Umwelt. Festgabe für Karl Georg Kuhn zum 65*. Edited by G. Jeremias, H.-W. Kuhn and H. Stegemann. Göttingen: Vandenhoeck & Ruprecht.

Henrichs, A. (1978). "Greek Maenadism from Olympias to Messalina." *HSCP* 82, 121–60.

Hezser, C. (2003). "The Impact of Household Slaves." *JSJ* 34.4, 375–424.

———. (2005). *Jewish Slavery in Antiquity*. New York: Oxford University Press.

Hilhorst, A. (1996). "Tertullian on the Acts of Paul." Pages 150–63 in *The Apocryphal Acts of Paul and Thecla*. Studies on the Apocryphal Acts of the Apostles 2. Edited by Jan Bremmer. Kampen: Kok Pharos.

Hillard, T. (1992). "On the Stage, Behind the Curtain." Pages 37–63 in *Stereotypes of Women in Power: Historical Perspectives and Revisionist Views*. Contributions to Women's Studies 125. Edited by B. Garlick, S. Dixon and P. Allen. New York: Greenwood Press.

Hillgarth, J. N. (1994). "Review of Amengual i Batle, *Orígens del cristianisme a les Balears i el seu desenvolupament fins a l'època musulmana*." *Speculum* 69, 729–31.

Hinde, R. A. (1999). *Why Gods Persist. A Scientific Approach to Religion*. New York: Routledge.

Hodge, C. J. (2007). *"If Sons, Then Heirs": A Study of Kinship and Ethnicity in Paul's Letters*. New York: Oxford University Press.

Hoff, J. (1994). "Gender as a Postmodern Category of Paralysis." *Women's History Review* 3, 149–68.

———. (1996). "A Reply to My Critics." *Women's History Review* 5, 25–30.

Hopkins, K. R. (1986). "Wet-nursing at Rome: A Study in Social Relations." Pages 201–29 in *The Family in Ancient Rome: New Perspectives*. Edited by B. Rawson. Ithaca: Cornell University Press.

———. (1987). "Graveyards for Historians." Pages 113–26 in *La Mort, les morts, et l'au-delà dans le monde romain: Actes du colloque de Caen*, 20–22 novembre 1985. Edited by F. Hinard. Caen: Université de Caen.

Horbury, W. (1999). "Women in the Synagogue." *CHJ* 3, 358–401.

———. and D. Noy (eds.) (1992). *Jewish Inscriptions of Greco-Roman Egypt*. Cambridge, UK: Cambridge University Press.

Hunt, E. D. (1982). "St. Stephen in Minorca: An Episode in Jewish-Christian Relations in the Early 5th Century AD." *JTS* n.s. 33, 106–23.

Ilan, T. (1995). *Jewish Women in Greco-Roman Palestine. An Inquiry into Image and Status*. TSAJ 44. Tübingen: Mohr Siebeck.

———. (1999). "Appendix: The Dead Sea Sect." Pages 38–42 in T. Ilan, *Integrating Women into Second Temple History*. TSAJ 76. Tubingen: Mohr Siebeck.

Ingersoll, J. (2003). *Evangelical Christian Women: War Stories in the Gender Battles*. New York: New York University Press.

Inowlocki, S. (2004). "Eusebius of Caesarea's *Interpretatio Christiana* of Philo's *De Vita Contemplativa*." *HTR* 97.3, 305–28.

Irshai, O. (2010). "St. Stephen and Gamaliel: Relics, Politics, and Polemics in Early 5th Century Palestine." In *"Ut videant et continant": Essays on Pilgrimage and Sacred Space*. (Hebrew).

Ivarsson, F. (2007). "Vice Lists and Deviant Masculinity: The Rhetorical Function of 1 Corinthians 5:10–11 and 6:9–10." Pages 163–84 in *Mapping Gender in Ancient Religious Discourses*, Biblical Interpretation Series 84. Edited by T. Penner and C. Vander. Leiden and Boston: Brill.

Jacobs, A. S. (1999). "A Family Affair: Marriage, Class and Ethics in the Apocryphal Acts of the Apostles." *JECS* 7.1, 105–38.

———. (2003a). "The Lion and the Lamb: Reconsidering Jewish-Christian Relations in Antiquity." Pages 95–118 in *The Ways That Never Parted*. Edited by A. H. Becker and A. C. Reed. TSAJ 95. Tübingen: Mohr Siebeck.

———. (2003b). "The Remains of the Jew: Imperial Christian Identity in the Late Ancient Holy Land." *Journal of Medieval and Early Modern Studies* 33, 23–45.

———. (2006). "'Papinian Commands One Thing, Our Paul Another': Roman Christians and Jewish Law in the *Collatio Legum Mosaicarum et Romanarum*." Pages 85–99 in *Religion and Law in Classical and Christian Rome*. Edited by C. Ando and J. Rüpke. Stuttgart: Franz Steiner Verlag.

James, W. (1902). *The Varieties of Religious Experience: A Study in Human Nature*. London: Longmans, Green and Co.

Janowitz, N. (2001). *Magic in the Roman World: Pagans, Jews and Christians*. London: Routledge.

Jastrow, M. (1903). (ed.). *A Dictionary of the Targumim, the Talmud Babli and Yerush- almi, and the Midrashic Literature*. London: Luzac; New York: Putnam.

Jay, N. B. (1992). *Throughout Your Generations Forever: Sacrifice, Religion, and Paternity*. Chicago: University of Chicago Press.

———. (2001). "Sacrifice as a Remedy for Being Born Female." Pages 174–94 in *Women, Gender, Religion: A Reader*. Edited by E. Castelli. New York: Palgrave.

Jeffery, P. (2004). "Philo's Impact on Christian Psalmody." Pages 147–87 in *Psalms in Community: Jewish and Christian Textual, Liturgical and Artistic Traditions*. Edited by H. W. Attridge and M. E. Fassler. Leiden: Brill.

Johnson, S. F. (2006). *The Life and Miracles of Thekla: A Literary Study*. Cambridge, Mass.: Harvard University Press.

Juschka, D. (ed.). (2001). *Feminism in the Study of Religion: A Reader*. New York: Continuum.

Kaestli, J. D. (1989). "Les Actes Apocryphes et la reconstitution de l'histoire des femmes dans le christianisme ancien." *Foi et Vie* 88, 71–79.

———. (1990). "Fiction litteraire et réalité sociale: Que peut-on savoir de la place des femmes dans le milieu du production des Actes apocryphes des apôtres?" *Apocrypha* 1, 279–302.

Katz, M. A. (1995). "Ideology and 'The Status of Women' in Ancient Greece." Pages 21–43 in *Women in Antiquity: New Assessments*. Edited by R. Hawley and B. Levick New York and London: Routledge.

Kearsley, R. A. (1986). "Asiarchs, Αρχιερεις and the Αρχιερειαι of Asia." *GRBS* 27, 183–92.

———. (1990). "Asiarchs, Archiereis and Archiereiai of Asia: New Evidence from Amorium in Phrygia." *Epigraphica Anatolia* 16, 69–80.

———. (1994). "The Asiarches." Pages 363–76 in *The Book of Acts in Its Graeco-Roman Setting*. Edited by D. W. J. Gill and C. Gempf. Grand Rapids: Eerdmans.

———. (2006). "Women and Public Life in Imperial Asia Minor: Hellenistic Tradition and Augustan Ideology." Pages 98–121 in *Ancient West and East*. Edited by G. R. Tsetskhladze. Leiden: Brill.

Kelley, N. (2006). *Knowledge and Religious Authority in the Pseudo-Clementines*. Tübingen: Mohr Siebeck.

King, U. (ed.). (1995) *Religion and Gender*. Oxford: Blackwell.

Kitch, S. (1989). *Chaste Liberation: Celibacy and Female Cultural Status*. Urbana: University of Illinois Press.

Klass, M. (1995). *Ordered Universes: Approaches to the Anthropology of Religion*. Boulder: Westview.

Klawiter, F. C. (1980). "The Role of Martyrdom and Persecution in Developing the Priestly Authority of Women in Early Christianity: A Case Study of Montanism." *Church History* 49.3, 251–61.

Kleiner, D. B. B., and S. B. Matheson. (2001). "Her Parents Gave Her the Name Claudia." Pages 1–16 in *I, Claudia II: Women in Roman Art and Society*. Edited by D. B.B. Kleiner and S. B. Matheson. Austin: University of Texas Press.

Koch, D.-A. (2006). "The God-fearers between Facts and Fiction: Two theosebeis-inscriptions from Aphrodisias and Their Bearing for the New Testament." *Studia Theologica—Nordic Journal of Theology* 60.1, 62–90.

Konstan, D. "Acts of Love: A Narrative Pattern in the Apocryphal Acts." *JECS* 6.1, 15–36.

———. (1997). "Defining Ancient Greek Ethnicity." *Diaspora* 6, 97–110.

Knust, J. (2007). "Enslaved to Demons: Sex, Violence and the Apologies of Justin Martyr." Pages 431–56 in *Mapping Gender in Ancient Religious Discourses*. Biblical

Interpretation Series 84. Edited by T. Penner and C. Vander Stichele. Leiden and Boston: Brill.

Kraabel, A. T. (1981). "The Disappearance of the 'God-fearers'." *Numen* 28, 113–26. Repr. in *Diaspora Jews and Judaism: Essays in Honor of, and in Dialogue with, A. Thomas Kraabel*. Edited by A. Overman and R.S. Maclennan. South Florida Studies in Judaism. Atlanta: Scholars Press, 119–30.

Kraemer, R. S. (1976). *Ecstatics and Ascetics: Studies in the Functions of Religious Activities for Women in the Greco-Roman World*. Ph.D. Dissertation, Princeton University.

———. (1979). "Ecstasy and Possession: The Attraction of Women to the Cult of Dionysos." *HTR* 72.1, 55–80.

———. (1980). "The Conversion of Women to Ascetic Forms of Christianity." *Signs: Journal of Women in Culture and Society* 6.2, 298–307. Repr. in *Sisters and Workers in the Middle Ages*. Edited by J. M. Bennet, E. A. Clark, J. O'Barr, B. A. Vilen, and S. Westphal-Wihl. Chicago: University of Chicago Press, 198–207.

———. (1985). "A New Inscription from Malta." *HTR* 78. 3–4, 431–38.

———. (1986). "Non-Literary Evidence for Jewish Women in Rome and Egypt." *Helios* 13.2, 85–101.

———. (1989a). "Monastic Jewish Women in Greco-Roman Egypt: Philo on the Therapeutrides." *Signs: Journal of Women in Culture and Society* 14.1, 342–70.

———. (1989b). "On the Meaning of the Term 'Jew' in Greco-Roman Inscriptions." *HTR* 82.1, 35–53. Repr. in *Diaspora Jews and Judaism: Essays in Honor of, and in Dialogue with, A. Thomas Kraabel*. South Florida Studies in Judaism. Edited by Andrew Overman and R. S. Maclennan. Atlanta: Scholars, 1992, 311–29.

———. (1991a). "Jewish Tuna and Christian Fish: Identifying Religious Affiliation in Epigraphic Sources." *HTR* 84.2, 141–62.

———. (1991b). "Women's Authorship of Jewish and Christian Literature in the Greco-Roman Period." Pages 221–42 in *"Women Like This": New Perspectives on Jewish Women in the Greco-Roman World*. Edited by A.-J. Levine. Atlanta: Scholars.

———. (1992). *Her Share of the Blessings: Women's Religions Among Pagans, Jews and Christians in the Greco-Roman World*. New York: Oxford University Press.

———. (1994). "The Other as Woman: Aspects of Polemic Between Pagans, Jews and Christians in Greco-Roman Antiquity." Pages 121–44 in *The Other in Jewish Thought and History*. Edited by L. Silberstein. New York: New York University Press.

———. (1998a). "Jewish Women in the Diaspora World of Late Antiquity." Pages 46–72 in *Jewish Women in Historical Perspective*, 2nd ed. Edited by J. Baskin. Detroit: Wayne State University Press.

———. (1998b). *When Aseneth Met Joseph: A Late Antique Tale of the Biblical Patriarch and His Egyptian Wife, Revisited*. New York: Oxford University Press.

———. (1999a). "Jewish Women and Christian Origins: Some Caveats." Pages 38–41 in *Women and Christian Origins*. Edited by R. S. Kraemer and M. R. D'Angelo. New York: Oxford University Press.

———. (1999b). "Jewish Women and Women's Judaism(s) at the Beginning of Christianity." Pages 50–79 in *Women and Christian Origins*. Edited by R. S. Kraemer and M. R. D'Angelo. New York: Oxford University Press, 50–79.

———. (2000a). "Acts 13:50: Devout Women of Psidian Antioch." In *WIS*, 461–62.

———. (2000b). "Acts 17:4: Leading Women Converts of Thessalonica." In *WIS*, 465–66.

———. (2000c). "Acts 17:12: "Greek Women (and Men) of High Standing in Beroea Who Become Believers." In *WIS*, 466.

———. (2000d). "Mark 6:3, Sisters of Jesus." In *WIS*, 425.

———. (2000e). "Matt 13:56, "Sisters of Jesus" In *WIS*, 410.

———. (2003). "Typical and Atypical Family Dynamics: The Cases of Babatha and Berenice." Pages 130–56 in *Early Christian Families in Context: An Interdisciplinary Dialogue*. Edited by D. Balch and C. Osiek. Grand Rapids: Eerdman's.

———. (2006). "Blaming Jewish Women for the Death of John the Baptist: A Christian (?) Theological Strategy?" *JBL* 125.2, 321–49.

———. (2008). "Women and Gender." Pages 465–92 in *The Oxford Handbook of Early Christian Studies*. Edited by S. A. Harvey and D. Hunter. Oxford: Oxford University Press.

———. (2009). "Jewish Women's Resistance to Christianity in the Early 5th Century: The Account of Severus, Bishop of Minorca." *JECS* 17.4, 635–65.

——— and J. Eyl. "Translating Women: The Perils of Gender-Inclusive Translation of the New Testament." Forthcoming in *Celebrate Her for the Fruit of Her Hands: Studies in Honor of Carol L. Meyers*. Edited by C. Carter and K. Bombach. Winona Lake, Ind.: Eisenbrauns.

———, and S. L. Lander. (2000). "Perpetua and Felicitas." Pages 1048–68 in *The Early Christian World*, vol. 2. Edited by P. A. Esler. London: Routledge.

Kraft, R. A. (1991). "Tiberius Julius Alexander and the Crisis in Alexandria according to Josephus." Pages 175–84 in *Of Scribes and Scrolls: Studies on the Hebrew Bible, Intertestamental Judaism, and Christian Origins*. Edited by H. W. Attridge et al. New York: University Press of America.

———. (2001). "Setting the Stage and Framing Some Central Questions." *JSJ* 32.4, 371–95.

Kron, U. (1996). "Priesthoods, Dedications and Euergetism: What Part Did Religion Play in the Political and Social Status of Greek Women." Pages 139–82 in *Religion and Power in the Ancient Greek World, Proceedings of the Uppsala Symposium 1993*. Edited by P. Hellström and B. Alroth. Uppsala: Ubsaliensis S. Academiae.

Krüger, G., and G. Ruhbach. (1965). *Ausgewählte Märtyrakten*. Tübingen: J.C.B. Mohr (Paul Siebeck).

Kuefler, M. (2001). *The Manly Eunuch: Masculinity, Gender Ambiguity and Christian Ideology in Late Antiquity*. Chicago: Chicago University Press.

Lagarde, P. (ed.). (1966). *Clementina*. Osnabrück: Otto Zeller. Originally published 1865.

Lake, K. (ed.). (1926–32). Eusebius, *The Ecclesiastical History*. LCL. 2 vols. Cambridge, Mass.: Harvard University Press.

Lampe, G. W. H. (ed.). (1961–68). *A Patristic Greek Lexicon*. Oxford: Clarendon.

Lampe, P. (2003). "The Woman from Justin's *Apology* 2.2." Pages 237–40 in *From Paul to Valentinus: Christians at Rome in the First Two Centuries*. Transl. Michael Steinhauser. Minneapolis: Fortress. Originally published as *Die Stadtrömischen in der erstsen beiden Jahrhunderten: Untersuchungen zur Socialgeschichte*. 2nd ed. WUNT 2/18. Tübingen: J. C. B. Mohr (Paul Siebeck), 1989.

Lander, S. L. (2002). *Ritual Power in Society: Ritualizing Late Antique North African Martyr Cult Activities and Social Changes in Gender and Status*. Ph.D. Dissertation, University of Pennsylvania.

Lanternari, V. (1963). *The Religions of the Oppressed: A Study of Modern Messianic Cults*. New York: Knopf.

LaQueur, T. (1990). *Making Sex: Body and Gender from the Greeks to Freud*. Cambridge, Mass.: Harvard University Press.

Larson, J. (2004). "Paul's Masculinity." *JBL* 123.1, 85–97.

Latour, B. (2004). "Why Has Critique Run Out of Steam? From Matters of Fact to Matters of Concern." *Critical Inquiry* 30, 225–48.

Le Bohec, Y. (1981). "Inscriptions juives et judaisantes de l'Afrique romaine." *Antiquités africaines* 17, 165–207.

LeClercq, H. (1921). *Les Martyrs. Vol. 1: Les temps Néroniens et le deuxième siècle*. Paris: H. Oudin.

Lefkowitz, M. R. (1991). "Did Ancient Women Write Novels?" Pages 199–219 in *"Women Like This": New Perspectives on Jewish Women in the Greco-Roman World*. Edited by A.-J. Levine. Atlanta: Scholars.

Leon, H. J. (1960). *The Jews of Ancient Rome*. Philadelphia: Jewish Publication Society.

Leonhardt, J. (2001). *Jewish Worship in Philo of Alexandria*. TSAJ 84. Tübingen: Mohr Siebeck.

Levarie, S. (1991). "Philo on Music." *The Journal of Musicology* 9.1, 124–30.

Levene, D. S. (1993). *Religion in Livy*. Mnemosyne, Bibliotheca Classica Batava Supplementum 127. Leiden: Brill.

Levi-Strauss, C. (1963). *Structural Anthropology*. New York: Basic Books.

Levine, A.-J. (1992). "Diaspora as Metaphor: Bodies and Boundaries in the Book of Tobit." Pages 105–17 in *Diaspora Jews and Judaism. Essays in Honor of, and in Dialogue with, A. Thomas Kraabel*. South Florida Studies in Judaism. Edited by A. Overman and R. S. MacLennan. Atlanta: Scholars.

Levine, L. I. (2000). *The Ancient Synagogue: The First Thousand Years*. New Haven: Yale University Press.

Levinskaya, I. (1996). *The Book of Acts in its Diaspora Setting*. Grand Rapids: Eerdmans.

Levinson, J. "Cultural Androgyny in Rabbinic Literature." Pages 119–40 in *From Athens to Jerusalem. Medicine in Hellenized and Jewish Lore and Early Christianity Literature*. Edited by S. Kottek and M. Horstmanshoff. Rotterdam: Erasmus.

Lewis, C. T., and C. Short (eds). (1879). *A Latin Dictionary*. Oxford: Clarendon.

Lewis, I. M. (1971). *Ecstatic Religion: An Anthropological Study of Shamanism and Spirit Possession*. Harmondsworth, Penguin. 3rd edition, as *Ecstatic Religion: A Study of Shamanism and Spirit Possession*. London: Routledge, 2003.

Lewis, N., Y. Yadin, and J. Greenfield (eds). (1989). *The Documents from the Bar Kochba Period in the Cave of Letters: Greek Papyri*. Judean Desert Studies 2. Jerusalem: Israel Exploration Society.

Lewis, S. (2002). *The Athenian Woman: An Iconographic Handbook*. London: Routledge.

Liddell, H. G., and Robert Scott (eds.), revised and augmented by Henry Stuart Jones. (1968). *Greek-English Lexicon*. Oxford: Clarendon Press.

Lieu, J. (1998). "The 'Attraction of Women' in/to Early Judaism and Christianity: Gender and the Politics of Conversion." *JSNT* 72, 5–22.

Lifshitz, B. (ed.). (1967). *Donateurs et fondateurs dans les synagogues juives, répertoire des dédicaces grecques relatives à la construction et à la réfection des synagogues.* Paris: J. Gabalda, et Cie.

———. (1970). "Du nouveau sur les 'sympathisants'." *JSJ* 1, 77–84.

———. (1961). "Inscriptions Grecques de Césarée En Palestine (Caesarea Palaestinae)." *Revue Biblique* 68, 115–26.

Linder, A. (ed.). (1987). *The Jews in Imperial Roman Legislation.* Detroit: Wayne State University Press; Jerusalem: Israel Academy of Sciences and Humanities.

Lipsius, R. A., and M. Bonnet (eds). (1891). *Acta Apostolorum Apocrypha.* 3 vols. Leipzig: Hermann Mendelssohn. Repr. Darmstadt: Wissenschaftliche Gesellschaft, 1959.

Lucius, E. (1879). *Die Therapeuten und ihre Stellung in der Geschichte der Askese: Eine kritische Untersuchung der Schrift De Vita Contemplativa.* Strasbourg: F. Bull.

Luck, G. (2006). *Arcana Mundi: Magic and the Occult in the Greek and Roman Worlds: A Collection of Ancient Texts.* 2nd ed. Baltimore: The Johns Hopkins University Press.

Luiselli, B. (ed.). (1968). *Tertullianus. De baptismo.* Corpus Scriptorum Latinorum Paravianum. 2nd ed. Turin: Aug. Taurinorum.

Luomanen, P., I. Pyysiäinen, and R. Uro (eds). (2007). *Explaining Christian Origins and Early Judaism: Contributions from Cognitive and Social Science.* Leiden: Brill.

Lutz, C. E. (ed.). (1947). *Musonius Rufus: The Roman Socrates.* New Haven: Yale University Press.

Lyons, D. (1997). *Gender and Immortality: Heroines in Ancient Greek Myth and Cult.* Princeton, N.J.: Princeton University Press, 1997.

MacCormack, C., and M. Strathern (eds). (1980). *Nature, Culture, Gender.* Cambridge, UK: Cambridge University Press.

MacDonald, D. R. (1983). *The Legend and the Apostle: The Battle for Paul in Story and Canon.* Philadelphia: Westminster Press.

———. (1984). "The Role of Women in the Production of the Apocryphal Acts of the Apostles." *Iliff Review* 41, 21–28.

MacDonald, M. Y. (1994). *Early Christian Women and Pagan Opinion.* Cambridge, UK: Cambridge University Press, 1994.

———. (1999). "Reading Real Women Through the Undisputed Letters of Paul." Pages 199–220 in *Women and Christian Origins.* Edited by R. S. Kraemer and M. R. D'Angelo. New York: Oxford University Press.

Mack, B. L. (2001). "On Redescribing Christian Origins." Pages 59–80 in *The Christian Myth: Origins, Logic and Legacy.* Edited by B. Mack. New York: Continuum.

MacLennan, R. S., and A. T. Kraabel. (1986). "The God-fearers—A Literary and Theological Invention." *BAR* 12.5, 17–26; 46–53.

Magness, J. (2005). "The Date of the Sardis Synagogue in Light of Numismatic Evidence." *American Journal of Archaeology* 109.3, 443–75.

———. (2003). *The Archaeology of Qumran and the Dead Sea Scrolls*. Grand Rapids: Eerdman's.

Mahmood, Saba. (2004). *The Politics of Piety. The Islamic Revival and the Feminist Subject*. Princeton: Princeton University Press.

Mandel, P. (2006). "The Tosefta." *CHJ* 4, 316–35.

Marsh, R. (1996). "Introduction: Women's Studies and Women's Issues in Russia, Ukraine and the Post-Soviet States." Pages 1–29 in *Women in Russia and Ukraine*. Edited by R. Marsh. Cambridge, UK: Cambridge University Press.

Marshall, J. (2008). "Hybridity and Reading Romans 13." *JSNT* 31.2, 157–78.

Martin, D. B. (1995). *The Corinthian Body*. New Haven: Yale University Press.

Martin, D. B., and P. C. Miller (eds). (2005). *The Cultural Turn in Late Ancient Studies: Gender, Asceticism, and Historiography*. Durham: Duke University Press.

Martin, T. (2004). "Paul's Argument from Nature for the Veil in 1 Corinthians 11:13–15: A Testicle Instead of a Head Covering." *JBL* 123.1, 75–84.

Mason, S. (2007). "Jews, Judeans, Judaizing, Judaism: Problems of Categorization in Ancient History." *JSJ* 38.4–5, 457–512.

Matthews, S. (2001). *First Converts: Rich Pagan Women and the Rhetoric of Mission in Early Judaism and Christianity*. Stanford: Stanford University Press.

———. (2002). "Thinking of Thecla: Issues in Feminist Historiography." *JFSR* 17.2, 39–55.

McCutcheon, R. (1998). "Redescribing 'Religion' as a Social Formation: Toward a Social Theory of Religion." Pages 51–73 in *What Is Religion? Origins, Definitions and Explanations*. Edited by T. A. Idinopoulos and B. C. Wilson. Leiden: Brill. Repr. in R. McCutcheon, *Critics Not Caretakers*. Albany: State University of New York Press, 2001, 21–42.

McDonnell, M. A. (2006). *Roman Manliness: Virtus and the Roman Republic*. Cambridge, UK: Cambridge University Press.

McDowell, M. (2006). *Prayers of Jewish Women: Studies of Patterns of Prayer in the Second Temple Period*. WUNT 2.211. Tübingen: Mohr Siebeck.

McGinn, S. E. (1994). "The Acts of Thecla." Pages 800–28 in *Searching the Scripture, Vol. 2: A Feminist Commentary*. Edited by E. Schüssler Fiorenza. New York: Crossroad.

McKnight, S. (2002). *Turning to Jesus: The Sociology of Conversion in the Gospels*. Louisville, Ky.: Westminster John Knox.

Menand, L. (2005). "Dangers Within and Without." *Profession 2005*, 10–17.

Meyer, M. (ed.). (1999). *Ancient Christian Magic: Coptic Texts of Ritual Power*. Princeton: Princeton University Press.

Mierow, C. C. (1939). "Tacitus the Biographer." *Classical Philology* 34.1, 36–44.

Miles, M. (1989). *Carnal Knowing, Female Nakedness and Religious Meaning in the Christian West*. Boston: Beacon.

Milgrom, J. (2000). *Leviticus 17–22: A New Translation with Introduction and Commentary*. The Anchor Bible. Garden City: Doubleday.

Mills, K., and A. Grafton (eds). (2003). *Conversion in Late Antiquity and the Early Middle Ages: Seeing and Believing*. Rochester: University of Rochester Press.

Mirecki, S., and M. Meyer (eds). (2002). *Magic and Ritual in the Ancient World.* Leiden: Brill.

Mitchell, M. M. (1993). "Review Essay on A. C. Wire's *The Corinthian Women Prophets." Religious Studies Review* 19, 308–11.

Mitchell, S. (2005). "An Apostle to Ankara from the New Jerusalem: Montanists and Jews in Late Roman Asia Minor." *Scripta Classica Israelica* 24, 207–23.

Mommsen, T. (1907). *Le Droit Pénal Romain.* Trans. J. Duchesne. Paris: A. Fontemoing.

Montserrat, D. (2000). "Reading Gender in the Roman World." Pages 153–82 in *Experiencing Rome: Culture, Identity and Power in the Roman Empire.* Edited by J. Huskinson. London: Routledge.

Moore, G. F. (1927–30). *Judaism in the First Centuries of the Christian Era: The Age of the Tannaim.* 3 vols. Cambridge, Mass.: Harvard University Press.

Munier, C. (1994). *L'Apologie de Saint Justin Philosophe et Martyr.* Paradosis 38. Fribourg: Éditions Universitaires Fribourg Suisse.

Musurillo, H. (ed.). (1954). *Acta Alexandrinorum: The Acts of the Pagan Martyrs.* Oxford: Clarendon.

———. (ed.). (1972). *The Acts of the Christian Martyrs.* Oxford: Clarendon.

Neyrey, J. (2003). "Jesus, Gender and the Gospel of Matthew." Pages 43–66 in *New Testament Masculinities.* Semeia Studies 45. Edited by S. D. Moore and J. C. Anderson. Atlanta: Scholars.

Ng, E. Y. L. (2004). "Acts of Paul and Thecla: Women's Stories and Precedent?" *JTS* 55, 1–29.

Niditch, S. (1991). "Women in the Hebrew Bible." In *Jewish Women in Historical Perspective.* Edited by J. Baskin. Detroit: Wayne State University Press. 2nd ed. 1998.

Nir, R. (2009). "Aseneth as the "Type of the Church of the Gentiles." Pages 1:109–37 in *Early Christian Literature and Intertextuality.* Edited by C. A. Evans and H. D. Zacharias. London: T&T Clark.

Nock, A. D. (1933). *Conversion: The Old and the New in Religion from Alexander the Great to Augustine of Hippo.* Donnellan Lectures 31. Oxford: Clarendon.

Noy, D. (ed.). (1993). *Jewish Inscriptions of Western Europe: Vol. 1: Italy (excluding the City of Rome), Spain and Gaul.* Cambridge, UK: Cambridge University Press.

———. (ed.). 1995. *Jewish Inscriptions of Western Europe: Vol. 2: The City of Rome.* Cambridge, UK: Cambridge University Press.

———, A. Panayotov, and H. Bloedhorn (eds). (2004). *Inscriptiones Judaicae Orientis. Vol 1, Eastern Europe.* Tübingen: Mohr Siebeck.

———, and H. Bloedhorn (eds). (2004). *Inscriptiones Judaicae Orientis. Vol. 3. Syria and Cyprus.* Tübingen: Mohr Siebeck.

O'Connor, J. M. (1992). "Lots of God-fearers? Theosebeis in the Aphrodisias Inscription." *Revue Biblique* 99, 418–24.

O'Donnell, J. J. (2005). *Augustine: A New Biography.* New York: HarperCollins.

Olyan, S. M. (1994). "'And with a Male You Shall Not Lie the Lying Down of a Woman': On the Meaning and Significance of Leviticus 18:22 and 20:13." *Journal of the History of Sexuality* 5, 179–206.

Ortner, S. B. (1974). "Is Female to Male as Nature Is to Culture?" Pages 67–88 in *Woman, Culture and Society*. Edited by M. Z. Rosaldo and L. Lamphere. Stanford: Stanford University Press. Repr. in S. Ortner, *Making Gender: The Politics and Erotics of Gender*. Boston: Beacon Press, 1996, 21–42.

———. (1996). "So, *Is* Female to Male as Nature Is to Culture?" Pages 173–80 in *Making Gender: The Politics and Erotics of Gender*. Boston: Beacon Press.

———, and H. Whitehead (eds). (1981). *Sexual Meanings: The Cultural Construction of Gender and Sexuality*. Cambridge, UK: Cambridge University Press.

Osiek, C., and M. Y. MacDonald. (2005). *A Woman's Place: House Churches in Earliest Christianity*. Minneapolis: Fortress Press.

Oster, R. E. (1988). "When Men Wore Veils to Worship: The Historical Context of 1 Corinthians 11:14." *New Testament Studies* 34.4, 481–505.

Overman, J. A. (1988). "The Godfearers: Some Neglected Features." *JSNT* 32, 17–26.

Oyewùmí, O. (2001). "The Translation of Cultures: Engendering Yorùbá Language, Orature and World-sense." Pages 76–97 in *Women, Gender, Religion: A Reader*. Edited by E. A. Castelli. New York: Palgrave.

Parker, H. N. (1997). "The Teratogenic Grid." Pages 47–65 in *Roman Sexualities*. Edited by J. P. Hallett and M. B. Skinner. Princeton: Princeton University Press.

Paton, W. R., and E. L. Hicks (eds). (1891). *The Inscriptions of Cos*. Oxford: Clarendon.

Penner, T., and C. Vander Stichele (eds). (2007). *Mapping Gender in Ancient Religious Discourses*. Biblical Interpretation Series 84. Leiden and Boston: Brill.

Perkins, J. (1995). *The Suffering Self: Pain and Narrative Representation in the Early Christian Era*. New York: Routledge.

———. (2007). "The Rhetoric of the Maternal Body in the *Passion of Perpetua*." Pages 313–32 in *Mapping Gender in Ancient Religious Discourses*. Edited by T. P. and C. V. Stichele. Leiden: Brill.

Pesthy, M. (1996). "Thecla among the Fathers of the Church." Pages 164–79 in *The Apocryphal Acts of Paul and Thecla*. Studies on the Apocryphal Acts of the Apostles 2. Edited by J. Bremmer. Kampen, the Netherlands: Kok Pharos, 164–79.

Petersen, W. L. (1986). "Can *arsenokoitai* Be Translated by 'Homosexuals'? (1 Cor. 6:9, 1 Tim. 1:10)." *Vigiliae Christianae* 40.2, 187–91.

Petropoulous, J. C. (1995). "Transvestite Virgin with a Cause: The *Acta Pauli et Theclae* and Late Antique Proto-'feminism'." Pages 125–40 in *Greece and Gender*. Edited by B. Berggreen and N. Marinatos. Bergen: The Norwegian Institute at Athens.

Pfuhl, E., and H. Mobius (eds). (1979). *Die ostgriechischen Grabreliefs*. Mainz am Rhein: Verlag Philipp von Zabern.

Pollard, E. A. (2001). *Magic Accusations against Women in the Greco-Roman World: From the First through the Fifth Centuries C.E.* Ph.D. Dissertation, University of Pennsylvania.

Pomeroy, S. (1975). *Goddesses, Whores, Wives and Slaves: Women in Classical Antiquity*. New York: Schocken.

Price, S. (1984). *Rituals and Power: The Roman Imperial Cult in Asia Minor*. Cambridge, UK: Cambridge University Press.

Pyysiäinen, I. (2001). *How Religion Works: Towards a New Cognitive Science of Religion*. Leiden: Brill.

Rajak, T. (1992). "The Jewish Community and its Boundaries." Pages 9–28 in *The Jews among Pagans and Christians: In the Roman Empire*. Edited by J. Lieu, J. North and T. Rajak. London: Routledge.

———, and D. Noy. (1993). "Archisynagogoi: Office, Title and Social Status in the Greco-Jewish Synagogue." *JRS* 83: 75–93. Repr. in T. Rajak, *The Jewish Dialogue With Greece and Rome: Studies in Cultural and Social Interaction*. London: Routledge, 2001, 393–430.

Ramazangolu, C. (1996). "Unravelling Postmodern Paralysis: A Response to Joan Hoff." *WHR* 5, 19–23.

Rawson, B. (ed.). (1986). *The Family in Ancient Rome: New Perspectives*. Ithaca: Cornell University Press.

Refoulé, F. (ed.). (1952). *Tertullian, Traité du bapteme*. SC 35. Paris: Éditions du Cerf. Rev. and corrected, 2002.

Rehm, B. (ed.). (1994). *Die Pseudoklementinen II: Rekognitionen in Rufins Übersetzung*. GCS. Berlin: Akademie Verlag.

Reiter, R. (ed.). (1975). *Toward an Anthropology of Women*. New York: Monthly Review Press.

Reynolds, J. M., and R. Tannenbaum (eds). (1987). *Jews and God-fearers at Aphrodisias: Greek Inscriptions with Commentary: Texts from the Excavations at Aphrodisias Conducted by Kenan T. Erin*. Cambridge, UK: Cambridge Philological Society.

Riaud, J. (1987). "Les Thérapeutes d'Alexandrie dans la tradition et dans la recherche critique jusqu'aux découvertes de Qumran." *ANRW* 2.20.2, 1189–1295.

Riley, D. (1988). *Am I That Name: Feminism and the Category of "Women" in History*. Minneapolis: University of Minnesota Press.

Ringrose, K. (2003). *The Perfect Servant: Eunuchs and the Social Construction of Gender in Byzantium*. Chicago: University of Chicago Press.

Robert, L. (1937). *Études anatoliennes: recherches sur les inscriptions grecques de l'Asie Mineure*, Paris: Coronet. 1937. Repr. Amsterdam: A. M. Hakkert, 1970.

Roberts, C. H. (ed.). (1950). *P. Antinoopolis*. London: Egypt Exploration Society.

Roberts, E. (2010). *Anger, Emotion and Desire in the Gospel of Matthew*. Ph.D. Dissertation, Brown University.

Rordorf, W. (1984). "Sainte Thècle dans la tradition hagiographique occidentale." *Augustinianum* 24, 73–81.

———. (1990). "Tertullien et les Acts de Paul (à propos de Bapt. 17,5)." Pages 151–60 in *Hommage à René Braun*. Paris, Les Belles Lettres, vol. 2, Edited by G. Jean. Repr. in *Lex Orandi, Lex Credendi. Paradosis. Beiträge zur Geschichte der altchristlichen Literatur und Theologie XXXVI. Gesammelte Aufsätze zum 60. Geburtstag*. Freiburg Schweiz: Universitätsverlag, 1993, 475–84.

———. (1993). "Terra Incognita: Recent Research on Christian Apocryphal Literature, Especially on Some Acts of Apostles." Pages 432–38 in *Studia Patristica XXV: Papers Presented at the Eleventh International Conference on Patristic Studies Held in Oxford 1991: Biblica et Apocrypha, Orientalia, Ascetica*. Edited by E. A. Livingstone. Leuven: Peeters.

———. (1989). "Was wissen wir über Plan und Absicht der Paulusakten." Pages 71–82 in *Oecumenica et Patristica, Festschrift für Wilhelm Schneemelcher zum 75*.

Geburtstag. Edited by D. Papandreou, W. A. Bienert and K. Schäferdiek. Stuttgart: Kohlhammer.

Rosaldo, M. Z., and L. Lamphere (eds). (1974). *Woman, Culture and Society*. Stanford: Stanford University Press.

Rosenblum, J. (2010). *Food and Identity in Early Rabbinic Judaism*. Cambridge, UK: Cambridge University Press.

Rouché, C. (1995). "Aurarii in the Auditoria." *ZPE* 105, 37–50.

Rousselle, A. (1988). *Porneia: On Desire and the Body in Antiquity*. Oxford: Blackwell.

Rubin, G. (1975). "The Traffic in Women: Notes on the 'Political Economy' of Sex." Pages 157–211 in *Toward an Anthropology of Women*. Edited by R. Reiter. New York: Monthly Review Press.

Runia, D. T. (1993). *Philo in Early Christian Literature: A Survey*. Minneapolis: Fortress.

Rutgers, L. (1995). *The Jews of Late Ancient Rome: Evidence of Cultural Interaction in the Roman Diaspora*. Leiden: Brill.

———. (2009). *Making Myths. Jews in Early Christian Identity Formation*. Leuven: Peeters.

Ryba, T. (2006). "Phenomenology of Religion." Pages 91–122 in *The Blackwell Companion to the Study of Religion*. Edited by R. A. Segal. Oxford: Blackwell.

Saller, R. (1982). *Personal Patronage under the Early Empire*. Cambridge, UK: Cambridge University Press.

———. (1998). "Symbols of Gender and Status Hierarchies in the Roman Household." Pages 85–91 in *Women and Slaves in Greco-Roman Culture: Differential Equations*. Edited by S. R. Joshel and S. Murnaghan. London: Routledge.

Santoro L'Hoir, F. E. (1992). *The Rhetoric of Gender Terms: "Man" and "Woman" and the Portrayal of Character in Latin Prose*. Leiden: Brill.

Satlow, M. L. (1994). "'They Abused Him Like a Woman': Homoeroticism, Gender Blurring, and the Rabbis in Late Antiquity." *Journal of the History of Sexuality* 5.1, 1–25.

———. (1996). "'Try to Be a Man': The Rabbinic Construction of Masculinity." *HTR* 89.1, 19–40.

———. (2002). "Fictional Women: A Study in Stereotypes." Pages 225–43 in *The Talmud Yerushalmi and Graeco-Roman Culture* III. TSAJ 93. Edited by P. Schäfer. Tübingen: Mohr Siebeck.

Saussure, F. de. (1976). *Cours de linguistique générale*. Edited by T. de Mauro. Paris: Payot.

Schäfer, P., and H. G. Kippenberg (eds). (1997). *Envisioning Magic: A Princeton Symposium and Seminar*. Leiden: Brill.

Scheiber, S. (1983). *Jewish Inscriptions in Hungary, From the 3rd Century to 1686*. Leiden: Brill.

Schiffman, L. (1994). *Reclaiming the Dead Sea Scrolls: The History of Judaism, the Background of Christianity, the Lost Library of Qumran*. Philadelphia: The Jewish Publication Society.

Schuller, E. (1994). "Women in the Dead Sea Scrolls." Pages 115–31 in *Methods of Investigation of the Dead Sea Scrolls and the Khirbet Qumran Site. Present Realities and Future Prospects.* Edited by M. O. Wise, N. Golb, J. J. Collins and D. G. Pardee. New York: Annals of the New York Academy of Sciences.

———. (1999). "Women in the Dead Sea Scrolls." Pages 117–44 in *The Dead Sea Scrolls after Fifty Years: A Comprehensive Assessment.* Vol. 2. Edited by P. W. Flint and J. C. VanderKam. Leiden: Brill.

Schürer, E. (1987). *The History of the Jewish People in the Age of Jesus Christ (175 B.C.–A.D. 135).* 3 vols. Revised and edited by G. Vermès, F. Millar, M. Goodman, and P. Vermes. Edinburgh, T&T Clark.

Schüssler Fiorenza, E. (1983). *In Memory of Her: A Feminist Theological Reconstruction of Christian Origins.* New York: Crossroad.

Schwartz, S. (2001). *Imperialism and Jewish Society 200 B.C.E.–600 C.E.* Princeton: Princeton University Press.

Scott, J. W. (1986). "Gender: A Useful Category of Historical Analysis." *American Historical Review* 91, 1053–75.

Sealey, R. (1990). *Women and Law in Classical Greece.* Chapel Hill: University of North Carolina Press.

Segal, A. (1990). *Paul the Convert: the Apostolate and Apostasy of Saul the Pharisee.* New Haven: Yale University Press.

Seigert, F. (1973). "Gottesfürchtige und Sympathisanten." *JSJ* 4, 109–64.

Sered, S. (1994). *Priestess, Mother, Sacred Sister: Religions Dominated by Women.* New York: Oxford University Press.

———. (1999). *Women of the Sacred Groves: Divine Priestesses of Okinawa.* New York: Oxford University Press.

Shaw, B. (1993). "The Passion of Perpetua." *Past and Present* 139, 3–45.

———. (1996). "Body/Power/Identity: Passions of the Martyrs." *JECS* 4.3, 269–312.

Sheridan, S. G. (2002). "Scholars, Soldiers, Craftsmen, Elites? Analysis of French Collection of Human Remains from Qumran." *DSD* 9.2, 199–248.

Shipton, P. (1997). "Fictive Kinship." Pages 186–88 in *The Dictionary of Anthropology.* Edited by T. Barfield. Oxford: Blackwell.

Sievers, J. (1996). "Individual Conversions to Judaism in Late Antiquity: Reconsidering the Epigraphical Evidence." *Dimensioni e problemi della ricerca storica* no. 2, 35–42.

Slingerland, E. (2008). *What Science Offers the Humanities: Integrating Body and Culture.* Cambridge, UK: Cambridge University Press.

Sly, D. (1990). *Philo's Perception of Women.* Brown Judaic Studies 209. Atlanta: Scholars.

Smallwood, M. (1959). "The Alleged Jewish Tendencies of Poppaea Sabina." *JTS* 10, 329–35.

Smart, N. (1983). *Worldviews: Cross Cultural Explanations of Human Beliefs.* New York: Scribner's.

Smith, B. H. (2009). *Natural Reflections: Human Cognition at the Nexus of Science and Religion.* New Haven: Yale.

Smith, D. (2003). *From Symposium to Eucharist: The Banquet in the Early Christian World.* Minneapolis: Fortress Press.

Smith, J. Z. (1988). "Sacred Persistence: Toward a Redescription of Canon." Pages 36–52 in *Imagining Religion: From Babylon to Jamestown*. Chicago: University of Chicago Press.

———. (1998). "Religion, Religions, Religious." Pages 269–84 in *Critical Terms for Religious Studies*. Edited by M. C. Taylor. Chicago: University of Chicago Press. Repr. in J. Z. Smith, *Relating Religion: Essays in the Study of Religion*. Chicago: University of Chicago Press, 2004, 179–96.

———. (2004a). "Trading Places." Pages 215–29 in *Relating Religion: Essays in the Study of Religion*. Chicago: University of Chicago Press.

———. (2004b). "When the Chips Are Down." Pages 1–60 in *Relating Religion: Essays in the Study of Religion*. Chicago: University of Chicago Press.

Snyder, J. M. (1989). *The Woman and the Lyre: Women Writers in Classical Greece and Rome*. Carbondale: Southern Illinois University Press.

Sophocles, E. A. (ed.). 1870. *Greek Lexicon of the Roman and Byzantine Periods*. Boston: Little Brown and Co.

Souter, A. (1924). "The 'Acta Pauli' etc. in Tertullian." *JTS* 25, 292.

Sparks, H. F. D. (ed.). *Apocryphal Old Testament*. Oxford: Oxford University Press.

Spiro, M. (1966). "Religion: Problems of Definition and Explanation." Pages 85–126 in *Anthropological Approaches to the Study of Religion*. Edited by M. Banton. London: Tavistock. Repr. in *Language Truth and Religious Belief: Studies in Twentieth-Century Theory and Method in Religion*. Edited by N. Frankenberry. Atlanta: Scholars, 1999, 137–75.

Staples, A. (1998). *From Good Goddess to Vestal Virgins: Sex and Category in Roman Religion*. London: Routledge.

Stark, R. A. (1996). "The Role of Women in Christian Growth." Pages 95–128 in The *Rise of Christianity: A Sociologist Reconsiders History*. Princeton: Princeton University Press.

———. (2001). "The Basis of Mormon Success: A Theoretical Application." Pages 207–42 in *Mormons and Mormonism: An Introduction to an American World Religion*. Edited by E. A. Eliason. Urbana: University of Illinois Press.

———, and W. Bainbridge. (1987). *A Theory of Religion*. New Brunswick, N.J.: Rutgers University Press.

———, and R. Finke. (2000). *Acts of Faith: Explaining the Human Side of Religion*. Berkeley: University of California Press.

Stephens, S. A. "Who Read the Ancient Novels?" Pages 405–18 in *The Search for the Ancient Novel*. Edited by J. Tatum. Baltimore: The Johns Hopkins University Press.

Stern, K. B. (2008). *Inscribing Devotion and Death: Archaeological Evidence for Jewish Populations of North Africa*. Leiden: Brill.

Stowers, S. K. (2007). "Review of Denise Buell, *Why This New Race?*" *JAAR* 75, 727–30.

———. (2008). "Theorizing the Religion of Ancient Households and Families." Pages 5–19 in *Household and Family Religion in Antiquity*. Edited by J. Bodel and S. M. Olyan. Oxford: Blackwell.

Strathern, M. (1990). *The Gender of the Gift*. Berkeley: University of California Press.

Streete, G. C. (2006). "Of Martyrs and Men: Perpetua, Thecla and the Ambiguity of Female Heroism in Early Christianity." Pages 254–66 in *The Subjective Eye: Essays in Culture, Religion and Gender in Honor of Margaret R. Miles*. Edited by R. Valantasis. Eugene, Or: Pickwick.

Swidler, L. J., and A. Swidler (eds). (1977). *Women Priests: A Catholic Commentary on the Vatican Declaration*. New York: Paulist.

Szesnat, H. (1998). "'Pretty Boys' in Philo's De Vita Contemplativa." *Studia Philonica Annual* 10, 87–107.

Tabbernee, W. (1997). *Montanist Inscriptions and Testimonia: Epigraphic Sources Illustrating the History of Montanism*. North American Patristic Society Patristic Monograph Series 16. Macon: Mercer University Press.

Takács, S. A. (2001). "Politics and Religion in the Bacchanalian Affair of 186 B.C.E." *HSCP* 100, 301–10.

———. (2007). *Vestal Virgins, Sybils and Matrons: Women in Roman Religion*. Austin: University of Texas Press.

Tannenbaum, R. (1986). "Jews and God-fearers in the Holy City of Aphrodite." *BAR* 12.5, 55–57.

Taylor, J. E. (1999). "The Cemeteries of Khirbet Qumran and Women's Presence at the Site." *DSD* 6, 285–323.

———. (2003). *Jewish Women Philosophers of First-Century Alexandria: Philo's 'Therapeutae' Reconsidered*. Oxford: Oxford University Press, 2003.

Theissen, G. (1978). *Sociology of Early Palestinian Christianity*. Trans. John Bowden. Philadelphia: Fortress.

———. (1991). The *Gospels in Context: Social and Political History in the Synoptic Tradition*. Trans. Linda Maloney. Minneapolis: Fortress.

Thompson, C. (1988). "Portraits from Roman Corinth: Hairstyles, Headcoverings and St. Paul." *Biblical Archaeology* 51.2, 99–115.

Tinh, V. T. T. (1971). *Le Culte Des Divinités Orientales a Herculanum*. EPRO 17. Leiden: Brill.

Trebilco, P. R. (1991). *Jewish Communities in Asia Minor*. Society for New Testament Studies Monograph Series 69. Cambridge, UK: Cambridge University Press.

Treggiari, S. (1991). *Roman Marriage: Iusti Coniuges from the Time of Cicero to the Time of Ulpian*. Oxford: Clarendon.

———. (2002). *Women and the Law in the Roman Empire. A Sourcebook on Marriage, Divorce and Widowhood*. London: Routledge.

Tremlin, T. (2006). *Minds and Gods: The Cognitive Foundations of Religion*. New York: Oxford University Press.

Trevett, C. (1996). *Montanism: Gender, Authority and the New Prophecy*. Cambridge, UK: Cambridge University Press.

Tribble, P. (2000). "Miriam 1." In *WIS*, 127–29.

Tylor, E. (1871). *Primitive Culture*. London: J. Murray.

Ullucci, D. (2004). "C. Musonius Rufus on Women." Unpublished Brown University Seminar Paper.

———. (2005). "Mary in the Cosmos, Women in the Church: Epiphanius on the Kollyridians." Unpublished Brown University Seminar Paper.

————. (2008). *The End of Animal Sacrifice*. Ph.D. Dissertation, Brown University.

van Bremen, R. (1985). "Women and Wealth." Pages 223–42 in *Images of Women in Antiquity*. Edited by A. Cameron and A. Kuhrt. Detroit: Wayne State University Press.

————. (1996). *The Limits of Participation: Women and Civic Life in the Greek East in the Hellenistic and Roman Periods*. Dutch Monographs on Ancient History and Archaeology 15. Amsterdam: J. C. Gieben.

van der Horst, P. W. (1978). *The Sentences of Pseudo-Phocylides*. Leiden: Brill.

————. (1991). *Ancient Jewish Epitaphs: An Introductory Survey of a Millennium of Jewish Funerary Epigraphy (300 BCE-700 CE)*. Kampen: Kok Pharos.

————. (1989). "Jews and Christians in Aphrodisias in the Light of their Relations in Other Cities of Asia Minor." *Nederlands Teologische Tijdschrift* 43, 106–21.

van der Weg, M. "A Wealthy Woman Named Tryphaena, Patroness of Thecla of Iconium." Pages 16–35 in *The Apocryphal Acts of Paul and Thecla*. Studies on the Apocryphal Acts of the Apostles 2. Edited By J. Bremmer. Kampen: Kok Pharos.

van Esbroeck, M. (1984). "Jean II de Jérusalem et les cultes de S. Étienne, de la Sainte-Sion et de la Croix." *Analecta Bollandiana* 102.1–2, 99–134.

Vanderlinden, S. (1946). "*Revelatio Sancti Stephani* (BHL 7850–6)." *Revue des Études Byzantines* 6, 178–217.

Vouaux, L. (1913). *Les Acts de Paul et ses Letters Apocryphes*. Paris: Librairie Letouzey et Ané.

Wallace-Hadrill, A. (1996). *Houses and Society in Pompeii and Herculaneum*. Princeton: Princeton University Press.

————. (2003). "Domus and Insulae in Rome: Families and Housefuls." Pages 3–18 in *Early Christian Families in Context: An Interdisciplinary Dialogue*. Edited by D. Balch and C. Osiek. Grand Rapids: Eerdman's.

Walsh, J. T. (2001). "Leviticus 18:22 and 20:13: Who Is Doing What to Whom?" *JBL* 120.2, 201–9.

Wander, B. (1998). *Gottesfürchtige und Sympathisanten. Studien zum heidnischen Umfeld von Diasporasynagogen*. WUNT 104. Tübingen: Mohr Siebeck.

Wankenne, J., and B. Hambenne. (1987). "La Lettre-encyclique de Severus évêque de Minorque au début du Vᵉ siècle." *Revue Bénédictine* 97, 13–27.

Wartelle, A. (ed.). (1987). *St. Justin, Apologies: introduction, texte critique, traduction, commentaire et index*. Paris: Études Augustiniennes.

Wassen, C. (2005). *Women in the Damascus Document*. Leiden: Brill.

Wasserman, E. (2008). *The Death of the Soul in Romans 7: Sin, Death and the Law in Light of Hellenistic Moral Psychology*. Tübingen: Mohr Siebeck.

Wegner, J. R. (1988). *Chattel or Person: The Status of Women in the Mishnah*. New York: Oxford University Press.

————. (1991). "Philo's Portrayal of Women: Hebraic or Hellenic?" Pages 41–66 in *"Women Like This": New Perspectives on Jewish Women in the Greco-Roman World*. Edited by A.-J. Levine. Atlanta: Scholars.

Wesseling, B. (1988). "The Audience of the Ancient Novels." Pages 67–79 in *Groningen Colloquia on the Novel*. Edited by H. Hoffman. Groningen: Egbert Forsten.

White, H. (1980). "Droysen's *Historik*: Historical Writing as a Bourgeois Science." *History and Theory* 19 (1980): 73–93. Repr. in H. White, *The Content of the Form: Narrative Discourse and Historical Representation*. Baltimore: John Hopkins University Press, 1987, 83–103.

———. (1984). "The Question of Narrative in Contemporary Historical Theory." *History and Theory* 23.1, 1–33.

Williams, C. A. (1999). *Roman Homosexuality: Ideologies of Masculinity in Classical Antiquity*. New York: Oxford University Press.

Williams, M. H. (1988). "'θεοσεβὴς γαρ ἦν,'—the Jewish Tendencies of Poppaea Sabina." *JTS* 39, 97–111.

———. (1992). "The Jews and Godfearers Inscription from Aphrodisias: A Case of Patriarchal Interference in Early 3rd Century Caria?" *Historia* 41, 297–310.

Wilson, B. C. (1998). "From the Lexical to the Polythetic: A Brief History of the Definition of Religion." Pages 141–62 in *What is Religion: Origins, Definitions and Explanations*. Edited by T. A. Idinopulos and B. C. Wilson. Leiden: Brill.

Wilson, S. G. (1998). "Early Christian Music." Pages 390–401 in *Common Life in the Early Church; Essays Honoring Graydon F. Snyder*. Edited by Julian V. Hills. Harrisburg: Trinity Press International.

Wilson-Kastner, P., et al. (eds). (1981). *A Lost Tradition: Women Writers of the Early Church*. Lanham, University Press of America.

Winkler, J. (1990). "The Laughter of the Oppressed: Demeter and the Gardens of Adonis." Pages 188–209 in *The Constraints of Desire: The Anthropology of Sex and Gender in Ancient Greece*. Edited by J. Winkler. New York: Routledge.

Winston, D. (ed.). 1981. *Philo of Alexandria. The Contemplative Life; The Giants; and, Selections*. Classics of Western Spirituality. New York: Paulist Press.

Wire, A. C. (1990). *The Corinthian Women Prophets: A Reconstruction through Paul's Rhetoric*. Minneapolis: Fortress.

Wittig, M. (1983). "The Point of View: Universal or Particular." *Feminist Issues* 3.2, 63–69.

———. (1992). "The Category of Sex." Pages 1–8 in *"The Straight Mind" and Other Essays*. Boston: Beacon.

Wolchik, S. L. (1998). "Women and the Politics of Gender in Communist and Post-Communist Central and Eastern Europe." Pages 297–303 in *Eastern Europe: Politics, Culture, and Society Since 1939*. Edited by S. P. Ramet. Bloomington: Indiana University Press.

Wright, D. F. (1984). "Homosexuals or Prostitutes? The Meaning of *arsenokoitai* (1 Cor. 6:9, 1 Tim. 1:10)." *Vigiliae Christianae* 32.2, 125–53.

———. (1987). Translating ARSENOKOITAI (1 Cor. 6:9, 1 Tim. 1:10)." *Vigiliae Christianae* 41.4, 396–98.

Yadin, Y., J. C. Greenfield, and A. Yardeni. (1994). "Babatha's Ketubbah." *Israel Exploration Journal* 44, 75–101.

Yonge, C. D. (1855–94). *The Works of Philo Judaeus*. London, H.G. Bohn. Available on-line at www.earlychristianwritings.com/yonge.

Zabin, S. (1996). "'Iudaea Benemerenti': Towards a Study of Jewish Women in the Western Roman Empire." *Phoenix* 50.3–4, 262–82.

Zias, J. E. (2000). "The Cemetaries of Qumran and Celibacy: Confusion Laid to Rest?" *DSD* 7.2, 220–53.

Zilm, J. (2008). "Blood, Bread, and Light: Female Converts in Early Judaism." *Women in Judaism: A Multidisciplinary Journal* 5.2, 1–21.

Index of Ancient Sources

Acts of the Apostles
2.36–37   250
5.34   161n20
6.8–7.60   153
13.50   222n144
16.3   199n69
16.13   222n144
17.4, 12   222n144
Acts of John
60.7   189n40
The Acts of Paul   169
Acts of (Paul and) Thecla
7   139
8   139
10   139
11   138
18   140
20   133
21   140
22   138, 140
23   140
24   141
25   136n73
26   142n91
32   132
33   138
34   138n79
29   134n69
30   134n70

38   138n79, 139n80
41   117, 142–43
43   133n67, 143
48   140n85
The Acts of Saint Eugenia
20   144n98
Acts of Thomas
13   41n27
55   34, 36–37
56   35, 38–41
58   38n20
Apollonius of Rhodes, Argonautica
3.876–83   170n51
Aseneth
15.7–8   248n20
Augustine, City of God
22.8   153n3

Babylonian Talmud Niddah
31a–b   45nn37–38

Chariton, Chareas and Callirhoe
2.2   248n19
7.5   248n19
8.8   248n19

1 Chronicles
6.3   102
Clement of Alexandria, Miscellanies
4.19   88n113
Codex Justinianus
1:9:12   189n36
Colossians
3.5–8   35n12
3.11   150n113
Consentius, Letters
Letter 12*   160n17
Letter 12*13.3–6   160n17
1 Corinthians
5.11   35n12, 52
6.9   52
7   38n19
7.12–13   50
7.12–16   50–51
7.13–15   49
7.13–16   51n57
7.15   50
7.16   50
7.19   199n68
11   171, 251
11.3–16   172n58, 247
11.5   63n25
11.6   136

1 Corinthians (*continued*)
14.26   250–52
14.33b–36   118, 172, 251
2 Corinthians
1.3   158
John Chrysostom,
    Against Judaizing
    Christians
2.3.3–6   182n17
4.7.3
Deuteronomy
11.19   42
16.11   63n25
16.16   246n13
20.1   91n119
24.1   51n56
24.3   51n56
Dio Cassius, *Roman History*
67.14.1–2   182n14
Diodorus Siculus,
    Historical Library
2.55–60   66n39
Egeria, *Diary of a*
    Pilgrimage
22–23   121n16
Ephesians
3.9   144n97
5.5   35n12
Epiphanius, *Panarion*
78.23   247n16
Eusebius, *Ecclesiastical*
    History
2.17.20   62n21
2.17.24   62n20
4.17   47n40
4.26.5   190n40
5.1.3–63   244n5
5.18.11   249n22
6.5.1–7   244n5
10.4.44   218n131
Exodus
14.31   95n137
15   66, 83–109
15.1   101, 104,
    108n162
15.1a   85, 95n137
15.1b   85, 87, 93,
    104–5, 108
15.1b–2   83
15.1b–18   105

15.2   101, 104
15.2–18   104
15.19   95n137
15.20   85, 96n138,
    101–2,
    250n24
15.20–21   83, 85,
    85n102,
    101–2
15.21   85, 87, 93,
    101–5, 108
15.23–25   171n54
23.14, 17   246n13
32.18   88n113
Ezekiel
13.17–23   250n24
Galatians
1.19   199n68
3.28   150
5.6   199n68
5.20   35n12
6.15   199n68
Genesis
1   115
1.26   150
1.26–27   115
1–3   66, 83, 114,
    263
3   168
Genesis Apocryphon
    45n37
Genesis Rabbah
17.7–8   265n70
Gospel of John
9.31   189n40
Gospel of Luke
1.48   250
5.37   170
8.1–3   254n38
16.18   51n56
24.11   167n39
Gospel of Mark
6.3   257
7.21–22   35
7.24–30   230
7.28   230n179
10.2–9   51n56
10.10–12   51nn56, 58
10.10–27   38n19
Gospel of Matthew
3   252

3.14   252
3.15   252
15.19   35n12
15.22–28   230
19.3–9   51
22.35   161n20
23.15   200
Gregory of Nyssa,
    Life of Macrina
2.33–34   121n17
Hebrews
6.4   144n97
Herodotus, *Histories*
1.86   189n40
2.37   189n40
Hippocrates, *On Regimen*
1.xxvii   17n61
Homeric Hymns
27.18   87n111
Isidorus of Seville, *Origins*
11.2.33   13n38
Jerusalem Talmud, *Sotah*
3.4   42n29
Jeremiah
9.1   158
Joel
2.28   66, 83
2.28–29   115
3.1–2   250n24
Josephus
    Against Apion
2.102–104   226n163
    Antiquities
2.346   86n107
3.276   207n96
12.137–44   198n66
13.171ff   65n37
13.298   65n37
13.311–13   65n37
16.164   91n119
18.81–84   181n11,
    225n158
18.255   170n48
18.259   58n4
19.276   58n4
20.17–53   181n10,
    222n143
20.34–35   226n164
20.92–96   181n10,
    222n143

20.100	58n4
20.139	199n68
20.189–90	224n156
20.189–98	181n13,
	222n149
20.191	224n157

Life

429	222n148,
	228n173

War

2.20.2	183n19
2.119–61	65n37
2.309–14	167n38
2.559–61	181n12
5.198–200	226n163

Judges

4.17–22	191n47

Julian

Letter 37	189n38
Letter 111	189n38
Against Heraclius the Cynic	189n38

Justin Martyr

Dialogue with Trypho

122.5	200n70

Second Apology

2.6	47n42
2.11	50n54
2.13–14	50n54

Justinian, *Novellae*

18.15	138n78

1 Kings

9.25	246n13

2 Kings

17.28	144n97
22.4	250n24

Letter of Aristeas

179.3	189n40

Leviticus

18.6–23	38
18.22	20
20.10–21	38
20.13	20
23.17	63

Livy, *Annals of Rome*

29.14	33n6
38.8	30n3
38.14	30n4
39.8–18	29n2

1 Maccabees

1.15	199n69

2 Maccabees

3.19	256

3 Maccabees

1.18–20	256

Nehemiah

6.14	250n24

Numbers

5.11–31	42
5.28	74n71
20.1	102
26.59	102

Origen, *Against Celsus*

3.44	51n59
7.5–6	249n23

Ovid, *Metamorphoses*

3.163–72	170n51

Passion of Saints Perpetua and Felicitas

2	206n91
20	167n38

Philo of Alexandria

Against Flaccus

89	167n38,
	256n46
121–22	107n159

Allegorical Interpretation

2.102	83n95,
	84n97

Hypothetica

11.14–17	76n78

Life of Moses

1.180	84n97,
	88–90, 96,
	99, 107
2.256	84n97, 89,
	95–97
2.256–57	89–90,
	98–99,
	105n152

On Agriculture

79	98
79–81	88
79–82	84nn97–98
80	92n124, 93,
	99
81	93, 95,
	100–101

81–82	92n129
82	85nn102, 104

On the Confusion of Tongues

36	84n97

On the Contemplative Life

1	76
2	58n6
13	61, 73n68,
	75nn74–75
18	61n16
21	58n7
29	93
30	111n166
31	58
32	60n13
33	74n69
34–35	58
37	58
65	59, 82n93
66	59, 60n14,
	62, 111n166
67	59, 62n18
68	60, 72
69	59, 61
72	61
75	59, 76n77
77	76
80	108n160
81	76
83	61, 93–95
83–88	59, 100
85	83n96,
	95n137
85–88	89
87	61, 96–97,
	106n155
88	95, 98
89	59

On Dreams

2.269–70	83n95,
	84n97, 89

On Drunkenness

111	84n97

On the Creation of the World

100	82n92,
	113n168

On the Embassy to Gaius

1.1	57n3

On the Migration of Abraham

Philo of Alexandria
   (*Continued*)
   151, 154   83n95
   On the Posterity of Cain
      and His Exile
   155–57   83n95
   On the Preliminary
      Studies
   104   83n95
   On the Soul
   58   57n3
   Special Laws
   3.62   74n71
   3.169–75   256n45
Pliny the Elder, *Natural*
   History
   5.17   65n37
Pliny the Younger,
   Letters
   10.96–97   248n18
Plutarch, *Life of Marius*
   38.3–4   49n49
Psalms
   9.7–8   156
   113–118   63n25
Pseudo-Clementines
   Recognitions
   7.32.2–4   230n177
   Homilies
   13.7.4   230n178

Romans
   1.26   36
   1.26–27   37
   1.29–31   35n12
   2.26   199n68

Juvenal, *Satires*
   6.542–47   250n25
   14.96–99   188n34

1 Samuel
   18.7   88n113
   21.11(12)   88n113
   29.5   88n113
The Sentences of
   Pseudo-Phocylides
   213–214   20n70
Severus of Minorca, *Letter*
   on the Conversion of
   the Jews
   5.1   154

6.2   161n20
6.6   154
7.2   155
8.2   178
8.5   155, 155n7
10.1–4   155
10.4–5   155
10.6   155
11.2   161n20
11.4   155n8
11.5   155n8
11.6   155
12.4   160n18
12.5–6   162
12.6   155n10,
         155
12.10   156n11,
         177
13.2   156, 156n12
13.3   156
13.7   156
13.3–12   165n34
13.11–12   156
13.12   157
16   177
16.2   157
16.4   157
16.7   157
16.8   157, 166n36
16.14–15   177
16.16   157
16.18   157n14
17.3   158
18.1   158
18.3   158
18.15   175
19.6   178
19.8–9   158
20.11   166n37
20.12   167n40
20.15   158
20.15–21   158
21.2   158, 168n43
21.3   159
23   159
24.1   168
24.2   170n52,
         171n55
24.4   170
24.5   170n53
24.10   171n56
26.1   159

27.1–3   172
27.2   172
28.5   174n63
30.2   153n24,
      159
31.2–3   159
Shepherd of Hermas,
   Commandments
   4.1.5–9   49n52
Sifre Deuteronomy
   46   42n30
Song of Songs
   6.8   155n9
Strabo, *Geography*
   7.3.3   189n40

Tacitus, *Annals*
   13.32   182n16
Tertullian
   On Baptism
   17   119n6
   On the Apparel of
      Women
   1.1   118n2
   On the Prescription of
      Heretics
   41   118n4
   On the Soul
   9   119n8, 172n58,
         252n32
   On the Veiling of
      Virgins
   9.   118n1
Testament of
   Naphtali
   1.10   189n40
Theocles
   8.62   87n111
Theocritus, *Idyll*
   15   255n43
Theodosian Code
   15.9.2   138n78
1 Timothy
   1.9–10   35n12
   2.12   125, 148
   4.7   125
   5.9   41
   6.4   35n12
2 Timothy
   3.2–4   35n12
   3.6   39, 125
   3.6–7   169n46

Titus

2.3 35*n*13

3.3 35*n*12

Tosefta *Megillah*

3.11 42*n*31

3.11–12 236*n*204

Xenophon, *Ephesian Tale*

4.3 248*n*19

5.4 248*n*19

INSCRIPTIONS AND PAPYRI

Note: Inscriptions catalogued in *JIWE* and *IJO* are not also indexed with the corresponding citations in *CIJ* (or elsewhere), which may be found in the footnotes. Only inscriptions not included in *JIWE* or *IJO* are indexed as *CIJ*, etc.

CIJ

1.159 208*n*102

1.576 203*n*7

1²731e 217*n*124

CIRB

70 208*n*100

71 208*n*100

73 208*n*100

CPJ

1.146 208*n*99

Gregg and Urman 1996

Fiq 22 191*n*48

JIWE

1.5 232*n*184

1.53 233*n*189

1.59 180*n*6

1.62 180*n*6

1.63 232*n*184

1.68 161*n*20

1.71 180*n*6

1.85 161*n*20

1.90 161*n*20

1.113 217*n*124

1.114 161*n*20

1.116 232*n*184

1.185 216*n*120

1.202 215*n*117

2.24 180*n*6

2.62 181*n*7, 203*n*78, 206*n*89

2.91 203*n*80

2.100 204*n*86

2.163 204*n*86

2.167 204*n*86

2.207 216*n*122, 217*n*126

2.209 161*n*20

2.210 161*n*20

2.218 203*n*78, 207*n*94

2.224 203*n*78, 208*n*101

2.251 232*n*184

2.288 161*n*20, 204*n*86, 233*n*189

2.364 191.48

2.392 203*nn*78, 82

2.489 203*n*78, 205*n*88, 209*n*104

2.491 203*n*78, 205*n*88

2.540 161*n*20

2.542 232*n*184

2.544 161*n*20

2.547 233*n*189

2.560 161*n*20, 204*n*86

2.576 161*n*20

2.577 179, 203*n*78, 232*n*184

2.578 161*n*20

2.579 161*n*20

2.584 161*n*20

2.626 214*n*112

2.626i 214*n*113

2.626ii 214*n*114

2.626iii 214*n*114

2.626iv 214*n*114

2.627i 217*n*124

IAph

11.55 191*n*43

IGR

4.1340 218*n*130, 219*n*133

IJO

I *Ach*3 232*n*183

I *Ach*40 210*n*108

I *Ach*66 210*n*109

I *Ach*67 210*n*109

I *Thr*3 180*n*6

2.6 217*n*128

2.14 191*nn*43, 47, 203*n*79, 221*n*142

2.27 191*n*48, 217*n*124, 218*n*130

2.36 258*n*54

2.37 210*n*108, 216*n*121

2.38 216*n*121

2.39 216*n*121

2.43 179

2.49 217*n*125

2.63 161*n*20

2.168 219*n*135

2.179 210*n*108

2.190 210*n*108

2.241 210*n*108

2.255 180*n*4

3 *Syr*9 200*n*72, 203*n*79

3 *Syr*72 201*n*72

3 *Syr*84 201*n*72

Lifshitz 1961

115–16 no.2 203*n*78

MAMA

6.264 219*n*135

Paton and Hicks 1891

278 217*n*128

PGM

4.685 189*n*40

SEG

17 (1960), 785 201*n*72

27 (1977), 1201 180*n*6

TAM

III.118 138*n*78

III.226 138*n*78

III.327 138*n*78

III.386 138*n*78

III.429 138*n*78

III.456 138*n*78

General Index

Acts of Andrew, 122, 146
Acts of John, 122, 146
Acts of Peter, 122, 146
Acts of Thomas, 27, 34, 122, 146, 243
   adultery, 38
   appropriate gendered behavior, 39
   as critiquing or negating gender constructions, 41
   false speech, 39
   homosexuality, 37–38
   punishments in, 40–41
   sexual practices, 36–38
   shame, 39
   sins, 35
   torments of hell, 34
adoptive parents, 212
adultery in antiquity, 38, 38n18
after-dinner discourses
   in Plato's and Xenophon's *Symposia*, 72
   of the Therapeutae, 79
afterlife torments, 34
akolastos, 47, 50
Alexander, 58
Alexander (Syriarches), 138, 141–42
Ameling, W., 201n75, 216n121, 217, 217n124, 218
Amengual i Batle, J., 154n5, 160n17
Amsler, F., 148n107
ancient Christianity

interpretations of, 8
scholarly reading of, 9–10
texts, 7–8
Annia, Paculla, 30
Anson, J., 19n67
anti-Jewish writings, 160
Aphrodisias inscriptions, 192
apocryphal *Acts*, 123
   Cooper's analysis, 130
apologetic treatises, 58
apostle Peter, 62
Arcadius, 163
archēgissa, 232
archisynagōgos, 180, 232–36, 239
Arjava, A., 38n18
arsenokoitai, 36
Artemisia, 159, 168
artistic representations of women, 3–4, 40
Asad, T., 21, 21n75, 180n2
ascetic celibacy of Christian women, 19, 149 (*see also* Thecla, story of)
   female autonomy, 150
   Tertullian's views, 117–20
   transgression of ancient gender conventions, 136–43
ascetic Christianity (*see also* Roman legal prosecution, of Christians)
   Christian wife in Justin's narrative, 52
   illicit sexual practices, 34

male homosexuality, 37
women in, 19 (*see also* ascetic celibacy of
    Christian women)
Aseneth, 189, 245
Atkindon, P.C., 115*n*170
Attridge, H., 144*n*97
Atwood, M., 247, 247*n*15
Aubin, M., 123*n*26, 133*nn*66–67, 136*n*72,
    139*nn*80–82, 140*n*85, 141*n*88,
    142*n*91
authorial intention, in reading of texts,
    8–9
Aymer, M., 123*n*26

Bacchae, 3
Bacchic rites, 27, 243
    decree related to, 29
    gendered elements, 29
    Livy's account, 30–31, 33
    prophesy, 31
    punishments rewarded to
        performers, 32
    revised rules, 29, 32
    women's participation, 32–33
Bacchus, 29
Baer, R. A., 64*n*29
Bainbridge, W., 21*n*74
Baker, C., 40*n*24, 255*n*42, 268*n*76,
    270*n*82
banqueting practices, 71–72
Barnard, L. W., 47*nn*40–41, 47*n*45, 50*n*55
Barthes, R., 10
Baskin, J., 265*n*70
Beard, M., 6*n*12, 7*n*14
Beavis, M. A., 66*n*39
Bellen, H., 190*n*42
Bernays, J., 190*n*42
Betz, H. D., 65*n*38
Biblical law, on homosexuality, 38
Blázquez, J. M., 163*n*24
Bleiberg, E., 259*n*55
Bloedhorn, H., 201*n*75
Blumenkranz, B., 160, 160*n*16, 183*n*19
b'nai Yisrael, 84, 86–87
Bodel, J., 202*n*77, 209*n*103, 246*n*14
Bonnet, M., 121*n*15, 133*n*67, 145*n*104
Bonz, M. P., 191*n*44
Boswell, J., 37*n*17
Boterman, H., 191*n*14
Boughton, L., 123*n*26, 126, 126*n*42,
    127*nn*44–45, 129*n*58, 143*n*92, 146
Bourdieu, P., 9, 9*n*21, 14*n*50, 16, 67, 69,
    78, 111*n*166, 137*n*75, 227*n*166, 240,

259–60, 260*n*56, 261, 261*nn*59–60,
    262, 262*n*61, 262*nn*63–65, 265,
    265*n*71, 266, 272*n*87, 273
Bouvier, B., 148*n*107
Bovon, F., 121*n*15, 148*n*107
Bowie, E., 124*n*33
Boyarin, D., 4*n*6, 7*n*14, 14*n*50, 15,
    15*nn*53–55, 20–21, 21*nn*76–77, 180*n*2
Boyd, B., 11*n*31
Boyer, P., 22*n*80
Bradbury, S., 153*n*3, 154*nn*5–6, 155*n*9,
    158*n*15, 160, 160*nn*16–19, 161*n*20,
    162, 163*n*24, 164*n*32, 165, 167,
    167*n*40, 168, 168*n*41, 168*nn*43–44,
    169, 170*n*52, 171*n*55, 173, 173*n*60,
    174*n*63, 175, 175*n*64, 178
Bremmer, J., 120*n*13, 121*n*18, 123*n*26, 127,
    127*n*44, 129*n*58, 132*n*64, 133*n*65,
    140*n*85, 141*n*90, 142*n*91, 146, 244*n*5
Brooten, B., 12*n*34, 35*n*12, 36*n*15, 37*n*17,
    51*n*58, 161*n*20, 175*n*65, 179, 180*n*44,
    183*n*19, 184–85, 191*n*47, 204*n*86,
    205, 221*n*142, 232, 232*nn*182–83,
    233–34, 237*n*206, 238, 258*n*52
Brown, P., 23, 128
Brumberg-Kraus, J., 79, 79, 79*n*88
Buckser, A., 187, 196*n*58
Buell, D., 186*n*31, 196*n*59
Burridge, K., 4, 4*n*4, 64, 64*n*28, 122*n*25,
    149, 149*n*111, 150
Burrus, C., 123*n*26, 125
Burrus, V., 123*n*26, 125*n*38, 126,
    126*nn*39–40, 129*n*58, 139*n*81,
    141*n*88, 146, 151
Butler, R., 14*n*50, 15, 15*n*55, 115*n*170
Bynum, C. W., 14*n*48, 14*n*50

Caecilianus, 158, 169
Caligula, Emperor, 68
Calzolari, V., 121*n*15
Cameron, Al, 216*n*121
Cameron, Av, 7*n*14, 128*n*50
Cansdale, L., 65*n*38, 77*n*79
Carson, A., 40*n*24, 137*n*77
Castelli, E., 14*n*50, 123*n*26, 135, 244*n*2,
    262*n*62
Celsus, 182
Chaeremon's work, 68
Chaniotis, A., 191*n*44
chōrizō, 50, 51*n*56
Christian, W. A., 21*n*74
Christian asceticism, 4
Christian monastics, 62–63

Christian rhetorical strategies, 135
Chrysostom, John, 182
Church, F. F., 119nn7–8
cinaedus, notion of, 18–19
circumcision practice, 198,
    199nn68–69
Clark, E., 7–8, 7n15, 8, 8nn17–19, 9,
    9n22, 10, 10nn23–29, 11, 11n30, 69,
    130n59, 147, 175n66, 223, 260n57
Claudius, Emperor, 67
Clines, D. J. A., 270n80
Cobb, S., 244n2
coerced conversion, 28
Cohen, S. J. D., 162n21, 180n2, 183n19,
    188n34, 192n50, 194–95, 197n61,
    198n67
Cohn, L., 57n1
Cole, S. G., 13n42, 27n96, 33n5, 204n84,
    246nn10–12, 246n14
Colson, F., 57n1, 58n9, 60nn11–12,
    60nn14–15, 85, 85n104, 90, 90n116,
    91nn118–19, 92nn125–28, 94, 96,
    98n143, 99n145, 111n166
Connell, R., 269n79
Connelly, J. B., 246n10
contextualism, 8n19
conversion of Jews. See Letter on the
    Conversion of the Jews
Conybeare, F. C., 57n1, 60n11, 63, 63n25,
    121n17, 144n98
Cooper, K., 7n14, 52, 52n61, 52nn63–64,
    53, 53n65, 123n26, 123n30, 127–33,
    127n44, 127nn46–48, 128,
    128nn52–54, 129, 129nn55–58,
    130, 130nn60–61, 131, 131n62, 132,
    132n63, 135, 140–41, 141n86,
    143n92, 145–48, 170, 170n47, 223,
    227, 227n167, 228n171
Corinthian women, 40, 136
Corley, K., 80n89
Corrington, G. P., 57n1
Cotton, H., 256n44
Crawford, S. W., 77n79
Crook, Z. A., 186n30, 187n32

Dagron, G., 121n17, 253n35
D'Angelo, M. R., 39n21, 40n24, 125n35,
    137n77, 151n115, 182n15, 254nn39–40
Daumas, F., 57n1
Davidman, L., 266, 266n74
Davies, P. R., 77n79
Davies, S. J., 123, 124, 126, 128, 129n58,
    141n87, 146, 150n112, 151

Davis, S. J., 121n15, 121n17, 122n19,
    122n23, 123, 123n26, 127n44,
    128n50, 129, 145n103, 146–47,
    147nn105–6, 150, 150n114, 152
de Palol, P., 163n24
dekania, 232
Delaney, C., 113n169, 197n62,
    262n61
Derrida, J., 8, 8n18
des Bouvrie, S., 33n5
Devreese, R., 121n15
Dillon, M., 246n10
Dionysos (Bakxos), 29
Divjak, J., 160n17
Divorce
    in Mosaic law, 49n51
    Paul's views, 50–51
Dodds, E. R., 3, 3n2, 4
Douglas, M., 5, 5n11, 25, 65, 78n86, 266,
    268
    grid/group theory, 65
DuBois, P., 113n169, 197n62
Dunn, P., 123n26, 126, 126n42,
    127nn44–45, 129n58, 146
Durkheim, É., 20, 20n73, 196n58, 245n7

ecstatic devotion, 4
Egyptian priests, 68
Eilberg-Schwartz, H., 198n67
Eisen, U., 237n206
Eliade, M., 24–25
Elliott, J. H., 4n6, 21n77, 22n78, 180n2
Elliott, J. K., 4n6, 21n77, 22n78, 180n2
Elm, S., 119n8
Engberg-Pedersen, T., 66, 66n39, 67,
    67nn40–45, 68–69, 69nn51–52,
    70, 70nn55–56, 71, 71nn59–61, 72,
    72n63, 77, 77n82, 78, 78nn85–87,
    79–80, 82, 82n94, 83, 107, 110, 114
Engberg-Pedersen's poststructuralist
    analysis of gender, 77–79, 82n94
Eno, R.B., 160n17
Ephrata cloister, Lancaster County, 63
Essenes, 65
Eusebius of Caesarea, 62, 68
Evans, E., 119n9
Exodus 15
    choirs, 91, 94–96, 103, 106–7
    exegesis of, 96–101, 105
    in Greek text, 87–88
    in Hebrew text, 84–87
    Life of Moses, Philo's treatment in,
        89–90, 101

Exodus 15 (*continued*)
  metaphors, 90–94
  Miriam's actions, 84–88
  On Agriculture, Philo's treatment in,
    90–94, 98–99
  On the Contemplative Life, Philo's
    treatment in, 94–96, 98, 107–9
  Philo's accounts of song and singers,
    88–96, 101, 105
  plural *hymns*, 90, 97, 107
  thanksgiving hymns, 89–90, 99
  verbs in, 86–87, 93
Exodus from Egypt, 158
Eyl, J., 61n16, 251n29

false speech, 39
falsehoods, 39
Faraone, C., 245n7
Feldman, L., 91n120, 183n19, 184n24,
    188n35, 189, 189n37, 190, 190n42,
    192n50, 199n68, 214n112, 222n143,
    222n150, 225, 225n159, 256n48
Felicitas, 180
female, active *vs.* passive, 18–19
female heroines in Greco-Roman
    novels, 123
female sexual gratification,
    rabbinic view, 46
feminine seed, 17
feminist study of religion, 4
  Clark's arguments on ancient accounts
    of, 8–10
Festival of Fifty. *See* Mareotic Feast of
    Fifty
Ficker, G., 172n57
Figueras, P., 200n72
Finke, R., 196n58
Finn, T. M., 190n42
Fischler, S., 227n167
Fishbane, S., 245n9
Flaccus, Governor, 107
Flavia Domitilla, 181
Florianus, 158
Foley, H. P., 133n68
Fontaine, J., 160n17
foster parents, 212
Foucault, M., 36n16, 52
Frankenberry, N. K., 25n92
Frazer, J., 21n74
Frey, J. B., 201n75, 203n78, 203n80,
    206n90, 213, 214n115, 217
Frier, B., 205n87, 207n98
Friesen, S., 239, 239n208

Gafney, W. C., 250n24
Gager, J., 123n26, 187n32
Galilaeus, 158
Gamble, H., 124n33
Gardner, J. F., 38n18, 197n64
Geerard, M., 121n15
Geertz, C., 21, 21n74, 24nn87–88
Gelenius, 119
gender, study of, 14–20
  ancient Mediterranean, 14–15
  biological bases, 14
  as a category of analysis, 14
  conversion, 196–98
  in cultural context, 15
  in early Christian martyrdom
    narratives, 135
  gender division of Therapeutae, 61,
    70n58, 71
  Parker's four-quadrant grid model,
    18–19
  representation of women in ancient
    narratives, 34–41
  Roman notions, 32
  social construction, 16
  unnatural sexual practices and
    hierarchical notions of gender,
    36–37
  gender identities, 17–18
Gentile women, interest in Judean
    practices. *See* non-Judean women,
    adopting Judean practices
gestation, theory of, 17
Gibson, E. L., 208n100
Gilbert, G., 191n44, 221n142
Ginzburg, C., 164n33, 176n67, 177n69
Glancy, J. A., 20n71, 39n21, 125n35
Glazier, S. D., 187n32, 196n58
Gleason, M., 18n65, 139n82
Goff, B., 13n42, 27n96, 33n5, 246n10,
    247, 247n15, 264
Golb, N., 65n38
Golden Bough (James Frazer), 21n74
Goldhill, S., 128n50
Goldstein, A. S., 183nn19–20, 187n32
Gomme, A. W., 238n207
Goodenough, E. R., 68n47, 215n118,
    218n132, 259n55
Goodman, J., 149n110, 249n22
Goodman, M., 182n16, 187n32, 192n50,
    200, 200n71, 201, 201n73
Graecina, Pomponia, 182
Graf, F., 245n7
Grafton, A., 187n32

Grant, R., 48, 48nn47–49, 49, 49n50, 49n53, 51, 51n57, 52, 52n60, 53n65
Greco-Roman Mediterranean vocabulary, 12
Greco-Roman period, women's religious behaviors, 4–6, 28, 30, 39–40, 40n24, 64
Greeks and the Irrational, The (E. R. Dodds), 3
Greek banqueting practices, 72
Green, G., 8n16
Greenfield, J., 256n44
Gregg, R., 191n48
Griffith, M., 266, 266n74
Groag, E., 219nn133–134
Grossman, M. L., 77n79
Grubbs, J. E., 38n18
Gunderson, E., 18n65
Guthrie, S. E., 23n84
Gutschow, K., 149n108, 266, 266n74, 268n76

Hague, L., 121
Haines-Eitzen, K., 145n99
Hak, D., 196n58
Halperin, D., 7n14, 15n51, 36n16, 80, 80n90
Hambenne, B., 160n17
Hänninen, M.-L., 33n7
Hanson, A. E., 12n35, 197n63
Harding, S., 14n45
Harnack, A., 121n18, 182, 182n18
Harraway, D., 14, 14n45, 14n49
Harrell, S., 14n48
Harrison, V., 65n30, 91n119, 113, 113n168, 265n72
Harvey, Y. K., 268n76
Hauptman, J., 45n39
Hay, D., 65, 65n33, 67n46, 82n94, 106, 109–10, 113
headcoverings, of women Greco-Roman period, 39–40, 40n24
Heine, R., 119n7, 172n57
Hengel, M., 88n113
Henrichs, A., 33n5
Her Share of the Blessings (R. S. Kraemer), 6, 27–28
hermeneutics, 7
Hezser, C., 207n93
Hicks, E. L., 217n128
Hilhorst, A., 119–20, 119n9, 120, 120nn11–12, 122n23, 129n57, 133, 144, 144nn95–96

Hillard, T., 227, 227n167
Hillgarth, J. N., 160n17, 163n24
Hinde, R. A., 22n80
historical narratives, 10
ho monos sōter, 95, 100
Hodge, C. J., 186n31, 196n59
Hoff, J., 11n31
hoi alloi, 108–9
homosexuality, views of
    in ascetic Christianity, 37
    Biblical law, 38
    Roman law, 38
Honorius, 163
Hopkins, K. R., 204n83, 208n99
Horbury, W., 88n113, 91n119, 201n75, 206, 233, 233n188, 235, 235nn196–98, 236, 236nn201–2, 236n204, 238, 238n207, 258nn52–53
human reproduction theory, 16–17
Hunt, E. D., 160n17

Iael, 191
idolatry, 36
Ilan, T., 42nn29–30, 77n79, 258n53
illicit sexual practices, in ancient narratives, 34–36
Ingersoll, J., 266n74
Innocentius, 168–69
Inowlocki, S., 60n11, 62n22
Irshai, O., 161n20, 177n69

Jacobs, A. S., 123n26, 153n2, 177, 177n68, 177n70, 181n9
James, W., 20, 20n73, 21n74, 22–23, 199n68
Janowitz, N., 245n7
Jastrow, M., 86n108
Jay, N., 198, 198n67, 246n12, 264, 264n69
Jeffery, P., 91n120, 95n136, 98n142, 105n152, 106n157, 108n161
Jewish scriptures, Christians in, 135
Johnson, S. F., 121n17, 123n26, 253n35
Jonah, 173–74
Jones, H. S., 12n36, 47n41, 60n11, 87n111, 91n111, 92n121, 92n122, 143n93, 144n97, 170n49, 201n73, 218n131
Judean, as alternative translation for "Jew," 26, 180
Judean contemplatives, 57, 68, 107–8
    (see also Therapeutae)
Juschka, D., 204n83, 262n62

Justin Martyr, story of Roman Christian matron, 47–55

Kaestli, J. D., 123n26, 124n34
Kearsley, R. A., 239, 239n208
Kelley, N., 231, 231n180
King, U., 14, 262n62
Kippenberg, H. G., 245n7
Kitch, S., 149n108, 268n76
Klass, M., 21n74, 24nn87–88
Klawiter, F. C., 119n7
Kleiner, D. B. B., 137n76
Koch, D. A., 189n36, 191n44, 192nn50–51
Konstan, D., 123n26, 180n2
Kraabel, A. T., 189n36, 190, 190n41
Kraemer, R. S., 4n3, 4n5, 5nn9–10, 7n15,
    14n43, 27nn94–95, 28n97, 42n28,
    54n68, 61n16, 65nn30–32, 74n71,
    77n79, 109n163, 115n170, 118n5,
    119n7, 122n21, 122n24, 123n28,
    124nn33–34, 126n41, 126n43,
    153, 173n61, 179, 180n3, 180n6,
    181n8, 181n13, 182n18, 184n24,
    186n31, 187n33, 189n40, 192n50,
    201n75, 204n83, 204n85, 205n88,
    210nn106–7, 211n110, 215n118,
    219n135, 227n169, 232n182,
    233n186, 244n5, 245n6, 247n17,
    248n20, 251n29, 256n44, 256n47,
    257nn50–51, 258nn53–54, 265n70,
    267n75, 272n86
Kraft, R. A., 58n4, 62n22, 63, 64n26,
    89n114
Kron, U., 204n84
Krüger, G., 47n40
Kuefler, M., 14n50, 15, 16nn56–59, 17,
    269n79, 271, 273

Lactantius, 17
Lagarde, P., 229n176
Lampe, P., 48, 48n47, 49, 49n51, 51n57,
    53, 53n65, 91n119, 182n14, 182n16,
    218n131
Lamphere, L., 14n44
Lander, S. L., 5n9, 115n170, 145n99,
    153n3, 244n5
Lanternari, V., 64n28
LaQueur, T., 16n59
Larson, J., 270n80
Latin vocabulary, 12–13
Latour, B., 11n31
Le Bohec, Y., 201n75, 214n115
LeClercq, H., 121n18

Lefkowitz, M. R., 5n9
Leon, H. J., 183nn19–20, 204n83,
    214n112
Leonhardt, J., 85n102, 85n104
Letter on the Conversion of the Jews,
    (Severus of Minorca), 153–54
    authenticity and historicity of,
        159–64
    burning of synagogue, 162–64
    conversion accounts of Jewish women,
        158–59, 164–74
    dreams, as evidence of divine origins
        and trustworthiness, 155
    social dynamics between Jewish and
        Christian communities, 155–58
    story of Jewish retreat and control of
        synagogue, 156–57
    story of the greedy slave, 156
    summary, 154–59
    violence, 156
Levarie, S., 91n120
Levene, D. S., 33n7
Levine, L., 232n184, 233, 233n188, 235,
    235n195, 235nn199–200, 236,
    236n204, 237, 237nn205–206,
    258nn52–53
Levinskaya, I., 190n41, 192n50, 216n121,
    217n123, 217n127, 219n134, 219n136,
    220, 220nn138–139
Levinson, J., 16, 16nn59–60, 17n61,
    18, 18n66, 113n169, 268, 268n78,
    272n86
Levi-Strauss, C., 128, 128n49, 129n58,
    260
Lewis, I. M., 4, 4n4, 122n25, 137n76
Lewis, N., 256n44
Lieu, J., 54n68, 182n18, 183n19, 184,
    184nn23–24, 185, 185nn25–27, 187,
    187n33, 202, 223
Lifshitz, B., 184n21, 190n42, 191n48,
    201n75, 203n78, 203n80, 217,
    217nn124–125, 219n135
Linder, A., 163nn25–28, 164,
    164nn29–31, 176n67, 183n20,
    189n36, 202n76, 207n93, 232n185,
    272n87
Lipsius, R. A., 121n15, 133n67, 145n104
literary-critical theory, 11
Livy, Titus, 27, 29–34, 54, 184
    defamation of Bacchanalia, 30–31,
        33–34
Lucius, E., 47–48, 50, 63, 63n24
Luck, G., 245n7

Luiselli, B., 119n9
Luomanen, P., 22n80
Lutz, C. E., 73n67
Lyons, D., 27n96

MacCormick, C., 14, 14n46
MacDonald, D. R., 121n18, 123n26, 124,
    124n34, 125, 125n37, 126n41, 129n57
MacDonald, M. Y., 53, 53nn65–67,
    128n52, 255n41
Mack, B. L., 6n13
MacLennan, R. S., 189n36, 190n41
Maenadism, 3
Magness, J., 65n38, 77n79, 221n141
Mahmood, S., 266n74
Mandel, P., 42n31
Mareotic community, 63, 67 (see also
    Exodus 15; Philo of Alexandria;
    Therapeutae)
Mareotic Feast of Fifty, 59–61, 80–81, 83
Marsh, R., 262n66
Marshall, J., 251n31
Martin, D. B., 7n14, 250n26
Martin, T., 40n26
Martyr, Justin, 28, 46, 200, 243
Marxist-based "cultural" theory, 11
masculine seed, 17
Mason, S., 4n6, 21, 21n77, 22, 22n78,
    26, 180, 180n2, 193, 193nn54–55,
    194–95, 194n56, 225n160, 271n84
Matheson, S. B., 137n76
Matthews, S., 52n62, 123n26, 126,
    126n41, 127n44, 128, 128nn50–51,
    129, 129n58, 146–47, 167–68,
    170, 174, 182n15, 185, 185nn27–28,
    204n85, 222n150, 223, 223nn151–55,
    227, 227n165, 228, 228nn171–72,
    229
McCutcheon, R., 6n13
McDonnell, M. A., 18n65
McDowell, M., 248n19
McGinn, S. E., 123n26
McKnight, S., 187n32
Meletius, 158, 168
men (see also Therapeutae; Therapeutae
    (masc. pl))
    active vs. passive, 18–19
    adultery, 38
    Bacchic service, 29–32
    and conversion, 196–98
    as God-fearers, 199
    male domination, 273
    masculinity, 18–20

Parker's grid, 18–19
proselytes, 198–99
prostitutes, 35–36
rabbinic paradigm of Torah study, 272
and religion, 21–22
Roman punishments, 32
Severus's representation, 158, 168–74,
    178
sodomites, 36
as subject to womanly influence,
    227–29
subordination of women, 15–16
theory of human reproduction, 16–17
Therapeutic singing, 108
Torah reading, 43–44
Menand, L., 11n31
Mesnartius, 119
Meyer, M., 245n7
Mierow, C. C., 182n16
Miles, M., 139n80
Milgrom, J., 20n70
Miller, P. C., 7n14
Mills, K., 187n32
Minorcan Jewish men, 272
Minorcan Jewish women, 165
    Artemisia, conversion to Christianity,
        170–72
    Innocentius's widowed sister-in-law,
        conversion to Christianity, 173–74
    stubbornness, 165
    Theodorus's wife, conversion to
        Christianity, 168–70
    violent behavior of unnamed groups,
        156, 165–67
Miquel, P., 57n1
Mirecki, S., 245n7
Miriam the prophetess, 84–88
    in Life of Moses 2 and Agriculture, 102–3
    On the Contemplative Life, 102–4
    in Philo's accounts, 101
    use of exarchein, 102–3
Mishnah, 41, 42
misrecognition, 9
Mitchell, M. M., 250n26
Mitchell, S., 193n53
Mobius, H., 217n123
Mommsen, T., 182
monastic Judeans, 57–58, 64, 70, 73n68,
    74
Moore, G. F., 183, 183n19, 189n36
Munier, C., 49n51
Musurillo, H., 47n40, 47n44, 48n49,
    182n15

Nature, Culture, Gender (C. MacCormick
    and M. Strathern), 14
Neyrey, J., 111, 111nn164–65, 270, 270n81
Ng, E. Y. L., 123n26, 127n44
Niditch, S., 7n14
Nir, R., 249n21
Nock, A. D., 187n32
non-Judean women, adopting Judean
    practices, 180–81
  Brooten's work, 184
  category of "God-fearers," 193, 195
  Cohen's arguments, 194–95
  Dio Cassius, writings of, 181–82
  conversion and veneration of gods,
    distinction, 186–87, 190, 193
  elite Roman women as patrons of
    Judeans, 229
  gender issues, 196–98
  Greek and Latin references, 189
  Hellenistic period, 194–95
  inscriptions, 190–92
  Josephus, writings of, 181, 183, 221–23
  Josephus's narrative of Fulvia,
    225–26
  Lieu's arguments, 184–85
  Mason's argument, 193–95
  Matthews' arguments, 185, 223,
    226–28
  in Pseudo-Clementines, 229–31
  punishments, 181–82
  Queen Helena of Adiabene,
    narrative of, 226
  rabbinic references, 188, 190
  relationship between ethnicity and
    devotion to deities, 194–97
  theosebēs inscriptions, 224–25
  theosebēs as general piety, 192–93
  veneration of Judean god, 195–96
normative sex, 36
Noy, D., 161n20, 179, 180n1, 191n48,
    201n75, 206n90, 206n92, 207n97,
    210n107, 214, 214n112, 214n114,
    215, 215n116, 215n119, 216n120,
    217n124, 232n182, 232n184, 233,
    233nn188–189, 234, 234nn191–193,
    235–36, 236n204, 237–39

O'Connor, J. M., 192n50
O'Donnell, J. J., 252n33
Olyan, S., 20n70, 85, 85n102,
    87nn109–10, 186n30, 246n14
On the Contemplative Life (Philo)
  allegorical interpretation of choirs by

Red sea, 84, 94–96, 98, 107–9
  authenticity of, 65–66
  Brumberg-Kraus' observations, 79
  divergent readings, 67–70, 72
  Engberg-Pedersen's poststructuralist
    analysis of gender, 67–71, 77–79
  Miriam and Moses, portrayal of, 102–4
  Philo's rhetorical purposes of
    contemporaneous practices, 72
  similarities with Chaeremon, 68
  Taylor's contextual approach, 67–73
  unspecified "hymns," 105
  women (Therapeutrides), description
    of, 60, 62, 64, 70, 72–73, 80–81
Ortner, S. B., 14, 260, 260n58
Osiek, C., 53, 53nn65–67, 128n52, 255n41
Oster, R. E., 40n26
Overman, J. A., 192n50
Oyewùmí, O., 12n34

Panayotov, A., 201n75
Parker, H., 13, 13n41, 18–20, 36n16, 118n3,
    149n109
Paton, W. R., 217n128
patristics. *See* ancient Christianity
Paulina, 181
Paul's Corinthian correspondence, 35
  views of separation/divorce, 50–51
Perkins, J., 5n9, 135, 135n71, 244n2,
    244n5
Pesthy, M., 121n17
Petersen, W. L., 36n14
Petropoulous, J. C., 121n18, 123n26,
    138n79
Pfuhl, E., 217n123
Philo of Alexandria, 57 (*see also*
    Therapeutae)
  accounts of song and singers, 88–96,
    101, 105
  choirs, characterization of, 94, 101
    (*see also* Exodus 15)
  debates on writings of, 62–66
    (*see also* On the Contemplative Life)
  exegesis of Exodus 15, 83–88, 96–101
  Therapeutae, representation of, 66,
    96–101, 109–14
  Therapeutic women philosophers,
    characterization of, 19
  Therapeutrides, characterization of,
    81 (*see also* Taylor's analysis of the
    Therapeutrides)
Plotina, Pompeia, 182
Pollard, E., 245, 245n8

Pomeroy, S., 14n43
Poppaea, Sabina, 181
postmodernism, 11
Price, S., 142n91
privilege authorial intentions, 9
prophesy, notion of, 31
proselytes in Greco-Roman inscriptions,
    180 (see also non-Judean women,
    adopting Judean practices)
    administrative tasks, 237–40
    ambiguities, 209–13
    Crysis, 208–9
    dating of inscriptions, 201–2
    dedications in, 208–9, 212
    Felicitas, 206–8
    hermeneutical issues, 210–11
    "honorary" titles, 184, 233, 235
    Justa, 230–31
    proportion of male and female, 202–4
    Rufina of Smyrna, 179–80, 184
    Sara of Cyrene, 181, 205, 209
    slaves, 207–8
    Sophia, 180
    term proselyte, 200–201
    Veturia Paula, 180, 204–5
prostatēs, 232
Pseudo-Clementines, 229–31
Ptolemaeus, 47–50
Pyysiäinen, I., 22n80

Queen of Adiabene, 181
Qumran, 45n37, 65, 77n79, 100

rabbis, 19
Rajak, T., 180n1, 233, 233nn188–89, 234,
    234nn191–93, 235–36, 236n204,
    237–39
Ramazangolu, C., 11n31
Rawson, B., 14n48
reading strategies, 8–9
Red Sea performance. See Exodus 15
Refoulé, F., 119n9
Rehm, B., 229n176
Reiter, R., 14n45, 57n1
religion, 20–28
    ancient terminology, 26
    as an ideological category, 21
    category of "Jew," 26
    cognitive theory of, 22–25
    definitions of, 20–24
    gendered as male, 6–7
    and gender issues, 246–59
    and power, 259–65

rabbinic view, 21, 21n77
    and social consequences of gender
        hierarchy, 266–74
    Stowers's definition, 23–24
religious practices, as compensation for
    deprivation, 64
religious practices, of women
    baptism, 252–53
    distinction between religion and
        magic, 245
    healing and exorcism of demons, 253
    issues of spatial differentiation, 255–59
    prayer, 248–49
    prophecy, 249–50
    singing hymns, 250–52
    traveling, 254–55
remarriage, 51n58
reproductive seed, 16–17
repudium, 47–48, 48n49
Reuben, 155, 157
Reynolds, J. M., 191n43
Riaud, J., 65n33
Richman, P., 14n48
Riley, D., 12n34
Ringrose, K., 249n22
Robert, L., 217, 217n127
Roberts, E., 271n83
Rohde, E. R., 123n30
Roman law, on homosexuality, 38
Roman legal prosecution, of Christians,
    47–55
Roman males, 18
Rordorf, W., 119, 119n10, 120nn12–13,
    121n15, 121n17, 122n23, 124, 124n32,
    129n57, 141n87
Rosaldo, M. Z., 14n44
Rosenblum, J., 171n54, 201n73
Rouché, C., 216n121
Rousselle, A., 16n59
Rubin, G., 14n45, 264n69
Rufina of Smyrna, 179–80
Rufus, Musonius, 73
Runia, D.T., 58n5, 62n22, 63n25
Rutgers, L., 181n9, 204n83, 215n118

Saller, R., 20n71, 227n165
Santoro L'Hoir, F. E., 13n40
Sara, 181
Satlow, M., 7n14, 19n68, 43–45, 245,
    245n9, 268, 268n78
Saussure, F. de., 260n57
Schäfer, P., 245n7
Scheiber, S., 180n4, 198n66, 215n116

Schiffman, L., 65n38, 77n79

Schneemelcher, W., 120n12, 121n18, 126, 126n43, 146

Schuller, E., 77n79

Schürer, E., 63, 220n139

Schüssler Fiorenza, E., 128n52, 250n26, 254n39, 255n41

Schwartz, S., 198n66

Scott, J., 14n50

Sealey, R., 38n18

Segal, A., 187n32

Segui Vidal, J., 160n19, 163n24

Seigert, F., 190n42

Senatus Consultum, 29, 32

Sered, S., 262n62, 266nn73–74, 268n76

Severus of Minorca, accounts on conversion. See Letter on the Conversion of the Jews

sex
  between men, 19
  rabbinic ideas, 45–46
  Roman definitions of, 19

Sexual Meanings: The Cultural Construction of Gender and Sexuality (S. Ortner and H. Whitehead), 14

sexuality in antiquity, 36
  women prophets, 149

Shaw, B., 135, 135n71, 244n5

Sheridan, S. G., 77n79

Shipton, P., 186n30

Short, C., 12n36, 13n38, 13n40

Sievers, J., 187n32, 200nn70–72, 201, 213n111

sins, in the Acts of Thomas, 35 (see also vices, ancient lists of)

slaves, 20

Slingerland, E., 11n31, 22n80

Sly, D., 64n29

Smallwood, M., 181n13, 190n42, 222n150

Smart, N., 21n74

Smith, B. H., 22n80

Smith, D., 80n89

Smith, J. Z., 3n1, 4n5, 6n13, 21n74, 22n79, 245n7

Snyder, J. M., 5n9

Sophia, 180

Souter, A., 129n57

Spiro, M., 21n74, 24n87

St. Stephen, 153, 155, 160

Staples, A., 27n96, 246n10

Stark, R. A., 21n74, 182, 182n18, 187n32, 196n58

Stephens, S.A., 124n33

Stern, K. B., 201n75, 214n115, 259n55

Stowers, S. K., 11n32, 21n74, 21n77, 23, 23nn84–85, 24, 24n89, 186n31

Strathern, M., 14, 14n46, 264n69

Streete, G. C., 123n26

Swidler, A., 123n27

Swidler, L. J., 123n27

synagogue officers, women, 181, 232–41

Szesnat, H., 19n69, 172n59

Tabbernee, W., 119n7

Takács, S. A., 13n42, 27n96, 29n1, 33n7, 246n10

Tannenbaum, R., 191n43

Taylor, J. E., analysis of the Therapeutrides, 57–58, 60–62, 65–70, 72–77, 81–86, 89, 96–100, 104–10, 113–14
  Alexandrian Jewish philosophical milieu, 75
  alternative Miriam traditions, 100
  being parthenoi, 74
  celibacy, 74
  childlessness, 74–75
  description of the "juniors," 76
  as "elderly virgins," 72–73, 77
  of inheritances, 75
  interpretation of Exodus 15, 85–86
  modesty, 74
  norms of the "good," 76
  On the Contemplative Life, contextual approach, 67–73
  Philo's description of singing of Therapeutae, 97–100, 105
  Philo's representation of women, 110
  Philo's use of the plural hymns, 97
  problematic married (and younger) women, 73
  theory of Philo's intentions, 69
  vs. Engberg-Pedersen's thesis, 77–78

Tertullian's prohibition of women's religious practices, 118–19

Thamyris, 139

Thecla, 19, 121–23, 244–45
  Boughton and Dunn's views, 126
  Bremmer's views, 127
  Brown's views, 128
  Burrus's views, 125–26
  confrontation with Alexander, 141–42
  Cooper's views, 127–33, 140
  Davies's views, 123–24
  descriptions of baptizing, 144
  fraught relationship of Thecla and Theocleia, 132–33

hairstyle and dressing, 136–37
literary testimonies and manuscript
    evidence, 121–24, 135
MacDonald's views, 124–25
as masculine, 139–40, 148
Matthews's views, 126, 128
renunciation of gender norms, 136–43
resisting of male figures of authority,
    138, 138n79
Schneemelcher's views, 126
Tertullian's views, 117–20, 129–31
textual issues, 119–20, 143–46
Tryphaena's support to Thecla, 132–35,
    142–43
Theissen, G., 80n89, 230n178, 254n37
Theodorus, 157–59, 168 (see also Letter on
    the Conversion of the Jews)
theory of mind, 22–23
theosebēs, 189, 191–92, 200
Therapeuō, meaning, 58
Therapeutae (see also Exodus 15)
    all-night vocal performance, 59–60
    ascetic diet, 70
    banqueting practices, 61, 71–72, 79
    behavior during prayers, 59
    choir, 59, 61, 81, 107
    communal room, 60, 70n58
    concluding day, 59
    description of the "juniors," 76
    Engberg-Pedersen's views, 67–71,
        77–79
    festival of seven sevens (Feast of Fifty),
        59–61, 80–81
    first six days, 58
    food and clothing of members, 58–59
    junior members of the society, 61
    garments, 70, 70n57
    historicity of, 65n33, 66
    hoi neoi and hoi eleutheroi, 76
    Philo's description of the community,
        61–62
    presbuteroi (elders), 61–62
    routine practices of, 70
    Taylor's views, 67–73
    therapeutic disciplining of the body, 70
    seventh day, 58, 70
    women (Therapeutrides), description
        of, 60, 62, 64, 70, 72–73, 111
Therapeutae (masc. pl), 4, 28, 58
Therapeutrides (fem. pl), 58
Thompson, C., 40n21
Torah, rabbinic debates on teaching
    women, 27, 272

ben Azzai's views, 42
contemporary commentators, 45–46
R. Eliezer's view, 42
R. Joshua's views, 42
in modern times, 43
public reading on Sabbath, 42
reading practice, 43–44
Satlow's views, 43–45
Tosefta, implication of, 42, 45
Tosefta, 42, 45
transvestite saints, 19
Trebilco, P. R., 189n40, 192n50, 216n121,
    218nn131–32, 219, 219n133,
    220n139
Treggiari, S., 38n18, 48n49, 207n95
Tremlin, T., 22nn80–82, 23n83, 23n86,
    24n90, 25n91
Trevett, C., 119n7
Trible, P., 102n148
Tylor, E., 20, 20n73, 24
Typhaena, Queen, 132

Ullucci, D., 73n67, 247n16, 264n69
urban prefect, 29, 47
Urbicus, 47, 50
Urman, D., 191n48
Uro, R., 22n80

van Bremen, R., 234n194, 239, 239n208
van der Horst, P. W., 20n70, 183nn19–20,
    192n50, 201n75, 203n78, 204n85,
    210n107
van der Weg, M., 133n66
van Rompay, L., 123n26
Vanderlinden, S., 153n2
veneration of Judean god, 195–96
    Greek theosebēs inscriptions, 216–21
    Latin inscriptions, 213–16
verisimilitude, 10
Veturia Paula, 180, 204
vices, ancient lists of, 35–36
Vigna Randanini catacomb, 204,
    204n86, 207–8
virtues, ancient lists of, 35
von Harnack, Adolf, 182
Vouaux, L., 121n15, 145n104

Wallace-Hadrill, A., 255, 255n42, 270n82
Walsh, J. T., 20n70
Wander, B., 192n50
Wankenne, J., 160n17
Wartelle, À., 47n40
Wassen, C., 77n79

Wegner, J. R., 42n31, 64n29, 258n53
Wendland, 57n1
Wesseling, B., 124n33
White, H., 10n27
Whitehead, H., 14
Williams, C. A., 18n65
Williams, M. H., 181n13, 192n50,
   222n150, 223
Wilson, B. C., 4n6, 21n74
Wilson, S. G., 91n120
Wilson-Kastner, P., 5n9
Winkler, J., 7n14, 14n48
Winston, D., 57n1, 60n12, 60n15
Wire, A. C., 250n26
Wittig, M., 14n50, 15, 15n52, 16
Wolchik, S. L., 262n66
women (see also religious practices,
   of women)
   ancient references and distinctions,
      12–13, 73
   ancient Roman perspective, 47–55
   artistic representations, 3–4, 40
   in ascetic Christian contexts, 19
   Clark's arguments on ancient accounts
      of, 8–10
   at communal meals, 80
   Corinthian, 40
   Greco-Roman Mediterranean
   vocabulary, 12
   hairstyle representations in Roman
      period, 136–37
   headcoverings, significance, 39–40,
      40n24
   interest in Christianity, 182
   Judean women, in Alexandria, 60, 62,
      64, 70, 72–73
   Latin vocabulary, 12–13
   ordination in ministerial and priestly
      offices, 4
   Palestinian rabbinic stereotypes, 7n14
   Philo's description, 60, 62, 64, 70,
      72–73, 80–81, 109–14
   philosophers, 73
   problems using ancient accounts of, 7–8
   proclivity for foreign religions, 185
   religious activities in ancient
   Greco-Roman Mediterranean,
      4–6, 28, 30, 39–40, 64
   representation in ancient narratives,
      34–41
   research sources on women's behavior
      in antiquity, 5
   role in importation of Bacchic rites, 31
   Severus's accounts of, 165–76
   stories in Hebrew Bible, 7n14, 10
   Taylor's analysis of Therapeutrides,
      72–75
   theory of human reproduction, 16–17
   Therapeutic singing, 108–9
Wright, D. F., 36n14

Yadin, Y., 256n44
Yonge, C. D., 91n119, 92n127

Zabin, S., 183n19, 204n83, 215n116,
   233n186
Zias, J. E., 77n79
Zilm, J., 183n19

Printed in the USA/Agawam, MA
December 19, 2011

563033.001